READINGS IN STATE AND LOCAL GOVERNMENT

PROBLEMS AND PROSPECTS

READINGS IN STATE AND LOCAL GOVERNMENT

PROBLEMS AND PROSPECTS

Edited by
DAVID C. SAFFELL
Ohio Northern University
and
HARRY BASEHART
Salisbury State University

Boston, Massachusetts   Burr Ridge, Illinois
Dubuque, Iowa   Madison, Wisconsin   New York, New York
San Francisco, California   St. Louis, Missouri

McGraw-Hill

A Division of The McGraw·Hill Companies

Readings in State and Local Government
Problems and Prospects

6 7 8 9 BKM BKM   09876543

ISBN 0-07-054479-4

This book was set in Melior by Ruttle, Shaw & Wetherill, Inc.
The editors were Peter Labella and Fred H. Burns;
the production supervisor was Denise L. Puryear.
The cover was designed by Rafael Hernandez.

Cover Photo Credit: John Coletti, Stock Boston/Town Hall
Middleborough, MA.

Library of Congress Cataloging-in-Publication Data

Readings in state and local government: problems and prospects/
   edited by David C. Saffell and Harry Basehart.
        p.   cm.
   Includes index.
   ISBN 0–07–054479–4
   1. State governments—United States.   2. Local government—United
States.   I. Saffell, David C., (date).   II. Basehart, Harry.
JK2408.R36   1994
353.9—dc20   93–37331

About the Editors

David C. Saffell is professor of political science at Ohio Northern University. He received his Ph.D. degree in political science from the University of Minnesota. He is the author of *State and Local Government: Politics and Public Policies*, 5th edition (McGraw-Hill). He is the author and editor of several other books dealing with American government. Recently he has published articles on legislative apportionment and rural politics in *Comparative State Politics* and *National Civic Review*.

Harry Basehart is professor of political science at Salisbury State University. He received his Ph.D. degree in political science from The Ohio State University. He is the author of several articles on state legislatures that have appeared in *American Politics Quarterly, Legislative Studies Quarterly,* and *National Civic Review*. He also directs an internship program that places undergraduate students in the Maryland General Assembly and other state and local governmental agencies.

Contents

Preface

Once described as the "fallen arches" of the federal system, state governments experienced a renaissance in the 1960s, 1970s, and 1980s. The structure and operation of their legislative, executive, and judicial branches were reformed; there was new creativity in solving social and economic problems; and in the mid-1980s there were sufficient revenue increases to fund new programs and, in some states, cut taxes.

Even worst-case cities such as New York, Chicago, and Cleveland, which faced bankruptcy in the 1970s, had brought order to their fiscal management by the mid-1980s. Despite cuts in federal assistance through the 1980s and a recession early in the decade, states and localities were set to enter the 1990s with healthy budgets and a new spirit of innovation. No longer fallen arches, states had become laboratories of democracy.

By 1991 resurgence had turned to distress. The recession, which began in 1990, led to a drop in revenues for all governments. Federal aid to states and localities had declined by about one-third in uninflated dollars from its peak in the late 1970s. The cost of programs such as Medicaid for states and aid to the homeless for cities skyrocketed. At the same time, old and new federally mandated programs put pressure on the states to raise revenue. In turn, state aid to cities and counties was cut while state-mandated rules and regulations severely strained cities.

By 1991 over half our cities' budgets were operating at a deficit and a new wave of tax increases was sweeping states, counties, and cities. Thirty states enacted new taxes in 1990. Programs were cut, employees were fired or furloughed, and even wealthy states such as California faced problems that a quick economic recovery would not cure. Unlike the federal government, all states except Vermont must balance their annual budgets, while cities face the added problem of having their taxing authority limited by the state.

The end of the Persian Gulf War brought new attention to a host of domestic problems that were showing the cumulative effects of years of neglect—education, child care, toxic waste disposal, crime, highways, city infrastructure, housing, medical costs. States and localities had little expectation of more federal help for these problems. Moreover President Bush mentioned only two domestic proposals—crime control and highways—in his speech to Congress following the end of the war in March 1991. Any "peace dividend" following the end of the Cold War seemed unrealistic in light of the recession, the federal deficit, and continued military expenditures. To a substantial degree, failure of his administration to take action on the home front to confront a weakened economy and problems in cities (highlighted by riots in Los Angeles early in 1992) led to George Bush's defeat in the 1992 presidential election.

Although President Clinton's campaign focused on domestic issues, as his administration began in 1993 it was beset by a host of international problems and a huge federal deficit that made it difficult to fund new federal programs to help states and localities. As approved in 1993, Clinton's comprehensive economic plan called for about $250 billion in tax increases and $250 billion in federal spending cuts over four years. The good news for states and cities was his call to invest in "roads, bridges, transit facilities; in high-tech information systems; and in the most ambitious environmental cleanup of our time." The bad news was that federal cuts, including the shutdown of military bases across the country, will have an adverse affect on state finances.

So it is that we approach the organization of this book with the theme "problems and prospects." There are many reasons to be apprehensive as states and localities face the decade of the 1990s. At times, problems seem overwhelming; still, there is room for optimism. The economy is improving and reforms of the past thirty years will serve governments well in the future. There is evidence that the tax revolt has lost much of its steam, and voters may be willing to support tax increases if they can be assured that the money will go to specific policy areas. Many innovative programs are in place and working well. States and localities cannot expect more money from Washington, so it is critical that they manage government carefully and earn the trust of their residents. Our concern will be to analyze states and localities in terms of how they respond to the pressures of changing intergovernmental relations and loss of revenue.

This book is organized to correspond with most introductory state and local government textbooks. Readings are reprinted close to their original length so that the meaning remains the same. Compared to other books of readings, there are relatively few selections. This permits readers to focus on a manageable number of readings without becoming confused by a great number of short pieces. Selections are free of the kind of jargon and technical terms that may turn off students in introductory courses. Each chapter introduction describes how the subject matter fits into the general theme of the book, and then places the chapter readings in that framework. There is a mixture of academic and more popular readings, with an attempt to provide background understanding of topics and still focus on contemporary issues.

We want to thank Peter Labella and Bertrand Lummus of McGraw-Hill for nurturing this project. In addition, Fred H. Burns and Carol Berglie improved the book by their direction of the production process. The following reviewers helped us make decisions that we believe improved the selection of readings and the organization of the book: John H. Baker, Southern Illinois University; Janet Clark, University of Wyoming; Donald Laws, Southern Oregon State University; Carl Lieberman, University of Akron; Timothy Mead, University of North Carolina, Charlotte; Roger Pajari, Georgia Southern University; Kenneth T. Palmer, University of Maine; Richard Scher, University of Florida; Charles H. Sheldon, Washington State University; and Nelson Wikstrom, Virginia Commonwealth University. Finally, other key people need to be acknowledged for their assistance. They include Robert Long, Department of Social Work at Salisbury State University, David Warner, Department of Legislative Reference, Maryland General Assembly, Gary Moncrief, Boise State University, and Barbara Roberts at Ohio Northern University.

David C. Saffell
Harry Basehart

READINGS IN STATE AND LOCAL GOVERNMENT

PROBLEMS AND PROSPECTS

CHAPTER 1

The Setting of State and Local Government

The study of states, cities, and counties should be exciting because they have the major responsibility for dealing with our most important and most controversial domestic problems. These responsibilities include trying to limit crime and imprisoning criminals, deciding under what circumstances women can have abortions, organizing schools and educating children and adults, disposing of hazardous waste, and providing shelter for the homeless.

In order to understand how states and localities organize their governments and how they respond to an almost limitless variety of social problems, we need to examine the setting in which they operate. This will help us explain how individual cities or states act, and will help us make comparisons among 50 states, 3,000 counties, and 19,000 municipalities. The governmental setting is affected by a host of historical, cultural, economic, geographical, demographical, regional, and ecological factors. Thus political scientists must borrow knowledge from many other academic disciplines in order to understand political systems.

Historically, it still makes a difference that the eleven Confederate states seceded from the Union and fought a war against the North. Culturally (and historically), the development of unique societies in states such as Alaska, Hawaii, Texas, and Louisiana has affected the way their governments operate and the kind of people they elect to public office. The fact that blacks constitute about 36 percent of the population in Mississippi and less than 1 percent of the population in Maine, New Hampshire, and Vermont directly impacts on public policy in those states. Population size, density, and mobility clearly influence what governments do. The presence of natural resources such as oil or rich farmland makes politics in Oklahoma and Iowa different from politics in Maryland. Of course, several historical, cultural, and economic factors may be linked together to give whole geographical regions unique settings.

Because of population mobility and improved transportation and communications, many cultural, economic, and regional differences have lessened since the end of World War II. Still, many of these differences persist and other factors linked to the physical characteristics of certain states remain unchanged. The two readings in this chapter deal with changes in the setting of states and localities in terms of political culture and population.

All state and local government textbooks discuss political scientist Daniel Elazar's classification of political subcultures and how they have affected state and local politics. Elazar (*American Federalism: A View from the States*, first published in 1966) identifies three subcultures—traditionalistic, individualistic, and moralistic—that were brought to the United States by early settlers and then spread unevenly across the country as groups of people moved westward. Briefly, the traditionalistic view (originating in the South) believes that government should help maintain the old social order and political power should remain in the hands of a political elite based on family ties or social position. The individualistic view (Middle Atlantic states) sees governmental power as a means to advance economic self-interest. The moralistic view (New England states) sees an active role for government to promote the public good and it encourages broad-based citizen protection. Both traditionalistic and moralistic cultures discourage widespread political participation and they tolerate a certain amount of political corruption. While few states are pure examples of a subculture, Elazar identifies predominate cultural patterns in states and local areas that continue to affect the nature of politics.

Although Elazar's classification scheme has been criticized for being too impressionistic (lacking mathematical precision or verifiability), being dated, not distinguishing subcultures down to local levels, and being circular in the sense of using past measures to describe the present, it continues to be widely quoted and tested. Political culture has been shown to be related to levels of economic development, political corruption, voter participation, spending for various public services, and even corporal punishment in public schools.

In Reading 1, political scientists John Francis and Clive Thomas explore what factors influence politics, power, government, and public policy in the American West. While recognizing that Elazar's classification is useful in explaining politics in the Western states, Francis and Thomas find that it also has serious limitations. For example, they note that many Westerners do not have family origins in the European settlements on the East Coast; they believe that physical environment strongly influences government; and they feel that Westerners change their opinions about government more frequently than people in other sections of the country.

The decennial census produces a wealth of information that keeps demographers and politicians busy for at least five years, after which we begin to get estimated data for the next census. Politically, the census is important because it determines the number of Congress members in each state, it affects the apportionment of state legislatures, and it helps determine the allocation of federal and state funds to state and local governments. Because the census affects political power, it invites challenge.

According to an adjustment survey of 165,000 households, completed in 1991, the 1990 census missed 5.4 percent of black men, 5.8 percent of Hispanic men, and 2 percent of nonblack men. The undercount for the entire population was 2.1 percent, or about 5.3 million persons. Among cities with populations over 100,000, 70 percent showed undercounts larger than the national average.

Secretary of Commerce Robert A. Mosbacher decided not to adjust the 1990 census figures. Many experts questioned the way in which the adjustment would have been calculated, contending that the sample wasn't large enough to furnish good data for smaller demographic units. In addition, it was argued that adjustment would increase cynicism among minority persons who would then view the census as a process to be manipulated by statisticians.

In Reading 2, Bryant Robey of the Population Reference Bureau outlines some of the major findings of the 1990 census and then discusses the nature of the undercount. Robey notes the unprecedented level of accuracy in the 1980 and 1990 censuses and he appears to argue against adjustment.

QUESTIONS FOR DISCUSSION

1. Based on the Francis–Thomas model, try to develop a set of influences on your section of the country.

2. Discuss the frontier ethos and how it makes the West different from other sections of the country. Is it possible that Francis and Thomas overstate the uniqueness of the West?

3. Discuss the accuracy of the 1990 census in your local area and in major cities in your state. Should the figures of the 1990 census have been adjusted? What is the position on adjustment taken by Clinton administration Secretary of Commerce Ron Brown? How can accuracy be improved in the 2000 census?

4. What are some of the major political consequences of the 1990 census findings as reported by Robey?

1.   Influences on Western Political Culture

John G. Francis and Clive S. Thomas

THE CONCEPT OF POLITICAL CULTURE: AN OVERVIEW

Since the time of Aristotle in ancient Greece, political observers have recognized that the general culture in a nation, region, state or locality has an

SOURCE: From "Influences on Western Political Culture" by John G. Francis and Clive S. Thomas from *Politics and Public Policy in the Contemporary American West*, University of New Mexico Press, 1991, pp. 24–51. Reprinted by permission.

important impact on politics. In this respect we can define the culture of the American West as the particular values, attitudes, beliefs and life-style of those living in the region. In turn, the general culture of a society will shape that society's political culture, which in essence is a shared set of knowledge, attitudes and symbols that help to define the procedures and goals of politics.

A major reason why countries, and often political subdivisions within countries, have different forms of government and produce different types of policy is because of variations in political culture. As a consequence, political scientists have paid considerable attention to the study of political culture in recent years. Like many concepts in social science, however, it exhibits problems of definition and measurement. Despite these limitations, political culture can tell us much about the nature of political attitudes and processes.

Over the past thirty years several definitions of political culture have been used by political scientists.[1] Probably the two most often used are those developed by Daniel Elazar and Joseph Zikmund, and by Sidney Verba. Elazar and Zikmund define political culture as "the particular pattern of orientation for political action in which each political system is imbedded."[2] Verba defines the concept as "the system of empirical beliefs, expressive symbols and values which defines the situation in which broader action takes place."[3] Both definitions share the idea of political culture as identifying values that orient people in a fundamental way to politics.

There are two principal levels of analysis in political cultural studies. One level focuses on the individual's orientations; while studies on the other level consider the political culture of a system, organization, or society.[4] Here we employ political culture to mean orientations found at the level of the individual Westerner.

Political culture at the level of the individual has a psychological focus. Such studies often focus on three sets of orientations: toward governmental institutions, toward others in the political system, and toward one's own competence and efficacy in politics. Researchers such as Almond and Verba, Huntington, and Inglehart have argued that societies with wide support for governmental institutions, significant levels of trust in other members of the society, and a strong feeling that political partici-

pation is effective for the individual citizen, are likely to possess a stable democracy.[5]

Discussions of political culture lead to two important questions. First, once a political culture has been described, what are the limits to generalization? Are there segments of the population who do not share at all or share only partially in the core values of the culture? Second, political culture is by definition a set of values that endures, yet politics is often concerned with change. How, therefore, do students of political culture account for political change?

Limits To Generalization

As to the limits to generalization, several studies in comparative politics report on countries that have two or more cultures existing within their borders. Canada is often described as having two cultures: Francophone Quebec and the Anglophone provinces to the west and east of Quebec.[6] Other studies describe a political culture that has a number of significant variations within one nation, variations that are described as subcultures. Subcultures are defined as a segment of the population that possesses important differences in outlook from the majority's viewpoint and in which both the majority and the subculture are conscious of these differences in outlook. The United States is often described as having a national political culture with a number of important subcultures.

Perhaps the best-known description of American political culture and its subcultures is that by Elazar.[7] He argues that the American political culture is rooted in two contrasting conceptions—those of marketplace and commonwealth. The marketplace orientation views public relationships as products of bargaining among individuals and groups acting out of self-interest. In contrast, the commonwealth orientation understands government as realizing certain shared moral principles.

Three distinctive types of subcultures result from the tension between these conceptions. The individualistic subculture emphasizes that the American democratic order is a marketplace and government is instituted for strictly utilitarian reasons. Government should play a restricted role that encourages private initiative and widespread access to the marketplace. In contrast, traditionalistic political culture is rooted in a mixed view about the marketplace linked with an elitist conception of the commonwealth. Popular participation in government is not widespread. Good government is that which maintains traditional patterns of social relationships. Finally, moralistic political cultures stress the value of political participation for the betterment of the commonwealth. Good government is measured in terms of the degree to which it promotes the public good. Principled political participation rather than party loyalty is valued in moralistic political culture. No state has a pure subculture of any one type, but Elazar argues that one type or a combination of two types will predominate in each state.[8]

There is also a close correlation between these subcultures and political ideologies based on a conservative-liberal scale. Traditionalistic states, which until very recently included most southern states, tend to be more conservative and have less activist governments. These also tend to allow more freedom of action to groups and individuals in pursuing their goals, which may extend to bribery and corruption. At the other end of the scale, predominantly moralistic states like North Dakota, Minnesota, Oregon and Michigan often have more activist governments, and place greater strictures on what are and what are not acceptable political tactics. Predominantly individualistic states like Connecticut, Nevada, Illinois and Pennsylva-

nia, and those manifesting a significant individualistic element like California, Montana, Kansas and Iowa, fall somewhere in between.

Elazar's critical working assumption is that culture is rooted in the historical experience of the people, and that once rooted it will survive migrations to quite different parts of the country. In certain sections of the country, a particular subculture will be dominant, which reflects the streams and currents of migration that have carried people of different origins and backgrounds across the continent in more or less orderly patterns.[9]

The Problem of Political Change

The second question is the problem of political change. Inglehart makes a number of important claims about political culture and political change. He argues that political culture is the crucial link between economic development and democracy. Cultural patterns once established influence subsequent political and economic events. "But culture is not a constant. It is a system through which society adapts to its environment. Given a changing environment, in the long run culture is likely to change."[10] Inglehart argues that postwar prosperity in North America and Europe engendered a cultural shift toward post-materialist values that has led to less emphasis on economic growth. In sum, political culture helps shape political and economic environment.

With this basic knowledge of the concept of political culture we can move to examine the particular influences that have shaped the political culture and subcultures of the West and thus the politics, governmental institutions and public policies of the region. Then we will be able to pose the question of the extent to which there is a distinct political culture in the West.

NATIONAL AND TRADITIONAL AMERICAN INFLUENECES

The West has undergone considerable change since World War II and particularly since the 1960s. Some of these changes are peculiar to the West itself, but most are the result of national trends. To understand recent changes in western politics we need to be aware of these major national trends and influences. Here we list ten of the most significant national developments since the 1960s:

1. Population has increased. The growth was 11.4% for the nation as a whole during the period of 1970–80.
2. Increasing urbanization continues. This has been partly responsible for a power shift from rural to urban areas.
3. Despite the message that we often get from the media, both the standard of living and the level of education have been rising for the United States as a whole. This has largely been due to major advances in technology, especially in computers.
4. The national economy continues to diversify, and some states and regions have made great progress in this regard.
5. Since the early 1970s there has been an increasing national trend toward conservatism. Two manifestations of this have been a decline in union membership and the rise of the Republican party in many areas at the expense of the Democrats.
6. Political parties, however, have experienced a decline in membership and effectiveness since the 1960s.
7. The power vacuum left by the parties has been filled to a large extent by interest groups. This includes the rise of so-called "single issue" groups and political action committees (PACs).
8. Government has increased its role considerably since the mid-1960s. This has led to an increasing reliance on government for funds and employments in some areas of the nation. Intergovernmental cooperation at all levels has also increased.
9. There has been a marked increase in the level of professionalism of elected and appointed government officials as well as of lobbyists.
10. Probably the most significant political development of the last twenty-five years is an expansion in political pluralism. That is, despite what we often read in the papers, hard evidence demonstrates that there are more people and groups participating at all levels of the American political process than ever before.

It is, of course, not just the last twenty-five years that the action as a whole has had an impact on western politics. From the time of the early pioneers the political debate in the West has been influenced by traditional American values and the national political heritage. Those who came to the West brought with them not only economic and social values but also a set of political values that had been molded back in the East or even in Europe. In other words, these settlers brought with them a political culture—or more precisely, a set of political subcultures. A major aspect of this political culture and its subcultures was a commitment to representative and responsible government. Such values were reinforced by the fact that Congress vetted each state's constitution before approving its admission to the Union, and rejected any constitution that deviated too much from national norms.

So it was that national political traditions and values came to make a lasting mark on western politics. However, as these political traditions and values were applied to local circumstances, needs and conflicts, they underwent some modifications. Westerners adapted them, as far as they felt appropriate and possible, to meet their own needs. Similarly today, national attitudes and trends, like the ten identified above, will be modified or adapted in the West as the result of a host of regional factors, including historical, social, cultural, economic and political needs and realities.

THE FRONTIER ETHOS

The various aspects of the frontier ethos have given a particular complexion to western culture and thus to the political culture and subcultures of the region. The idea of a frontier ethos or spirit is an ambiguous and elusive concept. Nevertheless, both academic and popular writers have long recognized that there was a difference in attitude between those who lived in the relative security of long-established settlements back East and in Europe, and those who ventured west and to the frontier. We can identify six major elements in this ethos: progress, optimism, individualism, *laissez faire*, pragmatism, and a qualified egalitarianism. All were part of the general American culture, but were interpreted and adapted to meet the needs of Westerners.

As products of the Enlightenment of the late eighteenth century, the ideas of progress and optimism center on the belief that human beings can affect their environment to improve the human condition; and that they have control over the rate of progress. This contrasted with previously held beliefs that human beings were subject to conditions over which they had no control. A fervent belief in progress and its concomitant optimism has always been part of the American ethos. It was particularly important in the birth and early development of the nation. And nowhere was it a more prominent part of the culture than among western pioneers and settlers. Few people would have ventured west if they had not strongly believed that it was in their power to create a better life for themselves; and that it was their own efforts that would determine the extent of their success.

The American version of individualism mainly emphasized freedom from government control in all aspects of life and especially in the political sphere. It also lauded self-reliance and private initiative as keys to both personal and national success. Those who came west not only exemplified this creed (at least in theory) but enhanced it with such laudable traits as courage, tenacity and endurance to produce their own unique brand of individualism—rugged individualism.

Closely associated with individualism is *laissez faire*. This is the concept that the role of government should be limited to providing law and order and national defense, a concept that dominated nineteenth-and early twentieth-century America. It became, and in many respects remains, a hallmark of American capitalism and political conservatism. The frontier's and later the developing West's espousal of *laissez faire* has been tempered perhaps more than in any other region by practical necessity. While rarely, if ever, openly admitted, in essence this means that many Westerners do not want to pay taxes or have their activities controlled and regulated by the government. Yet they certainly want—and actively seek—government aid and support not only to enhance their lives, but in many cases to make existence possible in the first place.

Pragmatism and egalitarianism were largely a product of the environment and conditions of the West. Pragmatism is a major characteristic of the American ethos in general, but it became an even more integral part of life out West and on the frontier. Here a person had to adapt his or her old ways of thinking and acting in order to meet new challenges and conditions. A person's life and his or her acceptance by other Westerners often depended on the willingness to adapt—to be pragmatic.[11]

The harsh physical conditions and the premium placed on adaptability and survival had a socially leveling effect on frontier society. Certainly, American society was known for its lack of a class structure, but there were still social stratifications in large cities and particularly in the South. The frontier and the West could not afford these to the same degree. It did not matter who one had been or what one had done back in the East or in Europe. The important question was: What can you contribute here? As with most frontier societies, that was how people were judged. As a result, the frontier and the West emphasized social and political equality to a greater degree than did the rest of the country. The West was, on the surface at least, more egalitarian.

This, however, was a qualified egalitarianism reserved for white only. Western white society was no more tolerant of racial minorities than was the rest of the nation. In fact, in many ways it was less tolerant as will be seen below. Furthermore, the West's pioneering of the extension of the franchise to women (beginning in Wyoming in 1890), which is often cited as evidence of the region's egalitarianism and toleration, was more the result of necessity than of any philosophical commitment to equality. So, as a result, the West had a particular brand of egalitarianism that was essentially the product of pragmatism. Like the frontier ethos in general, it contained both ambiguities and contradictions.

THE PHYSICAL ENVIRONMENT

We know from western movies that the physical environment had a tremendous effect on the life-style and attitudes of Westerners. Despite the advent of modern technology, this physical environment continues to exert a great influence on the life-style and politics of the West today. Five key aspects of the physical nature of the West have worked their effects on western politics and public policies.

First, there is the sheer physical size of the West. The region contains over half of the nation's land area, but only 20% of the national population. Size and distance push up the costs of roads, the exploitation of natural resources, and the costs of consumer goods and services. This situation is exacerbated by the second factor—the nature of the terrain. Mountain ranges in particular increase the costs of building roads and power lines. The third factor is the climate, which in itself affects the terrain. The West, of course, contains an array of climates from frigid arctic cold in interior Alaska to rain forests on the Pacific Coast to hot deserts in the Southwest. Coping with problems of climate and terrain often requires the expenditure of massive public resources. The fourth factor is very much the product of climate. The vast area of the West receives only 20% of the nation's rainfall, so there are vast arid lands or deserts resulting from lack of moisture. Consequently, the effect of aridity and the need for water has been and remains a central theme in western politics. Fifth, this vastness, terrain, climate and to some extent aridity, have affected decisions about where people have chosen to live in the West.

DEMOGRAPHIC FACTORS INCLUDING THE PRESENCE OF MINORITY POPULATIONS

The composition and distribution of the population affects western politics in a number of ways. The size of the population will partly determine the tax base. Size will also have an effect on campaign styles: the larger the population the less personal the electioneering process. The age distribution will affect the demand for services such as education, health care, and family services. The density and geographical distribution of the population will affect the type and cost of services. Population growth and decline also affects politics. On the one hand, rapid growth can bring a demand for limits on suburban and industrial growth and an attempt to protect the environment more carefully. Population decline lowers the tax base and makes for problems in attracting businesses and creating jobs. The racial and ethnic composition will impact the political culture and the policy focus of governments.

The West is very sparsely populated and most people are clustered in a number of what has been termed "urban oases."[12] Over 55% of Westerners live in California, and almost another 30% live in Arizona, Colorado, Oregon and Washington. In the 1970s, the West experienced a population growth almost three times that for the nation as a whole, 32.8% compared with 11.4%. This has slowed down considerably in the 1980s; but it is still twice the national average.

One in five Westerners is nonwhite and therefore of non-European extraction. The oldest non-European communities are the American Indian communities found throughout the West, but in significant numbers in Alaska, Arizona and New Mexico. Asian communities have long been dominant in Hawaii, and they are significant components of California's present-day population. In some areas Hispanic communities antedate the migrations from the East, but throughout the West, notably in the Southwest, these communities have greatly expanded both by successive immigrations and by natural increase. After World War II, black migration westward paralleled white migration. Today, significant black populations are found in the San Francisco Bay area, Los Angeles, Las Vegas and Denver. Over the years, the existence of these various minority populations has had a significant influence on western politics and policy.

The term minority has two distinct but often interrelated meanings in American politics. One is that of a numerical minority in relation to the total population of the nation, a region, a state or a locality, such as the non-European groups considered above. The second meaning is that of a group which does not enjoy the same political, civil and legal rights and opportunities as other Americans. In this latter sense a group may actually constitute a majority of the population—as is the case with women, a numerical majority who are often referred to as a "minority."

In both senses of the term, minorities have always had an important influence on American public policy. Until recently, however, it has been the existence of minorities, rather than the direct political activities of minorities themselves, that has brought about this influence. Until the 1960s the existence of minorities tended to unite the dominant political element in America—white males—in order to exclude these groups from an equal share of the political and economic benefits of American life. This was the dark side of American pluralism and of the American dream.

From the first years of the settlement of the West, minorities in the region were very much subject to such exclusion. The western states, in fact, were at the forefront of the movement to exclude minorities from many of the benefits of American society. California, for example, began to restrict the civil and legal rights of the Chinese in 1852—just two years after achieving statehood. Later the Chinese Exclusion Act of 1882 (extended in 1892 and 1902) was pushed through Congress after anti-Chinese sentiments on the Pacific Coast spilled over into violence. The Act itself was not repealed until 1943. The Japanese also suffered discrimination, particularly through the policy of internment during World War II.

As has been the case in the rest of the country, since the 1960s minorities in the West have been brought more into the mainstream of American society. Minorities themselves have begun to exert direct influence on western public policy.

DOMINANT FEDERAL PRESENCE

The federal government has always played and continues to play a dominant and crucial role in the West's development and particularly its economic development. One particularly significant aspect of the federal presence in the West is its ownership of land. The western states rank one through thirteen of the fifty states in the percentage of their land area that is federally owned. This ranges from 85.1% in Nevada to 19.9% in Hawaii. In ten of the states at least a third or more of the land is in federal hands. Only one other state in the Union, New Hampshire with 12.2%, even reaches double digits in this respect.[13]

When we combine the factors of development and land ownership, it becomes obvious how dominant the federal presence has been and continues to be in the West. Add to this the prime importance of land to much of the West in terms of its natural resource extraction, its agricultural and its tourist economy, and the federal influence on western politics becomes even more obvious.

DEPENDENCE ON EXTERNAL FORCES

Because of the tremendous amounts of capital required to develop the West, of which very little was available in the region itself, plus the natural resource extraction and agriculturally based economy, the West has long been dependent on external forces for its well-being. There have been three such forces in particular: the federal government, investors and banks from back East and from abroad, and world markets and the world economy in general.

Capitalists from back East, as well as some foreign capitalists, financed and controlled many western railroads, mines, banks and businesses. These groups often made decisions that were not in the interests of many Westerners.

Consequently, to Westerners it appeared that their region was a colony that the rest of the nation used to supply important natural resources, and that was to be exploited for profits regardless of the welfare of its inhabitants. Such was the feeling regarding discriminatory railroad freight rates levied on many western communities. Also the West has always been at the mercy of world markets for the prices of its raw materials and agricultural goods. Because these prices were and remain subject to supply and demand forces outside the region, low prices engendered a feeling of helplessness and anger against the faceless forces.

THE BOOM AND BUST ECONOMY

This feeling of frustration was exacerbated by the fact that so many western state economies have been based almost entirely on natural resource extraction and agriculture. So when world prices are high these economies boom; but when prices fall, slumps and sometimes depressions afflict the region. To be sure, California has broken this cycle and Arizona, Colorado, Washington State and Hawaii are moving in that direction. But this boom and bust cycle still afflicts many western states. Over the years, their reacting to and trying to break out of this state of dependence and its volatile economy has profoundly influenced western politics, government and public policy.

THE ROLE AND SIGNIFICANCE OF GOVERNMENT

In the early years government aid took the form of the U.S. Cavalry used in subduing the Indians, and the huge land grants to the railroads to subsidize the development of the first major western transportation lifeline. Later came massive federal funds for water and irrigation projects, hydroelectric systems and roads. In World War II came major military installations and federal research facilities like Los Alamos National Laboratories in New Mexico. After the war came more military installations; more federal scientists; space engineers; workers for a host of federal agencies, ranging from the Bureau of Land Management to the National Weather Service; and major federal defense contracts for companies like Boeing of Seattle. The result is that today a lot of business profits and many a payroll would not have become a reality if it were not for past or present federal aid and, increasingly these days, state government spending.

This heavy dependence upon government in the West has been primarily a consequence of necessity and not of choice. As noted above, it has resulted largely from need—primarily economic need—rather than any philosophical belief in the intrinsic value of government in promoting social goals. Indeed, the antigovernment attitudes and strong strain of political individualism and conservatism that exist in many parts of the West, particularly the Mountain states, opposes such an intrinsic role.

This tension between dependence on government and political individualism and conservatism has produced the western political paradox. Over the years many of the most successful western politicians have built their careers on the two seemingly contradictory practices of securing huge amounts of federal funds while vocalizing anti-federal government sentiments. In particular, former U.S. Senator Barry Goldwater espoused *laissez faire* at the same time as he was securing millions of federal dollars for the Central Arizona Project and similar federal programs to develop water and other resources. As regards the policy process itself, a political culture that champions the pioneer while spurning the government is likely to affect both policy formulation and implementation.

Heavy dependence on government has other more direct and more easily measurable impacts on western politics. One of these is that even slight changes in government budgets can seriously impact the economy of the region, a subregion or a state. This is particularly the case with federal spending cuts. But it is becoming increasingly important with reductions in state spending, and even local government spending, which is impacted by federal and state cutbacks. The fact that state and local governments are the major employers in many states means that budget cutbacks often lead to major layoffs of public employees. Because public payrolls are a greater percentage of the income of most western states than of states in the rest of the nation, this reverberates throughout their economies in a much more damaging way than it would in states like Pennsylvania or Indiana, which are much less dependent on government employment.

Both western voters and politicians are, of course, very aware of the devastating effects this economic dependence on government can unleash. That is part of the reason why western politicians have an obsession with economic development and diversification. The irony, however, is that in order to advance development and diversification, government aid and investment—in the form of roads and other transport facilities, business loans and tax incentives—are often required. In addition, the fact that large numbers of voters are public employees is not lost on western politicians. Neither is the fact that many of the major campaign contributors and the most effective interest groups in the region are public sector unions, such as schoolteachers and state employee associations. All these and other factors work to reinforce another characteristic of western politics among the public and politicians alike—that of political pragmatism.

So within the context of political individualism and conservatism that predominates in many parts of the West, what this all-pervasive role of government has produced, in effect, is a nonideological equivalent of Western European statism. That is, the recognition, if only tacitly and reluctantly in the West, that the transformation or development of society, and particularly its economic welfare, is impossible without the active and constant participation of government.

• • •

SUBREGIONAL FACTORS IN WESTERN POLITICS

We have noted on several occasions that while the West displays common elements in its politics, government and policy preferences, it also exhibits much diversity. This diversity stems from many sources including historical experience; economic factors, cultural, racial and ethnic differences; and adaptation to the physical environment. When these are combined with geographical location they have often produced a subregional perspective on various aspects of life including politics. These subregional political perspectives—which reflect variations in political culture—influence the nature of politics and policymaking. This is the case, for example, when regional associations or coalitions are formed around some common interest. These differing political perspectives also provide insights into understanding political variations within the West.

Various subregions have been identified over the years. The exact boundaries of these are, like those of the West itself, subject to dispute, and consequently they often overlap. Probably the best-known of the subregions are those based upon clusters of states such as the Southwest, the Northwest, the Pacific states subregion, and the Mountain states subregion. Sometimes a distinction is made

within this Mountain subregion between the northern Rocky Mountain and the southern Rocky Mountain states.

Two recently developed subregional divisions transcend political boundaries. One is between the Sunbelt area of the Southwest, Hawaii and parts of the coastal area of the three contiguous Pacific states, and the Snowbelt (sometimes referred to as the Frostbelt), which covers most of the rest of the West. The other is Joel Garreau's division of North America based on economics, culture and political interest. Here the West falls into four of his nine regions, which he describes as "nations." "Ecotopia" is a "nation" dominated by concerns about ecology. It includes the coastal strip from southeast Alaska to around San Francisco. "MexAmerica," where Spanish-American culture is pervasive, embraces much of the Southwest and southern California. The "Empty Quarter," where population is relatively sparse, includes much of the Mountain states and most of Alaska. The fourth "nation" is the "Breadbasket," which includes the eastern portions of Montana, Wyoming, Colorado and New Mexico. Hawaii, according to Garreau, is difficult to classify. It is as much an Asian aberration as it is a North American aberration. He sees Hawaii as a place of Ecotopian possibilities, with MexAmerican growth values and limits, run by Asians.[14]

While both of these subregional divisions certainly have important implications for the present, the Sunbelt-Snowbelt division and the one developed by Garreau are more futuristic and both have broader implications than just the political life of the region. As far as politics is concerned, over the years and particularly in the last two decades, several observers have noticed significant differences between the Pacific states (Alaska, California, Hawaii, Oregon and Washington) and the Mountain states (Arizona, Colorado, Idaho, Montana, Nevada, New Mexico, Utah and Wyoming).[15]

A study on cultural regionalism conducted as long ago as the 1930s drew attention to the relatively high level of prosperity in California and to a lesser extent in Oregon and Washington State in comparison with other sections of the nation and certainly in comparison with the low incomes of people living in the Mountain states.[16] The relative wealth of the West Coast still stands in contrast to the boom and bust economies of many of the Mountain states. Other differences between these two subregions include an increasing conservatism and support of the Republican party in the Mountain states, plus a stronger antigovernment attitude in that subregion. Several of the chapters in this book draw a comparison between these two subregions as a means for understanding contemporary variations in western politics and policy.[17]

WESTERN POLITICAL CULTURE AND SUBCULTURES

Do all the influences that we have considered above produce a distinctive political culture or subculture that distinguishes the western states from the rest of the nation? Expressed another way, have the various aspects of western culture produced a unique orientation toward politics in the West?

The answer to those questions at present is a qualified no. It is a qualified negative because there is very little survey information of either popular or elite attitudes that can be used to identify a distinctive political subculture in the western states. The surveys that have been conducted suggest that westerners' orientations to politics share much with those found in other regions of the nation. Nevertheless, as with our consideration of the frontier ethos, there is enough evidence of the existence of certain distinctive features of western political culture to justify our separate focus on the politics of the western states.

Earlier we indicated the appeal of Elazar's three subcultures to many scholars who are seeking to understand American politics. In fact, a number of the contributors to this volume rely on Elazar's formulation. Elazar concludes that the individualistic, the traditionalistic, and the moralistic subcultures are all to be found in western states. Elazar argues, for example, that the South being the center of traditionalistic culture, migrants from that region carried its political subculture values with them as they moved west to parts of New Mexico and California. Those from New England and the upper Midwest carried the moralistic culture to parts of Oregon, Washington State, Idaho and Montana. And those from the Mid-Atlantic and lower Midwest carried the individualistic subculture to all parts of the region. Elazar's assumption that as people move westward they carry their political values along with their possessions seems to make intuitive sense and is supported by studies of other migrations.

This conception of cultural transfer is reinforced by the relatively young age of western political communities. Much of the West only began to attract major migration in the last century and in many areas only during the past forty years. Many Westerners were born elsewhere, or their parents were born elsewhere.

The Elazar classification of subcultures certainly has some explanatory value. For example, Ira Sharkansky found some limited success in utilizing the classification to predict public policy outcomes, but expressed reservations about the reliability of the subcultural designations as applied to some states.[18] We also see considerable value in Elazar's classification for understanding western politics. At the same time, like Sharkansky, we have concerns about the explanatory value of Elazar's theory. Three of these concerns, as they affect the western states, are considered below.

Non-European Political Cultural Influences

First, significant numbers of Westerners do not have their familial origins in the European settlements of the east coast: most significantly Hispanic, Asian, black and American Indian communities. These communities are not explored as well as they might be in Elazar's work. In the case of all four, we simply lack the knowledge to offer generalizations about the attitudes of individual members. It may be that further investigation will require the formulation of several additional subcultures in addition to the ones advanced by Elazar. Indeed, as some commentators have observed, there may be grounds for believing that there is a quite distinct Mexican-American culture.[19] It is highly likely that we are witnessing in the western states new patterns in political participation and in political relationships. Such increased participation by what are now described as minority groups, which might some day be the majority at least in California, could lead to a new era of politics in the western states.

Culture and the Environment

Second, as Inglehart contends, there is a complex interplay between culture and environment. This is another area that Elazar does not treat extensively. We contend, however, that political attitudes and institutions, particularly governmental institutions in the West, have been strongly influenced by the environment. Take, for example, a recent study of Idaho political culture by Robert Blank. By using the three aspects of the political culture of individuals described at the beginning of the chapter—orientations to government, to others, and toward one's own activities—Blank took Elazar's subculture of individualism and explored how it had developed in the state.[20] He found that people in Idaho

hold fast to the values of self-reliance that were reinforced by the conditions of the frontier experience. This supports Elazar's theory. But Blank argues that commitment to self-reliance produced an orientation of distrust and suspicion of those persons and groups who were different. Blank also draws attention to what, in effect, is the existence of the western political paradox in Idaho: That is, the seemingly ambivalent attitude toward the federal government. Indeed, Blank describes it as a love-hate relationship. Idahoans, like many other Westerners, apparently combine deeply felt patriotism with deep suspicion of federal intervention. Yet they favor and even demand certain sorts of federal financial support for infrastructure developments such as irrigation and highways.

Another example of the relationship of culture and environment that appears to be particularly important in the West, but cannot be explained within the Elazar scheme, has to do with the interplay between economic well-being and policy change. We noted earlier that Inglehart observed that the sustained prosperity of the post-World War II period produced an economic climate that contributed to what he describes as post-industrial values—a concern for the quality of life notably in the area of the environment.[21] What we know about the western states gives us some appreciation of Inglehart's analysis. Conflicts over environmental politics are to be found in all sections of the nation. But in the western states, conflicts over the goals of environmental regulation are front-page news. These conflicts are very much a clash of the contending orientations that are present in every western town and city. Such clashes not only reflect a very deep division among Westerners over their respective orientations as to what they want out of politics, but may also reveal the powerful force that the landscape has had on the people living in the West.

Public opinion surveys during the past twenty years have indicated significantly greater support for environmentalist positions at both the mass and the elite level in California than is reported for the Mountain states. In recent years, however, there has been growing support, particularly in the urban areas of the Mountain states, for environmentalist positions. But opposition to restrictions on economic development continues to remain relatively high in the rural areas of this subregion.

Fluidity of Political Loyalties

Our third concern with the explanatory value of Elazar's theory of political culture as it relates to the West is the greater willingness of westerners to change their partisan loyalties and policy views than appears to be the case in other sections of the country. Miller and others have remarked on the magnitude and rapidity of what they regard as realignment in the Mountain states from being one of the most Democratic regions in the nation to being one of the most Republican regions in the country.[22] What is important to note about realignment, occurring in the late 1960s, is that both migrants and residents who were born in the region shifted partisan loyalties. On the basis of survey findings DeGrazia observed in the early 1950s the relative weakness of party loyalties in the West.[23] Kleppner believes that westerners carried their party attachments as they moved west, but that the policy content of party attachment simply made less sense in a frontier that generated a very different set of problems.[24] The widespread use of initiative and referendum weakened the power of parties and legislatures in shaping the political agendas of western states. Westerners became more inclined to look to issues and personalities, and the force of an issue or a striking personality seemed to bring about frequent shifts in party attachment.

THE CONNECTION BETWEEN INFLUENCES AND ENDURING CHARACTERISTICS

In summary, we can make five observations about the relationship between these influences and the characteristics that they have produced.

First, each characteristic of western politics is not the result of one influence, but of several. For example, the fragmented policy process is not just the result of weak political parties and strong interest groups, but in part also results from political pragmatism, individualism and regionalism. Likewise, political pragmatism is the result, in part, of the frontier ethos, the physical environment, the nature of the western economy, and the influences of the general American ethos.

Second, while we can show a cause and effect relationship between influences and characteristics as Robert Blank demonstrated in his study of individualism in Idaho, we cannot definitively measure the extent to which each influence contributed to each characteristic of western politics. We cannot say, for example, that the western political paradox is due 50% to the role of the federal government, 20% to the spirit of individualism, and so on. What we can say with some degree of certainty about this and other characteristics of western politics is that they are shaped by a complex set of factors. What makes the situation even more complicated is that not only do the influences we identified shape the characteristics of western politics, but one characteristic will often impact another. The characteristic of candidate-oriented elections, for example, will constantly help to undermine the influence of parties and help bolster the power of interest groups. In turn, the characteristic of candidate-oriented elections will be reinforced by weak parties and strong interest groups.

Third, despite the difficulty in mea-

16 John G. Francis and Clive S. Thomas

surement and the complexities of relationships, the combination of influences that constitute the western political culture has established a particular context of political life in the West. That is to say, while some of the characteristics of western politics may not be unique to the region, the way in which they manifest themselves in the West is usually distinctive. For instance, the use of methods of direct democracy is certainly not unique to the West. But no region makes more use of these devices, and nowhere is their impact in terms of public policy formulation and the way that they affect the attitudes of government and governed alike more significant than in the West. Similarly, all regions of the nation exhibit antigovernment sentiments and a skepticism toward the federal government. But the nature of the western experience with federal authority has given a particular orientation to the antigovernment feelings of the West.

Fourth, while all thirteen states well exhibit to some extent the ten characteristics of western politics identified in the first chapter, the importance of these will vary from state to state. This is largely due to the fact that some influences are more important in some states than in others. In other words, the political cultural make-up of the states differ.

• • •

This brings us to our fifth and final observation. If the impact of various influences varies from state to state and results in some characteristics of politics being more important in some states than in others, will a significant change in one or more influences result in changing characteristics of western politics? The answer is obviously yes. We alluded to this in the sections on political change in our consideration of political culture, especially comparing the Pacific and Mountain subregions.

NOTES

1. Discussions of the concept of political culture and its value and evolution in political science are found in: Gabriel A. Almond, "The Intellectual History of the Civic Culture Concept," in Gabriel A. Almond and Sidney Verba, eds., *The Civic Culture Revisited* (Boston: Little, Brown, 1980); Samuel C. Patterson, "The Political Cultures of the American States," in Daniel J. Elazar and Joseph Zikmund II, eds., *The Ecology of American Political Culture* (New York: Thomas Y. Crowell, 1975); Alan I. Abramowitz, "The United States Political Culture Under Stress," in Almond and Verba, eds., *The Civic Culture Revisited*; David J. Elkins and Richard E. B. Simeon, "A Cause in Search of Its Effect or Does Political Culture Explain?" *Comparative Politics* (January 1979), 127–165.
2. Elazar and Zikmund II, eds., Introduction to *The Ecology of American Political Culture.*
3. Sidney Verba, "Comparative Political Culture," in Lucian Pye and Sidney Verba, eds., *Political Culture and Political Development* (Princeton: Princeton University Press, 1963), 513.
4. Walter A. Rosenblum, *Political Culture* (New York: Praeger, 1975).
5. Gabriel A. Almond and Sidney Verba, *The Civic Culture: Political Attitudes and Democracy in Five Nations* (Princeton: Princeton University Press, 1963); Samuel P. Huntington, "Will More Countries Become More Democratic?" *Political Science Quarterly* 99, 2 (Summer 1984), 193–218; and Ronald Inglehart, "The Renaissance of Political Culture," *American Political Science Review* 82, 4 (December 1988), 1203–30.

6. David V. J. Bell, "Political Culture in Canada," in Michael S. Whittington and Glen Williams, eds., *Canadian Politics in the 1980's*, 2nd ed. (Toronto: Methuen, 1980), 155–74.

7. Daniel J. Elazar, *American Federalism: A View from the States*, 3rd ed. (New York: Harper & Row, 1984), esp. chap. 5, "The States and the Political Setting."

8. *Ibid.*, 134–37.

9. *Ibid.*, 128–29, for a map showing the transfer of political subcultures across the nation.

10. Inglehart, "The Renaissance of Political Culture," 1223.

11. Perhaps coincidentally rather than intentionally, the West exemplified the philosophy of pragmatism developed by C. S. Peirce (1839–1914), William James (1842–1910) and John Dewey (1859–1952). This was a home-grown American philosophy that attempted to explain the meaning and justification of beliefs through the practical effects of holding them. In large part this philosophy was an attempt to explain and justify the uniqueness of the development and the underlying characteristics of the American economic, social and political system. It has been very influential on the course and methods of American politics. It was philosophical pragmatism that provided the justification and methods for achieving many populist, progressive, and later, New Deal reforms. For a fuller explanation of philosophical pragmatism and its interrelationships with practical politics see A. J. Beitzinger, *A History of American Political Thought* (New York: Dodd, Mead, 1972), chap. 20; and David W. Minar, *Ideas and Politics: The American Experience* (Homewood, Ill.: The Dorsey Press, 1964), chap. 11.

12. Gerald D. Nash, *The American West in the Twentieth Century: A Short History of an Urban Oasis* (Englewood Cliffs, N.J.: Prentice Hall, 1973; University of New Mexico Press, 1977).

13. Alfred N. Garwood, ed., *Almanac of the Fifty States* (Wellesley Hills, Mass.: Information Publications, 1987), 421.

It is important to note that the specific percentages of federal land in each state varies according to which federal agency's data one consults. This accounts for the variations in percentages in the various chapters of this volume. While such variations may be a serious point of conflict for policy makers, as the differences are only one or two percent, they do not affect the points regarding federal land ownership being made in this book.

14. Joel Garreau, *The Nine Nations of North America* (Boston: Houghton Mifflin, 1981), 117–18, and maps of the "Nine Nations" following p. 204.

15. John G. Francis, "The Political Landscape of the Mountain West," in *The Politics of Realignment: Party Change in the Mountain West*, Peter Galderisi, Michael Lyons, Randy T. Simmons and John G. Francis, eds. (Boulder, Colo.: Westview Press, 1986).

16. Howard W. Odum and Harry E. Moore, *American Regionalism: A Cultural Historical Approach to National Integration* (New York: Holt, 1938).

17. For another perspective on western regionalism, see the interesting new regional division of America in Michael Barone and Grant Ujifusa, *Almanac of American Politics, 1988* (Washington, D.C.: National Journal, 1987).

18. Ira Sharkansky, "The Utility of Elazar's Political Culture: A Research

Note," in Daniel Elazar and Joseph Zikmund II, eds., *The American Cultural Matrix* (New York: Thomas Y. Crowell, 1975), 262.

19. See Rodolfo O. de la Garza, *Ignored Voices and Public Opinion Polls and the Latino Community* (Austin, Texas: The Center for Mexican American Studies, The University of Texas, 1978).

20. Robert H. Blank, *Individualism in Idaho: The Territorial Foundations* (Pullman, Wash.: Washington State University Press, 1988).

21. Inglehart, "The Renaissance of Political Culture," 1225–30.

22. Arthur Miller, "Public Opinion and Regional Political Realignment," in Galderisi et al., eds., *The Politics of Realignment: Party Change in the Mountain States.*

23. Alfred DeGrazia, *The Western Public, 1952 and Beyond* (Stanford: Stanford University Press, 1954). Other older standard works make the same point: Thomas Donnelly, ed., *Rocky Mountain Politics* (Albuquerque: University of New Mexico Press, 1940); Frank Jonas, eds., *Western Politics* (Salt Lake City: University of Utah Press, 1961); Frank Jonas, ed., *Politics in the American West* (Salt Lake City: University of Utah Press, 1969).

24. Paul Kleppner, "Voters and Parties in the Western States, 1876–1900," *Western Historical Quarterly*, 14 (January 1983), 49–68.

2. Two Hundred Years and Counting: The 1990 Census

Bryant Robey

WHAT THE 1990 CENSUS WILL SHOW

The national population growth rate has slowed considerably in comparison to the 1800s. The 1980 Census counted a total population of 226.5 million. For 1990, the Census Bureau projects a population of 249.9 million, 10.3 percent more than in 1980.

As the economy has changed and the large industrial cities of the Northeast and Midwest have peaked, the population has grown most in California, Texas, and Florida. The 1990 Census probably will confirm that these three states account for over half of the nation's total population growth during the 1980s. Projections have the Northeast growing less than 3 percent and the Midwest only 1.5 percent during the 1980s, while the south will gain nearly 16 percent and the West, 21 percent.[1]

California, Texas, and Florida together will have a 1990 population of nearly 60 million, almost as many people as lived in the nation as a whole a century ago, in 1890.

The national median age in 1980 was 30 years. By 1990, the median age is projected to rise to 33 years. Census Bureau projections anticipate a continued rise in the median age into the next century, as life expectancy rises, the birth rate remains low, and the baby-boom generation (the more than 75 million Americans born between 1946 and 1964) grows older. By 2010, the median age will be 39 years.[2]

SOURCE: From "Two Hundred Years and Counting: the 1990 Census" by Bryant Robey in *Population Bulletin*, April 1989, pp. 8–10, 32–36. Reprinted by permission.

We have become a nation of small households, with fewer children per family, fewer families as a percentage of all households, and more people living alone. The population grew 11 percent between 1970 and 1980, while the number of households grew 27 percent. The 1980 Census was the first in history to record an average household size of fewer than three people. In 1980, the average family contained 3.3 persons. By 1990, the typical American family—if it is still possible to speak of a typical family—probably will consist of only three people.[3]

Immigration has provided the United States with over 50 million new residents during the past two centuries, but the great majority of these new Americans arrived before the 1920s. A century ago, the 1890 Census recorded that nearly 15 percent of all Americans had been born abroad; by 1980, the proportion had dropped to just 6 percent. But of late the proportion is rising once again because American fertility is at record lows while the number of immigrants has risen rapidly in the past 20 years. The Census Bureau estimates that immigration accounted for 28 percent of the nation's total population growth in the first half of the 1980s.[4]

Successive waves of immigrants, followed by generations of intermarriage, have altered the nation's ethnic and racial character. Over two-thirds of all immigrants to the U.S. have come from Europe. So great has been intermarrriage among them that only 11 percent of Americans counted by the 1980 Census listed their sole ancestry as English. Only 8 percent said they were exclusively German. However, some 50 million, or more than one in five, have some English ancestry, and about the same share, German.

Today, about half of all new immigrants are coming from Asia. The total U.S. population grew 11 percent during the 1970s, for example, while the Asian American population grew 141 percent. The 1980 Census counted some 3.5 million Asian Americans: The 1990 Census is likely to count over 6.5 million.[5]

The 1980 Census also counted nearly 15 million Hispanics, about 6 percent of the total U.S. population. Providing consistent historical census information about America's Hispanic population is difficult because "prior to the 1970 Census, the concept of Hispanics as a group barely existed."[6] That census was the first to ask whether a person considered himself or herself Hispanic; earlier estimates were based on such concepts as surnames, foreign language spoken, or country of birth. Hispanics have long been part of America, of course. In 1848, Mexico ceded to the United States the territory that is now Texas, New Mexico, Arizona, California, Nevada, Utah, and part of Colorado. Immigration as well as high birth rates among U.S. Hispanics has led to rapid growth of the Hispanic population. Recent projections show a Hispanic population of 21 million in 1990. 8 percent of the total U.S. population.[7]

The first census in 1790 counted 757,000 blacks, 92 percent of them in slavery. The black population was then about 19 percent of the total population. The 1980 Census counted 26.7 million blacks, under 12 percent of all Americans. Over 90 percent of all blacks lived in the South in 1790; by 1980 the proportion had dropped to just over half, but 1980 Census data also confirmed that more blacks are now moving into the South than out of the region.[8]

Census Bureau projections anticipate that by the time of the 1990 Census the black population will be over 31 million, or about 12.4 percent of the total U.S. population. The black population nationally is projected to grow some 16 percent. The black population of the West is projected to rise the fastest, increasing 29 percent between 1980 and 1990.[9]

Much of what the 1990 Census will reveal is already known—because the Census Bureau through its Current Population Survey provides reliable up-to-date statistics about many of America's population characteristics—but primarily at the national and regional levels. Only the census provides detailed and consistent statistics for small geographic areas nationwide.

Moreover, each census contains its share of surprises. For example, the 1980 Census counted 5.5 million more people than had been estimated and revealed that migration from the Northeast and Midwest to the South and West during the 1970s was much greater than had been thought. Estimates and projections can be inaccurate for many reasons; we need the census to set us straight. "The national census, taken once every ten years, is one of the most important signposts on the road from past to future. In its charting of the characteristics of the American people, each census is a mirror of society at a single point in history. Over the decades, the succession of censuses reveals the changing face of the American people."[10]

• • •

ACCOUNTING FOR UNDERCOUNT

No matter how hard we try, it will prove impossible to obtain an accurate count of every American as of a single day, April 1, 1990. No census has ever been 100 percent accurate, and none ever will be.

It may also be too much to expect that every group in our society will be counted with exactly the same degree of accuracy. Voting behavior, social attitudes, family structure, income, education, and many other characteristics differ by age, sex, ethnicity, and race. So does participation in the national census. It is relatively easy to enumerate the middle class in their suburbs, because they live at easily-identified addresses, and are likely to receive and return their census questionnaire. But it is much more difficult to enumerate the poor and the alienated, because it is both harder to locate them—they live disproportionately in isolated rural areas and inner-city slums—and more difficult to enlist their cooperation when they are located.

Throughout our two centuries of census taking, states and localities have periodically complained that their areas were undercounted by the census. From time to time, evidence of serious undercounting has appeared. For example, the 1870 Census was thought to have seriously undercounted the population of the South. "Interpolation back from the 1880 figures indicate a potential total undercount of 1.2 million in the South and a black undercount of .5 million— over 10 percent of the black population," according to social historian Margo J. Anderson.[11]

Census Bureau studies after the 1980 Census showed that 99 percent of whites had been enumerated but only 94 percent of blacks. The Bureau's studies showed the highest undercount rates were for black males between the ages of 25 and 54, fully 15 percent of whom were missed.[12] The Hispanic population was probably also disproportionately undercounted by the 1980 Census.

Even before the 1990 Census questionnaire went to the printer, a lawsuit was filed that seeks to force the Census Bureau to adjust the actual count using statistical methods, in anticipation of another undercount that will vary by race. Following the 1980 Census, a total of over 50 similar suits were filed. In each of these cases, some of which took nearly the entire decade to complete, the courts found in favor of the government position not to adjust for undercount.[13]

Another suit filed more than a year before Census Day, 1990, seeks exclusion of illegal aliens from the 1990 count. The government's position is that the Constitution requires that all persons be enumerated. Further, even if the courts were to direct the Census Bureau to exclude illegal aliens, "any proposed method would be likely to have significant errors that could affect the allocation of one or more congressional seats."[14]

While successfully defending its decision not to adjust the 1980 Census tally, the Census Bureau began intensive research into whether it could develop statistically reliable methods to make adjustments for undercount by the time of the 1990 Census. If the research concluded that developing and using new statistical adjustment techniques could achieve a more accurate count of the true number of inhabitants than not adjusting, then the nation's political leaders and the courts would have the option of adjusting for undercount.

Testifying before Congress in July 1986, the Census Bureau's Associate Director for Statistical Standards and Methodology at that time, Barbara A. Bailar, said of the Bureau's 1990 Census efforts: "We will attempt to take the best census possible and to count everyone, but we also will do what is necessary to be prepared to adjust the counts if we determine that adjustment will improve them."[15] Then-Census Director John G. Keane used the same words in testimony before a Senate committee in September 1986.[16]

Dr. Bailar told Congress that the Bureau would have to establish methods that could accurately measure census coverage for small geographic levels and a variety of population and housing characteristics. Further, it would have to establish and publish standards for evaluating the quality of both the unadjusted and the adjusted census data. Finally, she said, "We have to implement the adjustment, compare the adjusted and unadjusted data in light of the standards, and then release one of the sets of data as the official 1990 Census results."

If there were two sets of official census results—one before and one after adjustment—the decision which to use could become hopelessly politicized. The goal of accuracy would be lost in the calculations of which localities and politicians would gain or lose by using which of the two sets of statistics. Any adjustment decision would need to be firmly agreed to *before* the outcome of the census were known or else we risk endless rounds of second-guessing, political maneuvering, and lawsuits that could seriously weaken the credibility of the census.

The Census Bureau began its adjustment research in 1984. By the summer of 1987, the researchers concluded that it might be possible technically to make statistical adjustments to the census counts that would come closer to the true number of inhabitants than not making an adjustment. However, many operational and policy questions remained.

Because the Bureau appeared to be making progress in developing satisfactory adjustment methods, advocates of adjustment began to take new heart. "Census Bureau is Urged to Adjust 90 Count to Include Those Missed," headlined a New York Times article on August 20, 1987. It noted that while statisticians remained divided, Democratic officials generally supported adjustment and Republicans opposed it. Representative Mervyn Dymally, a California Democrat who chaired the House Subcommittee on Census and Population, introduced a bill ordering adjustment, but it was never brought to a vote.

The Staff Director of the House Subcommittee on Census and Population, TerriAnn Lowenthal, told state and local officials, "Based on several hearings before our subcommittee and numerous consultations with the experts, we believe a consensus has emerged that a full-scale Post Enumeration Survey is a statistically valid and technically feasible method of adjusting the raw census counts. The time has come to carry out an adjustment of the decennial census figures to eliminate known undercounts and overcounts of the population."[17]

But late in October 1987, the Department of Commerce, the Census Bureau's parent agency, announced that the government had decided not to adjust the results of the 1990 Census. "Adjustment may create more problems than it solves, and may divert resources needed for enumeration," said the Under Secretary for Economic Affairs, Robert Ortner.[18]

Additional reasons offered by Ortner included the likely controversy that adjustment would generate, the suspicion it might create about the reliability and integrity of census statistics, and the fact that, even without adjustment, the Census Bureau expected to achieve a 99 percent accuracy rate. Under Secretary Ortner said, "Adjustment is a threat to the customary process of reapportionment which has been one of the foundations of our political system. The census count has traditionally been accepted as the best count available regardless of the political consequences. Adjusting the count may create the appearance of changing the numbers to achieve a desired political outcome by the party in office."[19]

Following this decision, the Census Bureau's Barbara Bailar, who had guided the research into adjustment methodology, resigned from the government in protest.

In July 1988, C. L. Kincannon, Census Bureau Deputy Director, issued a statement giving the official Census Bureau position on the undercount issue and the Commerce Department decision. He recalled that the Census Bureau had been researching the adjustment issue since 1984, and was continuing its research program in the summer of 1987, before the Commerce Department made its announcement. Based on this research, the Census Bureau Director concluded that the Bureau could "reasonably expect

to have the technical capability in 1990 of assessing the undercount." However, "the decision on whether we would actually adjust the 1990 Census would occur in 1990."[20]

Noting that some members of the Bureau's senior staff were not in complete agreement among themselves on the feasibility of adjustment, C. L. Kincannon reported that at a meeting of top Bureau officials held on July 15, 1987, before the Commerce Department decision, a majority agreed "that an adjustment could not be attempted in time for legal deadlines without placing the census itself at unacceptable risk. Most of the group strongly agreed that basic census operations should not be changed and that the efforts to adjust the 1990 Census by legal deadlines should not proceed. In light of the above, the Department of Commerce decided not to adjust the results of the 1990 census," Mr. Kincannon said.[21]

Early in November 1988, when the group of states, cities, and interest groups sued in Federal District Court in Brooklyn to force adjustment to the 1990 Census because of undercounting, Barbara Bailar, now the Executive Director of the American Statistical Association, filed an affidavit to accompany the suit charging that the Commerce Department decision was arbitrary, secretive, and substantively flawed."[22]

TO ADJUST OR NOT TO ADJUST?

The two sides of the undercount issues have persuasive proponents. While both would agree that the nation should obtain as accurate a count of the population as possible, they disagree about the extent to which the government should attempt to compensate for the failure of the census to count the American underclass as well as it counts the great majority.

The Census Bureau has been a leader

in measuring the degree to which the census has fallen short of perfection. Not every country's census, and not every government program, is as forthcoming about its shortcomings. The Bureau has also been a leader in using computerized statistical programs to improve the accuracy of enumeration. The Bureau's computer programs that impute residents and their characteristics, when they are known to exist but information cannot be gathered directly, are statistically sound and proven to be effective.

The Constitutional requirement for a census was drawn up long before the era of the computer or the development of demographic methods or sampling techniques. The Founding Fathers could not have expected an errorless census. The 1790 Census, which took 18 months to complete, yielded a total of 3,929,326, but the government suspected an undercount. "I enclose you also a copy of our census, written in black ink so far as we have actual returns, and supplied by conjecture in red ink, where we have no returns; but the conjectures are known to be very near the truth," wrote Thomas Jefferson to George Washington in 1791. "Making very small allowance for omissions (which we know to have been very great), we are certainly above four millions."[23]

Error has been part of every enumeration for 200 years, and occasionally the errors have been major, but the nation has always agreed to abide by the findings of the actual enumeration, just as it has agreed to abide by the outcome of free elections, without statistically adjusting their results for known demographic differences in voting behavior.[24]

There is irony in the fact that as the census has reached unprecedented levels of accuracy, the cries have become louder for even greater perfection. Pressures for statistical adjustment of census counts have grown as more federal money is allocated to states, cities, and local governments from benefit programs based on census statistics. Knowing that census statistics contain inaccuracies, legislators nevertheless placed more responsibility on these statistics.

The courts will have to decide whether the government is required to statistically add people to the census count. That decision will be historic and will influence census taking in the 21st century.

NOTES

1. Signe I. Wetrogan, "Projections of the Population of States, by Age, Sex, and Race, 1988 to 2010," *Current Population Reports*, Series P-25, No. 1017, October 1988.

2. *Ibid.*

3. Bryant Robey, *The American People: A Portrait of a Changing America and the Next Demographic Trends Around Us* (New York: E.P. Dutton, 1985) p. 39.

4. Leon F. Bouvier and Robert W. Gardner, "Immigration to the U.S.: The Unfinished Story," *Population Bulletin*, Vol. 41, No. 4 (Washington, DC: Population Reference Bureau, Inc., November 1986) p. 16.

5. Robert W. Gardner, Bryant Robey, and Peter C. Smith, "Asian Americans: Growth, Change, and Diversity," *Population Bulletin*, Vol. 40, No. 4 (Washington, DC: Population Reference Bureau, Inc., February 1989 reprint).

6. Cary Davis, Carl Haub, and JoAnne Willette, "U.S. Hispanics: Changing the Face of America," *Population Bulletin*, Vol. 38, No. 3 (Washington, DC: Population Reference Bureau, Inc., June 1983) p. 5.

7. "U.S. Population: Where We Are; Where We're Going," *Population Bulletin*, Vol. 37, No. 2 (Washington, DC: Population Reference Bureau, Inc., June 1982) pp. 6-7; and Rafael Valdivieso and Cary Davis, "U.S. His-

panics. Challenging Issues for the 1990s," *Population Trends and Public Policy* report Number 17 (Washington, DC: Population Reference Bureau, Inc., December 1988).

8. Wetrogan, *Projections* . .

9. *Ibid.*

10. Robey, *American People* . . ., p. 5.

11. Anderson, *American Census* . . ., p. 89.

12. U.S. Bureau of the Census, "The Coverage of Population in the 1980 Census," by Robert Fay, Jeffrey Passel, and J. Gregory Robinson, PHC80-E4 (Washington, DC: GPO, February 1988).

13. U.S. Bureau of the Census, "Chronological Listing of 1980 Lawsuits," July 20, 1988.

14. Memorandum from Sherry L. Courtland, Chief, Program and Policy Development Office, U.S. Bureau of the Census, "Why the Census Bureau Cannot Exclude Illegal Aliens from the 1990 Census," February 10, 1988.

15. Statement of Barbara A. Bailar before the Subcommittee on Census and Population, Post Office and Civil Service Committee, U.S. House of Representatives, July 24, 1986.

16. Testimony of John G. Keane before the Subcommittee on Energy, Nuclear Proliferation, and Government Processes, U.S. Senate Committee on Governmental Affairs, September 4, 1986.

17. TerriAnn Lowenthal, "State and Local Government Participation in the Census," October 14, 1987, p. 6.

18. Statement of Robert Ortner, Under Secretary for Economic Affairs, Department of Commerce, on the 1990 Census, Washington, DC, News Release, October 30, 1987, p. 2.

19. *Ibid.*, p. 3.

20. C. L. Kincannon, "U.S. Bureau of the Census Statement on Adjustment in the 1990 Census," July 15, 1988, p. 1.

21. *Ibid.*

22. "Commerce Dept. is Sued to Force Adjustment of 1990 Census Plan," *New York Times*, November 4, 1988.

23. Kaplan and Van Valey, *Census '80* . . ., p. 12.

24. Bryant Robey, "Adjusting for Census Undercount: The Statistical Nightmare," *American Demographics*, February 1980.

Good overviews of the census process and the U.S. Bureau of the Census are:

Margo J. Anderson, *The American Census: A Social History* (New Haven, CT: Yale University Press, 1988).

Ann Herbert Scott, *Census, U.S.A.* (New York: The Seabury Press, 1968).

Carroll D. Wright and Williams C. Hunt, *The History and Growth of the United States Census, 1790-1890* (Washington, DC: Government Printing Office, 1900).

U.S. Bureau of the Census, *Census '80: Continuing the Factfinder Tradition* by Charles P. Kaplan, Thomas Van Valey and Associates (Washington, DC: GPO, 1980).

CHAPTER 2
Intergovernmental Relations

The term *intergovernmental relations* suggests interdependence among all levels of government. Increasingly, public policy matters are influenced by decisions made throughout our governmental system. Appropriations, regulations, and administration are provided by Congress, state legislatures, county commissions, and city councils.

The U.S. Constitution says very little about the allocation of power between the states and the federal government. Cities, which are creations of state government, are not mentioned in the Constitution. In the American federal system, the states and national government in Washington have independent power and overlapping (or concurrent) powers that have been shifting, or evolving, ever since the first Congress began passing legislation. While national domestic activity began to increase in the late 19th century, as late as 1930 state spending was double national domestic spending and local government expenditures were five times greater.

Beginning with New Deal programs to combat the Depression and then Great Society domestic programs in the 1960s, national expenditures for domestic affairs and regulations grew dramatically and had exceeded the combined expenditures of states and localities by 1980. It should be noted that a substantial part of national (or federal) domestic spending was transferred to state and local governments, which then administered programs. This "creative federalism" suggested much greater cooperation among governments (intergovernmental relations) than had existed in the first half of the century.

As a percentage of state and local budgets, federal aid peaked at 26.5 percent in 1978. In his 1980 presidential campaign, Ronald Reagan argued that federal spending and regulations should be cut and that the power of state bureaucracies should also be reduced. Thus Reagan's New Federalism (discussed in Readings 3 and 21) proposed to eliminate many federal grants-in-aid and to consolidate others into block grants that give more flexibility to state and local authorities.

Federal aid to state and local governments was cut in the early 1980s, and its rate of growth was slowed by the Reagan administration. By 1988 federal aid as a percentage of total state and local outlays had been cut to about 17 percent. Congress created ten new block grants by consolidating categorical grants. Through consolidation and outright elimination, total categorical grants were reduced by about 130. However, the Reagan administration was not able to get Congress to substantially cut federal regulation (mandates) of state and local government.

In response to federal cuts, many states raised taxes and state aid to localities increased greatly in the 1980s. From 1983 to 1988, federal aid to state and local governments increased by 24 percent, while state aid to local governments increased by 50 percent. If Reagan wanted to reduce all government activity, he did not succeed. States and cities became more innovative, and a host of experimental programs in education, welfare, health, and environmental control flourished in the 1980s. Clearly, government became more decentralized in the past decade.

In Reading 3, economist Alice Rivlin (former Director of the Congressional Budget Office and now Deputy Director of the Office of Management and Budget) takes a look at the current state of American federalism and concludes that we should give more responsibilities to the states. She bases her conclusion on the increased competence of states that we have noted, plus the need to reduce the federal deficit and her belief that the federal government should pay more attention to international affairs.

Rivlin presents three possible scenarios for federal-state relations in the 1990s. They include tinkering with the present system (a return to the 1980s), instituting a program of aggressive federal spending and taxation (a return to the 1960s), and taking a new approach to dividing responsibilities between Washington and the states. Not surprisingly, she picks the third scenario. Rivlin's innovative and controversial approach would focus federal energy in a few areas such as health care, and rely heavily on states to fund and administer education, transportation, and economic development. Implementation of her program would require a strong commitment from the president and a willingness on the part of Congress members to give up many federal grants that help them get political support in their states and districts.

In the Preface we mentioned the economic distress facing states and localities in the 1990s. One way the Bush administration (led by Secretary of Housing and Urban Affairs Jack Kemp) tried to respond to this was by its support of enterprise zones (see Chapter 9). Shortly after the 1992 election, however, President Bush vetoed legislation that would have created enterprise zones because it also contained tax increases he opposed. Enterprise zones are supported by President Clinton.

One goal of enterprise zones is to reduce government regulation as a means of encouraging economic redevelopment. Curiously, Congress prepared a record number of new rules under President Bush, including regulations regarding clean air, child care, airport noise, and disabled persons.

In Reading 4, political scientist Joseph F. Zimmerman reviews ways in which increased federal mandates and restraints have affected states and cities since the 1980s. Mandates are orders requiring certain actions (such as costly compliance with hazardous-waste-disposal procedures), while restraints prevent states and localities from taking certain actions (such as setting an age for mandatory retirement of public employees). The administrative costs of compliance often are especially burdensome to small governmental units, which simply do not have staff who are adequately trained or sufficient in number to carry out federal directives.

Cities are especially hard-hit because mandates come from all directions. Some come directly from the federal government, some are passed through from Washington to states, and still others originate with state legislatures and require local compliance. In all cases a major problem is that cities and states faced more mandates in the 1980s, with less federal funding.

After discussing the nature of the mandate problem, Zimmerman offers several suggestions for improvement. While many of the mandates are needed—for example, to improve environmental quality—Zimmerman believes the federal government has a responsibility to look out for the administrative and financial needs of small governments. As a former governor, President Clinton is sympathetic to the mandate problems faced by states, but it will take action by Congress to make major changes in the 1990s. Clinton's meeting with the nation's governors early in 1993 promised change, especially in health-care regulations.

QUESTIONS FOR DISCUSSION

1. Which of Rivlin's three scenarios do you think is most likely to occur in the 1990s? Can you think of other possible scenarios for intergovernmental relations in this decade?

2. How do you react to Rivlin's response to the concern that states, if given more responsibility, might neglect the needs of the less fortunate?

3. Why do you suppose both federal and state mandates increased in the 1980s even though prevailing public opinion called for less government regulation?

4. Discuss Zimmerman's argument that increased federal mandates has led to decreased citizen participation in local affairs.

3. Rethinking Federalism

Alice M. Rivlin

I have argued that, for a variety of reasons, the division of tasks between federal and state government urgently needs to be reexamined.

• Global interdependence requires the federal government to pay more atten-

SOURCE: "Rethinking Federalism" from *Reviving the American Dream: The Economy, the States and the Federal Government* by Alice M. Rivlin, The Brookings Institution, 1992, pp. 110–125. Reprinted by permission.

tion to international affairs, so states must play a stronger role in domestic policy.

• The policies needed to revitalize the economy, which include eliminating the federal deficit and increasing public investment in skills and infrastructure, cannot all be undertaken by Washington without a federal tax increase too big to be either likely or desirable.

• Top-down management by the federal

government is unlikely to bring about needed change in education, skill training, and other areas where reform is essential.

- Some objectives, though, such as reform of health financing and control of medical costs, cannot be attained by states on their own.
- Increased competence and responsiveness of state government have weakened the rationale for many federal programs.
- Citizens' lack of trust in government, especially at the federal level, is exacerbated by confusion over which level of government is in charge of what and how tax money is being spent.

THREE SCENARIOS

What might happen to the division of responsibilities between states and the federal government in the 1990s? Three scenarios illustrate the possibilities.

The Eighties Continued

In the early 1990s, federal policy continued to be dominated by a distressing legacy of the 1980s: the huge structural deficit in the federal budget. The deficit, combined with politicians' perceptions that the public would not tolerate increased federal taxes, required restraining discretionary spending and avoiding new federal initiatives. Rising social security reserves and declining defense spending provided some offsets, but escalating costs of medical care and bigger outlays for interest on the growing debt keep pushing spending up.

The first scenario assumes that federal tax and spending policies continue on the basic tracks established in the 1980s without important changes. Using similar assumptions, the Congressional Budget Office projects the federal deficit continuing at high levels into the next century. To be sure, the deficit is project-

ed to decline as the economy recovers from the recession of the early 1990s and the deposit insurance crisis is resolved, but beginning in 1997, the deficit again begins to rise faster than total output.

The surprising resurgence of the federal deficit expected at the end of the decade is not caused by declining revenues, which remain close to 19 percent of gross domestic product (GDP). Nor is it caused by future Congresses voting new spending programs or adding to old ones: the projections assume continuation of the stringent caps on discretionary spending imposed by the budget agreement of 1990. Nor is social security to blame. Social security outlays remain about constant at 4.8 percent of GDP—the influx of retiring baby boomers starts about a decade later—and growing social security surpluses continue to offset part of the general fund deficit.

The sole reason that federal spending is projected to rise faster than GDP (without any economic or policy changes) is that rapidly increasing medical care prices will continue to push up spending for medicare and the federal share of medicaid. The cost of these two programs is projected to rise from 3.4 percent of GDP in 1992 to 5.2 percent in 2000.

This scenario assumes that politicians continue to view federal tax increases as politically risky. Congress and the president tinker with the tax system, but do not enact major revenue increases. They enact a few revenue-losing changes in the name of incentive for saving or investing (for example, a cut in income tax rates for long-term capital gains or more generous individual retirement accounts). These are offset by some revenue gainers in the name of fairness or financing infrastructure (a surcharge on millionaires or another nickel or dime of gasoline tax). Without a significant redefinition of the federal role, however, it is hard to imagine either a president or Congress mustering the political courage to increase revenue much above 19 percent of GNP.

Similarly, Congress and the president go on tinkering with federal spending. They continue to reduce defense spending while adding modest new domestic initiatives (some education, some child care, some low-income housing) but no major commitments. Continued concern about the deficit and fear of major tax increases also precludes significant new spending for health finance reform. Without the ability to fund new programs, the federal government goes on using mandates to affect state and local policy. Without effective medical cost control, both federal and state health programs steadily grow more expensive. The cost of private health insurance rises and more people are uninsured.

Meanwhile, under this scenario, the states keep struggling with rising demands for services, the escalating cost of medicaid, and additional federal mandates. They raise taxes and fees as much as necessary to stay afloat but are not able to finance major new initiatives. The division of tasks between states and the federal government remains muddy. Citizens continue to be confused about whom to blame for unsolved problems. Activist groups and state and local officials go on lobbying Washington for additional spending on everything from preschools to mass transit but have only limited success. The economy, still suffering from insufficient saving and high real interest rates, continues to limp along.

"The eighties continued" is definitely not a scenario for healthy and widely shared growth in the standard of living. With private investment levels no higher than those in the 1980s and no serious effort to improve schools, job training, or public infrastructure, productivity growth does not accelerate. Family incomes grow slowly, if at all. Moreover, escalating medical costs lower the amount of income working people can spend for other purposes—either because employers pay lower wages in the face of the rising cost of medical benefits or because workers have to pay the bills themselves.

If no aggressive measures are taken to improve the education, skills, or health of low-skilled workers, their situation will probably continue to deteriorate relative to that of the highly skilled and educated. The federal debt will continue to increase, requiring high annual interest payments that reduce funds available for federal programs. Moreover, with the federal government borrowing a substantial fraction of the nation's saving, the United States will remain dependent on foreigners for capital and will have to pay them substantial sums (in interest, dividends, and profits) for the use of that capital.

Paul Krugman has sketched out some of the implications of a similar scenario, which he calls "drift":

If the domestic U.S. economy in the year 2000 may look fairly similar to its current state, the international economy—and the role of the United States in the international economy—will almost surely look quite different.

In the first place, foreigners will own quite a lot of America. Net foreign claims on the United States will be something like 20 percent of GNP, with interest and dividends on these claims nearly 2 percent of national income. . . . It would not be surprising if, by the year 2000, foreign firms account for 25 percent of U.S. manufacturing production and own 45 percent of our banking sector.

The widespread foreign ownership will be a blow to traditional views of America's place in the world. . . . By the year 2000, an increasingly unified Europe will have a larger GNP than America's and Japan will have a GNP that in dollar terms is 80 percent or more of the U.S. level. . . . So by many measures the United States will have sunk to the number three economic power in the world.[1]

Krugman expects that Americans will simply allow this deterioration to occur and will not muster the political energy needed to get the country on a more positive track.

Back to the Sixties

The second scenario assumes that the electorate, refusing to accept "diminished expectations," demands federal action, or that some calamity, economic or political, propels an activist president into the White House with a supportive majority in Congress. With the energy of a Franklin D. Roosevelt or a Lyndon B. Johnson, the new president puts together an aggressive program of federal spending and tax increases and steers it through Congress. The federal government launches major new grants to both state and local governments—to improve skills, subsidize low-and middle-income housing, modernize infrastructure, and reform the schools. Washington churns out checks for programs and projects all over the country, along with guidelines, rules, and reporting requirements. The federal government also enacts either national health insurance or some less expensive health financing plan that subsumes medicaid.

All this federal activity raises the share of federal spending to perhaps 26 percent by the end of the decade (more if full national health insurance is enacted). Federal domestic spending rises by more than total spending because defense spending continues to decline. Taxes are raised, not only to pay for the increased federal activity, but to narrow the deficit. A combination of increases in taxes in payroll, sales or value added, energy, and income raises federal revenue from 19 to 25 percent of GDP and cuts the deficit to 1 percent of GDP. Even this huge assumed rise in the federal tax burden does not move the federal budget

to surplus. Some economists argue, however, that major increases in public investment make borrowing more defensible under this scenario than in the 1980s, when public investment was low.

The combination of federal grants and relief from rising medicaid costs enables states and localities to reduce taxes. While federal revenue rises faster than GDP, state and local revenue rises more slowly. Policy action shifts back to Washington, along with intense lobbying by myriad interest groups, including state and local governments, for a piece of the additional federal funding. Able people seeking careers in public service, whether as civil servants, political appointees or elected officials, gravitate to Washington, because that is "where the action is."

If the "back to the sixties" federal programs were well designed and executed, they might energize the economy, accelerate productivity growth, and put the United States back on the track of higher expectations and leadership in the world community. The risks, however, are large. It is not clear that the federal government has the capacity to manage new programs that intervene in so many aspects of community life. Can Congress and the president exercise leadership in initiating so many domestic reforms and oversee their execution at the same time they are dealing with all the problems of leadership in an increasingly complex and interdependent world? Can they find a way between the twin dangers of loose federal controls that invite misallocation of funds and rigid controls that are often inappropriate in local situations? Past experience suggests strong doubts.

The most serious impact of pervasive federal activism might be on the quality of state and local government and on citizen motivation to work for change. There is certainly a danger that a "back to the sixties" scenario would reverse recent trends and lead to declining energy and capability at the state and local level. Both voters and politicians in states and localities might decide to "let Washington do it."

Whatever its advantages or disadvantages, "Back to the sixties" is unlikely to occur. It would take a major shift in people's willingness to pay taxes at the federal level. Given the current antagonism toward big government and lack of clarity about which level of government has responsibility for specific functions, this reversal of attitudes toward federal taxation is hard to imagine.

Dividing the Job

The third scenario is more realistic than "back to the sixties" and more workable than either of the other two. It is based on the premise that Washington has neither the managerial capacity nor the grass-roots support to simultaneously create a federal budget surplus, reform health financing, and implement the productivity agenda—while also managing increasingly demanding international responsibilities. It would be better to divide the job, focus the energies of the federal government on the parts of the task for which it has a distinct advantage, and rely on the states for activities they are more likely to carry out successfully.

"Dividing the job" would involve five major changes in policy. First, the federal government would take charge of reforming the nation's health financing system to accomplish two objectives: firm control of medical costs and universal health insurance. Cost control is crucial, since broadening coverage without controlling costs will only exacerbate medical inflation. Fees and reimbursement rates for all medical services would be set according to a negotiated formula that all providers would have to accept. Controlling the rate of increase of these fees and reimbursement rates would gradually reduce the rate of increase in medical spending to roughly the rate of growth of the economy as a whole. Universal coverage could be achieved by full national health insurance or, more like-

ly, by some combination of private and public insurance. The new program would supplant medicaid, relieving state and local government of an increasing burden.

Even a limited public role would require additional federal revenues. Since these taxes, like current social security and medicare taxes, would be clearly related to identifiable benefits, they would be more acceptable to the electorate than general taxes to finance unspecified spending or deficit reduction. The health taxes should be earmarked for health services and deposited in a health insurance trust fund that would take over the spending functions now financed by medicaid and other health programs for low-income people. The size of the tax increase required would depend on the type of health financing program chosen, but even a limited reform would shift public spending for health from state and local budgets to the federal one. With successful control of medical cost inflation, it would be possible to provide health insurance for the currently uninsured without increasing total government health spending above that currently projected for the end of the decade.

Second, the states, not the federal government, would take charge of accomplishing a "productivity agenda" of reforms designed to revitalize the economy and raise incomes. These reforms would address needs such as education and skills training, child care, housing, infrastructure, and economic development. Once clearly in charge, the states would compete vigorously with each other to improve services and attract business by offering high-quality education, infrastructure, and other services.

Third, the following federal programs would be devolved to the states or gradually wither away: elementary and secondary education, job training, economic and community development, housing, most highways and other transportation, social services, and some pollution control programs. Some specific programs where federal action is needed would be retained, even expanded; for example, higher education scholarships for low-income students and federal support for scientific research, including research on learning. A few transportation functions—especially air traffic control—would remain federal. Devolving these functions would reduce federal spending by at least $75 billion. Much more important, devolution would reduce future pressure on the federal deficit. Citizens and organizations concerned about better housing, training, and education would have to lobby in their state capitals, not Washington.

Fourth, the federal government would bring its budget from deficit into surplus (including social security). It would then be adding to national saving and reducing the federal debt held by the public. The federal deficit would be eliminated by a combination of devolving domestic programs to the states, imposing health insurance taxes and transferring medicaid spending to a health insurance trust fund, and reducing other federal spending (including defense) faster than currently projected. Interest costs would also decline. General federal taxes need not rise.

Fifth, the states, with the blessing or the assistance of the federal government, would strengthen their tax systems and increase revenue by adopting one or more common taxes (same base, same rate) and sharing the proceeds. Common shared taxes would reduce border concerns and could enhance the revenues of poorer states. One version is a uniform value-added tax (VAT), shared on a per capita basis and substituted for state retail sales taxes. Another is a single state corporate income tax, perhaps collected by the IRS along with the federal tax, and shared on a formula basis. Another one is a shared energy tax.

Compared with "back to the sixties," "dividing the job" implies a smaller federal government and a larger state-local

sector. Tax increases would be required under both scenarios, since the deficit is to be reduced and more services provided in both. In "back to the sixties" all the new revenue would be raised at the federal level. In "dividing the job" additional revenue would come from a combination of new federal taxes for health insurance and increased state and local taxes for the productivity agenda.

Despite its name, the "dividing the job" scenario does not involve a return to dual federalism. There are important areas in which cooperative federalism is necessary and desirable. One of those is environmental protection. Many hazards to the environment cross state lines and cannot be satisfactorily dealt with by states and localities acting alone. Others are of largely local concern.

Welfare for families with children (AFDC) also remains a shared state and federal responsibility in this scenario. Some would argue for making AFDC federal or at least for a basic federal program that the state could supplement. Joint responsibility, however, would give both levels of government incentives to try hard to reduce welfare dependency. To this end, the states should improve education, training, and child care for welfare mothers, and the federal government should adjust the income tax to increase the after-tax rewards for low-wage work.

THE RATIONALE FOR "DIVIDING THE JOB"

A major premise underlying "dividing the job" is that citizens are anxious to revive the American dream. They want to live in an economy that provides sustainable and widely shared growth in the standard of living. They are prepared to work hard and make sacrifices to that end if they see the connection between the effort and the result. People want high-quality public services—schools that teach modern skills, retraining opportunities for workers who lose jobs, efficient transportation, health care for those who need it—but they also want to know what happens to the taxes they pay and see some evidence close to home that public efforts make a difference.

Successful economic revitalization is hard to carry out or even to comprehend on a national scale. Many of those concerned about the lagging American economy have urged the federal government to adopt an explicit industrial policy. Proponents usually envision a huge federal bank with a board allocating funds to industries and areas. Such grandiose notions flounder on closer examination, however, in part because of the sheer size and diversity of the economy. Few would trust the federal government to allocate funds wisely or nonpolitically to development projects or programs. Washington cannot mobilize the community support, business-labor cooperations, or coordination that successful development requires.

Governors and mayors, however, are closer to the scene. They have more ways to generate business, labor, and community support for development and put together an effective program to increase investment and jobs. The best chance of having a successful industrial policy in a country this size is to have a lot of communities, states, and regions competing with each other to improve their own economic prospects.

Several scholars of federalism have argued that states are currently better suited than the federal government to undertake the economic development policies needed to ensure successful American competition in a global economy. David R. Beam has pointed out that although Americans came to rely on Washington for economic policy leadership in the Great Depression, the federal government did not have the answers when the economy began faltering in the 1970s.[2] The "supply-side" tax cutting of the early 1980s left the federal government with a paralyzing deficit. A national industrial policy was rejected out of fear that federal government efforts to choose and foster industrial "winners," as the Japanese supposedly do, would result in the government handing out political favors at taxpayers' expense. Meanwhile, however, states moved aggressively to improve their own economies and revenue bases. They set up public investment and venture capital funds, fostered technology and innovation, and sent missions abroad to attract foreign investment and promote regional exports. The new state development efforts emphasized skill training, education reform, business-university partnerships, and better transportation, rather than tax concessions to business.

Beam concluded that states are likely to do a better job in the economic development role than the federal government and ventures this hypothesis:

Under conditions of global competition and rapid technological change, a large nation composed of multiple political and economic centers, each striving to secure its own economic advantage, will be better able to advance the welfare of its citizens than a large nation dominated by a single political and economic center.[3]

In an earlier study, Paul Peterson and his colleagues examined federal grant programs in an attempt to discriminate between types of programs for which intergovernmental cooperation was productive and those for which it was counterproductive or unnecessary.[4] They found that "development programs" (vocational education, hospital construction, community development) were enthusiastically supported by state and local officials and easy to administer cooperatively. The federal government allowed state and local officials substantial discretion in using the money, and all parties thought the relationships were working well. "Redistributive programs" (compensatory education, rent subsidies, health maintenance organizations, special education) were much more contentious. These programs were directed at special groups with little political clout and mandated new kinds of services. States and localities usually tried diverting the funds to more general purposes. Then federal officials tightened the guidelines. Cooperation took time and effort.

Peterson and his coauthors concluded that federal development programs were unnecessary, except in occasional cases where the benefits spilled across state borders in a major way. In general, these programs would be undertaken by states and localities and run in much the same way without federal prodding. The "redistributive programs," however, accomplished national purposes that states and localities were resisting and would not have addressed without persistent intervention from Washington. The authors urged refocusing federal domestic policy to emphasize redistribution while confining federal economic development effort to a few special cases.

This analysis suggests a major worry about "dividing the job," often expressed by traditional liberals, that states will neglect the less fortunate, particularly by retreating from federal efforts to improve the life chances of poor children. The fear has some basis, but poor and minority young people will not be left out if states play an aggressive role in economic development. Improving education, skills, and opportunities for the future labor force necessarily involves concentrating on the futures of low-income and minority young people, because they will make up such a large part of that labor force. Indeed, effective action to improve the skills and job prospects of the poor, especially young people, seems more likely if it is seen as essential to community and state economic development than if it is seen as federally funded redistribution policy.

Moreover, "dividing the job" does not involve federal abandonment of the poor. Low-income people would benefit most from universal health insurance. Most uninsured workers are in low-wage jobs, and one of the barriers to leaving welfare is fear of losing medicaid without gaining employer-provided health insurance. The federal food stamp program and joint federal-state funding of AFDC would also remain.

TWO PREVIOUS ATTEMPTS TO SORT OUT RESPONSIBILITIES

The idea of reexamining federal and state responsibilities is, of course, not a new one. In the 1970s and 1980s, concern with the proliferation of grants and the confusion of state and local roles led two presidents to propose new ways of sorting out the jobs.

Nixon's New Federalism

The administration of President Nixon, at least until it was paralyzed by the Watergate scandal and the ensuing impeachment proceedings, put unusual emphasis on improving the efficiency and effectiveness of government. Nixon's first term (1969–73) was a high watermark for White House concern with evaluation of program results, experimentation with policy innovation, and serious discussion of alternative ways of structuring responsibilities—both within Washington and between the federal and state levels—to make government work more efficiently.

Nixon's conservative ideology led him to emphasize sorting out federal and state functions more clearly, a concept he called New Federalism. He espoused a stronger role for the federal government in income maintenance and health care, although neither his family assistance plan nor his health proposals ever passed Congress. He believed in returning decisionmaking power to the states by cutting the number of categorical grants and providing federal aid to the states with fewer strings. In addition to general revenue sharing, he proposed a series of consolidations of categorical grant programs called "special revenue sharing." One hundred and twenty-nine separate programs were to be grouped into six block grants that the states could use for broad purposes such as education, transportation, and law enforcement, with relatively little interference from Washington.

The block grants had little success in Congress. Lobbyists for existing categorical programs fought to preserve their separate identity. In the end, only two of the proposed block grants were enacted, both in somewhat altered form. The Comprehensive Employment and Training Act of 1973 pulled together various manpower training programs, most enacted in the 1960s, into a single grant. The community development block grant program, which subsumed model cities and other funds for urban renewal, was passed by Congress and signed by President Gerald Ford in 1974.

The Reagan Swap Proposal

President Reagan's first year was dominated by his dramatic budget proposals. Then in his second State of the Union address in 1982, Reagan announced another drastic set of proposals, a series of "swaps" designed to sort out federal and state roles more clearly and reduce the number of categorical grants. The swap proposals, ill timed and ill thought out, met with strenuous opposition, not only in Congress, but in some parts of the state and local community as well. One salient feature was federal assumption of the full costs of medicaid in exchange for devolution to the states of the AFDC and food stamp programs. Such an exchange would have reversed the 1970s trend toward greater federal responsibility for welfare programs, reflected in the growth of the federal food stamp program and the creation of supplemental security

income for the elderly, blind, and disabled poor in 1974. Most governors could see only fiscal catastrophe in agreeing to take on the full costs of AFDC and food stamps, especially in the recession year of 1982. If they had focused on the rapid escalation of medicaid costs that was already beginning to strain their budgets and worsened later in the decade, they might have found Reagan's deal more attractive.

Another feature of the swap was federal devolution of a diverse set of forty-four programs (125 separate grants) to the states in return for phasing out a group of federal taxes (alcohol, tobacco, and telephone taxes, part of the federal gasoline tax, and a windfall profits tax on oil and gas sales). Revenues from the designated taxes were initially to be deposited in a trust fund for the states, but the taxes themselves were to be reduced gradually and eliminated by 1991. If the states wanted to replace the lost federal revenue, they would have to raise their own taxes. States and localities, already adversely affected by recession and reductions in federal grants, were not enthusiastic about the swaps. After considerable negotiation and attempted compromise, the idea died.

Since President Reagan's ideas about federal-state relations bore some similarity to President Nixon's, both came to be described by the Nixon term, New Federalism. Both emphasized decentralization and restoring decisionmaking authority to state and localities. However, the Nixon proposals, especially revenue sharing, involved increases in the amount of money flowing from the federal treasury to state and localities. Reagan's intention, by contrast, was to reduce domestic spending at all levels. Nixon's revenue sharing program was eliminated and other grants were reduced. Reagan believed that devolving responsibilities to the states, especially for social programs, would lead to less total government spending because state and local taxpayers would be less willing than federal ones to foot the bill. His expectations were not realized, however. The federal retreat energized state and local government and led to higher state and local taxes.

HOW "DIVIDING THE JOB" DIFFERS

"Dividing the job" differs from both the Nixon and Reagan proposals. Moreover, changing economic and political circumstances make fundamental restructuring of the federal-state relationship both more necessary and more feasible in the 1990s than it was in the 1970s and 1980s.

"Dividing the job" involves devolution of whole federal functions to the states. The Nixon proposals, by contrast, merely combined specific categorical programs into more general block grants and perpetuated joint federal-state responsibility for the function in question. The Reagan plan did devolve specific programs, but did not offer any clear division of responsibility between the two levels.

The Reagan package would have diminished states' financial resources and added to the pressure on states to reduce services. The Nixon plan was more attractive to the states because it included general revenue sharing. However, as state officials are all too aware, GRS proved a fleeting boon.

Moreover, restructuring the federal-state relationship is more urgent in the 1990s than it was even a decade ago. The lagging economy must be revitalized and the federal deficit eliminated. "Dividing the job" is an attempt to improve the chances of attaining both objectives.

NOTES

1. Paul Krugman, *The Age of Diminished Expectations: U.S. Economic Policy in the 1990s* (MIT Press, 1990), p. 193.
2. David R. Beam, "Reinventing Federalism: State-Local Government Roles in the New Economic Order," paper prepared for the 1988 annual meeting of the American Political Science Association.
3. Beam, "Reinventing Federalism," p. 16.
4. Paul E. Peterson, Barry G. Rabe, and Kenneth K. Wong, *When Federalism Works* (Brookings, 1986).

4. Financing National Policy through Mandates

Joseph F. Zimmerman

Local governments always have been subject to mandates and restraints imposed by their state legislatures and the Congress. In several states, a significant burden is placed upon local governments by the cumulative effects of the mandates. In 15 states, municipalities

SOURCE: "Financing National Policy Through Mandates" by Joseph F. Zimmerman in *National Civic Review*, Summer-Fall 1992, pp. 366–373. Reprinted by permission.

have secured constitutional amendments to restrict the levying of all or certain types of mandates unless the state funds the associated costs or provides a new source of revenue.[1]

In examining the mandate problem, it is essential to distinguish a mandate from a restraint. The former is a legal order—constitutional provision, statute, or administrative rule—*requiring* a local government to undertake a specified activity or to provide a service meeting minimum state or national standards. The latter *prevents* completely or partially an action contemplated by a local government. Restraints also may impose significant costs upon local governments.

Similarly, a distinction has to be made between a federal mandate and a "pass-through" state mandate. The Congress may impose a mandate, such as fair labor standards, directly upon local governments or the mandate may be placed upon the states, which in turn impose the mandate by statute upon their political subdivisions (i.e., a pass-through).

In 1965, the Congress commenced to employ its powers of preemption in an innovative manner. National minimum standards were established and the states were allowed to exercise "regulatory primacy" only if they developed standards at least as stringent as the national one, along with an enforcement plan.[2] The state legislature imposes the standards by statute and/or authorizes a state agency to establish standards by rules and regulations. These mandates upon local governments may be labelled "pass-through" mandates. This type of partial federal preemption first was employed in the Water Quality Act of 1965 and subsequently has been employed in a number of regulatory statutes.

The mandate problem has been aggravated for local governments by the sharp increase in the number of national mandates since 1965. Most federal mandates involve significant costs for local governments and total federal restraints also may involve costs for these units. The most expensive federal mandates are minimum environmental standards that political subdivisions must comply with. A total restraint, such as the prohibition of regulation of bankruptcies, may involve no direct state or local governmental costs. Several total restraints, however, have significant costs for municipalities. The complete federal ban

on the dumping of sewage sludge in the oceans, for example, necessitates that coastal municipalities utilize more expensive means of disposing of sludge.

Total congressional preemption of a regulatory responsibility may result in indirect expenses for local governments. Congress has preempted totally the regulation of hazardous and radioactive materials, yet the national government lacks sufficient qualified personnel and equipment to respond immediately and effectively to transportation accidents involving such materials. Meanwhile subnational governments have a moral obligation to respond to emergencies involving these materials and incur expenses in responding.

MANDATED COSTS

It is difficult to determine the costs of mandates, in part because of a lack of data on the extent of local government compliance with the various federal mandates. Limited evidence suggests that there generally is voluntary compliance with many mandates, although occasionally a federal agency or a citizen with standing to sue brings an action in United States District Court to compel compliance.[3] The inspector general of the United States Environmental Protection Agency and the United States General Accounting Office have conducted studies revealing the failure of a number of subnational governments to comply with specific federal mandates.[4]

Determining the costs of mandates, furthermore, is a difficult task because of inadequate local government cost-accounting systems and the failure of federal departments and agencies to issue all rules and regulations authorized by law. In particular, the Environmental Protection Agency (EPA) has been slow in promulgating implementation rules.

Estimating the costs to local governments of compliance with various environmental regulations—such as hazardous waste disposal and prevention of ground-water contamination—is compounded by the fact that many environmental mandates overlap.

ENVIRONMENTAL MANDATES

Environmental mandates collectively are the most expensive federal requirements imposed upon local governments and have proliferated in number during the past two decades. In 1970, for example, municipalities were affected primarily by mandates relating to waste water treatment.

The most costly post-1970 federal mandates relate to drinking water and solid waste disposal. In 1986, for example, Congress directed suppliers of drinking water to control for an additional 83 contaminants. In 1990, the EPA issued regulations requiring the 173 largest cities and 47 counties with populations exceeding 100,000 to obtain permits to discharge pollutants into storm sewers and to submit plans for managing discharge systems.

The EPA released in 1988 a report estimating that use charges and fees per household will increase by an average of an additional $100 annually by 1996 to finance municipal compliance with environmental mandates.[5] The increase, however, will be $160 per household annually for municipalities with populations under 2,500 and an estimated 21 to 30 percent of these units will experience financial difficulties in attempting to comply with the mandates.

In 1990, the EPA reported that local governmental expenditures for environmental protection totalled $27.3 billion in 1981 and $32.8 billion in 1987, and are estimated to total $47.85 billion in 2000.[6] In addition to a sharp increase in the amount expended, there is a significant change in the share of the burden of environmental expenditures financed by local governments—from 76 percent in 1981 to 82 percent in 1987, and to an estimated 87 percent in 2000.

New standards were established by the EPA in 1991 to lower by ten-fold the level of lead in drinking water. These regulations require the 79,000 public water suppliers to monitor tap water in hundreds of thousands of homes throughout the nation and to adjust treatment techniques in accordance with the monitored results. It is anticipated that many suppliers will have to replace lead service lines to minimize lead levels at household taps. Furthermore, suppliers will be required to employ corrosion-control treatments using substances, such as lime and soda ash, to reduce water acidity by increasing pH and alkalinity. The EPA estimates that approximately 40,000 suppliers will be required to install or improve corrosion-control and deliver a public education program. Most of these systems serve fewer than 500 persons. Approximately 8,000 systems, chiefly in the Northeast and Midwest, may have to replace lead service lines. Total costs are in the range of $500 to $800 million per year.

Costs aside, small local governments do not have qualified staff, including municipal attorneys, to read and decipher the voluminous and detailed statutes and rules and regulations imposing mandates.

"Pass-through" mandates raise the question in states with constitutional provisions for state reimbursement of mandated costs whether the states must reimburse local governments for the costs of compliance. The EPA in 1991 promulgated final drinking water standards for 33 contaminants and revised standards for an additional five contaminants, thereby increasing the number of standards for contaminants to 60.

To comply with the new standards, the New Hampshire Department of Environmental Services proposed to implement new regulations requiring 32 small towns to filter drinking water at a cost of

$200 to $300 per family annually. The proposed regulation triggered local government demands that the states reimburse the towns for the cost of filtering drinking water under a 1984 state constitutional amendment requiring the state to reimburse cities and towns for the costs of implementing *state* mandates. State officials maintain the regulations do not constitute a state mandate because the regulations mirror federal regulations.

The filtering requirement also affects large cities. New York City, for example, is constructing a $600 million filtration plant which will have estimated annual operating costs of $5 million.

A final example of a costly federal environmental mandate relates to air quality. Approximately 14 percent of municipal waste is incinerated. The federal Clean Air Act of 1990 will necessitate the installation of expensive anti-pollution devices, at an estimated cost of $20 million per incinerator, in 100 large municipal incinerators.

The EPA estimated in 1990 that the cost of implementing environmental mandates by local governments will increase from $7.6 billion in 1972 to $32.6 billion in 2000, but local governments' share of environmental mandates costs will fall from 29 percent to 22 percent.

The United States Supreme Court's 1985 decision in *Garcia v. San Antonio Metropolitan Transit Authority*, which upheld the extension of the Fair Labor Standards Act to state and local governments, has had a major financial impact upon these governments. Additional costs totalled an estimated $1.1 billion in 1986, with overtime costs exceeding $700 million.

An expensive mandate for school districts is the 1986 federal requirement that asbestos be removed from all public buildings. The cost of removing asbestos from the Landing Elementary School in Glen Cove, New York was $200,000. Fur-

thermore, the Lead Contamination Control Act of 1988 requires that schools test drinking water and remove all water coolers not meeting national standards.

COSTS ASSOCIATED WITH RESTRAINTS

Most federal restraints impact state governments, but a few have a significant effect on local governments. Although the Social Security Act of 1935 did not mandate that state and local governments provide coverage under the Act to their employees, many subnational governments decided to provide such coverage. Because of increasing Social Security taxes and less expensive retirement benefits available from private firms, a number of subnational governments commenced to withdraw from the system. Congress amended the Act in 1983 to prevent subnational governments from terminating participation in the program and to increase the old-age, survivors, and disability insurance contribution rates in 1984, 1988 and 1989 over the scheduled rates. These changes cost state and local governments $470 million in 1984, $750 million in 1988 and $810 million in 1989.

In 1982, Congress decided to prohibit private and public employers from requiring non-policy-making employees to retire because of age. The prohibition of superannuation of state and local government employees may result in increased expenses for subnational governments if older workers are less productive because of their age and could be replaced by more productive younger persons who would receive lower salaries and wages.

The Marine Protection Research and Sanctuaries Act of 1972 restricts subnational governments by requiring that they obtain permits from the United States Army Corps of Engineers prior to dumping dredge materials in the ocean. While this legislation increased disposal costs to a limited extent, the Ocean Dumping Ban Act of 1988, prohibiting the dumping of sewerage sludge in oceans, has had major cost implications for municipalities in coastal areas. Several municipalities have been fined by the United States District Court for violating consent decrees involving the stoppage of ocean dumping of sludge.

Federal laws regulating development of wetlands have resulted in local governments' losing property tax revenues because of the inability of the developer of a major commercial or industrial project to obtain a permit from the Corps of Engineers, which is also charged with protecting wetlands.

THE LOCAL IMPACT OF FEDERAL PREEMPTION

Direct Congressional regulation of the states and their political subdivisions have become well-established since 1965. Congressional regulation of subnational governments expanded sharply during the 1980s and coincided with a significant decrease in the amount of direct and indirect financial assistance provided to these governments by the national government. State government participation in the General Revenue Sharing (GRS) program was ended in 1980 when the program was renewed, and the program for local governments was not extended in 1986. The impact of federal preemption also was accentuated by the Congressional decision not to fund a number of grant-in-aid programs and to reduce appropriations for other grant programs.

In sum, the Congress during the past quarter-century has changed from a generous supplier of funds to subnational governments to a preemptor. This preemption involves imposing costs that could bankrupt, within the next decade, many small local governments with little or no commercial and industrial tax base, as well as fiscally strained cities.

Federal mandates admittedly confer direct benefits upon residents of localities and indirect benefits for residents of neighboring jurisdictions affected by spill-over problems such as air and water pollution. The mandates also impose substantial compliance costs with no direct federal cost reimbursement. Furthermore, national intervention in traditional local affairs raises the important question of democratic control of the public purse at the local level. Federal mandates are negating the gains made by the home-rule movement in assuring general purpose local governments greater discretionary authority.

In 1980, *The New York Times* editorially identified local government budget distortion as an undesirable result of the increased number of federal mandates upon local governments:

Mandates often have perverse effects. They require local officials to spend local money on some worthy services at the expense of others, but take away their discretion as to which needs the money more . . . Uncle Sam is in no position to balance these claims. Nor can he simply say, 'raise taxes.' He does not know when local taxes become so onerous that taxpayers are driven out. Both tasks call for balancing that must be left to local politics.[7]

The ability of many local governments to finance federally mandated costs is restricted by state constitutional property and tax-levy limits. Even in the absence of such restrictions, the availability of the initiative to voters in many local governments ensures that a tax revolt will occur if the property tax burden becomes too great.

A related problem is the decline in citizen participation in local affairs that may be attributable to the centralization of decision-making in Congress. Traditionally, opportunities for direct citizen participation in the governance process have been the greatest at the local government level. In small local governments, citizens may conclude that participation is a waste of time since a large portion of the local government's budget is mandated by the national and state governments. The reduction in attendance at New England open town meetings is associated with the proliferation of mandates.

Federal preemption shifts citizen control of their local governments to the remote Congress, where opportunities for citizen participation are limited and many economic interest groups have special access. Participatory democracy clearly suffers when national mandates arc imposed upon local governments.

The cumulative burden of federal mandates may force a number of small local governments and fiscally distressed cities into bankruptcy unless the Congress and/or the state legislatures initiate remedial action. The former could reimburse the local governments for some or all of the mandated costs or provide special grants-in-aid to the heavily impacted units.

CONCLUSION

The Congress lacks an incentive to control mandated costs in the absence of a reimbursement requirement. The federal deficit precludes reimbursement of all mandated costs, but a strong case can be made for reimbursement of costs associated with new mandates or enhancement of existing mandates. However, there should be no federal reimbursement for costs flowing from mandates designed to ensure due process of law, civil rights and voting rights.[8]

Relative to small local governments with restricted tax bases, state legislatures could promote the merger of small political subdivisions, provide additional state financial assistance to these units, or transfer responsibility for a number of functions subject to federal mandates to the counties or to the state.

In conclusion, Congress has two responsibilities toward small local governments: to exercise restraint in imposing mandates, and to reimburse localities partially or totally for some mandated costs.

NOTES

1. For details, see Joseph F. Zimmerman, *State Mandating of Local Expenditures* (Washington, D.C.: United States Advisory Commission on Intergovernmental Relations, 1978), and Joseph F. Zimmerman, "The State Mandate Problem," *State and Local Government Review*, Spring 1987, pp. 78-84.
2. Typologies of total and partial federal preemption are presented in Joseph F. Zimmerman, *Federal Preemption: The Silent Revolution* (Ames: Iowa State University Press, 1991), pp. 66-74 and 91-100.
3. Office of the Inspector General, *Non-Community Water System Program* (Washington, D.C.: United States Environmental Protection Agency, 1988).
4. Office of the Inspector General, *Report of Audit on the Lead in Drinking Water Program* (Washington, D.C.: United States Environmental Protection Agency, 1990), *and Drinking Water: Compliance Problems Undermine EPA Program as New Challenges Emerge* (Washington, D.C.: United States General Accounting Office, 1990).
5. Sector Study Steering Committee, *Municipalities, Small Business, and Agriculture: The Challenge of Meeting Environmental Responsibilities* (Washington, D.C.: United States Environmental Protection Agency, 1988), pp. 2-19.
6. A Preliminary Analysis of the Public *Costs of Environmental Protection: 1981-2000* (Washington, D.C.: United States Environmental Protection Agency, 1990), p. 10.
7. "Fighting Federal Mandates," *The New York Times*, August 16, 1980, p. 20.
8. Zimmerman, *Federal Preemption: The Silent Revolution*, pp. 152-158.

CHAPTER 3

Elections and Political Parties

Elections and political parties are of crucial importance in democratic political systems because together they are the principal way voters can influence what governments do. The concerns addressed in this chapter center on the future of state political parties, the voting patterns of ethnic groups in city elections, and the best procedures for allowing voters to participate directly in the making of governmental decisions (direct democracy).

Let's take the topic of direct democracy first. The most familiar elections are those that allow voters to choose who will govern them over the next two or four years. In many states and localities, however, voters are not limited to choosing among rival candidates for political office. They can also vote to approve or reject laws initiated by the voters or passed by the legislature, and can determine whether an elected official, whose term is not complete, should continue in office. These elections are known as the initiative, the referendum, and the recall.

The initiative and referendum exist in several different forms. The simplest are the direct initiative and the popular referendum. The direct initiative allows voters to bypass the legislature and propose a law by petition, and have it submitted to the voters for approval or rejection. The popular referendum allows voters to petition a new law passed by the legislature to the ballot for approval or rejection by the voters. Rejection by the voters means that the law will not go into effect. The recall enables voters to remove an elected official from office before his or her term is completed. If the required number of voters sign a petition, a special election is called and voters can decide if the official named in the recall should continue in office. The direct initiative is used in thirteen states; twenty-five states use the popular referendum, and fifteen states have the recall. A number of local governments have all or some of these options available to voters, too.

Although these techniques of direct democracy may seem worthwhile at first glance, it is frequently argued that voters are too poorly informed to decide complicated questions of public policy and, in reality, special interests and their money dominate the policymaking process, whether it is in the electoral or legislative arena. Political scientist Thomas E. Cronin, in Reading 5, presents several suggestions to improve the initiative, referendum, and recall. One suggestion for the initiative and referendum would require sponsors of a proposal to receive drafting advice from the state's attorney general before they can circulate a petition. Another suggestion would require the preparation and distribution of official voter information pamphlets to help voters make informed decisions. To ensure that the recall is aimed at removing only truly incompetent officials, Cronin offers a number of recommendations including the requirement that petitions contain the names of a high percentage of registered voters, perhaps 20 percent. Even with these new safeguards, Cronin concludes that the initiative, referendum, and recall should not be used on a frequent basis but only under extraordinary conditions.

Reading 6, by political scientists Charles S. Bullock and Susan A. Mac-Manus, examines the extent of racial bloc voting by blacks, Hispanics, and whites in municipal elections in Austin, Texas. One might expect the dominant pattern to be conflict: minority groups voting cohesively for candidates who share their minority status and whites voting cohesively for white candidates. Overall, Bullock and MacManus report that blacks and Hispanics had a similar voting pattern in almost half of the elections studied, with the remaining elections dividing almost equally between Hispanics and whites voting together and blacks and whites voting together. Interestingly, in elections won by Hispanic candidates, blacks and Hispanic voters tended to vote together, but winning black candidates found that Hispanic voters were not usually part of their winning coalition. Perhaps the most important finding in this study is that in 48 percent of the contests the leading vote-getter was also the leader among the three groups of voters. This lends support to the hope that the politics of ethnically diverse communities will be one of coalition and consensus building rather than conflict.

Political scientists Malcolm E. Jewell and David M. Olson, in Reading 7, address the future of political parties. Many students of the governing process argue that parties are indispensable as a link between voters and political leaders. In an ideal world, party government would characterize the politics of the states and the nation. For party government to exist, parties have to be reasonably competitive in elections and perform the following activities: (1) stand for certain programs and principles, (2) nominate candidates loyal to the party program, (3) conduct political campaigns so as to explain their programs to the voters, and (4) enact their programs into public policy when the voters give them control of the government.[1] But with the much-publicized decline of political parties in the past twenty-five years, can parties fulfill the role assigned them in the party government model?

Jewell and Olson, examining the vitality of today's political parties, see conflicting trends. For example, on the downside there is no doubt that the ability of parties to control who is nominated in the primaries is less today

---

[1] Sarah McCally McMorehouse, *State Politics, Parties, and Policy* (New York: Holt, Rinehart and Winston, 1981), pp. 30–31.

than in past years. In addition, fewer voters identify themselves as Democrats or Republicans and fewer voters use the party label as a guide in voting. Nonparty factors such as incumbency and candidate characteristics seem to be growing in importance for voters. On the positive side, the Democratic and Republican parties are more competitive in state election than they have been in the past, an essential condition for party government, and elected officials still frequently respond to public policy questions on the basis of their party affiliations. Jewell and Olson conclude that the future of political parties in the states is unclear, but the opportunity is present for improving the capacity of political parties so they can approach the party government ideal.

QUESTIONS FOR DISCUSSION

1. If the state (or city) you are living in allows the use of the initiative, referendum, or recall, name some of the issues that have been decided by voters in recent years. In your opinion, did voters understand the issues and make the right decisions?

2. If the state (or city) you are living in does not allow the use of the initiative, referendum, or recall, do you think these procedures should be adopted? Why?

3. Are there any communities you are familiar with that are becoming more ethnically diverse? Has this been reflected in the electoral and governing processes?

4. How competitive are the political parties in your state? Do the Democratic and Republican candidates, especially for governor, offer the voters different policies to choose from during election campaigns?

5.   Sound and Sensible Democracy

Thomas E. Cronin

SAFEGUARDS FOR THE INITIATIVE AND REFERENDUM

Initiatives and referenda are here to stay. Improvements, however, are needed to remedy their abuses and misuses. There are no magic formulas available, and inevitably those who want to can nearly always find inventive strategies to get

SOURCE: For permission to photocopy this selection, please contact Harvard University Press. Reprinted by permission of the publishers from *Direct Democracy* by Thomas E. Cronin, Cambridge, Mass.: Harvard University Press, Copyright © 1989 by the Twentieth Century Fund.

around or minimize the intent of any regulation. Also, some safeguards will be more appropriate for certain states than others. What makes sense for California may not make much sense for Maine. What makes sense for Inkum, Idaho, may not be desirable or workable for Los Angeles. Different jurisdictions have to adjust any safeguards to their own conditions.

Many of the following suggestions have been adopted in various locations. Many have been proposed by interest groups, writers, or legislative committees as ways to help citizen-voters to understand ballot issues better and to exercise the judgment required to make direct democracy live up to its potential. If direct democracy is to work properly, rules of fair play must be established in advance. Our efforts at self-government are never wholly achieved or defeated; every generation needs to make improvements and ensure that democratic principles are encouraged.

1. *Sponsorship and filing fee.* A proposed initiative and referendum should have a number of sponsors—between 100 and 200 individuals, depending on the size of a jurisdiction—and there should be a filing fee of between $200 and $1,000, again depending on the population size of the area. These nominal requirements are necessary to discourage frivolous or publicity-seeking petitions.

2. *Drafting advice provided by the attorney general's office.* Advice from a state attorney general need not be accepted, but it should be available, and petitioners should be required to obtain it. Some states now provide for a review board to go over draft language and eliminate confusing, misleading, or flagrantly unconstitutional wording. Although courts (in advance advisory opinions) could conceivably prejudge the constitutionality of a measure before it goes to court, various officials such as the attorney general and experts in a state's legislative counsel or legislative reference service can offer petitioners some helpful guidance at the drafting stage that may prevent litigation and court intervention at the election or postelection stages.

Some proponents of formal legal review point out that the attorney general at the state level or the city or county attorney may not be the appropriate official to conduct such a preview because of potential conflicts of interest. One group has suggested that legal review be provided free of charge by a voluntary *pro bono* panel of attorneys. "Such a

panel could conduct the review in an objective and professional fashion. This service might be provided in the same manner as the Office of the Public Defender, which provides volunteer attorneys to individuals who cannot afford legal assistance."[1] Other combinations of official and unofficial hybrids of these suggestions may work better, depending on the jurisdiction.

3. *Mandatory official statement and summary of the petition's contents.* After a measure is filed, a state official should be made responsible for giving the measure a title, preparing a concise and readable statement, and providing a slightly longer official summary of the meaning and consequences of the ballot measure. Some jurisdictions already require this, and, obviously, some political problems can arise. Groups who petition often want a glitzier title or a statement. Neutral wording, however, is essential for the integrity of the process and for voter understanding. A worthwhile additional step would be to require state officials to calculate the estimated financial cost of a ballot measure. Although this information must necessarily be approximate, it should be sought at the outset of a campaign.

4. *Reasonable signature requirements.* It should be neither easy nor nearly impossible to obtain the number of signatures necessary to get measures on the ballot. Six to 8 percent of the last vote for governor seems an appropriate requirement for statutory measures, 8 to 10 percent for constitutional measures.

5. *Geographic distribution requirements in certain states.* About half of the states permitting the initiative and referendum require some form of geographic distribution for petition signatures. Massachusetts, for example, has a simple stipulation that no more than 25 percent of the signatures may come from any one county, thus ensuring that not all the signatures would be collected in Boston. Arizona requires that 5 percent of signatures come from fifteen different counties. Missouri requires 8 percent to come from two-thirds of its six congressional districts for a constitutional initiative, and 5 percent for a statutory initiative. Geographic requirements are an additional obstacle for those who want to use direct democracy processes. But those who favor these requirements point out it is now possible in California or Colorado to qualify ballot measures by gathering signatures only in the most populous county or two of the state or in only one part of the state. Thus Orange County, California, or Denver, Colorado, could have an undue influence in the initiative process, one far exceeding the locality's representation in the state legislature.

Critics of a geographic distribution requirement dismiss it as an effort to make the initiative and referendum more difficult and more expensive to use. They say no section of a state should be denied access to the process just because it has a proposal of special concern to its region. California's attorney general says a geographic requirement is unnecessary: "If there is something wrong with the measure, let the voters vote it down. They've done it before. They'll do it again."[2]

Geographic requirements make sense in states such as New York, Texas, or Hawaii. Surely a petition in New York should include some signatures from localities outside New York City; a petition in Texas should have at least some support in the various regions of that sprawling state; and some percentage of petitions should come from some of the outer islands should Hawaii adopt the initiative and referendum. These requirements should be kept simple— along the lines of the Massachusetts requirement that no more than 25 percent of signatures should come from any one county or that an upstate/downstate or east/west requirement be stipulated— and minimal rather than high.

6. Stiff penalties for deceptive petitioning. The official wording and title of a proposed measure should be visible on all petitions, and signers should be instructed to read the statement beforehand. The message "Be Sure to Read This Statement before You Sign This Petition" should appear prominently at the top of each petition. Groups circulating a measure should be listed on the petition, and all circulators should sign an oath that all petition signatures have been submitted in accordance with the law.

7. Petition certification requirements. Secretaries of state or similar appropriate officials should be required to check the validity of signatures by means of standard statistical sampling techniques. A 5 to 10 percent base sample should be sufficient.

8. Required state legislative hearings. One way to make direct democracy processes more compatible with representative government would be to require state legislatures to conduct statewide hearings on the merits and drawbacks of a proposed ballot measure once it gets the necessary signatures. In many instances the legislature will have already held hearings on this or similar issues, but the initiative would provide the occasion for proponents and opponents to come together and examine evidence, fiscal estimates, minority rights, and other policy and tax consequences of the measure under consideration. It would allow, and sometimes force, legislators to get involved and make their views known and would allow grassroots groups as well as leadership elites to offer their views. Press and media coverage should be encouraged in order to educate the general public.

California has made an effort to conduct such hearings in recent years, but these have not lived up to expectations. Most legislators apparently prefer to be back home campaigning for reelection; others prefer to avoid controversial issues. Still others may believe such hearings only give publicity to single-issue groups they would prefer to get little or no attention. Whatever the reasons, the hearings in California have been cursory at best.

More experimentation with hearings is needed. Possibilities include televised hearings and regional hearings in major population centers. Either would be a way to get legislators involved debating the issues. Legislators should be able to inform and shape public opinion. In the many cases in which the legislatures have decided not to act on these or similar measures, representatives should make it clear to the public why they made that decision.

Mandatory hearings could have undesirable consequences in some states. In California, for example, where it is not unusual for a dozen or more measures to be on the ballot, holding hearings on every issue would be costly. In most states, however, only a few issues are usually on the ballot, and hearings would be far more manageable. It would appear feasible to hold several general "town meeting" style hearings in a few of the major population centers or regional centers in a state, concentrating at least on the most controversial initiatives. In short, what California has tried, if not succeeded with, other states might successfully adapt for their own region.

9. Voter information pamphlets. A clearly presented official information pamphlet is essential to enable voters to make wise policy choices. In Massachusetts, Oregon, and Washington such pamphlets are read, used, and often mentioned as a key guide in voting decisions. Properly prepared and designed, they provide each household with the text of an initiative, the basic arguments for and against it, and its projected costs and consequences. Efforts should be made both to simplify the statements and analyses and to provide 100-word "ballot digests," such as are used in some California cities.

A less expensive alternative, and possible one more likely to reach less well-educated voters, might be for states and localities to print ballot digests in local newspapers or to air them on radio and television. But the real challenge for states remains to provide both readable and informative voter pamphlets.

10. Mandatory financial disclosure. States and localities should require that all contributions of $200 or more be disclosed during and after an initiative and referendum campaign. Disclosure satisfies the public's right to know who is supporting and who is opposing a ballot measure. The public deserves to know as much as possible about the way an initiative got on the ballot and how it is being promoted or opposed. The size and source of contributions are often important issues in initiative and referendum campaigns. Grossly excessive contributions from a single source or single industry may well promote backlash among voters, and reasonable full disclosure remains "one of the best guarantees available against the excessive influence of money on election outcomes."[3] To keep reporting and enforcement burdens to a minimum, some figure should be set for the specific disclosure of individual donations. Overall expenditures, however, should also be disclosed. The majority of contributions raised before the election should be reported early enough that the public can appreciate the significance of the information. A final disclosure statement should also be required after the election and upon the termination of the respective campaign committees. States may also want to require immediate public disclosures of notable large contributions (perhaps over $2,500 in large states, or $1,000 in smaller states).

11. Expenditure floors and public financing. A fair initiative and referendum campaign should allow both sides to make their case to the public. Although it may not be politically and financially possible to allocate public funds to both sides of every ballot issue campaign, some form of assistance, such as a floor, could be put into effect in one-sided issue campaigns when one side raises more than a specified amount. Such a provision would prevent one group or view from dominating the public debate and the flow of information to prospective voters.[4] Political scientist Austin Ranney makes a persuasive case for this form of regulation:

> The absence of parties and party labels in referendum campaigns means that the voters enter the campaigns with less information and fewer guideposts than in candidate elections. And the campaigns are therefore significantly more important as suppliers of information and arguments that make for interested voters and informed votes. Accordingly, the prime object of government regulation of referendum campaigns should be to ensure that both the proponents and opponents of each proposition should have enough resources to make at least adequate presentations of their cases.[5]

12. A reinstituted fairness doctrine. Because most voters get much or most of their information about ballot issue campaigns from radio and television, fair access to media outlets is essential. Broadcasters should hold themselves to tough access standards in initiative and referendum campaigns, precisely because voters need even more information

on ballot issues than they do about the candidates for office. If they fail in this obligation, the FCC should again be charged to regulate toward this end.

13. Stiff penalties for false advertising. State and local legislatures should pass laws providing for prosecution against false advertising in initiative and referendum campaigns. The integrity of ballot issue elections is too often compromised by misleading claims, phony statistics, and misrepresentations to the voters. Well-publicized fines and penalties for the obvious violators of these laws will go a long way toward encouraging better-informed debate. Information about the identity of sponsors should be disclosed on the face of all advertisements.

14. Restriction of statutory and constitutional initiatives to general elections. Turnout is highest in general elections and considerably lower in primary or special elections. Many voters registered or identifying with neither major political party fail to turn out for primary elections because they are not that interested in intraparty personnel decisions; and in some states only those who are registered with a party affiliation are allowed to vote in primary races. Thus, states should place initiative issues on the ballot only in general elections. Some states already have such a requirement. Although some states would consequently have a long list of issues on the ballot at the general election, this somewhat daunting effect should be offset by two factors: a voter information pamphlet would have to be published only once every two years, and the maximum possible number of voters will be involved in the decisions.

OTHER CONSIDERATIONS

An *advisory referendum* system, such as that used in some European nations, is sometimes recommended as a better means than our current initiative and referendum to involve the general public yet keep the legislatures in charge of lawmaking. "The advantage of this approach," according to David B. Magleby, "is that the public can indicate its preference for general policy, and the legislature can handle the statutory or constitutional steps necessary for the implementation and administration of policy."[6] Magleby advocates putting simple questions before the public, and sometimes even multiple-response questions, thereby encouraging voters to offer general policy guidance and communicate the direction and intensity of their preferences. The functions of drafting and deciding on specific laws, however, would be left to the legislature.

This alternative to direct democracy would be more than a mere public opinion poll, but much less than advocates of direct democracy would prefer. It would, however, stimulate public debate, attract voter interest, and allow the public to play at least some role beyond selecting the people sent to the state legislatures. Although the results of such elections would be nonbinding, issues that won approval by significant majorities would place the legislature under pressure either to go along or to explain its opposition.

The advisory referendum is an unlikely candidate for adoption in states that now permit regular direct democracy elections; voters in those states would view such a move as a clear diminution of their political rights. On the other hand, if the signature requirements were decidedly less, perhaps just 3 or 4 percent instead of the usual 8 or 10 percent for binding referenda, there would be some merit to viewing the advisory referendum as a complement to rather than a substitute for the regular system. Certainly, the advisory referendum could be a reasonable experimental alternative for states and communities that do not now provide for the initiative and referendum.

Another alternative to the most familiar type of initiative and referendum system is the indirect initiative. Whereas under direct initiative a measure automatically goes on the ballot when enough petition signatures are obtained, under the *indirect initiative*, when enough signatures are filed the proposal first goes to the legislature, which may approve, modify, or reject the measure. Maine, Massachusetts, Michigan, Nevada, and South Dakota, among others, permit some form of indirect initiative. Some of these states allow for modification or amendment; others require the measure to be approved or rejected exactly as it came to the legislature. If rejected or sharply amended, sponsors may force the measure to a vote of the people. Often, however, proponents have to go through the petition process before the measure is certified for the ballot. "The indirect initiative is no panacea," writes Neal R. Peirce, "but there are powerful arguments in its favor." It involves legislators further in the lawmaking process. "It strengthens, rather than weakens, representative democracy for forcing legislators to come to grips with an idea they may have sought to avoid before. It brings into play the forces of moderation, compromise, common sense so often lacking in direct initiatives."[7]

The indirect initiative concept is endorsed by the League of Women Voters and the National Municipal League, but critics see it as just one more obstructionist hurdle raised by those who do not really want direct democracy procedures to be used at all. They claim that where it has been used, state legislatures almost always reject the initiatives, thus protracting an already lengthy process. Critics also point out that a legislature already has the option of passing its own form of legislation addressing the problems raised by petitioners. A responsive legislature would encourage the petitioners to withdraw their ballot measure or undermine their efforts to win petition support for the measure by having acted in a representative fashion.

The indirect initiative does indeed delay legislative change. But it also provides an opportunity for measures to get a formal hearing and to benefit from the experience of veteran legislators and their staffs.[8] It is a sensible option for states not permitting the direct initiative.

A few states have prohibited paying people to circulate and gather signature petitions. Advocates of banning *paid circulators* believe the process should be run by volunteers. They say there is too great a risk that paid circulators will be less candid or even untruthful when gathering signatures. If you have enough money, they argue, you can get just about anything on the ballot. Clearly, the early intentions of direct democracy have been compromised in states such as California, where petition by paid professionals has become a profit-making big business.[9]

Those who favor paying signature gatherers say any restriction against it violates freedom of speech; they note, too, that there is no such restriction on workers in candidate elections. In 1988 the U.S. Supreme Court, in *Grant v. Meyer*, struck down a Colorado law that made it illegal to pay people for gathering signatures. Such a law, the Court ruled unanimously, restricts freedom of expression, guaranteed under the First Amendment; it restricts access to the most effective, fundamental, and perhaps economical avenue of political discourse, direct one-on-one communication. Colorado's secretary of state, Natalie Meyer, decried the ruling and predicted it would create a flood of unnecessary and unrepresentative ballot measures. But several conservative groups hailed the decision as one restoring the freedom of all individuals in all states to use their efforts to get initiatives on the ballot.

Each side offers valid points in this debate. Yet the consensus Supreme Court ruling settles the issue, at least for the near future. And as a practical matter, it is necessary anyway to permit paid circulators in the larger states.

A final consideration is whether it will be impossible to *limit large contributions* to initiative and referendum campaigns. Courts have struck down efforts to restrict or limit corporate or individual financial contributions to ballot measure campaigns, but many groups such as Common Cause continue to press for such limits. Large contributions, they say, give an unfair advantage to the side able to attract "big money." Big spenders overwhelm the initiative process and may cause voter apathy. California Common Cause recommends contribution limits on corporations and unions but not on individuals, arguing that corporate, not individual, spending is overwhelming the initiative process in California. The group also believes that courts might eventually be stricter on corporations and unions.

Those who object to limiting contributions contend such a restriction is an infringement of individuals' or organizations' rights to express and support their political preferences; although it is not as severe a limitation as prohibiting them from making any contribution, it is still a significant infringement. If an initiative might significantly damage a group, industry, or individual, surely that group or individual should have the right to contribute any amount desired to defeat it.

We need to determine more accurately the influence, and perhaps the corrupting influence, of "big money" in initiative and referendum campaigns. Valuable preliminary studies have already been done; more will be needed before the courts can be persuaded to allow limits on contributions. Meanwhile, the question of money will best be treated by effective financial disclosure laws and some form of partial public financing or subsidies.

RECOMMENDATIONS FOR IMPROVING THE RECALL PROCESS

Recall is in many respects the most controversial of direct democracy practices. Yet it is plainly in the tradition of American concern for keeping public officials accountable. Although existing requirements have limited its use primarily to the local level, it has been used occasionally at the state level in Arizona, California, Idaho, Michigan, and Oregon, and usually with sensible results. Its use to force out of office an insensitive and irresponsible governor in Arizona suggests the positive virtues of the recall at the state level.

Of course the recall has been occasionally misused. In San Francisco, for example, a strident, intense, and irresponsible group used the recall mainly to embarrass Mayor Dianne Feinstein. Some public officials, understandably enough, complain that the presence of the recall in their jurisdiction encourages a zero-risk or overly timid neutrality in elected officials.

On balance, however, the recall has been mainly used to weed out incompetent, arbitrary, or corrupt officials. It is a positive device reminding officials that they are temporary agents of the public they serve.

Perhaps the most bogus of the critics' claims is that the recall discourages able citizens from running for office. There are plenty of factors dissuading thoughtful individuals from running for office, but the recall is far down the list. Able elected officials find that they have considerable latitude to define issues, shape the public policy agenda, educate citizens, and persuade people of their general positions.

The recall remains a sometimes mildly helpful but crude safety valve, and its use should be restricted to true emergencies. The essential objective is to encourage recall efforts only in those serious situations when a public official has been inexcusably negligent or has become incompetent. The recall can play an important, if minor, role in our political system, but the possibilities for misuse and abuse are considerable and must be monitored.

Although polls indicate Americans would like to have recall for federal officials, the recall device is not necessary or desirable for members of Congress or for the president. Because of their two-year terms, members of the House of Representatives are already nearly always running for reelection. For a variety of reasons, some of which may not be so healthy, they customarily retain a "candidate's state of mind." U.S. Senators, elected for six-year terms, serve in a chamber that was deliberately designed to take a longer view of the national interest. Recall would alter that view and the federalist principles that justify the existence of the Senate. And presidents can be overridden by Congress, checked by the Supreme Court, or impeached.

The recall is occasionally proposed as a vote of no confidence that would permit the removal of presidents who have lost the ability to govern. But the potential abuses outweigh the potential merits. If, however, presidents were granted six-year terms and House members were allowed four-year terms, some form of recall would become more feasible, and for the same reasons the recall was championed eighty years ago at the state and local levels. "That longer terms of office and a freer range of discretion are conducive to administrative efficiency is everywhere accepted," wrote Charles A. Beard, "and the recall seems to offer to democracy the proper safeguards against usurpation which will warrant the granting of longer terms and larger powers to executive authorities."[10]

Safeguards for the recall device will necessarily vary from place to place, depending on political traditions, and especially between the state and community levels because of the varying populations and time requirements. Still, if we are to permit the recall, these minimal regulations are necessary to ensure its soundness.

1. Petition statement and identification of petitioners. A recall petition should contain an explicit statement of the grounds on which the removal of the elected official is sought. The names of the persons or groups sponsoring the petition should appear clearly on the petition, as well as the message "Be Sure to Read This Statement before You Sign This Petition."

2. High signature requirements. A large percentage of signatures should be required for recall elections to keep costly elections to a minimum and to discourage sour-grapes and personal, retaliatory efforts. Signatures should be of registered voters—perhaps 25 percent of those voting in the last election for governor, or for the particular office in question, or 20 percent of registered voters in general—or whichever is higher.

3. No recalls during first six months in office. No recall petitions should be filed against any officer, state or local, within the first six months of an official's term. This provision would help prevent sour-grapes efforts or the variation of continuous recounts.

4. No circulation of recall petitions for six months after an unsuccessful recall election. This limitation would prevent continued harassment of officials and encourage voters to wait until the next election.

5. Stiff penalties for making false statements about the petition. Criminal penalties should exist for misrepresenting or making false statements about the

petition to gain signatures, for filing petitions known to contain false signatures, or for using a recall petition as a threat to extort money or special factors and contracts.

6. Financial disclosure. Ten days before and a week after a recall election, sponsors should file documents listing any contributions over $200. This information, made available to the local or state media, should allow citizens to discern if one or more single-interest groups were the primary supporters of the recall effort. It would also inhibit persons who have some reason to conceal their interest from investing in the recall campaign. In the absence of other limits or financial restrictions, financial disclosure should be imperative.

7. Signature verification. Officials from the secretary of state's office or election clerks at the local level should be authorized to verify recall petitions by using accepted professional statistical sampling techniques.

8. "Cooling off" period. Depending on the size of the jurisdiction, there should be a "cooling off" period after signature filings, before the date for the recall election is set. This might be forty or fifty days at the city level, seventy-five days or more at the state level. It would prevent hasty action in light of a single controversial vote, personnel decision, or budget decision and would allow for emotions to cool and the record and overall performance of the official in question to be appraised. It would also allow for media analysis of the controversy.

9. Public hearings. Depending on the availability of an ethics committee, a campaign fair-practices commission, or some similar relatively neutral and professional body, an open hearing should be scheduled on the merits of the recall. At such time both the petitioners and the targeted official could present their arguments. This discussion and evaluation would make information available to permit citizen-voters to make a more reasoned judgment.

• • •

SENSIBLE DEMOCRACY

The initiative, referendum, and recall have made modest contributions to American democracy. They have become so deeply rooted in the political culture of the many states and cities allowing them that they will undoubtedly continue to be used, and probably used more often, in the future. As in the past, their use will be tied to cycles of citizen impatience and frustration and to periods of social upheaval and economic uncertainty. If these populist devices are to serve us better than they have in the past, they must be subject to the kinds of safeguards outlined in this [reading]. Additional states should not adopt these processes without carefully considering the very real abuses detailed in earlier chapters and establishing regulations that will prevent them.

States that have employed these popular democracy practices should continue to do so, with modifications that will improve their integrity. Those states not now allowing the initiative, referendum, and recall should consider them, yet they should prudently weigh their assets and liabilities. Each state and locality will have to decide whether and how these practices would mesh with its own traditions and political culture. The nation has considerable variations and diversity, and no set of uniform policy or structural prescriptions need be imposed on dissimilar states and communities.

These devices should be used only when glaring deficiencies have occurred in basic governmental practices. Thus, recall of public officials should be rare. Initiative petition drives should be launched only when groups have tried to achieve their goals through their regular representative institutions. Legislatures should refer matters to the public reluctantly, understanding that it is primarily their own job to tackle tough policy issues. Too-frequent referrals will undermine the legitimacy of the republican principle. And none of these devices or practices will work well unless voters understand and respect the process and have access to the information necessary to make informed decisions.

• • •

NOTES

1. Coro Foundation, *Local Initiative: A Study of the Use of Municipal Initiatives in the San Francisco Bay Area* (San Francisco, 1984), p. 47.
2. John K. Van de Kamp, California attorney general, speech to Symposium on Initiative and Referendum Reform, Center for the Study of Law and Politics, San Francisco, December 7, 1984 (Mimeograph), p. 7.
3. Austin Ranney, "Regulating the Referendum," in *The Referendum Device* (Washington, D.C.: American Enterprise Institute, 1981), p. 92.
4. See Daniel H. Lowenstein, "Campaign Spending and Ballot Propositions: Recent Experience, Public Choice Theory, and the First Amendment," *UCLA Law Review*, 29 (February 1982), 578–582.
5. Ranney, "Regulating the Referendum," p. 95.
6. David B. Magleby, *Direct Legislation: Voting on Ballot Propositions in the United States* (Baltimore: Johns Hopkins University Press, 1984), p. 195.
7. Neal R. Peirce, "The Indirect Way for Americans to Take the Initiative," *Sacramento Bee*, February 12, 1979, p. B11.
8. Nick Brestoff outlines one of the best variations on the indirect initiative in "The California Initiative Process: A Suggestion for Reform," *Southern*

California Law Review, 48 (1975), 922–958.

9. Larry L. Berg and C.B. Holman, "Losing the Initiative: The Impact of Rising Costs on the Initiative Process," *Western City*, June 1987, p. 44.

10. Charles A. Beard, Introduction to

Charles A. Beard and Birl E. Shultz, eds., *Documents on the State-Wide Initiative, Referendum, and Recall* (New York: Macmillan, 1912), p. 69. See also Herbert Croly, *Progressive Democracy* (New York: Macmillan, 1914), pp. 324-327.

6. Voting Patterns in a Tri-Ethnic Community: Conflict or Cohesion?

Charles S. Bullock III and Susan A. MacManus

Many southwestern and western communities are tri-ethnic.[1] Of the 499 cities in the South and West with over 25,000 population, seven percent now have black and brown populations exceeding 10 percent; three percent have 15 percent or greater. The emergence of tri-ethnic communities has raised important questions about ethnic voting patterns: 1) how often do minority groups (black, brown) align more closely with each other than with whites; 2) how often does a minority group (black, brown) more closely align with whites than with the other significant minority group; 3) how often does a plurality/majority of each group (black, brown, white) support the same candidate; and 4) what are some plausible explanations for the ethnic voting patterns which have emerged.

This research report examines the level of intragroup and intergroup electoral conflict and cohesion in municipal elections in a tri-ethnic community, Austin, Texas, from 1975–1985. In 1980 the city was 71 percent white, 18 percent Hispanic, and 11 percent black. Between 1970 and 1980. Austin's Hispanic popu-

lation grew 65 percent, its white population 44 percent, and its black population 41 percent.

A black has been on the Austin City Council since 1971 and there has been a Hispanic member since 1975. The six council members and the mayor run for designated slots. There is a majority vote requirement for municipal elections with runoffs held when no candidate for a position receives a majority.

We do not contend that Austin is representative of ethnic political patterns for Texas, or the Southwest, although it may be. The Austin data may, however, stimulate additional research into this area which would reveal whether the Austin experience is typical of America's emerging tri-ethnic communities.

THEORIES OF ETHNIC VOTING PATTERNS

Most studies of ethnic and racial voting patterns have been bi-ethnic[2] or bi-racial.[3] Relatively little empirical work has compared electoral patterns of multiple ethnic groups within the same community since the studies of Tom Bradley's 1969 and 1973 mayoral election campaigns in Los Angeles.[4] Those studies found that Mexican American voting patterns more closely resembled those of whites than of blacks. Mexican Americans were a less cohesive voting

SOURCE: From "Voting Patterns in a Tri-Ethnic Community: Conflict or Cohesion? The Case of Austin, Texas, 1975–1985" by Charles S. Bullock III and Susan A. MacManus from *National Civic Review*, January/February 1990, pp. 5–22. Reprinted by permission.

block than blacks, but more cohesive than whites.

The Los Angeles election studies reported that black turnout exceeded that of Hispanics and whites.[5] This finding parallels other studies contrasting the organizational participation rates of whites, blacks, and/or Hispanics.[6] In general, black participation rates equal or exceed those of whites and far exceed those of Hispanics. The participation differentials are "explained" by assimilation-, generational-, socioeconomic-, cultural-, legal-, and relative deprivation-based theories, among others.[7]

Unfortunately, most of these studies are based on socioeconomic and participatory data from the 1960s and early 1970s. They do not reflect the vast improvements in minority socioeconomic status (especially education) which occurred in the 1970s. Nor do they reflect the significant gains in minority registration, turnout, and electoral success which followed passage of and amendments to the Voting Rights Act.

Ironically, in the period following the 1975 amendments to the Voting Rights Act the tendency of the courts, the U.S. Justice Department, and scholars has been to treat the concerns of minorities (racial and language—blacks and browns) as one and the same. A partial explanation for this tendency may be that the strategies followed by Hispanic activists in the 1970s seemed to parallel those successfully used by black activists in the 1960s.[8] Similar treatment of the preferences of blacks and browns was also an integral part of Jesse Jackson's rainbow coalition.[9] Yet, the 1984 CBS-*New York Times* exit polls of voters in the Democratic presidential primaries found that 78 percent of the blacks supported Jackson, compared with 14 percent among Hispanics, which was similar to the white vote for Jackson, nine percent. Should we really expect electoral preferences of the two groups to be identical when other literature suggests

that *policy* preferences are not?[10] Even when there is a tendency for blacks and Hispanics to share policy preferences, this agreement may be overridden by the social distance between the two minority groups.[11] A closer look at the premises underlying the formation of various ethnic coalitions is important to our understanding of this apparent inconsistency.

PREMISES OF ETHNIC COALITION THEORIES

Black-Brown Coalitions

The assumption that minority groups will coalesce is derived from the premise that since both groups have been discriminated against by whites, they will favor the same candidates in their search for political and economic influence. The minority-supported candidates tend to be minority, Democratic, and/or liberal, white candidates.[12]

Leaders of both minority groups have urged their members to "work together on issues of common interest, such as affirmative action, employment, job training, housing, and health care."[13] The inference is that these common policy preferences are strong enough to stimulate formation of minority electoral coalitions, particularly when candidates run against whites. (Interestingly, there have been few examinations of what happens to the coalition when black and brown candidates run against each other or in races where all three ethnic groups have at least one candidate.)

Minority-White Coalitions

The assumption that the common experience of ethnic discrimination or of being disproportionately disadvantaged economically suffices to unite blacks and Hispanics is suspect. The history of other ethnic groups suggests instead, that those who share common disadvantages may view one another as *competi-*

tors. In the Northeast, for example, the Irish and Italians often were political opponents. Moreover, ethnics have often adopted the stereotypes of other groups that WASPs had of them. Myrdal found that immigrants often became more hostile toward blacks than the native born population was.[14] Thus, despite both groups' being disadvantaged vis-a-vis whites, "their marginal status has also led to competition between them, accompanied by rancor and mistrust."[15]

Using data from a statewide Texas poll conducted in mid-1986, Dyer and Vedlitz conclude that "perhaps the most significant findings bearing on the coalition potential between blacks and Hispanics is the relatively low acceptance between blacks and Hispanics. Both groups are more accepting of Anglos than they are of each other."[16] Dyer and Vedlitz see social distance as impeding joint black-Hispanic action that could emerge from a general agreement on a number of spending priorities. Dreyfuss sees greater difficulty in unifying blacks and Hispanics: "The major obstacle to political alliance is the mistrust that the two groups have of each other. Other problems include differences on key political issues, competition for federal funds, and a sense of unequal power. While blacks are accustomed to complaining about their lack of influence, many Chicano leaders view with envy the gains that blacks have made."[17] Conflict over power and the policy agenda also characterizes the relationship between Cuban Americans and blacks in Miami.[18]

Each group's leaders periodically accuse the other of not being genuinely concerned with "minority issues" and of aligning with whites against them to get ahead faster.[19] Most of these conflicts occur over allocational decisions. As Herzog notes, "When the objective is to secure common material goals, there are very definite tensions that test a coalition. For example, when the goal is better job opportunity, the competition for scarce rewards produces severe conflict.[20] He also observes that black-brown coalitions become more tenuous as the possibility of electoral success for each group improves. Under those circumstances, each group is more inclined to build electoral coalitions with whites than each other.

Black-White Coalitions

There are a number of alternatives regarding black-white coalitions reflecting the different community socioeconomic conditions. Holloway reports that in some bi-ethnic, rural, lower-income communities, a basic strategy has been to form a liberal coalition linking blacks with "underdog whites" (poorer, less-educated) and white liberals.[21] This perspective assumes that "the 'underdogs' in the community are potentially a majority and should be able to unite in pursuit of common economic interests.[22] Hahn, Klingman, and Pachon refer to this strategy as "redistributive politics" that "aim to improve the position of persons at the bottom of the socioeconomic hierarchy at the expense of those who have been the traditional beneficiaries of public as well as private programs.[23] In other communities, the more pragmatic coalition may be among blacks and white elites (business and financial leaders, wealthier conservative whites).[24]

There is some evidence that black-white coalitions are more common than Mexican American-white coalitions, especially on issues.[25] Greater political sophistication of blacks in understanding the policy-formation process is the major explanation for this finding.[26]

Mexican American -White Coalitions

Other studies have asserted that Mexican American-white coalitions are more common.[27] Lopez argues that "the trend in Mexican American attitudes is away from an association with blacks and toward an alignment with Anglos" because whites are more accepting of Mexican Americans than they are of blacks.[28] According to Ambrecht and Pachon, Mexican Americans, to a greater extent than blacks, have been assimilated into white middle class communities and schools.[29]

There is some evidence of Mexican American-white coalitions. As noted earlier, in the Los Angeles mayoral elections of 1969 and 1973, white and Mexican American preferences more closely resembled each other than those of blacks.[30] But just as with black-white coalitions, Hispanics are concerned about whether to coalesce with poor and liberal white or the white elite.[31]

Shifting Alignments

Some studies have shown that racial groupings shift depending upon the nature of the policy area.[32] "On employment, government services, and educational issues (distributional issues), Hispanics and blacks are found to be competitive or conflictual, whereas on civil rights and law-enforcement issues (authoritative issues) they tend to be consensual."[33] Holloway notes two other conditions under which coalitions shift: 1) when local leaders experiment with alliances; and 2) when leaders do not reflect the opinions of their group members.[34] In other words, differences in intragroup cohesion may explain shifting intergroup coalitions. Whites and Hispanics are far less likely to be cohesive within their group than are blacks.[35]

Another stimulant to shifting coalitions may be the performance of minority candidates once elected. Sonenshein has observed that Tom Bradley's performance won over the white Republican business community and reduced the gap between blacks and moderate whites.[36] Finally, changes in the relative

size of ethnic groups within a community may alter the nature of their electoral coalitions. "Group size can affect the extent of voter mobilization, expectations of success, range of alternatives, extent of resources, and intensity of incentives."[37]

There is, then, reason to expect that voting alignments in tri-ethnic communities may be dynamic rather than stable. There are five possible voting patterns in communities having three ethnic groups: 1) blacks and Hispanics uniting in opposition to whites; 2) blacks and whites uniting against Mexican Americans; 3) Hispanics and whites uniting against blacks; 4) blacks, Hispanics and whites sharing a common preference; and 5) each group having a unique preference. We do not expect a minority versus white coalition to have been exclusive and persistent in Austin city elections over the past decade.

Research Design

Two measures of voting patterns will be examined here. One is the frequency with which possible pairs of groups agree on a candidate in opposition to the third group. This assessment determines the percentage point differences in support for the candidate who gets a majority or plurality of the vote. To illustrate, if the winning candidate got 38 percent of the black vote, 45 percent of the Hispanic vote, and 65 percent of the white vote, this would be counted as a situation in which blacks and Hispanics united against whites. The difference in support among blacks and Hispanics is seven points, compared with a 20-point difference between Hispanics and whites and a 27-point spread between whites and blacks.

A second measure considers the number of times that an individual was the most preferred candidate within each group. This second approach allows for the possibility that a candidate may be the winner with all three ethnic groups, or that each group has a different choice.

The analysis uses data from six Austin municipal elections held between 1975 and 1985. The unit of analysis is the contest for a position of mayor or council member. Estimates of the support for candidates among voters in the three ethnic groups were generated using ecological regression.[38]

FINDINGS

Of the 50 contests for mayor and council, the vote for the leading candidate was more similar among blacks and Hispanics in 24 instances. Each of the other two possible patterns occurred in almost 25 percent of the elections. Therefore, while the most common pattern was for blacks and Hispanics to be more similar to each other than to whites, this is not the only pattern.

Minority group similarity may not be typical of all elections, but it may have been more common when there was a minority candidate. Although minorities voted together and less like whites in just under half of the elections, minority unity may have dominated contests in which there was a black or Hispanic candidate. Analyses of voting patterns for minority candidates present two kinds of data. The first reports patterns for contests won by minority candidates; the second deals with minority candidates who lost.[39] In seven of eight contests in which a Hispanic triumphed (i.e., was a majority or plurality leader), Hispanics and blacks tended to vote together. There is, however, a distinctly different pattern in the seven contests won by blacks. In only one of these did blacks and Hispanics coalesce. The more common pattern was for less difference between Hispanic and white voting than between Hispanic and black voting. Of 35 elections won by whites, Hispanics and blacks were more alike 16 times while blacks and whites were most alike 13 times.

Turning to unsuccessful Hispanic can-

didates, for only one of these did blacks and Hispanics unite, while for two, Hispanics and whites voted more alike. The most common pattern was for blacks and whites to vote alike and this occurred five times. There were four blacks who lost to white candidates. For the two earlier ones, Hispanics and whites voted alike. In 1985, however, the least difference was between black and Hispanic voting. Black-brown coalitions were much less frequent for unsuccessful than successful minority candidates, occurring for only a quarter of the losing minority candidates.

While minorities vote together more than either group does with whites, this pattern accounts for just under half the elections studied. Even when there is a minority candidate and black-brown unity might be most likely, the minority candidate is opposed by a coalition of whites and the group of which the minority candidate is not a member in 16 of 27 contests. Black-brown agreements are most likely when there is a successful Hispanic candidate. Blacks support successful Hispanic candidates but Hispanics do not reciprocate when there is a black candidate. Instead, Hispanics tend to vote more like Anglos and less like blacks when there is a black candidate. If this pattern exists in the California cities studied by Browning, Marshall, and Tabb, it could further explain the animosities discovered between the two minority groups in some cities.[40] Not only might blacks complain that it appears Hispanics are more often given things that blacks have had to work for— initial Hispanic council representation in California was more often via an appointment than was initial black representation—but Hispanic voters are less supportive of black candidates.

The second perspective on voting patterns looks at whether a candidate was the leading vote getter with more than one ethnic group. The pattern for most favored candidates is different from that for differences in vote shares. Most frequently (48 percent of the time), a single candidate was the leader among all three groups of voters! The second most common pattern (one-third of the time) was for minorities to back one candidate while whites preferred someone else. Only once did each group have a unique preference.

Focusing on the favored candidate reveals even less of a minority/white split in the case of minority candidates than existed when we looked at vote shares. Most black and Hispanic candidates who attracted at least plurality support from more than one ethnic group were the leading vote getters among all three ethnic groups. This was true in all but one election won by a black and in five of nine contests in which Hispanics showed strength.[41] No black who was not elected was the leading vote getter among any ethnic group; there was one Hispanic who was the preferred candidate among both minority groups but was defeated by the white vote.

SUMMARY

Electoral results from Austin, Texas demonstrate that while blacks and Hispanics often share candidate preferences, tri-ethnic politics are not universally "minorities versus whites." If the distribution of voting patterns were random, minorities would vote most alike in terms of share of the vote one-third of the time. The minority coalition is particularly likely when a Hispanic is elected, but is infrequent when a black wins or when minority candidates lose.

If we look at ethnic voting patterns from another perspective, minority cohesion appears less important. *The most frequent pattern is for all three groups to support the same candidate.* Successful minority candidates—even more often than successful whites—evoke a positive response from all three sets of voters most of the time, but especially when a black is elected. In no instance would a white candidate have been elected in

place of a black even if we discount the minority vote. Minority votes are more important to the political success of Hispanic candidates. In two instances white votes kept Hispanic candidates from winning majorities in the first primary, and in one instance minorities elected a Hispanic in a runoff over white opposition. Minority votes are more significant for Hispanic than black candidates because blacks are more likely to support Hispanic candidates than Hispanic voters are to support black candidates.

While minorities tend to unite behind winning Hispanic candidates, this pattern did not carry over to black candidates or even to unsuccessful Hispanics. And while black and brown support of successful Hispanics was more alike than either group was with whites, five of the nine successful Hispanics polled at least a plurality from all three ethnic groups. There is, then, no consistent evidence that minorities vote against whites, even when a minority candidate opposes a white.[42]

Since blacks and browns together constitute less than one-third of Austin's population, the willingness of whites to support some minority candidates is critical to the ethnic diversity of the city council. Hispanic and black members on the council ensure that there is descriptive representation of these groups, but, taken alone, do not guarantee substantive representation of minority interests.[43] Enactment of policies desired by blacks and/or Hispanics requires the votes of some white members. The support given by one or both minority groups to most white municipal officials suggests that policy concerns of minorities are advanced by more than just the black or Hispanic council members. The variety of voting patterns that have elected Austin's mayor and council members alert candidates to the possibility of alternative groupings that could produce electoral success. The interaction of supporting groups and enthusiasm within each group means that serious candidates—both incumbents and challengers—dare not take any of the three ethnic groups lightly.

CONCLUSION: SIGNIFICANCE FOR OTHER COMMUNITIES

Many American cities (and suburban communities) are becoming more ethnically diverse. The termination of immigration quotas in 1965, and a surge in the number of immigrants and political refugees from Latin America, Asia, and Africa has drastically changed the face of many U.S. communities. For example, in the 1950s, Europeans constituted 59 percent of all immigrants; by the 1970s this figure had dropped to 18 percent. At the same time, Hispanics rose from 22 percent to 41 percent of all legal immigrants, and Asians from 6 percent to 36 percent.[44] As new immigrants are assimilated into the political system, the political dynamics of the host community change. The importance of building coalitions and consensus cannot be overstated. Studies such as this one of Austin, of who aligns with whom, when, and why can prove invaluable to community leaders responsible for building effective rainbow coalitions.

NOTES

1. Much has been made of the difference in the terms "race" and "ethnicity." While some scholars argue that the terms are quite different, (Lipset, 1987) others have regarded the two terms as interchangeable. As Meister notes (1981, p. 86), "Most sociologists use "ethnic" to include nationality, ethno-religious, and racial groups." Moreover, Horowitz (1985, p. 41) concludes that "comparison is facilitated by an inclusive conception of ethnicity that embraces differences identified by color, language, religion, or some other attribute of common origin."
2. See B.C.S. Ambrecht and H.P. Pachon, "Ethnic Mobilization in a Mexican American County: An Exploratory Study of East Los Angeles, 1965–1972," *Western Political Quarterly*, September, 1974, pp. 500–519; R. de la Garza, "Voting Patterns in Bi-Cultural El Paso: A Contextual Analysis of Mexican American Voting Behavior," in F. Garcia, Ed., *La Causa Politica* (Notre Dame: University of Notre Dame Press, 1974), pp. 250–265; J.A. Garcia, "Chicano Voting Patterns in School Board Elections: Bloc Voting and Internal Lines of Support for Chicano Candidates," Atisbos: *Journal of Chicano Research*, Winter 1976–77, pp. 1–13; and J.A. Garcia "An Analysis of Chicano and Anglo Electoral Patterns in School Board Elections," *Ethnicity*, June 1979, pp. 168–183.
3. See. H. Holloway, "Negro Political Strategy: Coalition or Independent Power Politics?" *Social Science Quarterly*, December 1969, pp. 534–547; B. Patterson, "Political Action of Negroes in Los Angeles: A Study in the Attainment of Councilmanic Representation," *Phylon*, Summer 1969, pp. 170–183; C. Davidson, *Biracial Politics: Conflict and Coalition in the Metropolitan South* (Baton Rouge: The University of Louisiana Press, 1972); V. Jefferies and H.A. Ransford, "Ideology, Social Structure, and the Yorty-Bradley Mayoralty Election," *Social Problems*, Winter 1972, pp. 358–372; T.F. Pettigrew, "When a Black Runs for Mayor," in Harlan Hahn, Ed., *People and Politics in Urban Society* (Beverly Hills: Sage Publications, 1972), pp. 95–117; R. Murray and A. Vedlitz, "Race, Socioeconomic Status and Voter Participation in Large Southern Cities, *Journal of Politics*, Vol. 39, 1977, pp. 1,064–1,072; R. Murray and A. Vedlitz, "Racial Voting Patterns in the South: An Analysis of Major Elections from 1960 to 1975 in Five Cities," *Annals*, September 1978, pp.

29–39; P. Kleppner, *Chicago Divided: The Making of a Black Mayor* (DeKalb: Northern Illinois University Press, 1985); and R.J. Sonenshein, "Bradley's People: Biracial Coalition Politics in Los Angeles" (presented at the 1985 annual meeting of the American Political Science Association).

4. See H. Hahn and T. Almy, "Ethnic Politics and Racial Issues: Voting in Los Angeles," *Western Political Quarterly*, December 1971, pp. 719–730; Ambrecht and Pachon, 1974; H. Hahn, D. Klingman, and H. Pachon, "Cleavages, Coalitions and the Black Candidate: The Los Angeles Mayoralty Elections of 1969 and 1973," *Western Political Quarterly*, December 1976, pp. 507–520; R.M. Halley, A.C. Acock, and T. Greene, "Ethnicity and Social Class: Voting in the 1973 Los Angeles Municipal Elections, *Western Political Quarterly*, December 1976, pp. 521–530; and Sonenshein, 1985.

5. Halley, Acock, and Green, 1976.

6. See J.A. Williams, Jr., N. Babchuk and D.R. Johnson, "Voluntary Associations and Minority Status: A Comparative Analysis of Anglo, Black, and Mexican Americans," *American Sociological Review*, Vol. 38, 1973, pp. 637–646; G. Antunes and C.M. Gaitz, "Ethnicity and Participation: A Study of Mexican Americans, Blacks and Whites," *American Journal of Sociology*, Vol. 80, 1975, pp. 1, 192–1,211; S. Welch, J. Comer, and M. Steinman, "Ethnic Differences in Social and Political Participation: A Comparison of Some Anglo and Mexican Americans," *Pacific Sociological Review*, July 1975, pp. 361–382; S.M. Cohen and R.E. Kapsis, "Participation of Blacks, Puerto Ricans, and Whites in Voluntary Associations: A Test of Current Theories," *Social Forces*, June 1978, pp. 1,053–1,069; R.D. Shingles, "Black Consciousness and Political Participation: The Missing Link," *American Political Sci-*

ence Review, Vol. 75, 1981, pp. 76–91; S.A. MacManus and C.A. Cassel, "Mexican Americans in City Politics: Participation, Representation, and Policy Preferences," *The Urban Interest*, Spring 1982, 57–69; and T.M. Guterbock and B. London, "Race, Political Orientations, and Participation: An Empirical Test of Four Competing Theories," *American Sociological Review*, Vol. 43, 1983, pp. 439–453.

7. For good reviews of these theories, see Hahn and Almy, 1971; D.E. Nelson, "Ethnicity and Socioeconomic Status as Sources of Participation: The Case of Ethnic Political Culture," *American Political Science Review*, December 1979, pp. 1,024–1,038; and Guterbock and London, 1983.

8. R.P. Browning, D.R. Marshall, and D.H. Tabb, *Protest is Not Enough: Struggle of Blacks and Hispanics for Equality in Urban Politics* (Berkeley: University of California Press, 1984).

9. See T.E. Cavanagh, *The Impact of the Black Electorate* (Washington, D.C.: Joint Center for Political Studies, 1984); T.E. Cavanagh and L. Foster, *Jesse Jackson's Campaign: The Primaries and the Caucuses* (Washington, D.C.: Joint Center for Political Studies, 1984); R. Smothers, "Alabama Black Leaders are Urging Pragmatism in Supporting Mondale," *New York Times*, March 12, 1984, p. B–9; and C.A. Broh, *A Horse of a Different Color* (Washington, D.C.: Joint Center for Political Studies, 1985).

10. See J. Florez, "Chicanos and Coalitions as a Force for Social Change," in Margaret M. Mangold, Ed., *La Causa Chicana: Change* (New York: Family Service Association, 1972), pp. 78–86; C. Davidson and C.M. Gaitz, "Ethnic Attitudes as a Basis for Minority Cooperation in a Southwestern Metropolis," *Social Science Quarterly*, March 1973, pp. 738–748; S.J. Herzog, "Political Coalitions Among Ethnic Groups in the South-

west," in Rudolph O. Garcia, Ed., *Chicanos and Native Americans: The Territorial Minorities* (Englewood Cliffs, N.J.: Prentice Hall, 1973), pp. 131–138: N. Lovrich, "Differing Priorities in the Urban Electorate: Service Preferences among Anglo, Black, and Mexican American Voters," *Social Science Quarterly*, December 1974, pp. 704–717; J. Dreyfuss, "Blacks and Hispanics: Coalition or Confrontation?" *Black Enterprise*, July 1979, pp. 21–23; C.P. Henry, "Black-Chicano Coalitions: Possibilities and Problems," *Western Journal of Black Studies*, Winter 1980, pp. 222–232; MacManus and Cassel, 1982; S.A. MacManus, "Shifting to State Block Grants: The Priorities or Urban Minorities," *Journal of Urban Affairs*, Spring 1985, 75–92.

11. J.A. Dyer and A. Vedlitz, "The Potential of Minority Coalition Building" (presented at the 1986 annual meeting of the Southern Political Science Association).

12. Hahn and Almy, 1971; Hahn, Klingman and Pachon, 1976; Halley, Acock, and Green, 1976; Sonenshein, 1985.

13. Dreyfuss, 1979, p. 21. See also Lovrich, 1973; Herzog, 1973; Henry, 1980; Dyer and Vedlitz, 1986.

14. G. Myrdal, R. Sterner, and A. Rose, *An American Dilemma* (New York: Harper, 1944), p. 603.

15. Davidson and Gaitz, 1973, p. 738.

16. Dyer and Vedlitz, 1986, p. 19.

17. Dreyfuss, 1972, p. 21.

18. C.L. Warren, J.F. Stack, and J.G. Corbett, "Minority Mobilization in an International City: Rivalry and Conflict in Miami," *PS*, Summer 1986, pp. 626–634.

19. Florez, 1972; Ambrecht and Pachon, 1974; Dreyfuss, 1979; MacManus and Cassel, 1982; MacManus, 1985; J. Mollenkopf, "New York: The Great Anomoly," *PS*, Summer 1986, pp. 591–597.

20. Herzog, 1973, p. 133.

21. Halley, Acock, and Greene, 1976.

22. Holloway, 1969, p. 537.

23. Hahn, Klingman, and Pachon, 1976, p. 511.

24. Holloway, 1969; Sonenshein, 1985.

25. MacManus, 1985.

26. Dreyfuss, 1979.

27. Davidson and Gaitz, 1973.

28. M.M. Lopez, "Patterns of Interethnic Residential Segregation in the Urban Southwest," *Social Science Quarterly*, March 1981, p. 59.

29. Ambrecht and Pachon, 1974, p. 503.

30. Hahn and Almy, 1971; Hahn, Klingman and Pachon, 1976; Sonenshein, 1985.

31. See Henry, 1980 and Florez, 1973.

32. Henry, 1980; MacManus and Cassel, 1982.

33. MacManus, 1985, p. 85.

34. Holloway, 1969, p. 535.

35. See Hahn and Almy, 1971; Ambrecht and Pachon, 1974; Hahn, Klingman, and Pachon, 1976; Halley, Acock, and Greene, 1976.

36. Sonenshein, 1985.

37. Garcia, 1979, p. 181.

38. For discussions of ecological regression, see L. Goodman, "Some Alternatives to Ecological Correlation," *American Journal of Sociology*, Vol 64, 1959, pp. 610–625; E.T. Jones, "Ecological Inference and Electoral Analysis," *Journal of Interdisciplinary History*, Vol. 2, 1972, pp. 249–269; J.W. Loewen, *Social Science in the Courtroom* (Lexington, Mass.: Lexington Books, 1982); and C.S. Bullock III and S.A. MacManus, "Measuring Racial Bloc Voting is Difficult for Small Jurisdictions," *National Civic Review*, 73:4, July-August, 1984.

39. Losing minority candidacies are limited to contests in which a minority was defeated by a white. Instances in which a minority lost to another minority are excluded.

40. Browning, Marshall, and Tabb, 1984.

41. In the one instance in which blacks and Hispanics preferred one candi-

date while another candidate got the bulk of the white votes, the candidate preferred by most whites was also black. Therefore, in no instance have most whites opted for a white over a black candidate.

42. The attitudes uncovered by Dyer and Vedlitz prompt the conclusion that there exists "a complicated picture of coalition potential among Texas's various ethnic groups. There are elements of commonality between all or parts of the various groups which could serve as the basis for joint political activities, but there are also elements of division between these groups or group segments which would mitigate cooperation" (see Dyer and Vedlitz, 1986, p. 19). These statewide findings may be appropriate for Austin and, if so, would help account for the variety of voting patterns observed in municipal elections.

43. Browning, Marshall, and Tabb, 1984.

44. B.E. Cain and D.R. Kiewiet, California's Coming Minority Majority," *Public Opinion*, February-March, 1986, pp. 50-52.

7.   The Future of State Politics

Malcolm E. Jewell and David M. Olson

Most of those who have gazed into the crystal ball of American politics in recent years have found it cloudy. There is no reason to expect our perceptions of the future of state politics to be any clearer. Rather than trying to make firm predictions that may prove to be faulty, we think it is more useful to call attention to some of the trends—often contradictory in their implications—that we find in American state politics.

We start with several assumptions. The most obvious point is that the future of state politics is closely tied to that of national politics. The states cannot escape the effects of changing levels of national party identification or changes in control of national government, for example. A second assumption is that the American states will continue to be important, independent centers of decision making, despite the influence of the federal government and the growing importance of metropolitan areas. In other words, state government remains important, and therefore the study of state parties and elections remains a subject of interest.

The American people have never been settled in their thinking or in their practices about the proper place of political parties in our government. However, as strong and important as parties may have been in our past, they have coexisted with strong antiparty sentiments. Our present confusion about parties is not new, but is a continuance of that strong American ambivalence toward parties (Gelb and Palley, 1975: 7–20; Ranney, 1975).

If parties are declining in importance, it is largely a consequence of, or at least coincides with, a similar trend at the national level. A number of commentators have raised questions about whether the party system still serves the needs that it once did in the political system. Among the more articulate of these is Walter Dean Burnham:

It is clear that the significances of the party as an intermediary link between voters and rulers has again come into

SOURCE: "The Future of State Politics" from *Political Parties and Elections in American States*, 3rd Edition by Malcolm E. Jewell and David M. Olson, The Dorsey Press, 1988, pp. 279–292. Reprinted by permission of the authors.

serious question. Bathed in the warm glow of diffused affluence, vexed in spirit but enriched economically by our imperial military and space commitments, confronted by the gradually unfolding consequences of social change as vast as it is unplanned, what need have Americans of political parties? More precisely, what need have they of parties whose structures, processes, and leadership cadres find their origins in a past as remote as it is irrelevant? (1970: 132–33)

Despite Burnham's pessimism there are a number of signs that state political parties are alive and well, though they may be developing in ways that are quite different from traditional party organizations. They are more competitive and better organized and financed than in the past, though they must compete for influence in the political system with a larger number of groups and organizations.

In the rest of this [reading] we will summarize both the evidence that state parties are growing stronger and the signs that they are growing weaker. And we will provide some perspectives and opinions that may shed light on the future role of the parties in state politics.

A COMMON PARTY SYSTEM AMONG STATES

Why does each state have two political parties? Further, why does each state have the same two political parties as all the others? Given the size of our nation and the diversity among the fifty states, we might expect a variety of state parties to form in response to the circumstances of their respective states and to gain control of state governments. We might expect three- and four-party systems in at least some states, and in those with two parties, those parties might be different from the main ones nationally.

The thrust of the preceding argument is that these developments are less likely now than at any time in our past. We have a greater degree of national uniformity of conditions now than previously. We have more centralized parties nationally than previously. The conditions promoting a consistency or party formation and alignments are greater now than ever before.

We created a nation from largely independent states before political parties had developed. Politics and elections centered on the individual states. Creation of a new nation created a new political arena—a common set of national offices. For the first time, politically ambitious persons in states could aspire to occupy national offices (especially in Congress). For the first time, political elites, previously restricted to their states, could aspire to and compete for a common set of offices. Once in office they interacted over common policies. No state, by itself, had a majority of votes in Congress to adopt the policies its elites preferred. They were forced to form alliances across state lines. Leaders of national policies, in turn, were forced to look to state leaders for support. Indeed, national leaders traveled through the states seeking allies and attempting to build local bases of support. Political parties, as we know them today, grew out of these developments in the early years of the new nation (Lipset, 1963: 29-51; Goodman, 1967; McCormick, 1967). The amazing development was that the same parties quickly formed in most of the states. It was in this early period that a wide variety of parties could most easily have formed in the states, and when each state could have developed distinctive party systems.

The presidential election has been a powerful catalyst in the formation of a common party system throughout the country. The device of selecting the electoral college separately within each state helped link in-state political elites to like-minded peers among all the states. Likewise, those seeking national office had a powerful inducement to attempt to organize and influence the course of intrastate politics as the means of influencing national politics.

But perhaps—we can only speculate— the selection of the U.S. Senate by state legislatures was an equally key ingredient in the development of a common party system throughout the states. For over a century, U.S. senators were elected by the state legislatures. Those persons elected in local districts to fill a state office were directly involved in the selection of national officials. Likewise, those elites attempting to shape national politics had to reach into the states to influence the selection of senators whom they preferred. The famous Lincoln-Douglas debates were not part of a presidential contest, but were part of a senatorial contest. They were seeking to be selected by the Illinois legislature as a U.S. senator from that state. This debate illustrates the concentration on national policy even in an intrastate contest, and also illustrates the often public means by which the state legislators' choices were shaped. The same incident illustrates also the extent to which the in-state electorate was involved by contesting elites in the issues and choices of national politics.

We have had distinctive state parties in our past. They have been formed in times of economic crisis in the Midwest and of racial turmoil in the South. Perhaps the surprising development is that we have not had more. Invariably, however, they have either died out or have merged with one of the two major parties. It is only in New York State that minor parties have continued to exist over a span of decades and to actively participate in their state's politics. We would guess that the conditions now are less favorable to the growth of distinctive state parties than at any time in our nation's past.

PARTY COMPETITION

Party competition has been growing in almost all of the states—first in the North as a delayed consequence of the New Deal and later in the South after national Republican candidates in the 1950s began making a serious effort to win votes there. The much more competitive character of state party politics is perhaps the most important difference between the states today and the nature of state politics before World War II. There are many reasons for believing that competitive state politics is here to stay, despite occasional slumps that minority parties may experience in particular states. The decline and fall of regionalism, the spread of urbanization and industry, the greater mobility of population, the decline of ethnic factors in party loyalty—all these developments contribute in one way or another to two-party competition at the state level.

In the mid-1970s there was a Democratic trend that strengthened the level of competition in a number of states that had traditionally been under Republican control. On the other hand, this trend delayed the efforts of Republican parties to become fully competitive in southern states. During the 1980s state Republican parties have benefited from the electoral success of the Reagan administration, particularly in the South. Nevertheless, in the South and the West—the two areas of greatest support for the national Republican candidates—there has been enough split-ticket voting to enable the Democrats to control the governorships and/or the legislatures in a number of states.

Control of the governorship is the singlemost important measure of party competition. In the elections from 1964 through 1986, there has been some alternation in partisan control of the governorship in every nonsouthern state except Hawaii. In many of these states there have also been either changes in partisan control of the legislature or divided control between the executive and the legislature. In the North, state party competition appears to have been stronger in recent years than at any time in this century.

The South remains the one area where two-party competition is less than robust, but it has been stronger during the 1980s than at any time since the Civil War. During these years there has been turnover in partisan control of the governorship in almost every southern state. The Republicans have also succeeded in making substantial gains in several of the legislatures where they were weakest, though they have yet to win a majority in any southern legislative chamber. The success of the Reagan administration in the South, the growing independence of voters, and the growing vitality of southern state Republican parties have combined to create a much firmer foundation for competitive two-party politics than in the past.

NEW MODELS OF PARTY ORGANIZATION

It has become a truism that party organizations are declining in importance, and there is no reason to anticipate a reversal of that trend. The traditional party organizations of the eastern and midwestern cities no longer have a supply of new immigrants to provide votes in return for jobs and services. One by one, the old bosses are dying—witness Mayor Daley of Chicago [Richard J. Daley was mayor of Chicago from 1955 to 1976—Ed.]— and no one of comparable skill and power is replacing them. This does not mean that the organizational tasks performed by traditional party machines have become irrelevant. Despite the increasing role of the mass media, those who manage political campaigns still find it necessary to conduct registration drives, poll the precincts, and get out the vote. They still need workers to stuff the envelopes, run the banks of telephones,

and sometimes campaign door-to-door. But increasingly these jobs are performed not by a stable group of precinct leaders and party faithful, but by the volunteers who are mobilized by particular candidates. There is some continuity of party workers from election to election and candidate to candidate, but there is also considerable turnover. The new breed of political workers is motivated not by promises of jobs and other favors but by their interest in particular policies and their enthusiasm for particular candidates.

The old party machines recruited workers largely based on patronage, maintained strong organizational discipline, and used their corps of workers to mobilize large numbers of voters and get them to the polls. The new party organizations have few sanctions they can apply to volunteer workers and much less ability to mobilize a solid bloc of reliable voters. The new organizations may be less powerful, but they may be better adapted to modern politics and better able to use sophisticated techniques of organization and campaign management. While the strongest of organizations in the past were often located in large cities, we now are most likely to find effective party organizations at the state level.

Many state political parties have, in the past fifteen years, opened permanent headquarters. They have raised funds and employed professional staff. A number have attempted to provide support to their legislators in the state capitol, and most attempt to be involved and helpful in elections.

Some of the state parties have also tried to become involved in the new technologies of public opinion polling, of mass media production, and of professional campaign management. To the extent that parties are able to master (and finance) these skills, candidates will be encouraged to cooperate with their state party. The state parties have increased their budgets and headquarters staff, though Republican state parties, both North and South, have far outstripped their Democratic counterparts, both in absolute numbers of dollars and staff, and in rate of growth from 1960 to 1980.

An important ingredient in the revival of state party organizations, apparently, has been the discovery by state chairmen of one another. In both parties, but especially in the Republican, the state chairmen have formed regional associations through which they have met and helped one another. They have apparently learned of new activities and support available to them, and have improved their own morale as a group. They have formed a distinctive subgroup within their national party and have lobbied for and obtained membership on their national committee. Here is yet another way in which state and national politics will be linked. One result, especially among Republicans, will be an increased flow of services and aids from the national party to their state party organizations (Huckshorn, 1971: chap. 7).

PRIMARY ELECTIONS AND PARTY ORGANIZATIONS

What is the future of primary elections in this period of change? . . . The primary was established in a period of one-party domination in many states by reformers who distrusted party bosses and machines; but it is a partisan institution. The primary laws transferred control over nominations from the organizations to the broad mass of voters who identified with the party and (in most states) were willing to register with that party or at least publicly indicate their desire to participate in that party's primary. But, with the increasing proportion of voters who identify as independents and/or vote independently, are we likely to see a decline in voter participation in primaries?

In most states there does not seem to be any consistent trend in rates of participation in primaries, though where the level of party competition is growing, there may be a shift of primary turnout from one party to the other. In some southern states there has been a growth of turnout in Republican primaries; and in most of the South there has been some decline in Democratic primary turnout— presumably because that election is less likely to be decisive as the general election assumes more importance.

Some states have shifted from closed to open primaries or have abandoned the rigid deadlines on shifting party registration from one party to the other. Some states also make it easy for those registered as independents to vote in party primaries. Louisiana has gone to the extreme of permitting nonpartisan primaries. The effect of these changes has been to make it easier for a voter to vote in the primary of his or her choice and to shift back and forth from one primary to the other. We do not know whether, in reality, many voters take advantage of this opportunity to shift party primaries—but over the long run we would expect more of them to do so.

. . . Some state political parties try to influence the outcome of primaries by making preprimary endorsements of candidates. Is this becoming a more common practice, or a more effective one? It is difficult to say because the trends are contradictory. There are a few cases of states, like Massachusetts, where the practice of legalized endorsements has ended. There have also been changes in informal endorsement practices; the Wisconsin Republicans no longer consistently make endorsements while the Massachusetts Democrats have begun to do so. Recent judicial decisions in both Massachusetts and California have strengthened the authority of party organizations to make endorsements on their own.

A more interesting question is whether endorsements are having more or less effect. There have been several recent examples of endorsed candidates being defeated in state parties where the endorsement principle has traditionally been widely supported: both parties in Minnesota, the Massachusetts Republicans, and the Connecticut Republicans. Well-financed independent candidates who make extensive and skillful use of television to appeal directly to the voters present a serious challenge to the party and its endorsees. At the same time the threat that such candidates present to the party organization may strengthen its commitment not only to maintain the endorsement system, but also to provide more tangible assistance to endorsees. The endorsement system also remains an important technique for enhancing the role and gaining the loyalty of party activists.

The verdict is not yet in about the future of the nominating process. Large numbers of voters who consider themselves independents continue to vote in partisan primaries. If these voters were to take much greater advantage of the opportunity to shift back and forth between primaries, the integrity of the party system would be undermined. The endorsement system remains the strongest vehicle available to party organizations for asserting their authority over nominations, but there is no certainty that the parties can continue to make that system work as effectively as it has in the past.

CAMPAIGN FINANCE

Election campaigns are obviously lasting longer and costing more with every year. What is less obvious, however, is that the organization of campaign finance has been greatly altered in the past decade, and we can anticipate further changes in the coming decade.

While the sources of campaign finance are becoming more diverse, they are also becoming nationalized and to some degree centralized through the political parties. National organizations, usually functioning as political action committees, are coordinating state and local

groups and their individual members. The national groups themselves confer and coordinate with each other on endorsements and contributions. The political parties are increasingly active in channeling these groups' funds to their own candidates. In some cases the groups contribute to the parties directly, while more commonly the groups send contributions to the candidate after coordination with and through the national political parties.

Another recent development in campaign funding has been the adoption by sixteen states of some form of public finance. While this reform is not rapidly spreading, its continued use and the experimentation with it in a variety of states are creating the possibility that some workable system will be developed that other states will find useful.

PUBLIC ATTITUDES TOWARD PARTIES

There is evidence that the attachment of American voters to parties, as well as their confidence in partisan institutions, is declining. The proportion of voters identifying with a party has declined from approximately three-fourths to two-thirds in the period since the early 1960s. Surveys of voter opinion in a number of states have shown similar increases in the proportion who are independent. Part of the explanation for this trend is demographic, such as the increased geographic mobility in the country and the increasing proportion of younger persons (eighteen to thirty), who have weaker party loyalties than older persons. These younger voters are evidently much more likely to be independent than similar age groups were a generation ago. We do not yet know what the attitudes are of independents toward the party system. How many have simply broken away from the local environment and family ties that would reinforce party loyalty? How many have no interest in parties or see no purpose in identifying with them? How many are actually disillusioned with parties and clearly hostile to the party system? (Asher, 1980: chap.3).

We have more evidence about the behavior of voters and those who work in politics than we do about attitudes and perceptions, so we will concentrate on this behavior in an effort to understand what trends are occurring in the party systems of the states. First, it is evident that there is a decline in voting along party lines for state offices. The immediate consequence of this trend has been to strengthen two-party competition in some states—those that used to be dominated by a single party. The fact that a majority of voters in such states are no longer totally loyal to one party has enabled the minority party to capture the governorship and win more legislative seats, to establish a foothold as a competitive party. But in the long run the decline of voting along party lines may weaken both parties in the states, depriving them of dependable bases of voting strength and creating occasional landslides in support of popular candidates.

If party loyalty is less frequently the determinant of voting in state elections, what is taking its place? Voters may be more impressed by the fact of incumbency than they used to be in state elections, but governors do not usually gain the same advantages from incumbency that congressmen do. We have described some of the kinds of issues—taxation, for example—that sometimes play a large role in state elections. Issues are likely to remain important in gubernatorial elections, but there is no way to predict what kinds of issues will be salient in state elections of the future. The clearest trend probably is the increasing importance of the candidates' characteristics. The highly successful gubernatorial candidate of the future is apt to be one who is capable of appealing across party lines, who knows how to make effective use of the media, who has attractive personal qualities—rather than one who has climbed the ladder of political office by winning the support of party leaders and workers. It is not necessarily true that anyone who can afford an expensive television advertising campaign and who hires a good PR firm can win elections, but it is true that use of television and other media are frequently crucial to the success of campaigns. If the voters are relying less on party loyalty than on their perception of candidates, the care and feeding of the candidate's image become highly important. One has only to look at two recent governors of California, Ronald Reagan and Jerry Brown, to understand the importance of gubernatorial image.

If fewer voters identify with a party or vote along party lines, does this mean that they are likely to support, or approve of, political parties than in the past? Dennis (1986) has found that voters who identify more strongly with a party are more likely to be supportive of the party system. But he does not find that support for parties has been declining. Examining data on Wisconsin voters from 1964 to 1984, he finds that a majority still believe that political parties create unnecessary conflicts and confuse the issues—but that the size of this majority is declining. Most voters believe that two-party competition is a good thing. But few voters believe in the concept of party responsibility or believe that they should consistently vote a straight party line, regardless of the quality of candidates. We can probably best summarize public attitudes toward parties with one word: *ambiguous.*

PARTY IN GOVERNMENT

Governors and state legislators propose and vote on state policy consistently with their political party. They rarely attain a complete consistency of party alignment, and the rate of party voting varies among the states. But given the diversity among our states, officials tend to react to public policy questions more consistently by political party than perhaps we expect (LeBlanc, 1969; Flinn, 1964; Jewell and Patterson, 1986: chap.8).

Party discipline and party voting in Congress are less than in European democracies—in part, at least, because of the separation-of-powers system. This system is duplicated in each state, and provides one reason why party discipline is not absolute.

Population diversity is an important factor diluting party consistency on issues. As state legislators respond to their respective and different districts, they vote differently on legislation. But the political party remains a generalized statement of preferences on questions of public policy. Over a wide variety of issues and over a long period of time, the political party provides a frame within which public officials tend to think and act. We would guess that this policy coherence between parties in each of the states will tend to persist. We would guess that the parties across the states will tend generally to support consistent points of view simply because of the greater degree of national uniformity of party composition and socioeconomic conditions.

But political parties, perhaps especially in the United States, are not so much a means of making policy choices as they are a means of selecting public officials and or organizing government (Lowi, 1967). Here again the possibilities for evolving factions and combinations outside of and to displace the standard national parties have been almost endless. While one-party legislatures have formed factions and while some two-party legislatures have formed bipartisan factions in selecting their speakers and committee chairmen, all of these permutations have occurred within the two main parties. We suspect that the conditions are less propitious now than in our past for the emergence of third-party formations among the officials of state government.

THE NATIONAL PARTIES

Both national parties have made strenuous efforts to recover from their respective national disasters, the Republicans in the 1970s and the Democrats in the 1980s. With a head start the national Republicans have pioneered in supporting and financing candidates, with Democrats attempting to catch up with both the technology and the success of their party rivals.

The national parties have created a direct-mail funding program, whereby individual citizens contribute funds directly to the party and its several national-level committees. The national parties directly fund senatorial and congressional candidates, supply research and issues information, and conduct campaign schools and seminars. In addition, the national parties either commission, or conduct their own, public opinion polls within selected states and congressional districts. The national parties directly prepare commercial media advertisements. They provide campaign advice throughout the whole season and have staff out in the field to monitor ongoing campaigns.

This range of campaign support activity is mainly directed at the U.S. Senate and House. But in addition, both national parties have targeted state legislative races and both are trying to increase the organizational and technical capacity of the state political party's headquarters staff. We might expect to see increased activity in these areas by both national parties because the national level is increasingly effective in raising political money and thus has resources to funnel into the state parties and state elections.

There is, however, at least one potential development that would lessen the national parties' ability to act in these ways: they are always threatened with factional splits that destroy their effectiveness. If Democrats have run the greater risk in the past two decades, national Republicans may experience a similar threat in the post-Reagan period.

SUMMARY

As candidates for elective office seek to gather the resources with which to wage an effective campaign, the political parties are only one of many sources to which they may turn. Parties are becoming more important participants in the electoral process than they have been in the previous two or three decades. Beginning with national-level revitalization, state parties too are becoming better financed and more active than previously.

Candidates and parties do not share an identity of interest or perspective; the success of one does not necessarily mean the success of the other. The relationship between them is often uneasy, and each usually has many complaints about the other.

The condition and capacity of political parties in the American political system are among the most important issues in the organization and conduct of our political system. In the fifty states political parties will have, in the coming decades, many opportunities to experiment and to evolve productive working relationships with candidates and public officials on the one hand, and with the electorate on the other.

REFERENCES

ASHER, HERBERT (1980). *Presidential Elections and American Politics*, 2nd ed. Chicago, Ill.: Dorsey Press.

BURNHAM, WALTER DEAN (1970). *Critical Elections and the Mainsprings of American Politics*. New York: W. W. Norton.

DENNIS, JACK (1986). "Public Support for the Party System, 1964–1984." Paper prepared for annual meeting of the American Political Science Association.

FLINN, THOMAS A. (1964). Party Responsibility in the States: Some Causal Factors." *American Political Science Review* 58 (March): 60–71.

GELB, JOYCE, AND MARIAN L. PALLEY (1975). *Tradition and Change in American Party Politics*. New York: Thomas Y. Crowell.

GOODMAN, PAUL (1967). "The First American Party System." In William N. Chambers and W.D. Burnham (eds.), *The American Party System*. New York: Oxford University Press.

HUCKSHORN, ROBERT J. AND ROBERT C. SPENCER (1971). *The Politics of Defeat: Campaigning for Congress*. Amherst: University of Massachusetts Press.

JEWELL, MALCOLM E., AND SAMUEL C. PATTERSON (1986). *The Legislative Process in the United States*, 4th ed. New York: Random House.

LeBLANC, HUGH L. (1969). "Voting in State Senates: Party and Constituency Influences." *Midwest Journal of Political Science* 13 (February): 33–57.

LIPSET, SEYMOUR M. (1963). *The First Nation*. New York: Doubleday Publishing.

LOWI, THEODORE, J. (1967). "Party Policy and Constitution in America." In William N. Chambers and W.D. Burnham (eds.), *The American Party System*. New York: Oxford University Press.

McCORMICK, RICHARD P. (1967). "Political Development and the Second Party System." In William N. Chambers and W.D. Burnham (eds.), *The American Party System*. New York: Oxford University Press.

RANNEY, AUSTIN (1975). *Curing the Mischiefs of Faction: Party Reform in America*. Berkeley: University of California Press.

CHAPTER 4

State Legislatures and Interest Groups

It is true that the executive, judicial, and legislative branches of state government have changed enormously during the past three decades, however most observers of the states would agree that the legislative branch is the one that has changed the most. To understand this change it is necessary to describe the reapportionment revolution of the 1960s and how it affected state legislatures. Interest groups, of course, have always been an important factor in state politics, but in recent years a significant expansion in interest-group activity in the hallways and lobbies of state capitol buildings has occurred, renewing concern that legislators are too responsive to special interests.

What was the reapportionment revolution? Before answering this question, it is necessary to explain the term *apportionment*. Apportionment is deciding how the members of a legislative body will be allocated within the boundaries of the political jurisdiction. The U.S. Constitution allocates two senators to each state and the number of representatives a state has depends on its population, with each state guaranteed at least one representative. At the state level, a typical example can be found in the Maryland Constitution where, prior to the reapportionment revolution, the apportionment scheme allocated membership in the state senate by giving each of the twenty-three counties one senator and Baltimore six. The formula for the lower house, called the House of Delegates, also allocated representatives among the city and counties but was a little more generous to the fast-growing suburban counties of Baltimore and Washington, giving them a few additional seats.

The consequence of this apportionment plan, and similar plans in other states, was that state legislatures, with only a few exceptions, were controlled by representatives who were elected from rural areas. For example, in the Maryland State Senate, rural counties that accounted for approximately 25 percent of the state's population actually elected 66 percent of the members. In other words, the more populous areas in Maryland—Baltimore and several suburban counties—had little representation in the state senate. Because most state legislatures refused to reapportion themselves, sometimes even when their constitutions required it to take place after each federal decennial census, the U.S. Supreme Court was asked to intervene in the early 1960s. The court decided two landmark cases: *Baker* v. *Carr* (1962) from Tennessee and *Reynolds* v. *Sims* (1964) from Alabama. In these cases, the court started the reapportionment revolution by deciding: (1) apportionment of state legislatures was not a political question but a justiciable one, meaning that it was proper for the court to decide apportionment disputes; and (2) both houses of a state legislature must be apportioned on the basis of population so each legislative district has the same, or very close to the same, number of people (one person, one vote).

Obviously, the immediate impact of the court's decisions was a decrease in legislators elected from rural areas, an increase in legislators from large cities and their suburbs, and greater attention to urban and suburban issues by the legislatures. Also, a gradual change in the kinds of people who became legislators has taken place—more women, blacks, and Hispanics have been elected. In 1969, only 4 percent of state legislators were women, compared to 20 percent in 1993.

Reading 8 is part of a larger study of the impact of women in public office, conducted by the Center for the American Woman and Politics. The study reprinted here is based on a nationwide survey of state legislators, both female and male. Its focus is to determine the effect women have had on the kind of issues to which legislators direct their attention. In other words, does the presence of women legislators change the legislative agenda? The study documents that women were more likely than male legislators to have women's rights bills, health issues, and children and family issues as their top legislative priorities. Although women were a minority in state legislatures, bills dealing with their legislative priorities were as likely to pass as those of their male counterparts.

At approximately the same time as the reapportionment revolution, a nationwide legislative reform movement emerged based on the belief that state legislatures were ill-equipped to solve the complex problems facing modern state government. One observer noted that state legislatures were "largely nineteenth century organizations and they must, or should, address themselves to twentieth century problems."[1] Examples of specific recommendations made by the Citizens Conference on State Legislatures, one of the organizations involved in this reform movement, are as follows:

- Higher legislative salaries that reflect the importance of being a legislator and the time it takes to do the job right.
- Increased professional and clerical staff so members, leaders, and committees can obtain and use information to make intelligent policy decisions.
- Elimination of restrictions on the frequency and length of sessions so legislatures can meet as long and as often as is needed to solve public policy questions.[2]

[1]Alexander Heard, "Introduction—Old Problems, New Context." In Alexander Heard, ed., *State Legislatures in American Politics* (Englewood Cliffs, N.J.: Prentice-Hall, 1966), p. 3.
[2] Citizens conference on State Legislatures, *The Sometime Governments* (New York: Bantam Books, 1971), pp. 40–47.

The goal of these reforms was to move the states away from part-time citizen legislatures to full-time professional legislatures. In fact, most of the reforms advocated during the 1960s and 1970s were adopted by the states, especially those dealing with improved staffing. In 1988, over 33,000 staff employees worked for state legislatures. Although there is little doubt that these changes helped legislatures become a viable partner with the executive branch in determining public policy, there is the possibility that the changes had unintended consequences as well.

Higher salaries allow legislators to spend more time being legislators, and the provision of greater staff resources allows legislators to undertake more activities such as constituency service. *Constituency service* refers to legislators, communicating with, and providing assistance to, the people who live within their district. On the surface, this would seem to be something that elected leaders should be doing, but Alan Rosenthal, a well-known scholar in the state government field, argues in Reading 9 that constituency service may have a negative impact on the legislative institution. Rosenthal identifies a number of benefits for legislators as individuals, increasing their reelection chances being but one. But what happens to the institution if legislators spend more time on constituency service and less time on the important activity of law making? This new emphasis on constituency service, along with a preoccupation with reelection campaigns and the raising the money to finance campaigns, is referred to as *congressionalization*. This is a word that has been invented to describe the process by which state legislatures acquire some of the more troublesome characteristics of the U.S. Congress.[3]

A more active state government adopting public policies on an increasing number of issues is one of the reasons that interest groups have grown in number, and the job of being a lobbyist is becoming a full-time occupation. The representatives of interest groups can be valuable participants in the legislative process because they provide legislators with information concerning the impact new laws and changes in existing laws will have on the members of their groups. Nevertheless, it is the belief of almost every American that lobbyists are doing something wrong. Behind this belief is the idea that lobbyists cause legislators to be more interested in representing the views of lobbyists than the views of constituents, more interested in representing the interests of groups who contribute to their campaigns than in representing the public interest. Citizens with these views think lobbyists and lobbying should be tightly regulated by the states.

Reading 10 is part of an Issue Brief prepared by Common Cause. Common Cause, which refers to itself as a citizen's lobby and has a national office in Washington and chapters in forty-nine states, argues that state laws regulating lobbying are presently inadequate. Common Cause suggests that all

---

[3] B. G. Salmore and S. A. Salmore "The Transformation of State Electoral Politics." In C. E. Van Horn, ed., *The State of the States* (Washington, D.C.: CQ Press, 1989) pp. 188–194.

states should improve their laws by requiring full disclosure of lobbying activities. Full disclosure—that is, the registration of lobbyists and periodic reporting of their expenditures—would allow the public to determine if special interests have undue influence on the policies adopted by our political leaders.

QUESTIONS FOR DISCUSSION

1. Is gender still an important factor in determining legislators' priorities when a number of additional characteristics (such as ideology, occupation, and motherhood) are taken into account?

2. If you were a state legislator, how would you handle the competing demands of constituency service and law making?

3. How are PACs useful to those who want to influence legislative decisions?

4. Do you think the key elements in the lobby disclosure statute proposed by Common Cause would be effective in reducing the influence of interest groups?

8. Gender Differences in Legislative Agendas
Center for the American Woman and Politics

Time is a scarce resource for legislators. Thus, a legislator's priorities tell us what is most important to her or him and indicate the policy areas likely to be affected because this individual rather than someone else holds office. As the number of elected women gradually expands, the opportunity to shape legislative agendas to reflect women's interests also increases. The question is: Will women direct government's attention toward women's distinctive concerns?

By our definition, the priorities we call *women's distinctive concerns* are composed of: 1) *women's rights bills* (those that are feminist in intent and that deal with issues having a direct impact on women); and 2) *women's traditional*

SOURCE: From "Gender Differences in Legislative Agendas" from Reshaping the Agenda: Women in State Legislatures by Center for the American Woman and Politics, 1991. Reprinted by permission.

areas of interest (bills that reflect women's roles as caregivers both in the family and society and thus that address issues in health care, care of the elderly, education, housing and the environment). This [reading] examines lawmakers' personal legislative priorities to see whether the increased presence of women officeholders means that more legislators are paying greater attention to either or both subcategories of *women's distinctive concerns*.

We first examine the top priorities of legislators to see whether women's distinctive concerns—women's rights bills, and bills relating to women's traditional areas of interest—are more often priorities for women than men. Then we identify characteristics of individuals and the political environment that affect priorities and gender differences in priorities. Throughout our examination of the factors that effect priorities, we focus the discussion on the general category of women's distinctive concerns. The sub-categories of women's distinctive concerns—women's right bills and women's traditional areas of interest—are discussed only when important differences appear between them. Finally, we examine legislators' records of success in getting their priority bills passed.

A LOOK AT THE PRIORITIES OF FEMALE AND MALE LAW-MAKERS: DO WOMEN MAKE A DIFFERENCE?

To determine legislators' priorities, we asked them the following question:

> We'd like to find out about the bills that you've been working on during the current session. Although you may have worked on a number of bills, for the next few questions we want you to pick out the single bill that you would say has been your own personal top priority for the current session. First, can you very briefly describe the focus of this bill?[1]

When priorities were categorized as either women's distinctive concerns or other concerns (e.g., budget, finance, transportation), the gender differences in priorities became apparent.[2] Women indeed were more likely than men to mention a women's distinctive concern as their top legislative priority. This was true among Democrats as well as among Republicans.

The increasing presence of women in office seems to be altering legislative agendas by raising the priority given to issues that most directly touch women's lives. This view was expressed frequently by women lawmakers:

> I think more and more people are seeing problems of kids and families and women, [and there is a]...willingness to step forward and be involved and

discuss these. For a long time it seemed necessary to have the male model, but it's okay now to talk about education and child care and domestic violence.

There was some overlap among the types of policy priorities women and men mentioned, and some women were quick to point out that neither are women the only ones who care about these human concerns nor are women only concerned with these issues:

> I can think of a number of men in the legislature who felt as strongly about these [humanistic] issues as we women did...[Furthermore,] women aren't only interested in what we euphemistically call human services, health issues....I think it's important for women to develop an expertise in some areas, but I also think it's very important that they really get the big picture. And I mean the *big* picture.

One veteran woman legislator credited the influence of women and reinforcement by the public for increasing men's interest in women's distinctive concerns:

> I think the differences [between women and men lawmakers] are becoming less all the time because the male legislators are discovering that women get a lot of publicity with their kinds of issues. In my legislature the [men] try to beat us to them. We are always glad to have an advocate... We'll help to get the research and the material and baby them along...because it goes a lot quicker if a male stands up and advocates something for children and...families or health care or something like that. We have sensitized them to these issues and also made our issues more in the mainstream of public policy.

Regardless of the apparent "mainstreaming" of these issues, it was still women legislators who were more likely to have had a women's distinctive concern as a personal top priority. This was true within both subcategories of women's distinctive concerns. Ten percent of women, but only 4 percent of men, had a women's rights bill as their top legislative priority. Women also were more likely than men to have had a priority reflecting women's traditional areas of interest (41 percent vs. 33 percent). A number of issues are encompassed within this broad category. The most frequently mentioned priority of this type was health care policy, with 14 percent of women but only 6 percent of men mentioning this issue. A notable gender difference occurred as well on children and family issues, with 11 percent of women but only 3 percent of men mentioning these as priorities.[3] Among priorities not classified as women's distinctive concerns, the major difference was that men were only slightly more likely than women to have mentioned budget/tax issues as their top priority (13 percent vs. 9 percent).

African-American and white women were equally likely to have had a women's distinctive concern as their priority. Fifty-two percent of white women and 56 percent of African-American women legislators mentioned a women's distinctive concern as their top legislative priority. Thus, whether we focus on the activities of white or African-American women legislators, the story is the same—women are working to refocus legislative agendas toward greater attention to humanistic and feminist concerns.

While we can state with confidence that women officeholders are making a difference, some women may be more likely than others to have a distinctive impact on policy agendas. These variations arise both from a variety of individual characteristics and from the political environment within the legislature.

FACTORS AFFECTING PRIORITIES: A LOOK AT INDIVIDUAL CHARACTERISTICS

Do Women Have Different Priorities Than Men Because Women Are More Likely to be Liberals?

Among legislators with similar self-described ideological perspectives, women were more likely than men to mention a women's distinctive concern as a top priority. Thus, although liberals were the most likely to have given top priority to a women's distinctive concern, the effects of gender meant that conservative women were about as likely as moderate men to have had a women's distinctive concern as a priority, and moderate women were as likely as liberal men to have this type of priority.

Ideology did affect the subtypes of women's distinctive concerns that women had pursued, and so the reasons for the gender gap differed across the ideological groups. Among liberals, women's and men's priorities differed because women were much more likely than men to have had a women's rights priority (16 percent vs. 3 percent). Among conservatives, the gender gap was due primarily to the greater likelihood of women having worked on priorities reflecting women's traditional areas of interest (36 percent vs. 28 percent).

Some suggest that women's and men's divergent life experiences may cause gender differences in priorities regardless of ideology. However, while women's life experiences may bring them in closer contact with human needs, sometimes these concerns touch men's lives as well. This may lead them to do the unexpected, as one woman legislator explained:

One of the more interesting things that happened in the legislature this last time was that a man came in and sponsored a bill for a team for [investigating the] sexual abuse of children. He was a very conservative member and generally had not been terribly supportive of a lot of these issues, but had seen an instance of something that he found was really terrible. He did come in and support a bill—an appropriation to have what we call child abuse investigation teams.

Nonetheless, by and large, women legislators were more likely than their male colleagues cut from the same ideological cloth to have placed women's distinctive concerns at the top of their priorities.

This conclusion is reinforced by analysis using a second measure of ideology—attitudes on the General Policy Index. Regardless of whether they scored low, medium or high in support for liberal policies, women legislators were more likely than men with similar policy views to have listed as their top priority a women's distinctive concern. As one woman legislator observed:

Even conservative women in our legislature are supporting things like mammography screening and the WIC funding and things like that...I see abortion as the only thing dividing women in our legislature.

Overall the data suggest that when a man and a woman share similar policy attitudes and ideologies, the woman is more likely to give greater priority to women's distinctive concerns.

Do Women Have Different Priorities From Men Because They More Often Are Feminists?

Women are shifting the focus of legislative agendas to include more issues that reflect women's distinctive concerns, but their impact cannot be attributed soley to the presence of feminists among women legislators. Self-described feminist women were only slightly more likely than non-feminist women to have had a women's distinctive concern as their top priority.

However, feminist and non-feminist men diverged sharply in priorities. Feminist men (who were only 20 percent of the men sampled) were as likely as non-feminist women to have mentioned a women's distinctive concern as a top priority; in contrast, non-feminist men (the vast majority of males in the legislature) were the least likely to have done so. The similar importance placed on women's distinctive concerns among feminist women, feminist men and non-feminist women belies one important difference: feminist women are more likely than non-feminist women and feminist men to have had a women's rights bill as their priority (14 percent, 7 percent and 6 percent, respectively).

The gender differences were greater when we compared the priorities of lawmakers with similar policy attitudes on the Feminist Policy Index. The gender gap was greatest among low scorers on the index, suggesting that even women who oppose the cornerstone issues of the women's movement are shaping a different agenda than their male colleagues. Among those with higher scores on the Feminist Policy Index, the gender gap narrowed, but nevertheless remained.

Overall, the results suggest that men with an ideological leaning toward feminism are more likely than other men to give priority to women's distinctive concerns. But because so few men are feminists, the increased presence of women—feminist or not—in the legislatures seems certain to encourage government to focus more on issues that reflect women's distinctive concerns.

Do Women Have Different Priorities From Men Because They Are Connected to Women's Groups?

The answer to this question depends on whether we define this connection in terms of memberships in women's groups or campaign endorsements by women's groups.[4] The more women's groups to which a legislator belonged, the more likely it was that her top priority was a women's distinctive concern.[5] Nevertheless, women who belonged to no women's groups were still more likely than their male colleagues to have listed a women's distinctive concern as their top priority (44 percent vs. 37 percent).

The number of campaign endorsements by women's groups did not differentiate among those women who did and did not have a women's distinctive concern as their top priority. However, among women and men legislators with equal numbers of endorsements, women were more likely than men to have had such a bill as their priority. While the men endorsed by these groups may be valuable allies on roll call votes, women endorsees seem more inclined to attempt to reshape legislative agendas.[6]

Do Differences in Women's and Men's Roles in the Workforce Contribute to Gender Differences in Priorities?

Among both women and men, the top priorities varied according to occupation. Women in traditionally female occupations were the most likely to have mentioned a women's distinctive concern as their top priority, followed by the small group of men in traditionally female occupations and by women in traditionally male fields. Men in traditionally male fields, who were the vast majority of male lawmakers in our study, were the least likely to have mentioned such a priority. The twelve percentage point difference in priorities of women in the two types of occupations was due to the fact that women in traditionally male fields were less likely than women from traditionally female occupations to have had a women's traditional area of interest as their top priority. These two groups were equally likely, however, to

have mentioned a women's rights bill as their top priority.[7]

We also asked lawmakers if there were one or two other bills that were important priorities to them. This allowed them to mention up to three priorities, but it did not force them to mention bills about which they actually cared little. We combined responses to both questions in order to look at their top three priorities. The results indicated that women in traditionally male occupations and in traditionally female occupations were equally likely to have worked on a women's distinctive concern (79 percent and 80 percent, respectively). Women in both occupational types were equally likely to have mentioned both women's rights bills and bills addressing women's traditional areas of interest in their top three priorities. It may be that women in non-traditional occupations combine interests in areas generally associated with women's lives with other political concerns, resulting in a broader array of policy priorities. That women regardless of occupation were equally likely to have mentioned women's concerns as one of their top three issues suggests that women officeholders will continue to bring distinctive priorities and perspectives to government as their opportunities for employment expand.

Are Gender Differences in Priorities due to Motherhood?

Women legislators often attribute their different perspectives from men to their experiences as mothers. However, our data suggest that regardless of whether or not they have children, women are more attentive than men to legislation that focuses on women's distinctive concerns. Furthermore, among women and men legislators who are parents, women are more likely than men to give attention to women's distinctive concerns. This pattern holds for both types of women's distinctive concerns—women's rights priorities as well as priorities dealing with women's traditional areas of interest.

The Effects of Seniority and Age: Will Gender Differences in Priorities Last?

Regardless of age or seniority, women more frequently than their male counterparts mentioned as their priority a women's distinctive concern. The gender gap was particularly great among older and among more senior legislators. While the gender gap in priorities may be closing as new generations of men replace older men, the fact is that, regardless of age, women's distinctive concerns are more central to women's legislative agendas. These patterns suggest that , as younger women move into office, they will continue to devote substantial energy to women's distinctive concerns.

CONSTRAINTS ON DIFFERENCES IN PRIORITIES: A LOOK AT THE POLITICAL ENVIRONMENT

Do Women Have Different Priorities Than Men Because They More Often Represent Liberal Districts?

There was little evidence to suggest that gender differences in priorities were due to district influence. Legislators of both sexes representing liberal districts were more likely than those from conservative districts to have had priorities reflecting women's distinctive concerns. Yet, within each type of district, women were more likely than men to have mentioned a women's distinctive concern as a priority. This was particularly true in moderate and conservative districts.

However, even in liberal districts, where women's and men's priorities looked most similar, there were interesting gender differences in priorities. We looked more closely at the type of women's distinctive concerns mentioned, separating these priorities into the two subcategories: women's rights priority bills and priority bills reflecting women's traditional areas of interest. Women were much more likely than men representing liberal districts to have had a women's rights bill as a priority (17 percent vs. 5 percent) and were less likely than men to have had a priority dealing with women's traditional areas of interest (43 percent vs. 53 percent). Thus, it seems that, even in liberal districts, women are defining their representational mission differently than are their male counterparts.

Does the Proportion of Women Holding Office Influence Priorities?

The number of women who served in a chamber of the legislature had little effect on the extent to which women or men gave priority to women's distinctive concerns. Women were just as likely to have mentioned one of these as their top priority when women were less than 15 percent of legislators as when women were 15 percent or more of legislators. Furthermore, regardless of the proportion of women in office, women were consistently more likely than their male colleagues to have mentioned these concerns as their top priority. These trends suggest that, as the number of women in office increases, more women will share the responsibility of directing attention to women's distinctive concerns.

Can Women be Political Insiders and Still Have Priorities That Differ From Those of Men?

Some people are concerned that, as women are accepted into predominantly male institutions, their priorities will change; however, our data suggest that this does not occur. According to our two measures of insider status (identification with the label "political party insider" and holding a legislative leadership position), women in both parties were more likely than their male colleagues with similar party insider or legislative leadership status to have had a women's distinctive concern as their legislative priority. There is no evidence that women who take responsibility for representing the concerns of women are more likely to be excluded from insider positions than other women.

The challenge for women officeholders may not be holding to their principles once they become insiders, but rather attaining positions of influence. In some states this is more of a problem than in others, as one woman lawmaker from a conservative state controlled by "the good old boys" explained:

> There's a long, strong power hold among a few people...I believe whenever you do not have a lot of bargaining power or turnover, you don't have opportunity for change. People are not inclined to hand it to you. What I worry about is the ability of women to be able to maintain the leadership... [on] a lot of issues that are now in the forefront that women have been promoting for a long time: ethics, health care, aging. They don't often have positions of influence to maintain leadership on those issues.

Does Professionalism of the Legislature Affect Gender Differences in Priorities?

The degree of professionalism in the legislature (as measured by salary) had little impact on the gender difference in policy priorities. Women in semiprofessional and citizen legislatures were almost as likely as women in professional institutions to have used their position to make a difference in the legislative agenda.[8] Thus, it seems that the professionalism

of the legislature is not likely to affect the priorities that women bring into office.

Do Women's Caucuses or Other Policy-Centered Meetings of Women Legislators Play a Role in Encouraging Gender Differences in Priorities?

The absence or presence of a women's caucus and attendance or non-attendance at these gatherings does not seem to affect the likelihood that women legislators are working on issues of concern to women as a personal priority. About half of the women legislators listed bills focusing on women's distinctive concerns as their legislative priority (53 percent of attenders vs. 49 percent of non-attenders).

Nevertheless, caucuses and other informal meetings may help women pursue their humanistic and feminist policy goals more effectively. As one legislator whose caucus has worked on issues such as domestic violence, welfare, nutrition and housing pointed out:

> Our [women's] caucus has a retreat and brings in all of the organizations that women dominate throughout the state to tell us what they have as their priorities for legislation. Out of that day of hearings, we choose three, at most five, priorities. This gives all of the women an opportunity to really feel involved in at least these issues which are usually unanimously adopted. They are the big issues that we know we will be dealing with. The women's caucus not only supports them by its action of adopting them, but it also develops the means of bringing in the support. That means that women can then focus on their own constituent needs. They can go back home and talk about what they did on women's issues, but it also gives them the opportunity and the freedom to

work on transportation, the budget, economic development.

Women's caucuses also can provide an institutionalized structure for dealing with these issues, as one legislator explained:

[Our speaker] will turn to the caucus on any issue that deals with children, family and even other things like no smoking. He'll do what we ask him to do because we've established the kind of rapport and we don't hold it against him that he doesn't understand what we're talking about—he tries, but he's just macho. He's political enough to know that these issues are important to the Democratic party.

THE FATE OF LEGISLATIVE PRIORITIES

Women and men are equally likely to have achieved their policy goals. About two out of three legislators reported that their priority bills had passed their house of the legislature in a form satisfactory to them.[9] The pattern held for both women and men even after taking into account differences in ideology, party, feminist identification, age, years in the legislature, professionalism of the legislature and proportion of women in the legislative chamber. Furthermore, priority bills that represented a women's distinctive concern were as likely to have passed as bills representing other concerns.

However, the proportion of women in the legislative chamber did affect the success of bills dealing with women's distinctive concerns. Both women *and* men who pursued these priorities in legislatures where women were fewer than 15 percent of the members were less likely to report passage of a satisfactory bill than those in legislatures where women were more numerous. When women

were a smaller proportion of the legislative chamber, 59 percent of the women and 63 percent of the men with a women's distinctive concern as a priority reported passage of their bill in satisfactory form, compared with 70 percent of female and male legislators in chambers with memberships of 15 percent or more women. This suggests that legislatures in which there are more women may be more supportive of women's distinctive concerns.

Some women legislators see signs that the attitudes of their male colleagues are changing:

It was not too long ago in [my state] that we [women] would do all the preliminary work on these issues and then it would get down to the floor and we would ask a male to handle the legislation because it would have a much better chance of getting through...Now all of a sudden, women are at the same level as men are and they [the men] come to us and ask us to carry it, and we don't have to go to them anymore.

Despite these victories, the successes that women have achieved, even in legislatures where there are larger numbers of women, seem very fragile to some:

We have to keep up the pressure, every day of our lives. If we let go, it's like the minute you pull that breaker away and the tide is there and in a very short period of time you can't find our footprints. That is the discouraging part of being a woman veteran legislator.

Another added:

I used to feel...frustrated, until one day I said to myself, it's almost like when your kids are in school. If you could send your kid to go fight the battle with the teacher or when you had a baby if you could say to your kid,

"Here you get up at 2:00 A.M. and take your own bottle," you would. But the kid couldn't do it, so you had to do it for him. So now I just accept it as a fact of life—the reality that you have to be there constantly nagging and pushing and pulling. I just don't get all consumed by that. We [women] make things happen, but we have to work at it the same way we raised our families, the same way we live our private lives.

SUMMARY

Based on the legislative priorities of women lawmakers, our research suggests that the increased presence of women in public office is heightening legislative attention to those issues we label as "women's distinctive concerns"—priorities that include women's rights bills and women's traditional areas of interest.

Women do not have to be feminists to make a difference. Even women who do not identify themselves as feminists are pursuing priorities reflecting women's distinctive concerns. Furthermore, feminist men are about as likely as non-feminist women to list a women's distinctive concern as their top priority. However, feminist men are greatly outnumbered by non-feminist men, who attach less priority to these concerns.

Women are consistently more likely than their male colleagues to list a women's distinctive concern as important even after taking into account factors such as political ideology, campaign endorsements by women's groups, parenthood, occupational experiences, age, seniority, ideology of the constituency, professionalism of the legislature, proportion of women in the legislative chamber and political insider status.

Women and men are equally successful in getting their priority bills passed. However, when a women's distinctive concern is the top priority, it is more likely to pass in a chamber where women

are 15 percent or more of the members. This is true whether the bill is the priority of a female or a male legislator.

Will women continue to make a difference in reshaping legislative agendas? Overall the answer appears to be yes, although there are indications in our findings that the concerns of men and women are converging. Some of our data suggests that as women begin to move into traditionally male occupations in greater numbers, their legislative agenda may represent a combination of women's distinctive concerns and policy items more typically associated with male leadership. In addition, younger men seem more attuned to women's traditional concerns than older men. Nevertheless, even if the slight trends toward convergence of women's and men's priorities continue, it seems clear that women lawmakers will make a difference in public policy and in legislative priorities for decades to come.

NOTES

1. This question provides a snapshot of behavior in a single session. However, while individual legislators' priorities may change from year to year, the probability of subgroups of legislators having certain types of priorities in any given year should be captured in this snapshot.
2. [Editors' note: For more details concerning this classification see Center for American Women in Politics, *Reshaping the Agenda: Women in State Legislatures* (New Brunswick, N.J.: Eagleton Institute of Politics, 1991) pp. 101–111.]
3. Separating some women's rights bills from some bills dealing with families and children often was difficult given women's traditional roles as caregivers within the family. Therefore, in discussing children and family issues

and women's rights priorities in this paragraph, we assigned to both categories some priority bills that seemed equally appropriate in either category: day care, parental leave and teen pregnancy prevention. In the remainder of the study, these priorities were counted only as women's rights priorities. This had no effect on the proportion citing women's distinctive concerns since it included both subgroups.

4. Only women legislators were asked about membership in women's groups since most of their members are women. [Editors' note: For a discussion of questions used to determine group memberships and campaign endorsements see Center for American Women in Politics, pp. 101–111.]

5. This trend was more pronounced when memberships only in feminist groups were counted.

6. The same patterns appear if we look only at self-reported NOW and WPC endorsements and exclude reports of endorsements by other women's groups.

7. The patterns found among those in traditionally male fields also were found among women and men attorneys—a subset of this larger category.

8. The small differences were the result of women in professional legislatures being more likely to have worked on women's rights priority bills than women in citizen legislatures (13 percent vs. 8 percent).

9. After mentioning the priority bill, each legislator was asked: "Has this bill been passed by your house of the legislature?" Those who said it had been were asked a follow-up question: "Are you generally satisfied with the bill in its final form?" The responses were then classified into three categories: passed satisfactorily, passed but not satisfactory or not passed.

9. The Consequences of Constituency Service

Alan Rosenthal

More significant than any other public, in the eyes of legislators, are the people who live in their district—their constituents. A large part of a legislator's job has to do with representing his or her constituency and providing service to constituents. Service to this district is the name of the game, according to people in the business. It is the bread and butter of every elected office holder.

SOURCE: "The Consequence of Constituency Service" by Alan Rosenthal in *The Journal of State Government*, Spring 1986, pp. 25–30. Copyright © 1993 The Council of State Governments. Reprinted with permission from *State Government News*.

Few legislators today would omit mention of constituent service as one of their duties. For example, when asked recently to assess the importance of various legislative functions, 77 percent of the members of the Connecticut General Assembly rated constituent service as "very important" (with another 16 percent rating it as "somewhat important"). Along with making policy, appropriating funds, and exercising oversight, servicing constituents is one of the legislature's principal functions.

THE NATURE OF CONSTITUENCY SERVICE

What is meant by constituency service varies from state to state and from member to member. At a general level, service entails communicating with constituents—listening, explaining, and helping. It may involve writing letters, sending pamphlets, distributing newsletters, making visits, giving talks, and running district offices. At a specific level, service involves providing assistance to people who have run into some problem in their dealings with government: a matter of welfare, workmen's compensation, college admission, zoning, a contract, employment, or just where to go in order to get information. At that level it is generally referred to as casework.

Malcolm Jewell of the University of Kentucky in his book, *Representation in State Legislatures* (1982), examines the range of legislative service activities. Focusing on nine states, he concludes that service is of high priority in California, Massachusetts, Ohio, and Texas; of medium priority in Indiana, Kentucky, and Tennessee; and of low priority in Colorado and North Carolina. According to Jewell, legislators who are most service oriented are found in states where constituency service norms are strong and where greater staff resources are available. They tend to be experienced members with career ambitions.

In some states legislators still conduct their constituency service activities much as their predecessors did before them. They attend various meetings throughout the district and hold office hours once a month or so in a local town hall. They do not have personal staff to help them, but they still respond diligently to the requests that come their way. They are only part-time legislators, and they are also only part-time ombudsmen. The individual and institutional resources devoted to the service function in these states continue to be limited, but the function is performed nonetheless.

The trend, however, is in the development of the constituent service function, particularly casework, after the fashion of Congress. Indeed, one of the strongest tendencies among state legislatures today is that of providing members with personal staffing and district offices, which are used to reach out to constituents. As with many other elements of legislative modernization, these features were instituted first by California about 20 years ago. Since then 18 state Senates and 11 state Houses have undertaken to provide personal aides for members, and 10 legislatures have devised district office programs of one sort or another.[1]

Support varies in amount from place to place and from Senate to House, with allowances, furnishings, and supplies calculated differently depending on the particular state. At one end of the continuum, California members receive a lump sum for both capitol and district office expenses, including personnel, averaging $182,000 per Assembly member and $388,000 per Senate member. In addition, they are supplied with office equipment, telephones, postage, and funds for newsletters. In New York, staff allowances depend upon a member's leadership position, seniority, and affiliation with the majority or minority party. Senators have between one and six staff members, and $10,000 for district office rent and utilities. Assembly members are allocated a basic staff allowance of $22,000 per year and are furnished district offices, telephones, office equipment, supplies, and postage. At the other end of the continuum, Connecticut members are not provided with district offices per se, but are allocated $3,500 a year which usually is used to cover such expenses. Maryland members also receive modest amounts for offices and staff.

New Jersey offers as good an example as any of how legislators use offices and staffs for constituent service. Take William Schuber, one of New Jersey's Assemblymen, a Republican from a suburban county. Schuber is prodigious when it comes to constituent service. He puts in hour after hour, hopping from club meeting to parade to picnic, trying to get known and drumming up business for his district office. He mails copies of relevant legislation introduced in Trenton to fire departments, zoning boards, and local councils. He delivers copies of the state legislative manual to libraries, appears on local cable TV shows, and works to get his news releases to his district's weekly papers. His staff of six part-time people comb newspapers for announcements of weddings, births, promotions, and obituaries, so Schuber can follow up with appropriate letters to constituents.[2] Or take Matthew Feldman, a veteran Democratic senator from the same county as Schuber. In his district Feldman has one full-time secretary, one full-time office manager, and one part-time caseworker. His office reportedly generates 50,000 pieces of mail a year and handles 1,000 constituent cases.[3]

INDIVIDUAL AND INSTITUTIONAL EFFECTS

Although it is not possible to measure the change in constituent service activity this past decade, there can be little doubt that practically everywhere such activity has increased. Indeed, if the 1970s witnessed the development of committee and caucus staff in state legislatures, the 1980s is witnessing the development of personal service activity. Given the likelihood of this trend's continuation into the future, it is worthwhile to look at the effects of constituency service—both on the legislator as an individual and on the legislature as an institution.

First, constituency service takes up a large part of the time and energy legislators spend on their overall job. One might think that members devote relatively little of their own time to such tasks, leaving it to their personal staff. That is not the case, however. Even in Congress, with its abundant staffing, it is estimated that the average member spends 40 to 45 percent of his time on service activities. In fact, members spend, on the average, almost two out of five days back in their districts where, among other things, they tend faithfully to their constituents.[4] At the state level, time commitments vary tremendously. One study, conducted in 1977–78, reported that Minnesota and Kentucky legislators spent their time as is shown below:[5]

Table 9.1   Percentage of Legislator Time Spent on Constituent Service

Time Spent	Minnesota	Kentucky
Less than 25%	32	24
25 to 49%	64	38
50% or more	4	38
	100%	100%

The mean amount of time spent on the function was 25 percent in Minnesota, and 40 percent in Kentucky. The commitments were quite different, but substantial in both places.

If we define service to include just about any form of contact, as most legislators do, the range from 25 to 40 percent of one's time, depending upon the state, seems not too far from the mark. Take Wisconsin (which does not provide district offices) as an example at the lower end of the range. A 1983 questionnaire, distributed by the legislature's Compensation Study Committee, found that members spent about 48 hours a week on legislative business, with about 12 hours, or 25 percent, given over to constituent contact and services. Or take Florida (which does provide district offices) as an example at the high end of the range. As of 1979 it was estimated that an active senator could be expected to spend 200 days a year on legislative work, with 96 days, or 48 percent, of total time on district office and constituent work.

There are limits on the amount of time legislators have at their disposal. If time and energy are channeled into constituent service, then they are not available for other activities. This means that legislators will have to spend less on floor sessions, committee meetings, and caucuses—activities that relate to other legislative functions. If they are part-time legislators, they will have to spend less on their outside occupations. Or they will have to squeeze the extra amounts out of that which is normally allocated to family life and recreation. Whatever the case or combination, more time on constituency service means less spent elsewhere.

Second, constituency service provides legislators gratification they cannot otherwise achieve. Although some legislators undoubtedly regard service as a chore, most recognize the function as an essential one in a representative democracy. It is something that they, as elected representatives of the people, have an obligation to do, and thus take pride in doing it. Moreover legislators, as a breed, like helping people. While some do prefer to focus on law-related pursuits and analytical endeavors, may others are "people persons." They are concerned about individual people, like dealing with them person-to-person, and are inclined to enjoy constituency service.

A few years ago, an examination of what New Jersey legislators particularly liked and disliked about their jobs revealed that about half of the members and former members liked having contact with people and making a difference

in their lives. The results obtained from intervening with a state agency, or in some other way, on behalf of a constituent are a source of considerable satisfaction to a legislator. This is particularly true when something concrete is achieved in a constituent's favor. The legislative process itself can be frustrating, and extremely so for minority, freshman, and chronically impatient members. One's bills frequently go nowhere. Clear, identifiable victories can be rare. No wonder, then, that a successful intervention with bureaucrats in the state capitol can be a rewarding experience for an otherwise embattled legislator.

Third, and by no means least, constituency service helps an incumbent win re-election. There is a belief among a number of people that a congressman can get re-elected by what he does for folks back home. Few doubt that at least some electoral benefit is derived by congressmen from their constituency service activities. Granting that service at the congressional level helps, the question is, "How much?"

According to Richard F. Fenno, Jr., "Our best present estimate is that incumbency, or extra constituent service, adds an average of five percent to a House member's electoral total."[6] We do not know what the electoral payoffs are at the state legislative level. But it would appear that many legislators—even those in what might be regarded as relatively safe districts—feel insecure electorally. For that reason, among others, they are strongly motivated to provide constituents as voters with service.

Although the ostensible purpose of district offices and staff is not the re-election of incumbents, it is difficult to ignore the political potency of many of these operations. They are integral parts of what has been called "the campaign that never ends." Take the case of New Jersey.[7] The tendency of legislators here is to divvy up the $30,000 allotted for personal staff among more, rather than fewer, aides, retaining a goodly number of people on the payroll rather than only a few. Out of a total of 730 aides (excluding hourly employees) working for senators and assemblymen, only eight receive $20,000 or more in salary, while 396 receive $2,500 or less. The result is a distribution of aides among district offices as shown below:

Table 9.2   District Office Staff in New Jersey

Number of aides per district office	Number of District Offices	
	Senate	Assembly
One or two	8	7
Three to five	17	27
Six to ten	11	38
Eleven to fifteen	4	5
	40	77

It would appear that a number of New Jersey's aides are employed largely for political, i.e. re-election purposes.

Or take New York. Here a member of the legislature made use of his staff in a successful race for Congress. The U.S. Attorney, the Brooklyn District Attorney, and the Justice Department all became involved in this case. The member pointed out in his defense that the New York Legislature drew no distinction between the use and abuse of hired staff; and the *New York Times* editorialized (August 26, 1985) as follows:

A legislator's staff cannot and should not be hermetically sealed from campaign-related work. What's needed are guidelines from Albany.

But the *Times* also reasoned that what else could a legislator do but use staff for constituents and campaigns since, "A penny-wise legislature has historically refused to finance adequate staffs for its members."

The demarcation between constituent service on the one hand and re-election politics on the other is a fuzzy one. Not only is good service good politics, but much of the self-promotion and publicizing that legislators would place in the service category is political indeed. Furthermore, as the New York case indicates, and the New Jersey personnel figures suggest, district aides and other staff are readily convertible into electoral resources. The more of them, the merrier. And there is little doubt that, along with other factors, constituency service gives incumbents a real edge. It helps explain why anywhere from one-fifth to three-fifths of them, depending on the particular state, are not even challenged when they come up for re-election.

Fourth, constituency service has effects on the legislative process, in terms of both policy making and oversight. The dominant view is that effective service buys legislators freedom on policy matters. By trying to help, by appearing to help, and by actually helping people, representatives build up support that can be transferred to the policy arena. Thus they may be able to get out in front on an issue, or take a position contrary to views held by many of their constituents, and still not risk repudiation at the polls.

But the strength of legislators' district orientations and service responsiveness also may help to shape the way they behave in other domains. Accordingly, the more responsive they are to their constituents on requests for service, the more they will try to discern and represent constituency views on substantive issues too. If one adopts this line of reasoning, then instead of buying freedom, legislators simply become more parochial and tied to district apron strings across the board.

Casework, as one aspect of constituency service, can be considered a form of legislative oversight. Thus service may bear on the effectiveness of state programs and the performance of state agencies. One study explored this subject, finding substantial differences between Kentucky and Minnesota in the performance of casework and its conversion into oversight. Much of the casework amounted to asking for special favors and exceptions, but some of it led to administrators correcting themselves, to further examination of practices, or to the introduction of legislation to remedy a deficiency caused by a particular problem.[8]

For the most part, however, casework is an extremely particularistic approach to oversight. Ordinarily, it is not advisable to generalize from one case to an entire agency or program. Nor does a particular problem encountered by a constituent—even one's own constituent—necessarily justify a change in administrative behavior or modification of a statewide program. But on occasion this happens; a single case has more general consequences.

The fact is that constituent cases are treated as individual occurrences. Information is not cumulative across all the state's districts or over some period of time. Therefore, it is not possible to figure out whether a problem is part of a pattern, requiring a change in policy or practice. If legislatures made collective use of case work data, it could be integrated with other oversight information. Currently, however, administrators respond to individual cases raised by individual legislators, and not to findings arrived at by the legislature as a whole.

Fifth, individual constituency service affects the legislature as an institution. Although these institutional effects are subtle, over time the consequences may be considerable. Along with an electoral preoccupation, the concern with the constituency service function promises to change the composition of legislatures. The trend is toward full-time members, career politicians. Where legislative salaries make it at all possible, more members are serving on an essentially full-time basis. One assemblyman from New York, for example, in a discussion of professional and citizen legislators, said that it just was not possible in New York to be a part-time anymore. "When I'm in the district, people bombard me constantly with requests for one thing or another," he explained. "There's no way to say, 'Leave me alone, I'm just part-time.'"

The more resources legislators put into districts, the more demands they generate. It is difficult for elective politicians to resist local demands, and the tendency undoubtedly will be to spend more time at the job. In about one-third of the states, the transformation has already taken place. Legislatures have changed from being composed primarily of citizen members, attached to their districts both by residence and by outside occupation, to being composed primarily of full-timers; attached to their districts by residence also, but by service activity rather than by any private calling. Among the distinguishing characteristics of the contemporary professional legislature are district offices and personal staff.

Not only are legislatures becoming professional, they are also becoming fragmented. Constituency service reflects and promotes that fragmentation, along with single-member districts, the proliferation and intensification of interest groups, and electoral uncertainty. The closer legislators are tied to their district, the more difficult it may be for them to consider statewide interests or institutional concerns.

Sixth, and perhaps as significant in the long run as anything else, are the effects that constituency service has on public confidence in government. In this era of large, complex, and bureaucratic government, it is critical that people have someone with whom they can communicate on a personal, one-to-one basis. With an attentive representative, or even with the attention of a representative's staff, constituents have an opportunity to express themselves. As Frank Smallwood, a former member of the Vermont Senate, puts it, "People can get things off their chest. What people want to know is that someone is listening to them and is ready to come to their assistance."[9] Whether citizens have lost their confidence in government or have become alienated from government, a system of diligent representation can have ameliorative results. As Jewell writes, "If citizens discover that legislators are effective in making the bureaucracy more responsive, they may be expected to become more supportive of state government."[10]

The relationship between constituent services and public support for state government is a plausible one. The evidence supports the contention that service strengthens constituent support for the representative. But there is no evidence that support for the representative carries over to support for the legislature in which the representative serves. At the congressional level, polls show that while people like their congressmen they do not particularly like Congress.[11] At the state level, data suggest less than overwhelming support for state legislatures, despite the fact that incumbents are favorably regarded. It would be ironic, indeed, if the increasing popularity of the individual legislator and the unpopularity of the legislature as an institution were related phenomena. Are members buying their support at the expense of the institution of which they are a part? Even if they are not, there is little evidence that they are seriously trying to promote the legislature and the legislative process beyond their own interests, and perhaps those of their party.

CONCLUSION

Where the professionalization of legislatures is advanced and electoral considerations are powerful, constituency service tends to be a major operation. Where professionalization has not gone as far and electoral considerations are more muted, constituency service is a less prominent feature of the terrain. But the trend toward increased attention to the constituency service function by state legislatures is likely to persist.

The results overall are positive. Incumbents surely benefit, and constituents benefit as well. There is also the possibility that, because of direct contact with their representatives, citizens will develop more supportive attitudes toward government in general, and legislatures in particular. Thus far, however, the legislature as an institution has reaped few benefits from the constituent services its members assiduously perform.

This condition can and should be changed. But that will happen only if legislators, in rendering constituency service, take into account the needs of the institution as well as their own needs. They will have to work in the future to strengthen their institution, just as they work today to strengthen their individual positions.

NOTES

1. The following information on district offices and staff in several states has been collected by the National Conference of State Legislatures.
2. John Shure, *Record*, August 23, 1982.
3. *Star-Ledger*, January 6, 1985.
4. Richard F. Fenno, Jr., *Home Style: House Members in Their Districts* (Boston: Little, Brown, 1978), p. 32.
5. Richard C. Elling, "The Utility of State Legislative Casework as a Means of Oversight," *Legislative Studies Quarterly*, v. 4 (August 1979), p. 357.
6. Fenno, p. 109. See also Robert S. Erikson, "The Advantage of Incumbency in Congressional Elections," *Polity*, v. 3 (Spring 1971), pp. 395–405.

7. Data on New Jersey are provided by the Office of Legislative Services.

8. Elling, pp. 353–379.

9. Frank Smallwood, *Free and Independent* (Brattleboro, Vermont: Stephen Green Press, 1976), pp. 172–173.

10. Malcolm E. Jewell, *Representation in State Legislatures* (Lexington, Kentucky: University Press of Kentucky, 1982), p. 163.

11. One reason is that the criteria for evaluating Congress and those used in evaluating congressmen are very different. Congress is assessed on the basis of its policy performance, while the assessments of representatives tend to be based upon constituency service and the personal attributes of incumbents. Glenn R. Parker and Roger H. Davidson, "Why Do Americans Love Their Congressmen So Much More Than Their Congress?" *Legislative Studies Quarterly*, v. 4 (February 1979), pp. 56–57.

10. Lobby Disclosure Reform in the States

Common Cause

The right of citizens to petition their government—to lobby—is a fundamental right of a free people guaranteed by the U.S. Constitution.

Lobbying can enhance and benefit the legislative process in a number of ways. It can provide information and facilitate the exchange of ideas. It can expand citizen participation and encourage government responsiveness and accountability. It can educate and aid in the development of public policy. It can contribute to the building of consensus and help turn theory into reality. It can play an essential role in making our political system work.

However, citizens in a democracy have a right to know how their government works, and particularly how government decisions may be influenced by the activities of organizations heavily engaged in the legislative process.

Such information is at the core of a citizen's ability to hold government accountable. And it is important for government decision-makers as well, to enable them better to understand and evaluate the pressures being brought to bear on them.

Further, the knowledge that this information is being disclosed is crucial to protecting and strengthening public confidence in government—a confidence upon which our democratic system ultimately must depend if it is to survive and flourish.

Full public disclosure of the lobbying expenditures and activities of organized interests and the lobbyists representing them, as well as limits on gifts and campaign contributions that elected officials can accept from lobbyists, are essential to protect the public from potential problems of organized lobbying.

Full public disclosure helps to ensure that the public is aware of which special interests may be exercising an undue influence on government decision-making and how that influence is practiced. Disclosure of expenditures by lobbyists and their employers can help reveal possible links between special interests which give campaign contributions, gifts and reimbursement for travel expenses

SOURCE: From "Lobby Disclosure Reform in the States" by Common Cause from *State Issue Brief: Lobby Disclosure Reform in the States*, January 1993. Reprinted by permission.

to elected officials, only to return later to try, directly or indirectly, to influence the official's decisions.

Full disclosure of lobbying activities by special interests, together with restrictions on gift-giving and campaign contribution practices, can help prevent corruption and inappropriate influence peddling which otherwise may go undetected. As former Chief Justice Earl Warren wrote in upholding the federal lobbying disclosure law:

Otherwise the voice of the people may all too easily be drowned out by the voice of special interest groups seeking favored treatment while masquerading as proponents of the public weal.[1]

THE PROBLEM

Lobbyists often perform the important function of providing information not otherwise available to decision-makers. On the other hand, if such information comes primarily from those lobbyists hired by well-monied special interests, the policy-making process can be distorted.

Lobbyists often seek to enhance their access to and influence over government decision-making through political action committee (PAC) contributions or individual campaign contributions tied to organized lobbying efforts. Well-organized lobbying efforts, coupled with PAC contributions, can generate overwhelming pressures on legislators and other public officials and can tilt the process in favor of special interests. The result is that public policy decisions may be based solely on who has money and access to government officials, rather than on whether the policy is in the public's interest. This potential distortion of the decision-making process has become a growing problem for state governments in recent years.

There is today a widespread perception that elected officials are too obligated to monied private interests, which often operate behind the scenes. To many citizens, the power of these special interests frequently seems to drown out the voice of the average citizen. According to a *Washington Post*/ABC News poll conducted in October of 1992, 75 percent of those polled worried "a great deal/good amount" that: "Special interest groups have too much influence over elected officials."[2] According to a *New York Times*/CBS poll taken in October 1990, 71 percent of Americans believed that, "Government was controlled by big interests, compared with 21 percent who saw a government run for the people." And a 1991 Kettering Foundation study (based on focus-group discussions) reported:

Who, then, has control over public officials? To whom do they listen? Group participants have a clear answer: public officials are captives of lobbyists, special interest organizations, political action committees, among others. "Fifteen to twenty people may have a say on a bill, that's all. They don't take into account everybody," commented a Richmond [VA] woman. She continued, "They don't take us seriously."[3]

It is essential that powerful lobbying groups not dominate the policy-making process to such an extent that the average citizen's voice can no longer be heard—or to the extent that private interests are placed before the larger public good. . . .

The motivation for special interests to lobby state and local government is simple—the political process has an enormous economic impact on these interests and presents a significant opportunity for special interests to benefit economically from state and local government policies. Government funds must be allocated for building schools and roads, as well as water and sewage systems. Other government decisions establish regulations for specific industries which may have a far-reaching financial impact on those concerned. Special-interest groups and their lobbyists also have an interest in how the laws passed in the legislature are implemented and administered by the executive branch and its various agencies. Sometimes these regulatory decisions have a greater and more immediate economic effect than the law itself.

The problem of unregulated lobbying has become more acute because greater responsibility for policy-making has shifted to the state and local level in recent years. Important business, health, environmental, consumer, and other regulatory decisions increasingly are being made at the state and local level. As one expert put it:

Increasingly, the state legislatures are becoming the primary arena for policy-making and for financing governmental functions hitherto dominated by the federal and local government.[4]

With this increased responsibility delegated to state governments, even influential Washington-based lobbying firms have become active in the states. As one state-federal lobbyist explained:

If I had a client come to me and say, "You know, if we could get Congress to act, we could solve this problem nationally—or if we can get 12 state legislatures to act, we could solve 90 percent of our problems," I'd say, "Let's go after those legislatures." They've got less on their plate, there are fewer people competing for their attention, and they are closer to home."[5]

For a $1.5 million fee, this lobbyist's firm helped Gulf States Utilities avoid bankruptcy in 1987 by organizing a successful lobbying campaign resulting in a $57-million rate increase approved by Louisiana and Texas legislators.

In 1990, lobbyists based in the states outnumbered lawmakers by nearly six-to-one.[6] A 1990 Associated Press survey found more than 42,500 registered lobbyists at state capitols, an increase of 20 percent from four years earlier.[7]

The number of lobbyists and the amounts they spend to influence decision-makers have increased markedly:

- In *California*, people who employ lobbyists spent more than $193 million in 1989 and 1990 to influence state policy making. This was a 22-percent increase over the amount spent in the previous two years. In 1991, California lobbyists spent $116.4 million, or $10 million more than the previous year.[8]
- In *Maryland*, the total money paid to lobbyists reached $11.2 million in 1990, compared to $2.9 million in 1979, when records were first kept. More than 660 clients hired 498 lobbyists to represent them in 1991, an increase of 20 percent for both groups since 1988.[9]
- In *Minnesota*, lobbyists spent $4.4 million in 1991, compared to $2.15 million for the previous reporting period.[10]
- In *Mississippi*, spending by lobbyists increased from $2.4 million in 1991 to $4.2 million in 1992, an increase of 73 percent.[11]
- In *New Jersey*, lobbyists spent $12.4 million in 1991; expenditures by lobbyists have increased steadily since 1982.[12]
- In *New York*, 1,993 lobbyists were registered with the state in 1990, a 17-percent increase from 1989. They were paid a total of $29.3 million, a 12-percent rise over the year before and a five-fold increase since 1978.[13]
- In *Virginia*, lobbying expenditures rose from $4 million during the 60-day legislative session of 1990 to $5 million during the next 60-day session, which was held in 1992.[14] Between 1980 and 1992, the number of registered lobbyists increased by 62.8 percent, and the

amount they spent increased by 354.5 percent.[15]

- In *Wisconsin*, the number of registered lobbyists doubled from 300 in 1987 to 600 in 1991.[16]

THE ROLE OF POLITICAL ACTION COMMITTEES

Lobbyists and their employers seek to influence government decision-making by directly communicating with government officials. In many cases, they also try to ensure access or influence by making various kinds of financial contributions. For example, lobbyists often give personal gifts and campaign contributions to legislators. Between 1986 and 1990, lobbyists gave over $194,000 to Michigan legislators, according to Common Cause/Michigan.[17] To enhance their ability to influence government decision-making, lobbyists and their employers may also bind together to form a PAC which then contributes to statewide and legislative campaigns. PACs can wield this clout in the form of campaign contributions, often distributed by individual lobbyists, which open officials' doors that are often closed to the average citizen.

In Minnesota in 1990, lobbyists gave $225,000 to candidates for the state legislature; they combined this with $4.4 million spent on advertising, gifts, entertainment, and other lobbying expenses. Two lobbying firms alone gave more than $155,000 to successful candidates. One of these firms, North State Advisors, gave $61,000 through its PAC, and each member of the firm gave an additional $2,000 personal donation. North State's President, Thomas Kelm, said: "The only thing I ever ask for is, give us a hearing, let us come into the office and bring the client." In 1991, Northwest Airlines hired lobbyists from North State, as well as a former Minnesota Attorney General, to lobby for an $830 million state aid

package. In all Northwest Airlines reported spending $700,000 to influence the legislature. During the debate over the state aid package, legislators reportedly left the floor to meet with Northwest executives in a room just outside the Senate chambers. Opponents of the package complained that they had not received equivalent access.[18]

In some instances, the relationship between public official, lobbyist and PAC can be very close. In March 1988 in Iowa, for example, it was revealed that one state senator had accepted more than $8,000 and another, $6,000 in "consulting fees" from two PACs. Iowa Senate Minority Leader Calvin Hultman received the fee from the PAC of the Hawkeye Bancorporation, reported as "an influential player in the interstate banking bill" then pending before the Iowa State Legislature. Another legislator, Senator Jack Nystrom, received $8,392 from a PAC formed to recruit Republican candidates for the legislature and partially financed by General Contractors of Iowa and Deere & Co. Those two companies were lobbying the legislature in support of a gasoline tax increase at the time. This incident was the first time in Iowa that PAC money had been channeled directly to legislators as a fee rather than donated as campaign contributions, and raised new questions about the effectiveness of state ethics laws.[19]

There is strong evidence that PAC contributions are utilized by lobbyists and lobbying organizations to enhance their access to and influence over government decision-making. In 1988 a Washington, D.C.-based PAC director and lobbyist commented on his work, saying:

If you have a particular problem in getting to see a Senator you can always go to the Senate Campaign Committee, and all we say is "we want five minutes with Senator X." Like I say, we are not buying votes, we just want five minutes to see that person.[20]

A report by the California Commission on Campaign Financing entitled "The New Gold Rush: Financing California's Legislative Campaigns," noted the combined power PACs and lobbyists can wield:

> One veteran and well-placed lobbyist privately estimates that 50 or so bills each session are decided by how much is given by whom in campaign contributions that more accurately could be described as bribes."[21]

A study by Common Cause/Colorado highlights the potential impact of special-interest money on legislative decision-making in that state. In 1986, special-interest PACs accounted for 59 percent of contributions to state House candidates and 62 percent to state Senate candidates.[22] PACs are generally tied to organizations which lobby and PAC contributions are used as an integral part of an overall lobbying strategy. As one state legislator put it:

> Undue influence makes its appearance and manifestation in legislation that we pass here in the Assembly, and many times the taxpayers must pay a greater price for various forms of legislation because of the influence of those groups that have made campaign contributions.[23]

SUMMARY OF STATE LOBBY REGULATION LAWS

Registration and Disclosure

Rules governing disclosure of lobbying expenditures vary considerably in their effectiveness from state to state. For example, under Washington's law—one of the most comprehensive lobby registration and disclosure laws in the country—a record $15.6 million was reported spent by lobbyists in 1990.[24] But in Pennsylvania, a state with nearly twice

the population of Washington and extensive industrial and financial interests, lobbyists reported spending a total of only $402,728 that year.[25]

According to a Common Cause/Illinois study, "Desperately Seeking Disclosure," in contrast to the $293,198 in reported lobbying expenditures in Illinois in 1990, Missouri lobbyists reported spending $1.1 million, Virginia lobbyists reported spending $4 million, Massachusetts lobbyists reported spending $15.4 million and New York lobbyists reported spending more than $29 million.[26]

Although state lobby laws vary in scope and effectiveness, all states now have laws requiring lobbyists to be registered. Forty-nine states require some kind of reporting of lobbying expenditures (only Wyoming does not).[27]

In addition, at least 25 states and the District of Columbia have agencies which compile and publish data about lobbying activities supplied by these reports.[28] At least 26 states and the District of Columbia define the term lobbyist to include those who lobby executive branch agencies.[29] At least 25 state laws require those employing individual lobbyists to register (known as registration of principals).[30] At least 25 state laws require those employing individual lobbyists to file expenditure reports.[31] Laws in at least 35 states and the District of Columbia require expenditure reports to provide data by category of expenditures.[32] Laws in at least 35 states and the District of Columbia require expenditure reports to provide total expenditures.[33]

The Definition of "Lobbying"

An essential element of any lobby disclosure law is a clear, fair, and objective definition of "lobbying." A citizen who writes concerned letters to a state legislator clearly should not be required to register as a lobbyist. If it were necessary to file disclosure forms in such situations, citizens might be discouraged from expressing their views at all—and would thereby be deprived of their First Amendment rights. On the other hand, a large corporation should no be allowed to escape coverage even if it spends only a small fraction of its resources on lobbying.

A reasonable test might require disclosure whenever a set amount of money is spent to lobby the legislature or the executive branch, or whenever a set number of hours or days is devoted to such lobbying by paid employees. Such a provision could exempt volunteers, small organizations without paid employees, citizens communicating with the legislature on their own behalf, and small firms or organizations which lobby only occasionally.

At least 25 states and the District of Columbia require registration by anyone who receives compensation to lobby.[34] Twenty-six states and the District require registration by anyone who spends a threshold amount of money on lobbying.[35] And 19 states and the District use a minimum time standard.[36] In many states, two or three of these triggers apply simultaneously.

Washington State has one of the most effective lobby disclosure statutes in the country, the constitutionality of which has been upheld in court.[37] Under the Washington State statute, "lobbying" means attempting to influence government decisions, and anyone who does so is a lobbyist. However, certain classes of people who fit this definition do not have to register or disclose, including members of the press, those who lobby without pay, and those who spend no more than four days and $25 lobbying during a three-month period.[38]

The Council on Governmental Ethics Laws (COGEL) has written a model lobby disclosure law, under which anyone defined as a lobbyist would have to register. In the COGEL law, a lobbyist is defined as anyone who is paid to influence government decisions, or who represents an organization for the purpose of lobbying, or who is the sole proprietor of a firm with a financial interest in a government decision that he or she tries to influence.

Existing federal law requires registration only by those whose "principal purpose" is to lobby. Many large organizations therefore fail to register, arguing that lobbying is just one of their activities. As a result, federal law has failed to provide adequate levels of disclosure. However, a new bill was introduced in the U.S. Senate in February 1992 that would create a more specific and useful trigger for registration. Under this legislation, an organization would have to register as soon as it paid someone to make a "lobbying contact" with a government official. Thereafter, all related expenses would be subject to disclosure.

As well as defining *who* is a lobbyist, a disclosure bill must also define *what* is disclosable lobbying. An excessively vague definition of "lobbying activities" could cause a law to be ruled unconstitutional, since a vague law violates citizens' due process rights.[39] When the federal lobby disclosure law was challenged in court in the 1950s, the plaintiffs charged that its definition of "lobbying" was unconstitutionally vague. However, the U.S. Supreme Court ruled in *U.S. v. Harriss* that the law was clear, as long as "lobbying" refers to "lobbying in its commonly accepted sense—to direct communication with members of Congress on pending or proposed federal legislation."[40]

Citing this language in *Harriss*, the Deputy Attorney General of Vermont recently issued a narrow interpretation of the Vermont lobby disclosure law. He ruled that, if the law was to pass constitutional scrutiny, it could only apply to "disclosure of expenses immediate to actual contracts with legislative or executive officials about identifiable pending or proposed bills or regulations."[41] Therefore, the Deputy Attorney General advised an industry coalition that it did not have to disclose expenditures for an annual dinner for state officials unless "identifiable...bills or regulations" were discussed.

However, *Harriss* seems to permit a broader definition than the one proposed by the Vermont Attorney General's Office. In *Harriss*, the Supreme Court interpreted "lobbying" to mean "direct communication...on pending or proposed federal legislation." But the Court left unchallenged a broad definition of "legislation." Under the federal act, "legislation" means "bills, resolutions, amendments, nominations, and other matters pending or proposed in either House of Congress, and includes any other matter which may be the subject of action by either House."[42] Thus, it would seem to be constitutional to require disclosure of lobbying on potential areas of government action, and not just on pending or proposed bills.

Limits on Gifts

In many states, it is legal for legislators to accept unlimited amount of gifts, meals, trips, and the like from lobbyists. This practice can create a conflict of interest or the appearance of a conflict. Archibald Cox, Common Cause Chairman Emeritus, described the problem in 1986 testimony:

> Toleration of even the appearance of linking personal friendships or personal financial advantage with governmental decisions is the beginning of a long downhill slide into major corruption, public cynicism, and the collapse of confidence in public justice.[43]

In 1991, Associated Press reported:

> In a Media General-Associated Press poll, 75 percent of 1,071 adults across the nation said gifts from lobbyists create undue influence. Eight in 10 said

lawmakers sometimes vote the way lobbyists want them to in exchange for gifts. Eight in 10 said they would back a disclosure law requiring lobbyists to publicly report all contacts they have with state lawmakers.[44]

To address this problem, 34 states and the District of Columbia have restrictions on the receipt of gifts by officials or employees.[45] Certain states, such as Wisconsin and South Carolina, ban state officials and employees from soliciting or accepting anything of pecuniary value— lodging, transportation, food, meals, beverages, or money—from lobbyists. Other states set limits on the value of gifts a state legislator or employee can accept. For example, California prohibits elected state officers from accepting gifts with a total value of more than $250 from a single source in a calendar year. In Florida, Kansas, Nevada and Massachusetts, the limit on gifts from lobbyists to legislators is $100 per year. In Connecticut lobbyists may not spend more than $50 per gift. Texas law limits lobby expenditures on entertainment and gifts and prohibits "pleasure trips" for legislators that are paid for by lobbyists.

In-Session Ban on Lobbyists Contributions

Fifteen states—Arizona, Arkansas, Connecticut, Georgia, Iowa, Kansas, Louisiana, Maryland, Minnesota, Nevada, Oregon, South Carolina, Texas, Utah and Wisconsin—and the District of Columbia have adopted bans on lobbyists making contributions during the legislative session.[46]

In 1990, a Florida court found an in-session contribution ban unconstitutional.[47] The previous year, the Florida legislature had passed a law banning all campaign contributions during the legislative session. The law was aimed at preventing legislators from holding fundraising events during the session and soliciting money from lobbyists who had issues pending before the legislature. However, in 1990, a circuit judge ruled that, although the State has a compelling interest in regulating campaign financing, the statute was not tailored narrowly enough to meet the constitutional test of strict scrutiny.[48]

However, it should be noted that the Florida law was particularly broad: it banned all contributions of any kind from anyone (not just lobbyists) to any candidate (incumbent or challenger) or any office holder (including judges) during the legislative session. The Court found that the ban on contributions to challengers was "unnecessary" for the purpose of preventing corruption, and criticized other provisions of the law.[49] But a more narrowly tailored bill may withstand strict scrutiny.

It can be expected that constitutional concerns will be raised whenever political contributions are banned under specified circumstances. Challenges may range from the argument that First Amendment rights have been violated, to concerns about equal protection for lobbyists, to criticisms of the effectiveness of such provisions as anti-corruption measures. It is not clear yet how these arguments will be dealt with by the courts. For example, a contribution ban that was aimed solely at registered lobbyists might pass the strict scrutiny test more readily than a universal ban, but it might also interfere with lobbyists' right to equal protection.[50]

States have adopted various approaches to regulating contributions. Oregon prohibits lobbyists from contributing to current office holders and candidates alike during regular and special legislative sessions. Minnesota prohibits lobbyists from contributing to legislators or candidates for the legislature during the regular legislative session. And an Arkansas law prohibits all elected statewide and legislative officials from accepting contributions from any source during the period from 30 days before to 30 days after the legislative session or during any special session.

Enforcement

A large portion of lobbying activity in many states goes unreported because the disclosure laws lack necessary enforcement mechanisms. In 1990, The Associated Press reported that 28 states had conducted no investigations of lobby disclosure reports during the previous reporting period. State governments devote few resources to monitoring lobbying— 23 states assign only one full- or part-time staff member to conduct oversight activities.[51]

In Montana, where investigations into compliance with the state's lobby law are not mandated, a lobby disclosure audit has never been conducted.[52]

A report by Common Cause/Virginia, released in November 1992, noted: "Virginia currently does not conduct investigations" into compliance with lobby disclosure laws.[53] But, according to newspaper reports, the Better Transportation Association of Virginia spent at least $80,000 to support a transportation bill in the General Assembly in 1986, yet it did not file as a lobbyist.[54]

A 1990 Common Cause/Pennsylvania study that compared Pennsylvania to other states in terms of the size of the legislature, the number of lobbyists and the amount lobbyists reported, concluded that Pennsylvania's lobby law is "deficient in its ability to mandate and enforce the disclosure of information essential to public understanding of the magnitude of the effect of professional lobbying.[55] For example, the amount Pennsylvania lobbyists reported as having spent decreased from 1988 to 1989, even though the number of lobbyists increased.[56]

In some states, strong independent commissions enforce the law. In Washington State, for example, an independent commission was established to determine whether lobby disclosure reports are filed correctly, to investigate and report violations of the law either in response to a complaint or at its own instigation, and to enforce.

In a few states, violations of state lobbying laws have met with serious consequences. In Connecticut, for example, the Retail Merchants Association was fined $50,000 for "widespread" violations of the state's lobbying laws, including failure to disclose excessive gifts and lavish entertaining of Connecticut lawmakers. Connecticut's law prohibits legislators from accepting gifts worth over $50 in a year from a lobbyist.[57]

As often happens, strong enforcement may follow scandals. In South Carolina, where as of July 1991, 10 state legislators implicated in a bribery scandal had pleaded guilty or been convicted of bribe-related charges, the new Secretary of State, Jim Miles, announced that he would:

> Review the disclosure forms of every one of South Carolina's 300 registered lobbyists to see if they fully revealed what they lobbied for, which legislators they tried to influence and what they spent to influence them.[58]

COMMON CAUSE PROPOSALS

Common Cause believes that each state should adopt a comprehensive lobbying statute requiring full and timely disclosure of special-interest lobbying activities.

An effective lobby disclosure law would make the balance of money and power on either side of any issue more obvious to voters, decision-makers, and competing interests alike. An effective statute also would help to ensure a more accountable decision-making process by exposing lobbying activities to public scrutiny. It would thereby help to restore public confidence in the political process.

However, it is important to recognize that other critically important issues also must be addressed if the government is to deal with public concern about special-interest influence and restore public confidence in the political process. In addition to disclosing lobbying activities, it is important to pass tough campaign finance reform and conflict-of-interest legislation to address directly the ability of lobbyists and others to channel resources—e.g., campaign contributions, gifts, and honoraria—to legislators.[59]

- *Registration and reporting of expenditures by all persons and groups that receive or spend a significant sum of money on lobbying.* The public has a clear interest in knowing who is trying to influence governmental decisions and by what means. Employers of lobbyists and lobbyists themselves should file separate registration and expenditure forms. And an objective test should be established for triggering registration.

- *Coverage of those who attempt to influence the executive branch and the regulatory agencies in addition to those who attempt to influence the legislative branch.* The public's interest in knowing the activities of those who attempt to influence governmental decisions is no less important when the decision is made by the bureaucracy or the executive rather that the legislature. This is increasingly important because of the growing number of administrative agencies formulating policies to regulate consumer, health, environmental, and other problems.

- *Comprehensive and periodic disclosure of special-interest lobbying expenditures.* Lobbyists and their employers should report their sources and amounts of income, their expenditures (with major expenses itemized), and the matters they have attempted to influence. These reports should be made regularly—e.g., monthly—while the legislature is in session and quarterly during the rest of the year. In addition, efforts to generate grassroots lobbying should be disclosed. This will help ensure that citizens and public officials have the opportunity to judge special-interest pressures before legislation is considered.

- *Identification of public officials who receive gifts from lobbyists and a limitation on such gifts.* Gifts can be used by lobbyists to seek the kind of access to public officials that average citizens do not have. The date, beneficiary, amount, and circumstances of each gift valued over some minimal amount should be disclosed. No lobbyist should be able to give any official more than $50 in gifts in a single year.
- *Tough sanctions by an independent enforcement commission.* Effective enforcement is essential to any law that may affect powerful financial interests. A knowing violation of the law should be a criminal offense. The law should be enforced by an independent commission whose members are not otherwise public officials, with a full-time staff and strong enforcement powers. Citizens should have the opportunity to initiate civil action in accordance with the law under specified circumstances.
- *Lobby reports should be readily available and easily accessible to the public.* They should be kept together in one location for a period of at least 10 years, and be indexed by organization and issue. It should be possible to find out which groups have disclosed a lobbying interest on any bill by searching a computer file. Basic information from the disclosure forms should therefore be entered into a data base with cross-references, in order to make the information readily available and useful to citizens and elected officials.

NOTES

1. *United States v. Harris*, 347 U.S. 612, 625 (1953).

2. *The Washington Post*, November 3, 1992.
3. *Citizens and Politics: A View from Main Street America*; prepared for the Kettering Foundation by The Harwood Group, June 1991; p. 29.
4. William Pound, Executive Director, National Conference of State Legislatures; Common Cause/Delaware newsletter; July 1989.
5. *National Journal*; November 28, 1987.
6. Associated Press; June 25, 1990.
7. *Ibid.*; June 25, 1990.
8. *The San Francisco Chronicle*, March 27, 1991; *City and State*, May 18, 1992; *COGEL Guardian*, February 1992.
9. *The Washington Post*, April 1, 1992.
10. *COGEL Guardian*, February 1992.
11. *COGEL Guardian*, October 1992, p. 19.
12. *Ibid.*; June 1992, p. 22.
13. *The New York Times*; March 19, 1991.
14. *The Washington Post*; May 19, 1992.
15. Common Cause/Virginia, "Is the Virginia Lobby Disclosure Law Adequate?"; November 1992, p. 7.
16. *Milwaukee Sentinel*, March 2, 1992.
17. *Common Cause/Michigan*; vol. 18, no. 1, Spring 1992.
18. *St. Paul Pioneer Press*, Special Reprint Section, "Bankrolling the Legislature;" April 1992.
19. *The Des Moines Register*; March 10, 1988.
20. "PACs on PACs: The View from the Inside;" Center for Responsive Politics; Washington, DC; February 1988.
21. California Commission on Campaign Financing; *The New Gold Rush: Financing California's Legislative Campaigns*; Los Angeles, CA; 1985; p. 8.
22. "'PACed' Houses II: Common Cause Reports on Campaign Finance in Coiorado;" Common Cause/Colorado; January 1988.
23. *Pennsylvania Legislative Journal*; May 22, 1988; p. 1108.

24. "Desperately Seeking Disclosure;" Common Cause/Illinois; April 1991; p. 5.
25. Common Cause/Pennsylvania; June 11, 1991.
26. "Desperately Seeking Disclosure;" Common Cause/Illinois; April 1991; p. 5.
27. In 1992 Georgia enacted its first disclosure law, while Louisiana and Utah enacted disclosure laws in 1991.
28. These states include: Alaska, Arkansas, California, Connecticut, Florida, Idaho, Indiana, Kansas, Kentucky, Maryland, Massachusetts. Michigan, Minnesota, Nebraska, Nevada, New Jersey, New York, Ohio, Oklahoma, Oregon, Pennsylvania, Texas, Vermont, Washington, and Wisconsin.
29. These states include: Alaska, Arizona, Arkansas, California, Connecticut, Hawaii, Kansas, Louisiana, Maryland, Massachusetts, Michigan, Minnesota, Missouri, New Jersey, New York, Ohio, Oklahoma, Pennsylvania, South Carolina, Tennessee, Texas, Utah, Vermont, Washington, West Virginia, and Wisconsin. (*The Book of the States: 1992–1993 Edition*; Council of State Governments; Lexington, Kentucky; 1992; p. 205.)
30. These states include: Alabama, Arizona, California, Hawaii, Indiana, Maine, Maryland, Massachusetts, Michigan, Minnesota, Mississippi, Missouri, Montana, New Jersey, North Carolina, Oregon, Pennsylvania, Rhode Island, South Dakota, Utah, Vermont, Virginia, Washington, and Wisconsin. (Common Cause/Illinois study; "More Loophole than Law;" May 1989.) Minnesota passed this provision in 1990 and North Carolina did so in 1991.
31. These states include Alabama, Arizona, California, Colorado, Connecticut, Hawaii, Indiana, Maine, Maryland, Massachusetts, Michigan, Minnesota, Mississippi, Montana,

New Jersey, New York, North Carolina, Ohio, Oregon, Rhode Island, South Dakota, Vermont, Virginia, Washington, and Wisconsin. (Common Cause/Illinois study; "More Loophole than Law;" May 1989.) Minnesota, Ohio, and Washington passed laws on this in 1990 and North Carolina did so in 1991.
32. These states include: Alabama, Alaska, Arkansas, Colorado, Connecticut, Delaware, Hawaii, Idaho, Indiana, Kansas, Kentucky, Louisiana, Maryland, Massachusetts, Michigan, Minnesota, Missouri, Montana, Nebraska, Nevada, New Hampshire, New Jersey, New Mexico, New York, North Carolina, Oregon, Pennsylvania, Rhode Island, South Carolina, Tennessee, Texas, Virginia, Washington, West Virginia, and Wisconsin. (*The Book of the States: 1992–1993 Edition*; op. cit.; p. 207.)
33. These states include: Alaska, Arkansas, California, Connecticut, Delaware, Hawaii, Idaho, Indiana, Iowa, Kentucky, Louisiana, Maine, Maryland, Massachusetts, Michigan, Minnesota, Mississippi, Missouri, Montana, Nebraska, Nevada, New Jersey, New Mexico, New York, Ohio, Oregon, Rhode Island, South Carolina, Texas, Utah, Vermont, Virginia, Washington, West Virginia, and Wisconsin. (*Ibid*, p. 207.)
34. These state include: California, Colorado, Connecticut, Hawaii, Idaho, Indiana, Kentucky, Louisiana, Maine, Maryland, Massachusetts, Michigan, Missouri, New Hampshire, New York, North Dakota, Ohio, Oklahoma, Pennsylvania, Texas, Utah, Vermont, Virginia, Washington, and West Virginia. *Ibid.*; p. 205.
35. These states include: Arkansas, Colorado, Connecticut, Hawaii, Indiana, Louisiana, Maine, Maryland, Michigan, Minnesota, Missouri, Montana, Nevada, New York, North Dakota, Ohio, Oklahoma, Oregon, Tennessee, Texas, Utah, Vermont, Virginia,

Washington, West Virginia, and Wisconsin. *Ibid.*

36. Those states are: Alabama, Alaska, California, Connecticut, Hawaii, Louisiana, Maryland, Michigan, Minnesota, Missouri, Nevada, New York, North Dakota, Oregon, Texas, Utah, Virginia, Washington, and Wisconsin, *Ibid.*

37. *Fritz v. Gorton*, 517 p. 2d at 931 (1974).

38. Washington State Open Government Act, RCW 42.17.160.

39. This was the fate of a Montana law which was struck down in *Montana Auto Association v. Greely*, 632 P. 2d. 300 (1981).

40. 347 U.S. 612, at 620, citing *U.S. v. Rumely*, 345 U.S. 41.

41. Brian L. Burgess, memorandum; October 21, 1991.

42. 2 U.S. 261.

43. Testimony of Archibald Cox, Chairman Emeritus of Common Cause, before the Governor's Committee on Ethics in Government; Warwick, Rhode Island; June 2, 1986.

44. Associated Press; June 26, 1990.

45. As of 1991, these states included: Alabama, Alaska, Arkansas, California, Connecticut, Florida, Hawaii, Illinois, Indiana, Louisiana, Maine, Maryland, Massachusetts, Michigan, Mississippi, Montana, Nebraska, New Hampshire, New Jersey, New York, North Carolina, North Dakota, Ohio, Oklahoma, Oregon, Pennsylvania, Rhode Island, South Carolina, Tennessee, Texas, Vermont, West Virginia, and Wisconsin. (*The COGEL Campaign Finance, Ethics and Lobby Law Blue Book 1990–91*; December 1990; The Council of State Governments; Lexington, KY; Table 20.) When this paper went to press, the 1992 *COGEL Blue Book* was not yet available, but it will be obtainable

in early 1993 through the Council of State Governments. In 1992, Iowa enacted a gift provision.

46. South Carolina's law prohibits candidates from soliciting or accepting contributions from registered lobbyists throughout the year, regardless of legislative session.

47. *State of Florida v. Jack P. Dodd*, 561 So.2d 263 (Fla. 1990).

48. Strict scrutiny, in this case, means that since the law has an impact on a fundamental right, the statute must relate very closely to the legislative purpose.

49. *State of Florida v. Dodd*, at 265.

50. Laws have been upheld which ban contributions from particular classes of people—including casino employees and liquor licensees—on the ground that such contributions pose a special risk of corruption. A similar rationale could perhaps be worked out to ban contributions from lobbyists. See *In re Soto*, 565 A. 2d 1088 (N.J. Super. Ct. App. Div., 1989), *cert. denied* 110 S.Ct. 3216; and *Schiller Park Colonial Inn, Inc. v. Berz* 349 N.E. 2d 61 (Ill. 1976).

51. *Associated Press*; June 25, 1990.

52. "For the People"; Common Cause/Montana; 1991.

53. Common Cause/Virginia, "Is the Virginia Lobby Disclosure Law Adequate?"; November 1992, p. 16.

54. *Ibid.*, p. 14.

55. "Lifting the Shroud of Secrecy"; Common Cause/Pennsylvania; 1990.

56. Common Cause/Pennsylvania; June 11, 1991.

57. *COGEL Guardian*; April 30, 1991; p. 24.

58. *Governing*; February 1991; p. 12.

59. For further information on campaign finance reform and conflict-of-interest laws, see 1991 Common Cause issue briefs on these subjects.

CHAPTER 5

Governors and State Bureaucracies

The executive branch and the office of governor are the most interesting institutions in American state government. Men and women who serve as governors are at "the apex of the power structure of the state,"[1] and may very well use this office as a stepping stone to national office, perhaps even the presidency. Three recent presidents—Carter, Reagan, and Clinton—served as governors.

Today's governors, by virtue of their formal powers (both constitutional and statutory), are much stronger than those who served at the end of the Revolutionary War, when the writers of state constitutions were distrustful of executive authority because of its association with British rule during the colonial period. These early governors were frequently elected by the legislatures, not by the voters; had a short term of office, usually one year; and did not have the power of the veto that would allow them to prevent acts of the legislature from becoming law.

The creation of an executive with an array of formal powers, often referred to as a strong governor, did not happen quickly. Popular election of the governor, longer terms of office (at least two years), and acquisition of some form of the veto were important changes adopted in the nineteenth century. But the most significant expansion of gubernatorial power occurred in the twentieth century. The adoption of the executive budget in many states early in this century increased the authority of governors in budgetary matters. The term executive budget means simply that the governor has the responsibility to prepare the state budget and submit it to the legislature. This is an important power because it enables governors to develop budgets that reflect their policy priorities, not the priorities of a board of administrative officials or a legislative committee.

The most recent period of reform affecting gubernatorial powers took place from 1965 to 1987. The goal was to make the governor "the center of energy, direction and administrative management."[2] Some of the changes affected governors in a direct way, with more and more states allowing governors to serve four-year terms and paying them higher salaries along with

[1] Sarah McCally McMorehouse *State Politics, Parties and Policy* (New York: Holt, Rinehart and Winston, 1981), p. 203.
[2] James K. Conant "In the Shadow of Wilson and Brownlow: Executive Branch Reorganization in the States, 1965 to 1987," *Public Administration Review* 48, p. 893.

giving them increased staff support. For example, twenty-four states permitted governors to serve two four-year terms in 1981, contrasted to only six in 1955.

Gubernatorial power was also expanded by changes that took place within the executive branch. The agencies that had proliferated in earlier years were consolidated into major departments. Jimmy Carter, while governor of Georgia, persuaded the state legislature to enact a major reorganization of the executive branch that consolidated 300 separate agencies into 22 departments. This type of reorganization, although not always as extensive as in Georgia, occurred in many states. Equally important was the expansion of the number of departments and agency heads appointed by the governor. Previously many of these officials were elected by the people or appointed by boards or commissions. Appointment by the governor is important because it helps ensure that the secretaries of departments and the heads of agencies are more responsive to the policy concerns of the governor. (It is important to note that even though governors have stronger appointive powers, the heads of a number of important agencies in almost every state are not appointed by the governor. Perhaps the best-known example is the attorney general who is elected in forty-three states.)

Much of the political science literature has focused on the formal powers of governors. In the final analysis, however, governors are judged by their ability to provide leadership: to identify problems confronting their states, propose solutions to these problems, and convince the legislature to enact their proposals.

The process of identifying problems and proposing solutions, usually referred to as setting the agenda, culminates with the state-of-the-state addresses governors deliver at the beginning of the legislative session. These addresses review "the state's condition and highlights both current accomplishments and recommended initiatives for the future."[3] As part of agenda setting, governors develop a specific legislative program—proposals for bills that will be introduced in the legislature. Setting the agenda does not mean that there is a blank sheet of paper and governors can write down all their personal policy concerns. Economic and political factors place constraints on the agenda. If revenues are down, the possibility of proposing new programs requiring new funds is slim. Ideas for the agenda can come from a number of sources—campaign promises, the political philosophy of the governor and even members of the legislature, to mention a few.

Once the agenda is determined, governors must focus their attention on obtaining legislative approval. How is this accomplished? Political scientist Alan Rosenthal, in Reading 11, identifies what he calls "outside and inside strategies." The outside strategy is when governors attempt to build support for a proposal by attempting, in some way, to get the public concerned and

---

[3] James J. Gosling "Patterns of Stability and Change in Gubernatorial Policy Agendas," *State and Local Government Review 23* no. 1, p. 3.

involved. The inside strategy refers to governors persuading and bargaining with both legislative leaders and individual legislators to get the votes needed to have proposals enacted into law. As important as these strategies are, Rosenthal also points out that governors should have a legislative program that does not contain too many proposals; a focused program is more likely to receive legislative approval than one that tries to do everything at once.

One of the more interesting powers that many governors have is the item veto, which allows the veto of specific sections or items in an appropriation bill, but permits everything else in the bill to become law. Reading 12, by Tony Hutchison, a staff member of the National Conference of State Legislatures, argues that the original purpose behind the item veto was to allow governors to better control the budget by reducing some of the spending sought by legislatures. What appears to be happening in a number of states, however, is that governors are using the item veto to change the language in the appropriations bills that directs how money is to be spent—in other words, changing legislative intent. Perhaps in these states governors are becoming too powerful.

Reading 13, by political scientists Deil Wright, Jae-Won Yoo, and Jennifer Cohen, takes a look at administrators who head state agencies—those individuals who are part of the executive branch and, in terms of an organizational chart, serve just below the governors. These individuals have the responsibility of implementing public policies that have been adopted by the governors and legislators.

Collectively, these agencies are commonly referred to as the state bureaucracy. By way of example, we can look at three states: Colorado, Pennsylvania, and Wisconsin. One of the agencies in the state of Colorado is the Office of Economic Development, headed by a director, which encourages industry to locate in the state. In Pennsylvania, the Department of Environmental Resources is headed by a secretary; the purpose of the department is to manage the state's pollution-control program and to improve the overall quality of the environment. All of us are familiar with the motor vehicle administration in our own state, which is responsible for issuing and maintaining records relating to owning and driving automobiles. In Wisconsin, this agency is called the Division of Motor Vehicles and is headed by an administrator. Whether they are called directors, secretaries, or administrators, all are examples of what is meant by the general terms of state administrators and agency heads.

Wright and his colleagues discovered that today's agency heads are better educated, younger, and more diverse in terms of gender and ethnicity than those of the 1960s. Many have made a career of service in state government; in fact, one-third were serving in the agency immediately prior to becoming its head. On the other hand, the system is not entirely closed because some agency heads come from local or national governments and even the private sector. State administrators report working 50 to 55 hours a week. This article concludes that state administrators are equipped to handle the new burdens being placed on state governments as a result of the national government's reducing its role in domestic policy.

QUESTIONS FOR DISCUSSION

1.   Are there examples in your state of a governor informing the public about problems the state needs to address? (Rosenthal calls this conditioning.)

2.   According to Rosenthal, are governors usually successful in getting legislatures to pass their programs?

3.   Why was the item veto originally adopted by the states in the late nineteenth century? In what specific ways has its use in some states changed from its original purpose?

4.   The Wright, Yoo, and Cohen reading contains a lot of information concerning who state administrators are and the kind of activities they engage in. Do you think you might be interested in a career in state government? Why or why not?

11.   Gubernatorial Follow-through

Alan Rosenthal

Legislatures expect governors to lead. They rely on the governor to define issues and set the process in motion. Legislatures need not be weak or a rubber stamp to want gubernatorial leadership. If the issue is significant, the governor's presence and power may be vital in achieving agreement. "What does the governor want?" and "What does the governor want us to do?" are the customary questions raised by legislators in the capitol.

Gubernatorial leadership, at the outset, naturally requires the formulation of a program and the setting of an agenda. But beyond that, it requires that the governor steer the program through and succeed in having it adopted by the legislature. Therefore, as Madeleine Kunin

SOURCE: "Gubernatorial Follow-Through" by Alan Rosenthal from *Governors and Legislatures: Contending Powers*, 1990 Congressional Quarterly Press, pp. 103–116. Reprinted by permission.

points out, the governor has the ability "not only to define the agenda, but then to develop it, to actually make it happen." To make it happen, governors must have follow-through—the willingness and the skill to appeal to the public, persuade legislators, and do whatever they deem necessary to steer their proposals through the legislative process. Success does not always come on the first push. Sometimes a governor will lose in one legislative session and then reintroduce the proposal in the next. Accomplishment may take a governor's entire term.

Bruce Babbitt, who concentrated on a few issues in each of his years in office, described how he "used everything at my disposal—initiative, referendum, the bully pulpit, the press, browbeating, trade-offs, threats, rewards— to get what I needed."[1] That was Babbitt's way of following through. Other governors do it somewhat differently. There are a variety of ways to succeed, as the following cases of gubernatorial leadership suggest.

THREE CASES OF LEADERSHIP

Byrne and the Pinelands

Brendan Byrne's advocacy of the pinelands in New Jersey, more than anything else, was responsible for the passage of the Pinelands Protection Act in 1979. Having been influenced by John McPhee's book [*The Pine Barrens*], Governor Byrne mentioned the pinelands in his 1978 message to the legislature. From then on, he insisted on his goal of protecting and preserving an especially vulnerable area through the establishment of a regional planning and management commission.[2]

During the process, the governor indicated to his staff just how much he wanted the bill. He issued an executive order that established a planning commission and imposed temporary, but stringent, controls on development. That executive order was unparalleled for the reach of executive authority, even in a state where the governor is extremely powerful by virtue of the constitution. The purpose of the executive order was to pressure the legislature into passing a bill rather than face the possibility that the supreme court might uphold the governor's extraordinary action when the case was brought to court. The attorney general and his staff believed that the executive order was unconstitutional. But Byrne did not want to be deterred, so he never asked the attorney general for an opinion; instead, he simply forged ahead.

The process in New Jersey moved forward. Public hearings were held around the state. As a result, amendments were added to the bill to appease various groups, but no substantial changes were made. The governor's staff worked the legislature skillfully and, together with the legislative leadership, persuaded nearly all the members of the senate and enough members in the assembly to go along with Byrne's initiative. Governor Byrne got almost precisely what he wanted, partly because he went all out on behalf of his proposal.

A legislative staffer, Michael Catania, who was involved in the process, describes the role played by Byrne:

> Everybody thought we should preserve the Pines, but nobody thought the legislature would pass a bill until somebody had the guts to say, "I will make this my issue, I will make this happen, and I will make them know that I will not take no for an answer."

The pinelands had many friends, but their protection and preservation were on no one else's agenda. In reflecting on his term as governor, Byrne concluded that the pinelands legislation, like no other measure he proposed, "would not have been passed if I didn't take an interest in it." The governor normally is vital in the enactment of policy; in this case he was indispensable.

Ray and the Bottle Bill

Robert Ray of Iowa was a late convert to a bottle bill, an environmental measure to control litter in the state. But "without the governor's leadership," recalled one senate Republican supporter, "it would have been difficult to pass,"[3] As for many other bills, introducing and deliberating the bottle bill in the legislature would have presented no problem, but it is doubtful whether "we would have had the muscle to get the thing passed." A bottle bill was first raised in the early 1970s and was introduced every year by a conservative Republican, but it went nowhere. Late in 1976, the governor's office, in putting together a list of ideas for Ray's annual program, brought up the problem of litter control. The governor responded positively and, after staff review of alternative approaches, he committed himself to a bottle bill.

In order to build support, Ray pursued both an outside and an inside strategy. His backing of the bill put it in the spotlight throughout Iowa. "Suddenly it went from a bill that nobody paid much attention to," explained one of his aides, "to one that was discussed on the talk shows." That was the easy part of the job; the more difficult part was placating the various interest groups and dealing with the legislature.

The Republicans, in the minority for a second term, were anxious to find a measure to back rather than to stand in opposition to the majority Democrats. But beer distributors, soft drink lobbyists, and retailers—a number of whom had contributed to Republican legislators—were adamant in opposition. Organized labor, which was also against the bill, had close ties to the Democrats.

Ray managed to split the opposition. He did not want to hurt Iowa business and worked closely with Alcoa, which subsequently dropped its objections to the bill. That took some of the intensity out of the campaign by both manufacturers and the AFL-CIO and eased the way for passage of the bill. Its final enactment was one of Ray's major accomplishments. "It wasn't his idea, others had introduced it, there was nothing original about it," remarked the Democratic majority leader of the Iowa house. Nevertheless, he admitted, "it is fair for him to take a lot of credit for it." The bottle bill in Iowa would probably not have been enacted without gubernatorial leadership.

Kunin and Growth and Development

Growth policy in Vermont also demonstrates gubernatorial leadership. Rapid growth and development had caused problems in Vermont since the 1960s, and recent prosperity brought a new surge that appeared to require remedial action by the state. Governor Madeleine

Kunin decided that the time was ripe in mid-1987, shortly after she began her second two-year term in office. That summer she held a retreat attended by members of her administration, a few legislators, and several out-of-state experts on the planning process. (She believed that in developing policy and strategy, it was advisable to escape from the daily rhythm of the office.) The strategy devised at that retreat was pursued by means of both outside and inside campaigns. A top-down approach would not work; it had not succeeded in the past. Statewide land-use planning was such a polarizing issue that, without public debate, it would be neither politically nor practically feasible to enact into law. That thinking underlay the subsequent campaign.

Kunin's first step was to appoint a blue-ribbon group, the Governor's Commission on Vermont's Future, to provide a rationale and political cover for legislation. The commission, chaired by the dean of the state university's law school, included the president of the Vermont League of Cities and Towns, a representative of the state's ski resorts, a dairy farmer, two representatives of the business community, the editor of a state business magazine, a member of the governor's administration, the president of a local college, and a veteran legislator. Having to assess the concern of citizens regarding growth, establish guidelines for growth, and suggest mechanisms to help plan Vermont's future, the commission held a dozen hearings and focus groups and conducted several surveys. The process was purposely speedy, so that opposition would have little time to form. The commission, which organized in September 1987, had its report ready by January 1988.[4]

The initial response to the report was positive, and the predictable battle between environmentalists and developers did not take place, at least not at the outset. The ski industry and Vermont business appeared reconciled to some planning process. The public had been alerted and the interested parties had been softened up. It was now in the hands of the legislature, and the strategy shifted to an inside one.

The legislature had its own contribution to make—filling in the details, providing the nuts and bolts. The speaker and Democrats in the house had growth policy as a high priority, so they felt that the governor had chosen the right issue, their issue. They had come into their own, and benefiting from the publicity power of the governor, they stood to achieve their goals. To signal the importance of the issue to members, the speaker appointed a special committee, chaired by the majority leader, to develop legislation and to expedite the process.

Now, with an actual target—a piece of legislation—to shoot at, conflict arose. Opposition organized, and the issue quickly became a partisan one in the senate, with Republicans opposed to the governor's plan. Therefore, the initial thrust was in the house, where the governor worked with the Democratic leadership, and the speaker then dealt with the Republican leadership. One member of the governor's staff spent full time lobbying, with others serving as back-up. The governor, herself, dealt with individual legislators one on one, emphasizing that planning, as required in the proposed legislation, was not a partisan matter.

In addition to explanation and exhortation, bargaining was called for. The growth issue unleashed a concern in the legislature about agriculture. In return for supporting the governor's growth policy, the house extracted as a price the governor's backing of its measure to assist agriculture. The house wanted to provide dairy farmers with a subsidy, but the governor, concerned about excessive spending, refused to go along. Under pressure from Vermont farmers, not one legislator was willing to oppose the sub-sidy in public. So a compromise had to be worked out. Kunin's office developed as an alternative to a subsidy a tax-abatement program with a temporary subsidy. The house was agreeable to the compromise. Meanwhile, a number of liberal Democrats in the senate were insisting on property tax reform as a quid pro quo for supporting the growth bill. Kunin could not accede to their demand, but she did promise to form a committee to study the issue. The governor's office was prepared with additional inducements. "We had a whole batch of three-digit license plates stockpiled for the occasion," one aide remarked. But the plates were not needed.

During the final stages of the campaign the governor again went public, delivering a television address and meeting with newspaper editors. Not all Democrats were on board and most Republicans were opposed, but the bill passed by a narrow margin in the senate. Without doubt, leadership by the governor made the difference.

OUTSIDE AND INSIDE STRATEGIES

As indicated by these cases, and especially the Vermont growth legislation, on major and controversial issues governors are likely to deal with the public and relevant groups outside the legislature before dealing with leaders and rank and file within the fold. The two strategies are complementary. Going outside facilitates the bargaining that dominates the legislative process. The approach of many governors today may be thought of in terms of *conditioning, coalition formation*, and *consensus building*. The first step is to let the public know about problems that need to be addressed. A second step, combining outside and inside elements, is to involve interest groups and to begin discussions. A third step is to negotiate with legislative leaders and legislators, and perhaps other groups, in order to arrive at a program with sufficiently broad support.

Governors' appeals to the public do not mean that they are going over the head of the legislature. While they may occasionally do so, more frequently their appeals to the public are for purposes of laying a groundwork for a campaign. Many modern governors are in the habit of going public by establishing a theme and a program, packaging the issue so people will understand it, repeating the message continuously, and scheduling events to highlight the particular issue being promoted.

Some governors see themselves as educators. Minnesota governor Rudy Perpich is foremost among them. He takes issues to the public as a matter of principle, traveling throughout the state in the fall, holding hearings, and opening up major issues for public debate. Other governors think less of public education per se and more of accomplishing designated purposes. They go to the public on a few issues only—ones where a major change is being proposed or support is required or both, or where a governor can benefit politically by identifying his or her administration with a particular issue. Often these governors conduct their issue campaigns as if they were running for office themselves, hiring outside consultants and attempting to manage coverage in the press. Lamar Alexander of Tennessee, for example, raised money to retain the firm of Bailey, Deardorff for public relations. He was interested in developing labels and themes for his programs, and shaping people's perceptions accordingly. John Sununu, who served as governor of New Hampshire before moving to the Bush White House as chief of staff, maintained that in order to be successful in office, governors need the same communication skills that they need as candidates. "In the 1990s," he states, "a governor will be governing almost entirely in public, on stage."[5]

It is not surprising, then, that today's governors devote time and energy to speaking to the public. Governor Mike Hayden and his transportation secretary flew around Kansas and argued (unsuccessfully as it turned out) that both safety and economic development required adoption of his program.

In Vermont, Madeleine Kunin focused on educational finance in 1987, so that it was the only subject of her state of the state address. Her objective was to direct attention to funding for the schools, and that is what she talked about with whatever groups she met. Even though her audiences would groan as she belabored the topic, Kunin managed to create a public climate in Vermont that was favorably disposed toward dealing with the educational funding problem.

Over the years, Bill Clinton of Arkansas has become particularly adept in appealing to the public. His approach and techniques vary according to the legislative package or issues involved. On themes central to his administration, he spends months educating the public before the legislative session. In 1988 he succeeded in winning support from the public for a tax increase before a special session. Later that year, in anticipation of the 1989 session, he took his dog and pony show from one corner of Arkansas to another preparing people and the legislature for his "year 2000" program.

When governors neglect going outside on major issues, they risk failure. Kentucky's Martha Layne Collins proposed a tax program in 1984 to finance educational reform, but she never had a chance to engage in a speaking and media campaign or to mobilize public support. She lost in the legislature, but for the next sixteen months she went public before succeeding with her program in a special session the following year.

The real contest occurs on those relatively infrequent occasions when the governor appeals to the public over the head of the legislature. Sometimes the threat of appeal is enough to pressure the legislature into compliance. That was the case in a western state whose governor delivered the following ultimatum to his legislature.

> I believe that water policy is our most serious problem. I am willing to work with you on a solution, but whether or not you address the issue, I plan to. If we have not been able to act together during the coming two years, I will act alone, taking my case to the people.[6]

From time to time, there is cause to do battle. Governor Mario Cuomo of New York, for instance, appealed to the public over the head of the legislature on several occasions, most notably on ethics legislation. Objecting to a weakened ethics bill that emerged from a compromise between the senate and assembly, Cuomo took the high ground and with righteousness cast a veto. He then focused public attention on the issue through constant comment in the media, delighting the press and making legislators look bad. Given the nature of the issue and Cuomo's resolve and oratorical skills, there could be little question as to the outcome. The legislature was forced to agree to a bill that satisfied the governor's objections.[7]

Appealing over the head of the legislature will not always work, and the strategy itself entails risks. As a legislative leader in the New Jersey assembly put it: "If you go to the public, you better win; otherwise you'll lose your pants in the legislature." Whether they lose their pants or lose face, governors cannot afford to be bested once they throw down the gauntlet in a challenge to the legislature.

An outside strategy usually entails engaging the state's opinion leadership and its organized interests, as well as appealing to the mass public through the media. Governors travel across their states to meet with editorial boards of newspapers in an attempt to secure their endorsement for an incipient proposal, and thereby impress legislators who are not yet committed. They also work at wooing influential special interests, who in turn may help persuade legislators that the governor is on the right track.

One device that is frequently employed combines elements of both strategic approaches. Governors appoint commissions, task forces, committees, or the like, which pave the way for the governor's priorities with the public and also with the legislature. The blue ribbon commission has become a most popular device at the national level, used largely to furnish the president and Congress with political cover, a way to avoid blame. Special panels to address the social security system, obsolete military bases, federal criminal sentencing, and the budget deficit are examples. At the state level, governors have also made use of such bodies—sometimes to avoid dealing with a problem, sometimes to shield the executive from political heat, but increasingly to fashion programs and develop consensus. Moreover, such entities facilitate longer range planning, insulate discussion from the political maneuvering of a legislative session, and permit broad participation by representatives of business, academia, and other groups.

In resorting to a commission, governors cannot be certain as to what exactly will emerge, but they can have a reasonably good idea of the general dimensions of the product. At the very least, they can count on their interest being expressed by members of their administration whom they appoint to the commission, and probably by other appointees as well. The objective of many commissions—not all, since some are intended to shelve problems—is to come up with proposals, to accomplish something specific. The tendency is for members to endorse the governor's initiatives. In any case, members recognize that their recommendations will not get far without gubernatorial backing. All of this accounts for the governor's influence at this stage of formulation.

As a rule, a commission will include not only a member or two of the administration, but also representatives of significant and relevant interest groups, usually including business, and several key legislators. Once the commission has made its report, the governor can take the package of proposals to the press and the people for their endorsement. Meanwhile, commission members from the interest groups can be expected to become advocates and to line up their organizations and perhaps engage them in a campaign on behalf of the governor's package. Finally, the legislators who served and who approved the package will be responsible for providing leadership in moving legislation through the house and senate.

Commissions are widely used in the states, taking on economic development in Maine, transportation in Virginia, unemployment in New Jersey, and tort reform in Missouri. But probably no policy domain has been as well served by blue-ribbon commissions as elementary and secondary education. With the publication of *A Nation at Risk* in 1983, educational reform accelerated throughout the nation. In many of the states that underwent reform, commissions spearheaded the drive. Arkansas governor Clinton made use of a legislatively created citizen's committee on new educational standards and appointed his wife as chair. She took the committee on the road, holding hearings in all seventy-five of the state's counties. On the basis of the committee's recommendations, Clinton backed a teacher-testing bill and tax increases to pay for an expanded teaching force and for higher salaries. With the governor's firm leadership, the package passed the legislature.[8]

Reform began in Florida with a commission on secondary schools. The gov-

ernor, speaker of the house, and president of the Senate knew what they wanted from the commission and agreed on a chair who would seek their objectives. As a result, a comprehensive education package, including many of the commission's proposals, was passed by the legislature. In Georgia, Governor Harris established the Educational Review Commission, on which business would play a predominant role. He embraced the commission's report, championed it throughout the state, and managed its recommendations through the legislature, where the Quality Basic Education Act of 1985 passed without challenge.

Legislators' participation at this early stage appears highly desirable. In order to enhance their chances, governors give legislators a sense of ownership, encouraging their participation in the initial formulation of a program or a share of the credit for what is finally achieved or both.

Governor Kunin, for example, welcomed legislative involvement in educational finance and in growth and development from the very outset. She established a summer study commission on school funding, which included legislators as well as her own secretary of administration. Legislators were the ones to take the lead, hammering out a revised school aid formula. Because of their vigorous participation, they could help steer the governor's proposals—and their own—through the process. One of the products of Kunin's Commission on Vermont's Future was proposed legislation, presented not as a package of bills but rather as a set or working documents. It was left to a special legislative committee to transform these documents into bills. The committee did so, and as a result almost everyone's hand had been on the legislation by the time it came up for decision. That proved decisive in the struggle that ensued.

Ownership can also come about when a governor, such as John Ashcroft in Missouri, develops proposals on job creation, rural development, and education and divvies up the initiatives among individual legislators and interest groups, all of whom sign on and advocate the governor's program.

Governors, however, cannot rely completely on their appeals to the public, on blue-ribbon commissions, and on legislators having a sense of ownership. They still have to exercise leadership within the institution, and that entails intervening in the process and using the resources of gubernatorial office. Whatever the popularity of individual governors, as far as state legislatures are concerned, a time comes to shut the door and cut a deal.

Governors must deal first with leadership, and then with rank-and-file members. Occasionally leadership can accomplish whatever is necessary, but frequently governors must be personally involved. In Arizona, for example, Governor Babbitt could not leave such matters to anyone else. He proved effective, largely because he threatened to veto members' bills unless they backed his proposals. In Louisiana, Governor Edwin Edwards needed a two-thirds vote from the legislature for a constitutional amendment to make the superintendent of education an appointive officer. In the senate, the governor's bill failed by one vote. After a night of intense lobbying by Edwards, the bill was recalled under the rules the next day and passed with a vote to spare. In the house, it was defeated initially, but the governors overnight succeeded in changing six votes. Once again, the next day the legislation was recalled and passed.[9] It was the governor's doing, no one else's.

THE BOTTOM LINE

If governors are selective in what they propose, make use of the commission device, take their case to the people, and work the legislature from inside, we would expect them to achieve considerable success in having their programs enacted into law. Their cumulative powers surely give them a head start.

Officials of both the executive and legislative branches agree that today's governors are highly effective in steering their proposals through the legislatures. The record bears them out, as the following examples show.

- In Arkansas, governors since 1979 have succeeded with more than three-fourths of their major policy proposals.[10]
- In Hawaii, Governor Waihee had about 80 percent of his bills pass.
- Governor Branstad of Iowa had about an 85 percent success rate.
- Maine's McKernan steered through twenty of twenty-four initiatives in 1987.
- Maryland's Schaefer had twelve of fourteen important administration bills pass in 1988, including major breakthroughs in higher education, prisons, and transportation.
- In Minnesota, Governor Perpich was successful on ten of twelve initiatives.
- In Missouri, Governor Ashcroft managed to ensure that 80 to 85 percent of his priorities were enacted.
- Governor Kean of New Jersey won on such issues as an alternate route to teaching, high school proficiency examinations, minimum teacher salaries, school takeover, ocean clean-up, civil service reform, and inheritance tax changes—roughly 80 to 90 percent of priorities.
- Governor Lamar Alexander of Tennessee, despite being a "lame duck" Republican with a Democratic legislature, managed to steer nearly all of his proposals through the 1986 session.[11]
- Tennessee governor Ned McWherter received legislative approval for all his initiatives in 1987 and 1988, although

his program was limited to relatively few measures.

One of the poorest records—statistically, at least—was that of Mario Cuomo in New York. Only about 50 to 60 percent of his program bills were enacted into law by a divided legislature during the 1988 session. But Cuomo did well by comparison to his predecessor, Hugh Carey, who got only about 25 percent of what he wanted from the legislature.

A high executive batting average should not suggest that the legislature is a rubber stamp. Nothing could be further from the truth. One of the principal reasons gubernatorial success rates are impressive is because governors know how to accommodate their legislatures. And usually the legislature leaves a heavy imprint on the governor's initiative.

Such an imprint may not even be discernible when made early, before the start of the formal process. Many governors consult with legislative leaders and other key members before the opening of a session, and at that time they take into account legislative priorities and views. The process of modification is already under way before the process formally begins. Modification by the legislature continues, sometimes through amendments on the floor, and occasionally occurs as late as a conference committee between the two chambers. The process of negotiation is a continuing one.

If governors prove stubborn, they may lose. For example, in 1987, Governor Ashcroft of Missouri rejected a legislative change in his proposal for college savings bonds. As a result, nothing passed. The next year Ashcroft accepted the grafting into his plan of a Michigan-style prepaid tuition plan. The two notions were married, and the proposal was enacted into law. In other instances, too, governors have had to give way. Governor Edward DiPrete of Rhode Island wanted a new department of envi-

ronmental quality, with the consolidation of a number of commissions, and a department of environmental management. He got some of what he wanted, but by no means everything. Instead of a new department, he had to settle for a new deputy commissioner, the establishment of a study commission, and the possibility that he would get more of what he wanted in the future. DiPrete also had as a priority affordable housing. He could not persuade the legislature to require towns to allocate land to low-income housing, but he did succeed in obtaining a loan and grant program that accomplished some, if not all, of his objectives.

While most recent governors have been relatively successful, a few have not fared well at the hands of their legislatures. Mike Hayden of Kansas was beaten on some of his top priorities, and those of his proposals that became law in 1988 passed in "one battered form or another."[12] In New Mexico, Tony Anaya was about as unsuccessful as a governor could be with a legislature that rejected major parts of his revenue package and killed his plan to invite out-of-state banks into New Mexico.

Even in places where governors have compiled positive records, legislatures have drawn the line on one issue or another. Iowa's Branstad lost on criminal justice, tightening of the drunk driving laws, and caps on medical and tort liability, and he was not able to reach agreement with the Democratic legislature on workmen's compensation. Vermont's Kunin could not persuade her legislature to enact a parental leave bill, and Maine's McKernan was defeated on a reorganization plan involving energy resources. In Missouri, Ashcroft's big loss was an economic development measure, which failed on the last day of the session, and a secondary loss was a welfare reform plan.

Even Governor Schaefer, who surely dominated in Maryland during his first two years in office, suffered setbacks. He wanted to have savings and loan depositors paid at a faster pace; the legislature turned him down. He proposed a plan to revise the appointment of circuit judges; like governors before him, he lost on that issue too. But Schaefer's most important and bitter defeat was on his proposal for a residential "super" high school for math and science, to be called the Maryland School for Science and Technology. The governor argued that such a school would be a boon to economic development in the state. In the 1987 session the legislature put the governor's scheme on hold, setting aside $100,000 for planning rather than starting immediately. The following year Schaefer went out, appealing to the public. But the teachers' associations questioned the school, the senate budget and taxation committee was firm in its opposition, and finally legislative leadership came out against it. The governor made the issue a very personal one—"you're for the high school or you're against me"—and confronted the legislature. But the general assembly stood its ground, and Schaefer could not prevail, however vigorously he fought.

Governors are more likely to suffer losses on tax measures, or on proposals that require additional revenues, than on anything else. Bill Clinton, for instance, has been beaten on tax issues on several occasions. One reason for this is that in Arkansas, as well as in several other states, revenue bills require more than a majority vote in the house and senate. Clinton has been able to raise the "sin" taxes somewhat, but has not succeeded in capturing the revenues needed to fund the programs he believes are necessary.

Another governor who has had a particularly difficult time with taxes is James Thompson of Illinois. In his second campaign against Adlai Stevenson III, Thompson omitted any mention of taxes. Then right after reelection he called for the largest tax increase in Illinois history. With little preparation or campaigning, the proposal failed. Recently, the governor made two more attempts to put a tax package through the legislature. After taking office in 1987 for a fourth term, he proposed higher income and gas taxes and a new tax on services. He lost again in what was called "the single greatest defeat Thompson had suffered in a decade in office."[13] While he managed to obtain the support of the minority leaders and of Phil Rock, the Democratic president of the senate, he could not persuade the house speaker, Michael Madigan, to go along with his plan.

The Illinois general assembly finally enacted a tax package, increasing revenues by about one billion dollars, in 1989. It was not Thompson's income tax, but rather Speaker Madigan's, that passed. In May Madigan had suddenly announced his own tax-increase plan, which was smaller than the governor's. In a display of raw power, the speaker had his plan passed in the house that same day. Significantly, the new monies were earmarked for local governments and schools, and not for state agencies. Senate support for Madigan's bill could not be put together until the last day of the session, and the speaker obtained most of what he wanted. Governor Thompson signed the bill into law. Although the governor did not get the permanent tax increase that was part of his proposal, he did get gasoline and cigarette taxes that were part of his overall package. But the speaker and the legislature had prevailed.

Even with defeat in the legislature, governors still have recourse. If they persevere, there is a good chance that they will prevail in time. For example, Schaefer refashioned his proposal for Maryland's math-science school. No longer did he seek a high school per se; instead he sought a program to train math and science teachers. William F. Winter, one of Mississippi's new breed of governors, had as his principal goal educational reform. In the 1982 session his proposal for public kindergartens came up on the last day of the session. The speaker, C.B. (Buddie) Newman, adjourned the house, and the bill died. Thereupon, the governor launched a statewide campaign and managed to pass the measure in a special session of the legislature.[14]

Defeat for a governor is not the end of the line. "Defeat doesn't mean as much as a lot of people think," said a chief of staff to a New Jersey governor. "If the governor is persistent, he can win most of his battles." And most governors do.

NOTES

1. David Osborne, *Laboratories of Democracy* (Boston: Harvard Business School Press, 1988), 139-140.
2. The following section is based on Eagleton Institute of Politics, "The Pinelands Protection Act."
3. This section is based on Jon Bowermaster, *Governor: An Oral Biography of Robert D. Ray* (Ames: Iowa State University, 1987), 169-176.
4. Report of the Governor's Commission on Vermont's Future: Guidelines for Growth, January 1988.
5. Rod Paul, "John H. Sununu, New Hampshire's Governor Preaches High-Tech Solutions to Age-Old Problems," *Governing*, August 1988, 52.
6. National Governors' Association, *Transition and the New Governor*, 30.
7. Gerald Benjamin, "The Albany Triad," *Comparative State Politics Newsletter 9* (February 1988): 9-10.
8. Osborne, *Laboratories of Democracy*, 92-94.
9. Charles D. Hadley, "Louisiana," *Comparative State Politics Newsletter 6* (August 1985): 4.
10. Diane Blair, *Arkansas Politics and Government* (Lincoln: University of Nebraska Press, 1988), 139-140.
11. Steven D. Williams, "The 1986 Session of the Tennessee State Assembly," *Comparative State Politics Newsletter 7* (June 1986): 18-19.
12. The characterization is from the *Wichita Eagle-Beacon*, quoted in Sharon Randall, "From Big Shot to Boss," *State Legislatures*, July 1988, 36.
13. John M. Dowling, "Robert L. Mandeville: The Financial Wizardry (Or Sleight of Hand) of a Fiscal Spin Doctor," *Governing*, January 1989, 46.
14. Peter J. Boyer, "The Yuppies of Mississippi—How They Took Over the Statehouse," *New York Times Magazine*, February 28, 1988.

12. Legislating Via Veto

Tony Hutchison

Wisconsin's veto king, governor Tommy Thompson, defended his 290 partial vetoes in the 1987 budget bill by telling taxpayers that the Legislature was wasting their money. In reality, many of

SOURCE: "Legislating Via Veto" by Tony Hutchison from *State Legislatures*, January 1989, pp. 20–22. Copyright© 1989 by National Conference of State Legislatures. Reprinted by permission.

Thompson's vetoes don't save much money. Instead, they impose the philosophy of a governor of one party on a legislature controlled by the other party. And it's not just happening in Wisconsin. It's happening in California, New Jersey and Oklahoma and many more of the 40 states that allow the item veto.

Looking at 542 item vetoes exercised by Wisconsin governors between 1975 and 1985, University of Wisconsin political scientist James Gosling found that they were "used primarily as a tool of policymaking and partisan advantage rather than fiscal restraint." While the item veto did reduce some government costs during the period studied, fiscal restraint did not appear to be the primary goal of the vetoes, Gosling said. He discovered that the highest total cuts to the general fund budget resulting from item vetoes ranged from .006 percent to only 2.5 percent.

Legislative and executive branch battles over the item veto have been under way virtually since its conception. Although different state constitutional provisions, and different courts interpreting those provisions, make comparisons around the nation difficult, it seems clear that conflicts over the item veto are on the rise again—especially when legislators believe a governor is using it to change the meaning of a bill. This is due in part to increasing fiscal pressures in many states that have made budgetmaking more difficult than ever. But the real stimulus probably has more to do with the ascendancy of legislative bodies as state fiscal policymakers. Most state legislatures now have the resources to challenge the governor on nearly every issue relating to budget and taxes. In short, state legislatures now have the staff and information to carry out fully their constitutional roles in the appropriation process. This was not the case when the concept of the item veto was first introduced into state budgeting.

Authority for the item veto first showed up in the provisional constitution of the Confederate States. When the Civil War ended, several states wrote or amended their constitutions and the provision found its way into many of these. The idea continued to be a popular one due to a growing distrust of legislative institutions during the "Age of Spoils" that followed the Civil War. The item veto was seen as a way to prevent pork-barrel politics and logrolling in state legislature. The belief in its efficacy in curb-

ing legislative abuses was further cemented into our political culture by subsequent good government and scientific management movements that emphasized executive branch competency and efficiency and disdained legislative branch politicking.

Today, executive branch competency can hardly be argued as a valid reason for placing additional fiscal powers in the hands of a governor. That argument is out-of-date, given the last 25 years of professionalization of state legislatures. Logrolling and pork-barrel politics remain problems, but governors are just as likely as legislators to become involved in such political schemes. And no matter what history intended, modern governors have turned a tool of fiscal restraint into a tool of one-upmanship.

Many legislatures put policy language in appropriations bills to direct the spending of state money in a certain fashion or to impose reporting requirements on the executive branch in conjunction with a particular appropriation.

Increasingly governors are using their item veto powers to remove these policy directives rather than to delete actual appropriations. This trend often has partisan overtones. "The line-item veto is more likely to be used where the governor of one party faces a legislature wholly or partially controlled by the opposite party," say political scientists Glen Abney and Thomas Lauth in a study for the *Public Administration Review*. They found this to be true for both Democratic and Republican governors. The study concludes that the partisan use of the item veto "probably has had a minimal effect on making legislatures or state government more fiscally restrained."

The item veto, through its active use or the threat of its use, can be an instrument of fiscal restraint, since getting the two-thirds vote needed for an override of many marginal programs is harder than getting a simple majority. On the other hand, legitimate democratic processes can be frustrated by a governor who uses the item veto power to remove legislative intent. In such cases governors often do not delete or reduce appropriations at all but simply detach the spending controls that legislatures have attached to appropriated dollars.

Oklahoma Governor Henry Bellmon did this in 1988 when his numerous vetoes set a state record. Bellmon actually removed language expressing conditions of appropriations rather than the appropriations themselves. In doing so he cancelled a great deal of the legislature's oversight authority over those appropriations. In one case, an agency received $2 million and no direction on how to spend it—"the governor had vetoed the spending provisions," said Jerry Johnson, a fiscal analyst with the Oklahoma Senate. This leads to two major problems Johnson said—too much spending discretion for non-elected executive branch officials and reduced oversight capabilities by the legislative branch. "It's difficult to evaluate a program's effectiveness when there was never any intent given for its funding," he says.

The most extreme case of modifying legislative intent occurred in Wisconsin during the 1988 session. Unlike any other state, Wisconsin allows a "partial" veto, giving the governor the opportunity to make up new words with an assortment of letters left from vetoed sections of budget bills. Protesting against 37 of Governor Thompson's 290 item vetoes, the Legislature took him to court, pointing to sections of the bill where he had used that partial veto to change the intent of the legislation. For example, he changed the length of time a juvenile can be held in a secure detention facility or juvenile portion of a county jail from 48 hours to 10 days—more in keeping, legislators say, with the governor's tough stance on crime than any desire for fiscal restraint.

Wisconsin's high court, however, sided with the governor, saying that his partial veto power extends to individual letters, spaces and even punctuation marks in an appropriations bill. This creates a situation where the governor can not only change legislative intent by deleting items but can actively create new intent by forming new words. For instance, the phrase "there shall be no tax on cattle" could become "there shall be no tax on ale" by striking the t's and the c in cattle.

"Jefferson and Adams would be rolling over in their graves if they knew what this court has done," said Representative Marlin Schneider, co-chairman of the Wisconsin Joint Finance Committee.

The court upheld the governor's "creative veto" by a 4-3 vote. Wisconsin Justice William Bablitch, a former Democratic Senate majority leader, wrote the dissenting opinion. He argued that the constitution was not meant to allow such actions by the governor and that the majority's legal reasoning "strains the English language beyond the breaking point."

The majority of the court ruled that the governor could strike any letters, spaces and punctuation he liked, "so long as the net result of the partial veto is a complete, workable bill which the legislature itself could have passed in the first instance." The only restraints on the governor's powers are whether the result of his veto is a "complete, entire, workable law, and whether new language remained germane to the appropriation bill."

Representative Schneider sees numerous abuses to democratic processes coming out of this decision. "A governor who is clever and determined, as is ours, can unilaterally create new laws with the consent of one-third of one house of the legislature. I have a hard time believing this is what the people intended when they approved the item veto."

The Wisconsin case is an anomaly in the sense that other state courts are not likely to follow the reasoning regarding individual letters and spaces constituting parts or items in an appropriation bill. It is important, however, in that it represents a line of legal reasoning that holds that item vetoes by their nature may change legislative intent—a view diametrically opposed to the traditional view that the item veto should only delete or reduce appropriations, and never have any creative qualities.

In a 1984 case (*Karcher and Orechio vs. Kean*), before an appellate court in New Jersey, Justice Robert Matthews wrote in a decision siding with New Jersey Governer Thomas Kean, "The exercise of the line-item veto power also gives the governor power to shape governmental policy. Unquestionably, the exercise of the line-item veto will alter legislative intent, at least insofar as it is expressed in an appropriation at the time the budget initially passes the Legislature."

Other state courts have been less generous in their interpretation of gubernatorial veto power. The California Supreme Court in the 1987 case *Harbor vs. Deukmejian*, which involved the item veto of language directing the expenditure of AFDC appropriations, said,

"Unless permitted by the constitution, the governor may not exercise legislative powers." The California high court relied on legal reasoning which takes the literal meaning of the word veto from the Latin "I forbid." The court ruled that any veto should have the effect of "frustrating an act without substituting anything in its place."

The court went even further and said that in cases that involved an item veto of substantive language directing an appropriation, the governor's veto power extended only to the item of appropriation and not to the language directing the expenditure of that money.

Ample evidence is available to show that executive branch use of the item veto can create problems as bad as those it was designed to cure. It may be time for some states to redesign their item veto to fit the politics of today. As a local New Jersey editorial writer put it following the court decision in favor of broadening that state's executive veto power, "Governors are free now to wreak havoc with legislative appropriations and let the devil take the hindmost. If the constitution means what the court says it means, it needs to be changed."

13. The Evolving Profile of State Administrators
Deil S. Wright, Jae-Won Yoo, and Jennifer Cohen

The significance of the states in the 1980s was highlighted in numerous and diverse arenas. Author Carl Van Horn notes that state governments "are arguably the most responsive, innova-

SOURCE: "The Evolving Profile of States Administrators" by D.S. Wright, J.W. Yoo, and J. Cohen in *The Journal of State Government*, Jan./March 1991, pp. 30–38. Copyright© 1993 The Council of State Governments. Reprinted with permission from *State Government News*.

tive, and effective level of government in the American federal system."

The states' increased intergovernmental roles were firmly established by numerous studies. Their rising economic significance, domestically and internationally, also was clearly confirmed. Additionally, their political roles as laboratories of democracy were examined and applauded. The significance of the states from an administrative perspective, however, seems destined to remain largely untold.

This article documents a small part of the quiet revolution in state administrations occurring across the nation. Research has found that today's agency heads are better educated, and younger than their predecessors. The role they play in state government is one of a central actor keeping the government operating despite the power struggles between the executive and legislative branches. Recent state administrative developments continued the trends and patterns of the last three decades.

This article reports on recurrent surveys of agency heads across the 50 states. The surveys were conducted in 1964, 1968, 1974, 1978, 1984 and 1988. Response rates varied from a high of 60 percent to 70 percent in the earlier surveys to lows of 40 percent to 50 percent in the more recent years. Respondents to each survey ranged from 900 to 1,500.

STATE ADMINISTRATIVE GROWTH

For the past three decades, states have been the core governmental jurisdictions responding to citizen expectations for increased public services, benefits, social and economic regulations and infrastructure needs. This is confirmed by growth in full-time equivalent employment and expansion in the number, variety and types of state agencies.

State government employment has increased 300 percent since 1950. Only increases in elementary and secondary education approach the rate at which the number of full-time state employees has risen. Furthermore, employment by the states substantially exceeds federal employment. State employment surpassed federal employment in 1980.

A second description of administrative growth at the state level comes from a study of the creation of state agencies from the late 1950s to the early 1980s. Table 13.1 shows a consistent "core" group of 40 administrative agencies present in 45 or more states throughout this period. (Haas and Wright, 1989) In the mid-1960s, states begin establishing new agencies, including commerce, natural resources, federal relations and economic development.

By the early 1970s another 10 types of distinct agencies existed in 30 or more states, including those involving community affairs, human resources, criminal justice and drug abuse. Since the mid-1970s, an additional 16 agencies were established in half the states. These included consumer protection, mass transit, housing finance, ethics, arts and energy.

In sum, the administrative establishments of state governments have grown dramatically in two directions. First, there has been a massive expansion in terms of absolute number of state employees (appointed administrative persons). Second, those employees have been lodged in a rapidly growing and diverse number of separately identified state agencies. State-level administration has expanded because the level of state services has intensified and a wider range of services requires a more complex organizational structure.

CRUCIAL ADMINISTRATIVE LINKS

The increased number, variety, and size of state administrative agencies pose several issues for the states, individually and collectively. First there is the question of accountability—to whom and how are these agencies and their administrative heads held responsible? A second issue is one of responsiveness. As political leaders change through the electoral process, how responsive are state agencies and their personnel to the shifts in policy directions produced by electoral results? A further issue is one of effectiveness. How reliable and certain is it that administrative agencies will implement public policies with equity, efficiency and effectiveness?

These questions help focus attention

Table 13.1   Proliferation of State Agencies, 1959–1985

I.   1959–1985: Agencies that existed in 45 or more states

Adjutant General	Attorney General	Aging
Agriculture	Advertising (Tourism)	Banking
Budget	Auditor	Geology
Corrections	Civil Defense	Fishing
Food and Drug	Education	Health
Higher Education	Forestry	Insurance
Labor	Highways	Library
Library (Law)	Highway Patrol	Parks
Mental Health	Liquor Control	Parole
Water Pollution	Motor Vehicles	Purchasing
Public Assistance	Public Utilities	Taxation
Securities	Water Resources	Welfare
Secretary of State	Workmen's Compensation	Soil Conservation
Vocational Education	Employment Security	Treasurer

II.   1965–1985: Agencies that existed in 35 or more states

Administration/Finance	Aeronautics	Comptroller
Commerce	Natural Resources	Personnel
Planning	Federal Relations	Oil and Gas
Economic Development	Labor Arbitration	

III.   1971–1985: Agencies that existed in 30 or more states

Community Affairs	Court Administration	Drug Abuse
Human Resources	Information	Mining
Air Pollution	Criminal Justice	
Juvenile Delinquency	Economic Opportunity	

IV.   1975–1985: Agencies that existed in 25 or more states

Consumer Protection	Occupational Licensing	Housing Finance
Mass Transportation	Mental Retardation	Energy
Waste Management	Environment	Ethics
Vocational Rehabilitation	Transportation	Medicaid
Manpower	Railroads	Arts
Occupational Health/Safety		

on one set of crucial actors by whom and through whom these issues are filtered, mediated and resolved. Those critical actors, the key links between electoral politics and administrative operations, are the administrative leaders of each of the several hundred state agencies that house the 3.6 million state employees.

The central roles administrative leaders play in relation to accountability, responsiveness, and effectiveness make it important to know more about them.

PERSONAL PROFILE

Age, gender, ethnicity, and education are four distinctive characteristics that are frequently the focus of attention in describing the composition of an important cohort of persons. Previous research on state administrators reported that they were becoming younger, slightly more representative in gender and ethnicity, and clearly better educated. (Hebert and Wright, 1982; Haas and Wright, 1987) These trends appear to be continuing, although some shifts are slackening.

The "youth movement" among these top-level officials has been consistent and noteworthy. Both the mean and median ages have dropped by about 10 years between 1964 and 1988. In 1964 barely 40 percent of these administrators were under 50 years of age, whereas more than 60 percent were in this age bracket in 1988.

In gender terms, there continues to be a notable rise in the number of female agency heads. The proportion of women administrators was approaching 20 percent in 1988. This was in sharp contrast to only 2 percent in 1964. While there is increasing gender diversity among state agency heads, the movement toward greater ethnic/racial diversity appears to have slowed, if not actually stopped. The proportion of non-white administrative heads increased to about 10 percent in 1984 compared to only 2 percent in 1964. Little if any change occurred between 1984 and 1988.

These gender and ethnicity percentages mark the upper echelons of state administration as still the predominant preserve of white males. To the extent that there is a "glass ceiling" in the executive establishment of state government, it probably is more breakable than ones in local government, in the national government and especially in the executive suites of large private firms.

The rising educational qualifications of state administrators is one of the most pronounced shifts among the many personal attributes of these officials. In the early 1960s only about two-thirds of the agency heads held one or more college degrees. Two of every five held at least one graduate degree, often in law, and less often in medicine. By the 1980s, nine out of 10 held at least one college degree, while the proportion holding graduate degrees ranged around 60 percent. In general, the proportion of administrative heads holding law degrees has declined while those holding management/administration degrees (either business or public) have increased notably.

The composition and character of the top-level state administrative establishment is clearly changing. That cadre is better educated, younger and more diverse in terms of gender and ethnicity. These findings are consistent with the broader thesis that state administration has become more socially representative and more educationally professional.

PROFESSIONAL CAREER PROFILE

How do top-level state administrators arrive at their positions? What have been the predominant "paths to the top" as documented from the surveys?

First, administrators are entering public service at an increasingly younger age. The median age among 1964 heads when they first held a public position was 33. That figure had dropped to 26 by 1988. The median age at which agency heads first held a state government position similarly dropped from 37 in 1964 to 29 in 1988. As these figures suggest, it has become less common for state administrators to begin their public service careers outside state government.

In 1988 about 30 percent of the agency heads had held appointed posts in national or local governments, with city/town positions constituting the largest portion, 13 percent. Also, 13 percent had held popularly elected posts, all at the local government level.

These percentages for 1988 are at some variance from those for agency heads in 1964. Then, nearly 45 percent had held appointed posts, including 17 percent at the national level. Also, more than 20 percent had held elected positions, including a small number (1 percent) who had been elected members of Congress. The trend, while not dramatic, shows a decline in those holding elected or appointed positions in other governmental entities.

There is diversity in the careers of state agency heads. First, between one-fourth to one-third of the agency heads, from 1964 to 1988, entered their posts without experience in the public sector. There is no clear or consistent trend across the decades in these proportions. Second, another one-third of all agency heads moved into the top post from a subordinate position within that agency. (An exception was 1978 when more than 40 percent were "internal" successors.)

Third, a sizable proportion of agency heads, around 20 percent, came from a different administrative agency within the same state, while roughly 10 percent came directly from local governments to a top state post. Fourth, only small proportions (2 percent to 6 percent) of state agency heads are recruited from other states or the national government. To the extent that there is a trend among these last two sets of figures, it is complimentary, with slightly more attracted from other states and slightly fewer drawn from the national government.

How varied are the careers of agency heads within state government? About 50 percent have held positions in only one agency—the one that they now head. Another 40 percent have been slightly more mobile, holding posts in two or three state agencies. Finally, only about 10 percent are in a class that might be termed highly mobile, that is, they served in four or more state agencies.

Around one-sixth or one-seventh of

the administrators have held posts in other states. These proportions include those 5 percent to 6 percent of all administrators who have been recruited directly into the top agency position from another state. Here, too, stability rather than sharp change is the hallmark of career patterns and configurations across the three decades.

The stability theme persists in the final feature of career characteristics reported. The median number of years served in state government varies only slightly from the 1960s to the 1980s from 12-14 years. Likewise, the average amount of time spent in the agency that the administrator now heads is stable at about 10 years. This figure might suggest that these agency heads rose quickly within their agency. Recall, however, that only about one-third of the administrators came up through the ranks. The majority came to the top post from outside the agency and this, therefore, may greatly lower the average in-agency experience calculated for all agency heads.

POSITION PROFILE

How do these state administrators allocate their time? From a simple hourly standpoint these executive work at least 10-hour days or perhaps six-day work weeks.

It also is evident that routine administrative management tasks such as personnel decisions consume the bulk of an agency head's time compared to tasks such as policy development or intergovernmental relations.

Only in 1972 did the mean percentage for the administrative component fall below 50 percent. What is striking, however, is the stability with which the administrative component consistently falls in the narrow band of 50 percent to 55 percent across the surveys. A similar stability prevails in such areas as policy development, where roughly 25 percent to 30 percent of an executive's time is spent, and building public support, which occupies around 20 percent to 25 percent. . . .

POLICY RELATIONSHIPS PROFILE

A perennial question confronted by all but a very few public administrators is: Who's in charge? This straightforward query is another way of framing the issue of accountability. For agency heads in state government this broad question usually can be reduced to the alternative: Is it the governor or the legislature who exercises the greatest control over the agency? All respondents were presented with these two alternative with the additional response option: "Each the same."

Initially, in 1964, a notably high proportion reported greater legislative control and oversight. By 1974 the distribution was reversed in favor of the governor. Across the last three surveys the governor has continued to enjoy a modest plurality.

In the aggregate, it is evident that the constitutionally-grounded principle of separation of powers, present in every state, places state agency heads in a politically competitive framework. They perceive governors and legislators in a contest for control and guidance of the directions of state administrative agencies. (Hebert, Brudney, and Wright 1983; Brudney and Hebert, 1987) This competition thesis is reinforced by the consistent percentage of agency heads, about 25 percent, who report that each of these two sources of institutional power exercise about the same degree of control over agency affairs.

Clearly, of course, there is considerable variation in perceived control patterns across the 50 states and among the agencies. Preliminary analysis indicates that variables such as selection method and formal powers of the governor are two important factors that explain variations in perceived control. (Wright, 1967)

Other less obvious and less conventional factors also appear to influence perceptions of control. For example, agency size (in terms of budget or personnel), the amount of political visibility an agency has, and an agency's dependency on federal aid or earmarked revenue assist in understanding the pattern of legislative-executive competition for control over state agencies. (Hebert, Brudney, and Wright, 1983)

The mention of finances offers the opportunity to monitor, across three surveys (1974, 1984, 1988), the relative roles of the governor and legislature in the budget process. The main premise underlying the data on "budget request reduction" is that administrative agencies normally ask for more funds than they need. This administrative "padding" leads to a budget cutting process on both the executive and legislative side of the state capitols. Of course, since state governments have been subjected to "cutback management," the "tax revolt," and other types of fiscal constraints, the notion of "padding" is far from the sole premise or requisite condition for reducing budget requests.

We asked agency heads which of the two constitutional actors were the most zealous in reducing budget requests. The plurality of respondents indicated the legislature with considerable consistency between the 1974 and 1984 figures. The 1988 results show a slight plurality in favor of the governor in inducing fiscal constraints on state administrative agencies. Here, too, further analysis is called for. For example, the variations across states, especially ones under varying degrees of fiscal stress or cutback pressures (at the time of each survey) could indicate the contrasting political and institutional mechanisms by which administrative agencies are responsive and accountable to external forces.

The two distinctive variables of control/oversight and budget cutting are negative in their implications. Both connote or imply that state agencies must be held in check, either by fiscal or policy restraints. To redress this apparent negative tilt the surveys have consistently incorporated a measure of organizational support. That is, the agency heads were asked which political actor, the governor or the legislature, was "more sympathetic and supportive of the purposes and aims of your agency?"

Clearly, the governor enjoys a wide margin as the predominant provider of support for agency aims. A consistent majority, ranging from 56 percent to 63 percent across the six surveys, view the governor as the prime source of support for achieving agency purposes. The legislature as an anchor for agency support is reported by a minority of agency heads, varying from just under one-fourth to slightly over one-third.

The three indicators of policy and institutional relationships presented state administrators with limited and forced choices—the governor or the legislature (or each the same). But there has been, historically, another option often open to state agency heads with regard to policy control or oversight. The Progressive reform movement sought to remove administration from the realm of politics through numerous "independent" boards and commissions to oversee administrative operations and to set agency policies. These buffering, protective, or insulating boards/commissions were created at local, state and national levels. Many remain influential in state governments today. The prospect of working for or under this type of institutional setting offers state administrators an option to shield themselves from direct legislative or gubernatorial control. This shield, cover or canopy is intended to moderate if not neutralize much of the agency-directed influence emanating from executive branch halls and legislative chambers.

All this is by way of preface to the discussion of the response patterns reported. State agency heads were presented

with a hypothetical situation: "Suppose that your state's governmental structure was reorganized and you were able to select who would exercise the greater control over your agency. Which one of the following would you choose?"

With the exception of the 1964 survey, a majority of the agency heads selected the governor. Preferences for legislative control lagged far behind and was generally the least preferred option. Rather noteworthy is the substantial but slightly waning fraction of administrators who elect the independent commission. This subset of administrators, from nearly one-third down to one-fifth of all respondents, offers multiple avenues for analysis and exposition. What proportion already function under these semiautonomous organizational arrangements and simply wish to preserve the status quo? What proportions seek this "out" from existing executive or legislative control patterns? What are the agency and agency head characteristics of those who prefer this distinctive organizational arrangement? Identifying who these persons and agencies are could provide important indicators and insights about the issues and challenges facing state governors today and in the near future.

A POSITIVE OUTLOOK

What can be said about the character and caliber of administrative leadership in state governments over the past three decades? Our periodic surveys of large numbers of agency heads across the 50 states enable us to identify some major trends centered around the four profiles that provide the organizing scheme for this article.

1. Personal. The personal or individual attributes of state administrators reflect increasing and progressively greater diversity. While the rise in diversity may have slackened somewhat in the late 1980s, the avenues for greater openness seem well established.

2. Professional. Among the clearest and most confirmed trend over the past three decades is better trained and better educated administrators. This conclusion derives from educational levels and specialization as well as from the career paths followed by the majority of state agency heads. Clearly, state government is not, if indeed it ever was, an administrative backwater.

3. Position. State administrators operate in a spider web of relationships that is multidimensional, assuming a mix of demanding tasks and roles. The demands are partly but poorly indicated by the 50-55 hour work-weeks that they average. The policy networks in which state administrators are located are exceedingly complex. The state network is indicated by the variety and intensity of the contacts with numerous state-level actors such as governors, legislators, lobbyists and state agency officials. The intergovernmental network is reflected in administrative involvements in state-local and state-national relationships, especially the receipt of and dependence on federal aid.

4. Policy Relationships. State administrators are the focal points for the convergence of powerful institutional actors in state governments. The governor and legislature are prime contestants in the struggle for control and guidance over the actions of agency heads. Administrators' responses to questions relevant to the influence policy decisions have on their jobs clearly reflect the skillful balancing act that agency heads must perform at the administrative peak-points in state governments. A modest but diminishing minority even prefer an institutional arrangement, guidance by an independent commission, that would buffer them from direct gubernatorial and legislative control.

There have been significant and positive changes in the character and composition of top-level public administrators in state governments. In this respect, the states seem well positioned, administratively, to cope with the increased burdens that have been thrust upon them by national actions and local-level pressures. The states often are said to be "in the middle" of the federal system. This phrase usually is taken to mean sandwiched between the national and local levels of government in a horizontal, layer-cake sense. From a domestic policy and public service delivery standpoint it is probably more accurate to think of the states as the center ring or circle in a series of concentric but overlapping circles.

Helping to anchor and otherwise stabilize the state in serving as central actors is the administrative establishments of state government. The decade of the 1990s is likely to put severe demands upon the states, and helping to bear the stress and strain of these demands is a respectable, responsive and accountable corps of top-level administrators.

REFERENCES

BRUDNEY, JEFFREY L. and F. TED HEBERT (1987). "State Agencies and Their Environments: Examining the Influence of Important External Actors." *Journal of Politics.* 49 (February): 186-206.

HAAS, PETER J. and DEIL S. WRIGHT (1987). "The Changing Profile of State Administrators." *State Government,* 60 (November/December): 270-278.

HAAS, PETER J. and DEIL S. WRIGHT (1989). "Administrative Turnover in State Government: A Research Note." *Administration and Society,* 21 (August): 265-277.

HEBERT, F. TED, JEFFREY L. BRUDNEY, and DEIL S. WRIGHT (1983). "Gubernatorial Influence and the State Bureaucracy." *American Politics Quarterly,* 11 (Fall): 243-264.

HEBERT, F. TED and DEIL S. WRIGHT (1982). "State Administrators: How Representative? How Professional?" *State Government*, 55 (Spring): 22-28.

OSBORNE, DAVID (1988). *Laboratories of Democracy.* Harvard Business School Press.

VAN HORN, CARL E. (ed.)(1989). *The State of the States*, Congressional Quarterly Inc.

VAN HORN, CARL E. (1989a). "The Quiet Revolution," pp. 1-13 in *The State of the States.* Congressional Quarterly Inc.

WRIGHT, DEIL S. (1967). "Executive Leadership and State Administration." Midwest (American) *Journal of Political Science*, 11 (February): 1-26.

CHAPTER 6
Courts and Criminal Justice

As in most areas of state and local government, it is difficult to make generalizations about courts because they are so diverse. Even within a single state there often are differences in methods of judicial selection, case-load management, and fairness in dealing with certain classes of litigants.

Despite this diversity, certain problems are shared by nearly all courts. The major difficulty is the growing number of cases to be processed. As crime rates continue to increase (many crimes, of course, are drug-related), there is added pressure on courts to improve procedures and settle cases before they go to trial. Increased civil case-loads mean delays of up to three years in some jurisdictions. This has encouraged the diversion of cases to arbitration or mediation boards, and even to private judging where the parties hire retired judges to hear their cases. Many courts have begun to use various computer systems and other modern technologies to improve the flow of cases.

Still, much of what courts do (and how efficiently they do it) can best be understood in terms of personal interaction among attorneys, judges, police, and court administrators. As discussed in Reading 14, viewing courtrooms as organized workgroups can help us understand better how courts dispose of their case-loads and how they "do justice." Political scientists James Eisenstein and Herbert Jacob explain how the operation of courtroom workgroups helps reduce uncertainty and maintain group cohesion among people who work with each other on a daily basis. If the group is working smoothly, it can facilitate negotiation and move cases to quick and fair resolution. Often the workgroup reduces the uncertainty of a trial by the use of plea bargaining in criminal cases and pretrial settlements in civil disputes. Of course, the system may break down if personnel are not stable or if the workgroup has some collective biases. Eisenstein and Jacob note that individual biases against blacks, women, Hispanics, or certain types of criminals become operative only when permitted to do so by the norms and actions of the collective courtroom workgroup.

Seeking to improve the justice system, academics and political reformers have devoted a great deal of attention to the means by which judges are selected. There are a wide variety of choices that include election by partisan and nonpartisan ballots, appointment by the governor and confirmation by the legislature, appointment of municipal judges by city councils, selection by the state legislature, and the use of some sort of merit plan. *The Book of the States, 1992–93* reports that over half the states and the District of Columbia use judicial nominating commissions that present candidates for judicial office (supposedly based on merit) to the governor for appointment. In general, reform proposals recommend moving from some kind of election or appointment system to a merit system, often modeled on that adopted by Missouri in 1940.

Given all the time, effort, and money spent to change the method of judicial selection, it is curious that virtually all studies done by political scientists conclude that the method of selection has little impact on the characteristics of judges or their quality. In part, this is true because even in election systems a majority of judges were first selected in an interim appointment by the governor. Still, there is growing concern about the nature of judicial elections. As suggested in Reading 15, even if merit systems don't produce "better" judges, they would improve the selection process, which in many states is marked by mudslinging, campaign gimmicks, and outright corruption. Because expensive, hard-hitting elections still occur in merit systems, this reform alone (without some public reeducation and campaign guidelines) would not solve all existing problems. In large part, judicial selection reform is seen as a battle between interest groups that benefit from the status quo and interest groups who are losing.

During the 1980s there was strong sentiment to "get tough" with criminals. This affected criminal courts because state legislatures passed laws providing longer mandatory sentences, especially for drug-related crimes, and this has reduced judicial discretion in sentencing. At the same time that convicted criminals were being given longer and more certain prison sentences, the crime rate skyrocketed. In part, this was because of the number of men in their twenties (the prime prison-prone age) in the 1980s was very high. As a result, while the U.S. population increased by 28 percent from 1960 to 1990, the number of people in prison increased over 150 percent. By the end of 1990, 771,000 people were in state prisons. California had nearly 100,000 people imprisoned. One of every twenty-seven men in the United States was under some form of correctional supervision. Proportionate increases in the number of persons on probation and parole placed even greater financial burdens on state governments. Probation—supervised community living for those found guilty of a crime—is the most common way in which criminal cases are disposed. Over 3 million Americans are on probation, including nearly 300,000 in Texas. Several states have eliminated paroling prisoners, and with more mandatory sentencing the number of people on parole is declining.

Prison overcrowding has created pressure to build more prisons, but it has also led to emergency-release programs to relieve crowded conditions in several states. In addition, many states have given judges authority to impose intermediate sanctions such as house arrest, electronic monitoring, and "boot camps" (a military-type environment for young first-time offenders) as alternatives to prison sentences.

Overcrowded prisons create severe financial strains at a time when state and local budgets are being cut. Corrections costs were up 19 percent in 1990 and 14 percent in 1991. Politically, politicians don't want to seem soft on crime, yet budget deficits make prison alternatives to incarceration more attractive. As Reading 16 suggests, perhaps what we need is "smarter" punishment. Political scientist John J. DiIulio, Jr., begins by reviewing the increased reliance on community-based supervision (furloughs) of criminals in the 1980s and the high economic cost of keeping criminals in prison. He suggests that most prisons are run in ways almost calculated to reinforce inmates' criminalistic behavior. As a result, DiIulio recommends "punishing smarter" by using house arrest in which the offender is subject to electronic surveillance, placing offenders in closely supervised community service programs, and utilizing intensive supervision probation and parole. DiIulio believes that we will need to treat corrections as a major domestic problem, as with welfare or health care, in order for significant change to occur.

QUESTIONS FOR DISCUSSION

1. Argue against an adversarial system in criminal proceedings. What might replace it?

2. How does the courtroom workgroup encourage plea bargaining? What are the advantages and disadvantages of plea bargaining? How does this relate to the goals of workgroups?

3. How does the experience of judicial elections in your area compare with those described by Watson in Florida and North Carolina?

4. Argue in favor of popular election of judges.

5. Discuss the concept of "geography of crime," as explained by DiIulio.

6. Which of DiIulio's alternatives to institutionalization seem most promising?

14.   The Courtroom Workgroup

James Eisenstein and Herbert Jacob

Courtroom workgroups have characteristics commonly found among other organized workgroups.

1. They exhibit authority relationships.
2. They display influence relationships, which modify the authority relationships.
3. They are held together by common goals.
4. They have specialized roles.
5. They use a variety of work techniques.
6. They engage in a variety of tasks.
7. They have different degrees of stability and familiarity.

SOURCE: From *Felony Justice: An Organizational Analysis of Criminal Courts* by James Eisenstein and Herbert Jacob, Little, Brown and Company, 1977, pp. 20–38. Reprinted by permission of the author.

These traits establish a complex network of ongoing relationships that determines who in the courtroom does what, how, and to whom.

COURTROOM AUTHORITY PATTERNS

The judge is the formal leader of most courtrooms.[1] In a sense, the courtroom belongs to him; he enjoys considerable formal powers to force others to conform to his desires. Most decisions the courtroom produces, including those made by others that affect the disposal of cases, usually require formal judicial approval. The judge must ratify the defendant's decision to enter a guilty plea, the prosecutor's decision to dismiss some or all charges, and an agreement on sentence. Finally, by participating in a number of decisions affecting case outcomes, judges gain influence over other courtroom organization members. Judges make preliminary decisions on bail, on motions and hearings. They rule on specific objections during courtroom proceedings and thus influence whether a compromise is reached—and if so, its content—as well as the verdict when no bargain is consummated.

Judges are universally considered the linchpins of courtroom workgroups. They are the formal leaders of the court and have the formal responsibility for making decisions that affect the flow of cases. They set dates for motions, hearings, trials, and other proceedings. The courtroom's work load is affected by their willingness to grant or deny extensions of deadlines, the time they take to render decisions on motions and in hearings, the procedures they use to empanel juries, the degree to which they cut short attorney's examination of witnesses, and the amount of time they are willing to work. Judges also govern courtroom conduct. They are responsible for the actual behavior of attorneys, witnesses, spectators, and defendants; for example, they regulate voice level and physical move-

ment, and decide when conversations will be allowed.

Attorneys represent interested parties to a conflict, but the judge is the neutral arbiter; even in criminal trials, he is not supposed to favor the state, even though he is a public official like the prosecutor. He represents the ideals of justice; he sits above the others, wears a robe, and requires all others to show visible respect for him by addressing him as "your honor" and by rising when he enters and leaves the courtroom. No one may openly criticize him in the courtroom; he may charge those who do with contempt of court (not contempt of the judge) and fine or imprison them on the spot. Moreover, this formal authority is often reinforced by the age and experience of the judge. He is often older and more experienced in the law than the attorneys who practice before him.

The judge, however, has less authority than many superiors in workgroups. He does not hire or fire others who work in the courtroom. Almost all of them are assigned by independent authorities— we call them sponsoring organizations— such as the state's attorney, the public defender, the clerk of courts, the sheriff (who assigns the bailiffs in many courtrooms), and the marketplace, which brings private attorneys representing individual clients to the courtroom. Each of these sponsoring agencies imposes its own requirements on the participants it sends to the courtroom workgroup. Consequently, the judge's authority is quite limited.

Judges also have few budgetary controls over the courtroom. Unlike most workgroups, courtroom workgroups typically do not have their own budget. Each participant brings his own resources to the workgroup and uses them himself or shares them with others. Neither judges nor anyone else in the courtroom workgroup can decide to install a new public address system or to hire several additional clerks; judges cannot reward hardworking prosecutors or bailiffs with a salary raise, nor can they directly withhold salary increments from malingerers. Lacking personnel and budgetary powers, judges have less authority than many workgroup supervisors.

Even on legal matters the judge's authority is not absolute. He renders decisions, of course, and they have the force of law. But they are subject to reversal by other judges. Attorneys sometimes seek to influence their content by citing statutes and appellate decisions. In addition, a judge generally can rule only when someone else raises the issue and requests a decision. Thus, his legal decisions are molded by the activities of others.

COURTROOM INFLUENCE PATTERNS

The influence of other participants in the workgroup limits the formal authority of the judge. Their influence stems from formal authority that the law also provides them, and from superior information or control over access to the courtroom.

The law gives the state's attorney the right to determine whom to prosecute and what charges to press. In addition, the prosecutor routinely has more information about a case than anyone else in the courtroom. He possesses the police report, records of previous arrests and convictions, witness reports, laboratory tests, and the physical evidence if there is any. The prosecutor, more than anyone else, knows what the strength of a case is and when it is ready for disposition. Thus in many courtrooms, the prosecutor controls the scheduling of cases and the dispositional pattern. The judge—although possessing greater formal authority—responds to the prosecutor's actions. No experienced prosecutor will routinely overlook the judge's sentiments about how the courtroom is to be run, but many run it instead of the judge.

Even where the judge maintains more control, he must take into account the prosecutor's opinion of what should be done.

Defense counsel also possess considerable influence in the work of the courtroom. They are charged with representing their client in a number of crucial proceedings. The defense attorney has a duty to insist that evidence seized illegally be thrown out of court and may ask for a hearing to accomplish that end. He can demand a hearing to determine the legality of an arrest or confession. A conscientious and skilled defense counsel may make the work of a prosecutor much more difficult and may require detailed rulings on the law from the judge.

The defendant is notably absent from most interactions of courtroom workgroups, assuming the role of a very interested spectator with a front row seat.[2] But he possesses several rights—the right to a jury trial being the most important—which cannot be waived without his formal direct participation in a ceremony. Before a defendant can waive his right to a jury trial or enter a plea of guilty, he must be questioned directly by the judge and answer in his own voice, not his attorney's. But defense attorneys may convince defendants to waive these rights and may school them in the proper responses to the judge's questions. If defense counsel is unwilling or unable to influence and control clients most of the time, the smooth operation of the workgroup is jeopardized.

Under some circumstances, clerks also possess some influence in the courtroom workgroup. In busy courtrooms where dockets are not arranged by a central computer, the clerk often determines which case will be heard next. The order in which cases are heard is important for busy lawyers who want to avoid fruitless hours of waiting for their case to be called for a two-minute ritual. Where the sequence of cases has an effect on the outcome (because one case is affected by the outcome of the case just before), the clerk's decision may also lead to more or less severe results for the defendant.

Finally, police have significant influence on the operation of criminal courts. In many cities they determine who will be sent to court by the arrests they make; at the least, they share that determination with the prosecutor. They also are the most frequent witnesses in criminal court. Their appearance or absence, their demeanor, the care with which they preserve evidence—all have a considerable effect on the work of the courtroom. Prosecutors, especially, depend on the police, but defense counsel and judges also have a considerable stake in how the police act in the courtroom.

The precise pattern of influence in courtroom workgroups varies with the degree to which each of the participants possesses these resources and how he uses them. When everything else is equal, an aggressive defense attorney will exert more influence than a reticent one. A diligent prosecutor exerts more influence than one who forgets details of the cases he is handling. An assertive judge retains more of his authority than one who sees his role solely as responding to the initiatives of others in the courtroom. Some courtrooms appear to be governed almost entirely by their judges, although that appearance almost always is an exaggeration. Other courtrooms are ruled by the prosecutor; a few are dominated by defense counsel. Many are governed by a collective decision-making process encompassing judge, prosecutor, defense attorneys, clerks, and police.

SHARED GOALS OF COURTROOM WORKGROUPS

Courtroom workgroups have a job to do. Like most people pressed for time, their members do not often pause to philosophize about their ultimate purpose or goals. It is difficult enough just to keep going. Although they may not realize it, all courtroom workgroups share values and goals.[3] These shared perspectives undermine the apparent conflicts generated by the formal roles of workgroup members—the prosecutors' push toward convictions, the defense attorneys' quest for acquittals, and judges' inclination toward neutrality.

Four goals present in courtroom workgroups are summarized in Table 14.1. They are produced by the interaction of two dimensions: the function performed (expressive or instrumental) and the origins of the goals (external or internal to the group).[4] Expressive goals serve symbolic functions and infuse meaning into activity. Instrumental goals serve material functions and help get things done. Externally oriented goals are produced by the need of the members to share perspectives that sustain the organization itself.

External goals reflect pressures on the workgroup from outside the immediate bounds of the courtroom and from the sponsoring organizations that send the major participants to the courtroom. The police, the media, governmental agencies, including the legislature and appellate courts, and ultimately the general public, all expect results from the courtroom workgroup. These "outside" groups impose both instrumental and expressive goals on courtroom organization. The most important instrumental goal is that cases should be handled expeditiously. Many people believe that expeditious disposition will deter crime. In addition, quick convictions or acquit-

Table 14.1 Goals of Courtroom Workgroups

Functions of Goal	Origins of Goal	
	External	Internal
Expressive	Doing Justice	Maintaining Group Cohesion
Instrumental	Disposing of Case Load	Reducing Uncertainty

tals tie up fewer resources of the police. They also fulfill requirements imposed by appellate courts for a speedy trial and might reduce appellate business. They produce a steady flow of news to the media and assure the public that the courts are doing their job. Disposing of cases without attracting undue attention or criticism from outsiders is also interpreted by many as doing justice.

All members of the courtroom workgroup are interested in disposing cases, although the reason for this interest varies. Judges and prosecutors want high disposition rates in order to transmit an aura of efficiency and accomplishment. Prosecutors also prefer speedy dispositions because as cases age, memories dim and witnesses scatter, weakening the evidence and lowering the chances of conviction.

Retained attorneys face a more complicated set of incentives. Most attorneys who specialize in criminal cases depend on a high turnover of clients who can afford only modest fees. Without high volume and the investment of a modest amount of time in each case, many a private defense counsel would go broke. Yet private counsel must maintain a reputation for vigorous defense in order to attract new clients. Public defender organizations charged with representing all indigent defendants prefer quick disposition because their manpower barely suffices to handle their case load. But they also seek to establish a reputation for effective representation of defendants.

The expressive goal imposed by the external environment is to do justice. All the principal participants are attorneys, and are bound to that goal by their professional training. For that matter, nearly everyone in American society values doing justice. The specific content of the term, however, is ambiguous. For some, justice is done when criminals are caught and severely punished regardless of procedures. For others, adherence to the principles of due process and equal treatment produces justice. The ambiguity and disagreement contained in the notion of justice in society are mirrored in the varying perspectives of workgroup members. For the defense, doing justice may mean either obtaining an acquittal or a mild sentence for its clients, or forcing the prosecution to prove its case beyond a reasonable doubt. The prosecution often sees doing justice in terms of its conviction rates, because it is convinced that most defendants are in fact guilty. Judges generally see this goal as requiring impartial behavior, although their definition of impartiality often favors either the defense or the prosecution. Thus surface agreement within the courtroom organization on the goal of "doing justice" often engenders behavioral conflict.

Internally oriented goals facilitate the functioning of the courtroom workgroup. The expressive form of these goals is maintaining group cohesion.[5] Pervasive conflict is not only unpleasant; it also makes work more difficult. Cohesion produces a sense of belonging and identification that satisfies human needs. It is maintained in several ways. Courtroom workgroups shun outsiders because of their potential threat to group cohesion. The workgroup possesses a variety of adaptive techniques to minimize the effect of abrasive participants. For instance, the occasional defense attorney who violates routine cooperative norms may be punished by having to wait until the end of the day to argue his motion; he may be given less time than he wishes for a lunch break in the middle of a trial; he may be kept beyond usual court hours for bench conferences. Likewise, unusually adversarial defense or prosecuting attorneys are likely to smooth over their formal conflicts with informal cordiality. Tigers at the bench, they become tame kittens in chambers and in the hallways, exchanging pleasantries and exuding sociability.

The instrumental expression of internal goals is reducing or controlling uncertainty.[6] The strong incentives to reduce uncertainty force courtroom members to work together, despite their different orientations toward doing justice. More than anything else, trials produce uncertainty. They require substantial investments of time and effort without any guarantee of the result. The difficulty of estimating how long they will last makes everyone's schedule very uncertain. Even bench trials require some preparation of witnesses and throw the other participants at the mercy of these witnesses, whose behavior on the witness stand is unpredictable. What witnesses say and how they say it may make the difference between conviction and acquittal. Jury trials are even worse, because attorneys must deal with the jurors as well as the witnesses. In ordinary cases very little is known about the jurors, and jury decisions are proverbially unpredictable. Even after presenting a "dead bang" case to a jury, prosecutors suffer nervous hours while the jury deliberates. The judge is also committed to avoiding uncertainty. Most judges like to have some control over their dockets; they like to see where actions are heading and what further activity is required of them.

The desire to reduce uncertainty leads to the development of several norms designed to make behavior predictable. One is "stick by your word and never mislead deliberately." Attorneys who violate this norm find they are punished. Another is "no surprises." It is often illegal to call surprise witnesses or to introduce evidence that the opposing counsel is unaware of; it is almost always regarded as a dirty trick.

The instrumental goals we have identified are generally mutually supportive. Caseload disposition and reduction of uncertainty go hand in hand; the former is often articulated (partly because it is directed at the external environment),

whereas the latter is more often an unspoken commitment by courtroom members. Expressive goals, however, are not as frequently mutually supportive. The quest for justice often threatens courtroom cohesion, and the desire to maintain a cohesive workgroup may seem to jeopardize the quest for justice. The general political culture more explicitly legitimates the externally oriented goals. There is much public discussion of the need for justice and for the clearing of dockets in criminal courts. Organizational maintenance goals are almost furtive by contrast. They are rarely articulated in public by members of the courtroom organization; they can best be deduced from private statements and courtroom behavior. Although they are not illegitimate, they have not yet been publicly legitimated.

Courtroom workgroups vary in their adherence to these goals. For instance, some workgroups value cohesion less than others because they find conflict less threatening to their survival. But in general we believe that the variation is not great. Nevertheless, it is important to identify these goals, because common adherence to them keeps the groups together.

WORKGROUP SPECIALIZATION

Although courtroom participants have common goals, they play radically different roles. The participants rigidly adhere to the specified role differentiation. The judge maintains an air of impartiality; he responds to requests for rulings on the law and makes decisions when called on by others. He may intervene in the scheduling of cases or in questioning witnesses, but he may not take sides. The prosecutor, on the other hand, represents only the state and never the defense. Defense counsel only defend and never prosecute. There is no alternation of roles in the criminal courtroom.

However, the three leading members of the courtroom workgroup—the judge, prosecutor, and defense attorney—are all lawyers and possess the professional qualifications to do each other's work. Although role orientations are distinct and specialized, the work these three principals do is very similar. All of them manipulate information in order to reach decisions on the cases before them. They ask questions of witnesses—in private interviews or on the witness stand. They search out relevant aspects of code and case law and seek to apply them to their cases. All three are familiar with the techniques employed in adversarial proceedings; they are equally familiar with negotiations.

Little disagreement exists in the courtroom about this division of tasks and roles. It creates a situation in which everyone quickly fits into his accustomed place and in which the principals readily understand each other's work. Even novices readily fit into the work routine of a courtroom. The clerk keeps records. Although judges and lawyers may keep their own, the clerk's record is the official one. He records decisions, the dates when they occurred, and the motions and appearances that are filed with him. Together with the stenographic record of the proceedings, the clerk's file is the official record of the case and is used by everyone in the courtroom to determine what has happened in the past and what still needs to be done to complete disposition of the case. In addition, the court reporter—often a private contractor—makes a stenographic record of public proceedings. Those records, however, are not transcribed unless the defense or the state asks and pays for the transcription. Finally, bailiffs work in the courtroom to maintain decorum and guard prisoners who appear as defendants or witnesses.

Each of these members of the courtroom workgroup knows his task, role, and physical location in the courtroom.

He knows it before he enters the courtroom. Little formal training or socialization occurs in the workgroup. If a participant needs additional skills, he learns them informally.

THE WORK TECHNIQUES OF COURTROOM ORGANIZATIONS

Organizations are more than stable groups of people who share goals and divide tasks in a purposive manner. Organizations also employ a technology, which in turn helps shape them.[7] The technology consists of procedures to manipulate resources into desired outputs. For courtrooms, resources consist principally of information and the authority to make decisions that bind others. The outputs are dispositions. The courtroom organization's task is to transform information and authority into dispositions by applying its work techniques.

Courtroom workgroups require an externally validated, comprehensive, readily available, and generally accepted set of techniques, because the participants are sometimes unfamiliar with one another. This unfamiliarity means that they have not developed common patterns of interaction. When strangers meet and interact, they fall back on commonly accepted formulas to guide their behavior. The procedures embodied in statute and case law relating to the conduct of trials and the hearing of motions provide such formulas. These techniques are not only justified because they employ norms and values relating to equal justice and due process; the very nature of courtroom workgroups also requires that some work techniques be codified and generally accepted.

Courtrooms use three sets of techniques: (1) unilateral decisions, (2) adversarial proceedings, and (3) negotiations. Each of them required highly specialized knowledge and involves courtroom members in intense interactions.

Any attorney member of the courtroom workgroup may make unilateral decisions that eventually turn into dispositions. The defense counsel may file a motion; the prosecutor may file a dismissal; the judge or clerk may call up one case rather than another in his docket. In each instance, the participant uses his information and authority to impose a condition on other members of the courtroom team. The extensive interdependence of workgroup members, however, restricts their ability to impose unilateral decisions on the group. Consequently, unilateral decisions play a rather minor role in the courtroom's work.

Adversarial proceedings play a much more prominent role. They may be invoked by any of the three attorney members. Some of them are preparatory proceedings, such as preliminary examinations or hearings on motions; others are full-scale trials before a judge or jury. Adversarial proceedings are highly stylized interactions for revealing and sharing information that can become the basis for a disposition. During adversarial proceedings, information must be elicited in the approved manner, through oral arguments on legal points or questioning of witnesses. Neither prosecution nor defense ordinarily knows the full story a witness may tell, but the side presenting the witness generally knows more about what he might reveal than the opposing party. The judge knows almost nothing. Each side attempts to elicit information most favorable to its cause while blocking the presentation of damaging information. This activity requires a high degree of skill in questioning and a thorough knowledge of the technical rules of evidence which guides courtroom hearings. Participants whose skills are inadequate not only jeopardize their case, but also hinder the output rate of the courtroom. It is common to see a judge take over questioning from inept prosecutors or defense counsel, or to cut them off when he thinks that sufficient

evidence has been presented to reach a disposition. Similarly, counsel often advise judges about the legal basis for a decision.

Hearings require considerable coordination by the prosecutor or defense counsel rather than the judge. Witnesses must be assembled and prepared; each side must have an overview of its argument so that witnesses can be called in the most convincing sequence. Witnesses who might make an unfavorable impression or who appear fragile are often held in reserve and used only if absolutely necessary. If the hearings involve legal as well as evidentiary matters, the attorneys must read up on the law and have appropriate appellate citations at their fingertips. All of this preparation involves coordinating many people outside the ordinary ambit of the courtroom workgroup. Consequently, coordinative skills are almost as valuable as debating skills in adversarial proceedings.

Negotiation is the most commonly used technique in criminal court-rooms.[8] Plea bargaining—although most widely publicized—is only one use of negotiation. Continuances and the date of hearings are often bargained; the exchange of information is also commonly negotiated. Negotiation involves persuasion and the search for common ground. The common ground is generally based on agreement about the courtroom's goals; most members of the courtroom implicitly agree on the need to dispose cases and to reduce uncertainty. They also recognize the value of accommodating those on whom they are partially dependent. Each party to the negotiation attempts to convince the other that his solution is acceptable; in the course of negotiations, both parties are likely to move from their original positions toward a mutually acceptable outcome.

Information and the ability to make unilateral decisions that affect others significantly are the principal resources in negotiations. Courtroom participants utilize two types of information. One type is information about legal matters: the character of admissible evidence, the authorized sentence for a particular offense, the meaning of "lesser included offense," and similar matters. Most attorneys who specialize in criminal cases routinely possess this legal information. They also need to know the factual details of the case. Normally the prosecution possesses more information about the incident, on the basis of police reports and sometimes as a result of preliminary interviews with witnesses. Often there are disputes about what "really" happened, with the defense attorney attempting to put a less serious interpretation on the events than the prosecutor. At the same time, the character of the defendant is also in question. The defense attorney often claims to know more about that; he will tell of his client's family background, his employment record, his standing in the community, in addition to any disadvantages he has had to overcome. The prosecutor usually possesses only the defendant's police record. Negotiations proceed through a careful manipulation of this information. Even when both prosecutor and defense make "full disclosure," they often interpret the information at their disposal rather than simply laying it out on the table.

Information about the way in which other courtrooms handle similar incidents is also important in negotiations. What happens in other courts of the city or state is communicated principally through these negotiations. If other courtrooms readily grant continuances, that constitutes a useful argument that a continuance ought to be granted in the case under discussion. If, in an adjoining courtroom, aggravated assault seems to carry a normal sentence of two to four years, defense counsel will try hard to achieve at least as low a sentence. Because prosecutors usually work in a single courtroom, whereas private defense counsel circulate throughout several courtrooms in the city, some defense attorneys posses more of this kind of information.

Negotiations also invoke claims on workgroup cohesion. None that we witnessed did so overtly, but many were impregnated with hints that the continuing need to work together required reasonableness in negotiation. Participants joked about it; at the end of a negotiation, they often stood around and chatted about other matters as if to imply that they were still friendly partners of the same workgroup. Only when negotiations broke down did either prosecutor or defense counsel occasionally stalk out without the usual social amenities.

Clearly the techniques of presentation, the manipulation of information, and the invocation of common workgroup values are quite different in negotiations than in adversarial hearings. Not only are the negotiations much less formal, but they also depend less on the rules of evidence and other legalistic formulas that pervade so much of the adversarial performance. In negotiations much more depends on the long-run relationships between bargaining member of the workgroup. Trust, empathy, mutual understanding are important in negotiations, but matter little in adversarial proceedings. In bargaining, information is narrated; formal testimony from witnesses is the principal mode in adversarial proceedings.

Implicit threats to make unilateral decisions underlie the uses of information in all negotiations. The ability to take such actions gives weight to the efforts to control the exchange of information. Judges can render decisions that affect the outcome of specific cases and the work life of attorneys in general. The prosecutor can proceed to trial on the original charges if the defendant does not plead guilty to them. And the defense attorney can insist on a full jury trial regardless of what anyone else does, unless a complete dismissal is forthcoming. Without the existence of these threats, negotiations based on the exchange of information would carry little weight. Indeed, much of the manipulation of information is directed toward demonstrating what would happen if the case went to trial. . . .

WORKGROUP FAMILIARITY

Courtroom workgroupings almost always contain some persons who are quite familiar with one another and some who are more like strangers. The familiarity among major participants is an important characteristic of workgroups, because it has a significant effect on the manner in which they work. The more workgroup members are familiar with one another, the better they can negotiate; the more familiar, the less they need to rely on formalities and the more they can utilize informal arrangements. The more familiar courtroom members are with each other, the more likely it is that they will agree about courtroom values and goals and the less they will conflict with one another.

Workgroup familiarity depends on two factors. The first is the stability of the workgroups themselves.[9] The second is the size of the pool from which workgroup members are drawn; the smaller the number of judges, prosecutors, defense attorneys, clerks, and others working in the courthouse, the more familiar courtroom members will be with each other.

Generally the most stable assignment is that of the judge. Except during vacation or illness, a single judge ordinarily sits for a year or more in a single courtroom. However, in courtrooms hearing misdemeanors, assignments may last for as little as a month; in other courtrooms, where the judges are elected or appointed to the criminal court itself, the assignment may extend over many years. The stabilizing effect of long assignments of judges is well illustrated by what happens when one is temporarily replaced by another judge. Work routines become substantially altered. Everyone suffers from more uncertainty about what to do and how to do it, because an important stranger is in their midst. Where possible, the remaining members postpone significant proceedings until the judge returns. If action cannot be delayed, proceedings switch into an adversarial mode, because the unknown qualities of the substitute judge can best be neutralized in a jury trial.

The assignment of prosecutors and defense attorneys is much more variable. These differences have profound consequences.

The less change there is in a workgroup personnel, the more interaction will occur. Frequent interactions produce familiarity with each other's intentions and probable behavior. In stable courtroom workgroups, the principal actors know each other's preferences; they have been able to develop standing accommodations with each other. They work together enough to share organizational maintenance goals; they learn to understand the pressures that each must bear from his sponsoring organization. Thus, prosecutors and defense attorneys learn what information the judge wants in routine cases; they know the sentence he will likely mete out. They know how to present a case in order to provoke the harshest response or the mildest reaction from the judge. They know what plea offers were made in the past, and can evaluate the present case in the light of that common past. The uncertainty in negotiating with each other is considerably reduced by their familiarity with one another. In addition, frequent interactions provide innumerable informal opportunities for negotiation. Prosecutor and defense counsel may talk about a case not only when it is on the docket but during the many other occasions at which they encounter each other. They can test possible compromises informally, without putting the case on the judge's desk for formal decision. By contrast, in fluid workgroups information about each of the participants is much more sparse; members of the courtroom workgroup deal with each other more as strangers than as friends; formal roles govern them more completely. In fluid workgroups, members work in a much less certain context. They are less likely to know the judge's preferences or each other's. They do not have a great storehouse of common experiences by which to evaluate the present case. They have not had an opportunity to develop a set of shared accommodations or an understanding of each participant's work pressures.

Finally, low interaction means that no one heavily depends on the actions of any other individual to accomplish his work. Where the same individuals interact continually, however, strong patterns of mutual dependence and accompanying abilities to influence one another emerge. In addition, if interaction is high, circulation of defense counsel and prosecutors from one courtroom to another will be low. A lower circulation, in turn, facilitates the development of distinctive styles of behavior within the rather isolated courtrooms located in the same building.

Even in unstable workgroups members may be quite familiar with each other, if the pool of active participants in the courthouse is fairly small. Where there are only a handful of judges, a half-dozen prosecutors, and a dozen defense attorneys, familiarity develops as if the workgroups were the same every day. But the familiarity found in smaller cities and in rural areas can be approximated in 19 large cities if a small group of specialized attorneys monopolizes the work.

SUMMARY OF WORKGROUP CHARACTERISTICS

All courtroom workgroups confront the same basic task—to dispose of defendants' cases. All have the same composition—a judge, prosecutor, and defense attorney, who are familiar with each other's roles but who specialize in their own tasks. They share expressive and instrumental goals generated from within the workgroup and from the external environment. Workgroups utilize three work techniques—adversarial proceedings, negotiations, and unilateral decisions. These characteristics are found regardless of city. But workgroups also differ in several significant respects. Nowhere do judges completely dominate influence patterns within the workgroup, but the precise distribution of influence does vary. When the membership of workgroups is stable, patterns of mutual dependence develop, resulting in a more even distribution of influence. Stability also produces familiarity, but familiarity can exist even when workgroup composition is fluid, if the total number of people who form workgroups is fairly small and unchanging. When members are familiar with one another, negotiations are facilitated. When they are not, adversary proceedings are more likely.

Courtroom workgroups are like many other organizations. They are labor-intensive, are staffed by professionals, and provide services rather than products. Courtroom workgroups have an authority structure that is modified by influence relationships, but they are not hierarchies. The judge does not rule or govern; at most, he manages, and often he is managed by others.

Although workgroups dispose of many cases during a day, they are not assembly lines. Even routine decisions involve discretion. Setting bond, for instance, does not involve putting the same nuts and bolts into a piece of sheet metal (as on a typical assembly line); rather, it requires fitting a variety of factual assertions into a limited number of possible bail-bond decisions. The information required for such decisions may be communicated rapidly, and decisions may follow one another in quick succession. But it is no assembly line. On an assembly line, one worker simply relies on all the others doing their jobs; an assembly line requires few verbal or social interactions. Workgroup members must interact with one another to reach a decision.

NOTES

1. The judge's formal role is the focus of much legal literature. It is epitomized by Bernard Botein, *The Trial Judge* (New York: Simon and Schuster, 1952).
2. Note the analysis of criminal proceedings from the defendant's perspective by Jonathan Casper, *American Criminal Justice* (Englewood Cliffs, N.J.: Prentice-Hall, 1972).
3. We are conceptualizing goals as incentive mechanisms and the goal structure as multifaceted. They help orient the calculus of decision-makers and serve to bind organization members together. An insightful discussion of the problems associated with operationalizing goals and placing them in a theoretic scheme is Petro Georgiou, "The Goal Paradigm and Notes toward a Counter Paradigm," *Administrative Science Quarterly* 18 (1973): 291–310. Despite Georgiou's arguments, we find the concept of goals and incentive structures essential to the organizational paradigm.
4. This discussion reflects what Mohr calls transitive and reflexive goals. Lawrence B. Mohr, "The Concept of Organizational Goal," *American Political Science Review* 67 (1973): 470–481, esp. 475–476.
5. For partial evidence in support of the following see "Lawyers with Convic-

tions," in Abraham S. Blumberg, *The Scales of Justice* (Chicago: Aldine, 1970), pp. 51–67; George F. Cole *The American System of Criminal Justice* (North Scituate, Mass.: Duxbury Press, 1975), pp. 238–241 and 271–272; Carter, *The Limits of Order*, pp. 75–105; Jerome Skolnick, "Social Control in the Adversary System," *Journal of Conflict Resolution* 11 (1967): 51 ff; Lynn M. Mather, "The Outsiders in the Courtroom: An Alternative Role for the Defense," in Herbert Jacob (ed.), *The Potential for Reform of Criminal Justice* (Beverly Hills, Calif.: Sage Publications, 1974), pp. 268–273.
Note, however, that cohesion is not the only goal of actors and that it sometimes conflicts with others.
6. Cf. Carter, *The Limits of Order*, pp. 19–21.
7. See especially James O. Thompson, *Organizations in Action* (New York: McGraw-Hill, 1967).
8. We have drawn from descriptions of courtroom negotiations by Blumberg, *Criminal Justice*, Casper, *American Criminal Justice*; Carter, *The Limits of Order*; Mather, "The Outsiders in the Courtroom;" and Albert W. Alschuler, "The Prosecutor's Role in Plea Bargaining," *University of Chicago Law Review* 36 (1968): 50–112.
9. Stability or cohesiveness is taken for granted by many organizational analysts. For instance, the much-cited article by D.S. Pugh, D. J. Hickson, C. R. Hinings, and C. Turner, "Dimensions of Organizational Structure," *Administrative Science Quarterly* (June 1968): 65–106 does not count stability as one of the dimensions of organizational structure.

15.   The Run for the Robes

Tom Watson

It was Christmas 1985, and the leaders of the Philadelphia Roofers Union were feeling flush with the holiday spirit. Indulging the joy of giving, they drew up a list of their favorite judges in the city and decided to spread a little of the union's largess around.

The judges who were chosen received bundles of between $300 and $500 in cash, stuffed into envelopes marked "Season's Greetings." A lawyer for the union called the envelopes Christmas presents. Unfortunately for the Roofers and their beneficiaries, federal prosecutors called them bribes.

Even in a city where corruption is commonplace, the so-called Roofers scandal registered as an especially sleazy affair. Eventually, two judges went to federal prison. Another nine were forced from the bench or decided to resign. The *Philadelphia Inquirer* called the episode "a whole new chapter in the annals of municipal graft."

Today, six years later, the impact of the Roofers scandal is still being felt in the governor's mansion, in the chambers of the Pennsylvania legislature and in the offices of some of the most powerful lawyers and interest groups in the state. Democratic Governor Robert P. Casey has called for replacing the state's traditional method of choosing judges—partisan election—with an appointive system giving the governor the power to pick from a list of candidates drawn up by a nominating commission. Champions of "merit selection," as it has long been known, say it could help prevent incidents like the Roofers scandal from happening again.

SOURCE: "The Run for the Robes" by Tom Watson from *Governing*, July 1991, pp. 49–52. Reprinted by permission.

Pennsylvania has plenty of company. Judicial selection is re-emerging as an issue in many parts of the country this year after a relatively quiet decade of the 1980s. The reason is simple. Complaints about judicial elections—their cost, their ethics, and their consequences—are streaming in from contests for the lowest municipal trial courts to state Supreme Courts across the land.

"There's been impetus in a number of states because of scandals...or just new evidence that things aren't working that well," says Steve Goldspiel, staff director for the Judicial Selection Committee of the American Bar Association. "It's when things start failing that you galvanize change. People start saying there's got to be a better way."

These days, it seems, everyone has a horror story to tell about judges' campaigns.

In North Carolina, it involves the tone of the electioneering. Last fall, two Republican candidates for the state Supreme Court tore into two sitting Democratic justices, accusing them of having dragged their feet in doling out the death penalty to convicted murderers. North Carolina's politics are known for being among the roughest in the country. But coming from judicial candidates, the charges struck nearly everyone as excessive.

In Florida, the worry is that judicial elections do too little to screen out unqualified candidates, letting practically anybody grab a seat on the bench. State bar association leaders highlight a recent Hillsborough County case to stress the point. A young candidate who had barely been practicing law long enough to be eligible for a county judgeship came out of nowhere to win on the strength of an aggressive campaign strategy that included flying over sports stadiums in a hot-air balloon.

Even in Wisconsin, whose Progressive Era traditions make direct democracy an article of faith, judicial elections are coming in for closer scrutiny. The typically placid tone of last year's judicial campaign season was shattered when a state Supreme Court justice, Donald W. Steinmetz, aired an advertisement branding his opponent a tool of "rich personal-injury lawyers" who were bankrolling his campaign. It turned out that Steinmetz had gotten his facts wrong—he had overstated the amount that the opponent, state Appeals Courts Judge Richard S. Brown, had actually received from the personal injury bar. The Dane County district attorney wound up investigating to determine whether Steinmetz was guilty of false advertising. That probe was eventually dropped, but judges, lawyers and journalists all began to question whether their beloved electoral system was foundering. Meanwhile, Steinmetz won the election by a vote of 355,000 to 330,000.

All of these strategies—stirring up popular passions about capital punishment, slinging mud against other jurists, using the flimsiest campaign gimmicks to attract attention—strike reasonable people in many places as conduct somehow unbecoming to a judge or anyone who aspires to be one. They are routine, of course, in contests for most political offices in this country, but there is widespread feeling that judges should be different, that their office should impose a certain dignity on them, even when the law requires them to run for election.

Slowly, however, a sad truth is dawning on those who work in and watch over judicial elections. The special status that traditionally has lifted contests for the bench above those for other political offices is fast eroding. Today, running for a judgeship is a lot like waging any other political campaign.

"We always thought of judges in a different light, more dignified, like they were on a different plane," says Sherman Stock, communications director for the Wisconsin Academy of Trial Lawyers. "But the kind of complaints we are hearing here suggests that judges' campaigns have become like regular races. They're getting more and more like the kind of circus political campaigns have become."

There is, of course, one dramatic change that proponents say would end the circus once and for all: Stop electing judges and choose them all through some form of appointive or "merit" system. For many critics, perhaps most, it is the only real solution. But this reform has one drawback: In much of the country, it is not going to happen anytime soon, no matter how desirable it might be.

Advocates of merit selection have been pushing for its adoption for the last 80 years. Yet 39 states still use the ballot box to select at least some of their judges. An array of powerful interests, ranging from minority groups and organized labor to trial lawyers and anti-abortion forces, have blocked the path to merit selection, branding it an elitist system that threatens voters' right to choose.

So in the current climate of discontent with judicial elections, there is somewhat less attention than in the past on scrapping the system and more focus on regulating it to temper its excesses. Some reformers are pushing special committees to monitor complaints arising from the conduct of judicial elections. Others want to establish better mechanisms for disciplining judges who stray beyond the bounds of decorum on the campaign trail. There are even some who argue that the way to improve judicial campaigns is to loosen traditional restrictions on what judges can talk about during campaigns, in hopes that voters will be able to learn more about the candidates and make a more intelligent choice.

"All anybody ever pays attention to is

whether 'merit' is coming or not coming," says Roy A. Schotland, a judicial selection specialist at Georgetown University Law Center. "There's so much energy spent on that question that it has distracted from efforts to reduce the mounting problems in campaigns, which are considerable. Anybody who refuses to deal with those problems these days is clearly at home in cloud cuckooland."

Those problems are not new ones. They echo more than a century and a half of U.S. history. At the very beginning of the American experience, it is true, all 13 colonies chose their judges by gubernatorial or legislative appointment. But by 1850, Jacksonian democracy had taken root; every new state entering the Union was opting for elected judges, and that pattern held until 1959, when Alaska won its statehood.

Complaints that judicial elections enabled political parties to pack the bench soon began rolling in. Tammany Hall, the Democratic organization that ran New York City from the mid-1800s into the 1930s, provided critics with some of their best evidence. Tammany's leaders regularly directed their foot soldiers to vote out qualified judges who strayed off the reservation and replace them with candidates whose only relevant credential was loyalty to the machine.

In 1906, a Nebraska lawyer named Roscoe Pound gave voice to the growing sense of frustration. By "putting courts into politics, and compelling judges to become politicians in many jurisdictions," Pound argued, the nation had "almost destroyed the traditional respect for the bench." Seven years later, Pound's disciples formed the American Judicature Society, dedicated to righting the wrongs he perceived. The group developed the merit selection plan and began shopping it around.

The going was slow, stalled by those who saw appointments as an elitist way of preventing ethnic and religious minorities from reaching the bench. One judge greeted the news that Missouri had adopted an appointive system by composing a biting song:

> *Oh, the Old Missouri Plan*
> *Oh, the Old Missouri Plan*
> *When Wall Street lawyers*
>   *all judicial candidates will*
>   *scan*
> *If you're not from Fair Old*
>   *Harvard*
> *They will toss you in the can...*

Despite such eloquent opposition, appointment eventually caught on to some extent; by the mid-1970s, merit selection was being used to pick at least some judges in 28 states. But lately, the pace of victory for AJS and its allies has slowed. The number of states that elect judges has remained essentially constant for the past five years; New Mexico in 1988, was the last state to adopt a merit system to fill both initial and interim state judicial vacancies. A movement that once promised to sweep the nation is now fighting for small victories in the trenches, and having to secure them against determined opposition over long periods of time.

"The pace of adoption has definitely slowed," says Kathleen Sampson, a spokeswoman for AJS, which is headquartered in Chicago. "All the easy states are in." Accustomed to having their hopes dashed in recent years Sampson and her allies are loath to make predictions about notching another significant win anytime soon.

Some of the reasons why are plainly on display at the moment in Pennsylvania.

On paper, conditions could not be riper for an attack on judicial elections. In the aftermath of the Roofers scandal, Governor Casey convened a special commission to study how best to address the rising tide of complaints about the judiciary not only in Philadelphia but elsewhere in the state. The legislature began considering a merit selection system in earnest, prodded by the state bar association and an alliance of business and self-styled "good government" groups. Editorial writers shifted into overdrive.

Together, their efforts helped push a plan for appointing judges as far as the floor of both chambers of the legislature in 1990. This year dawned even brighter. Casey, previously a champion of electing judges, did a high-profile turnabout in his annual State of the Commonwealth address, calling for a referendum on whether to start appointing them, at least at the appellate lever. Casey also urged that voters in each county decide how best to select members of the local courts of common pleas.

That came as welcome news to many members of Pennsylvania's legal community, who have long grumbled that the state's system for selecting judges gave too much power to the political parties. A number of the complaints come from Philadelphia, where judicial candidates historically have been "maced"— forced to contribute to their party's mayoral candidate if they want their names to appear on the sample ballots handed out by ward-heelers working on the mayoral campaign. Rather than forego a golden opportunity for free publicity and risk alienating the party's power structure, many judges over the years have gone along with the mace.

In Pennsylvania, as in other places, the reformers wade into battle armed with arguments from the state legal establishment. Judges complain about the difficulty of having to solicit thousands of dollars from lawyers, then trying to turn around and mete out impartial rulings when these same lawyers appear before them in court. Knowledge of who gave and who didn't weighs on the judges, they say, even if they try to ignore the issue.

"I tried to insulate myself from information about who contributed," says Edmund B. Spaeth Jr., who quit as presiding judge of Pennsylvania's second-tier appellate court in 1985, citing concerns about the election system. "For fund raising, I had a committee and would try to get other people to do that for me. I had an accounting firm prepare the records. But sometimes you know, and sometimes the lawyers tell you."

Judges aren't the only ones who worry. Bar association leaders cite Spaeth as a prime example of one of their worst fears about judicial elections: that the demands of politicking will drive some of the best and brightest from the bench, clearing the path for novices and zealots. And partners at major law firms complain that they are frequently forced for political reasons to give to more than one contender in a judicial contest, a requirement that is painfully expensive.

Still, despite their rhetoric and their political momentum, merit selection advocates are dubious about their chances for victory. "This isn't a 40-yard dash," Governor Casey says. "This is a marathon." For him and for his allies, that passes for optimism.

Part of the problem is procedural: To abolish judicial elections, Pennsylvania, like many states, must amend its constitution. That means that the legislature must pass identical reform bills in two consecutive sessions, always a difficult stumbling block. More fundamentally, though, there is the argument that merit selection is merely a way of taking the power to pick judges from the electorate and turning it over to legal and political elites.

Among those making this argument in Pennsylvania and other states are organized trial lawyers, anti-abortion activists and organized labor—which remains a potent force in this battle, the Roofers scandal notwithstanding. "Just because there are three bad apples in a bushel, that doesn't mean the whole system is rotten," says Bill George, president of the state chapter of the AFL-CIO.

"If you go around the country, the number of corrupt judges under the merit system outweighs those under elections anyway. . . . The constitutional right that exists in Pennsylvania to elect judges is something we treasure. We have a system here we think is working."

To George, judicial selection is simply a matter of interest group politics. The groups that are currently winning are happy with the system. The groups that are losing are not. "When corporate Pennsylvania had control of the elections process," George argues, "the elections process was OK. Historically, companies would dump their corporate attorneys—attorneys who had become non-productive—into the judiciary. They dumped their garbage...It's the losers saying, 'Change the system.'"

That said, George and his allies know that the pressure for some form of change may prove too great to forestall, even if they manage to keep merit selection at bay. The pressure is generating a variety of proposals, both within Pennsylvania and elsewhere around the country; some are more politically sellable than others. But taken together, the proposals represent an unusual consensus that the way America chooses judges needs improvement.

To cope with the spiraling cost of judicial campaigns, Governor Casey has proposed introducing public financing into contests for the courtrooms. Only three states currently provide public financing for judges: Montana, North Carolina and Wisconsin. And Casey's proposal thus far has met with opposition from a variety of critics, including some who fear it will detract from the more important cause of merit selection. Nonetheless, Casey regards it as a significant interim step in controlling the special-interest politics he says has tainted the state's judicial system.

Elsewhere, the focus of short-term reform is on establishing committees to monitor judicial campaigns and handle any complaints that might come up. Last year, North Carolina established the first statewide watchdog group in the country, building on local models in California's San Mateo and Santa Clara counties; Rochester, New York; and Columbus, Ohio. Roy Schotland, the Georgetown law professor who work with leaders in North Carolina to establish the group, says it could help stave off a repeat performance of the negative campaigning that plagued last year's judicial elections.

Perhaps the most pronounced new reform effort has been geared toward better educating the electorate about judicial contests. Last year, North Carolina became the first state to distribute a voter's guide devoted specifically to judicial candidates. It distributed some 550,000 copies of a 12-page pamphlet as an insert in Sunday papers around the state. The interest group that published the guide also sponsored a debate among judicial candidates on public television.

Pennsylvania has now gone a step further. In March, Samuel C. Stretton, a contender for the Chester County common pleas court, successfully challenged a state law restricting what judicial candidates can say about their views on political and legal issues. A federal court ruled that the law abridged Stretton's First Amendment right of free speech. Similar challenges have been launched in Florida and Kentucky in recent months.

Codes of judicial conduct have traditionally prohibited incumbents or candidates from saying anything that might suggest how they would rule in a particular case. One consequence of the rules, however, has been the trivialization of the campaigns, along with a disproportionate advantage for those with big campaign treasuries and partisan organizations behind them, as well as for those willing to engage in campaign gimmickry. "You feel very foolish," says Edmund Spaeth, the former Superior Court judge in Pennsylvania. "What can you say? 'If

I'm elected, I'll do my best to be fair. I'll read the briefs and be as conscientious as I can be.' So what else is new?"

Those who want to "unshackle" judicial candidates argue that if they were allowed to discuss the issues on a serious basis, the tenor of the campaigns could not help but improve. Voters would have a better sense of how capable the candidates are, and more of them would be able to cast an intelligent vote on Election Day. "There is a perception that voters will be more likely to vote for judges if they know where judges stand on particular issues," says Linda Glyman of the American Bar Association. The ABA loosened its own restrictions on campaign speech in 1990.

To others, though, the move toward free speech for judicial candidates is a step in precisely the wrong direction. It injects more politics, they say, into a system whose main problem is that it is far too political already. It is bound to frustrate the many lawyers and judges who lament that the once-pronounced differences between judicial elections and other political contests seem to be dissolving by the day.

"There is a gulf" between judges and other political officeholders, "and there should be," says Richard S. Brown, the Wisconsin judge who lost out for the State Supreme Court partly because of the false campaign ads run by his opponent. "What the electoral process does is make judges political animals even if they are not interested in being political animals."

16. Punishing Smarter: Penal Reforms for the 1990s

John J. DiIulio, Jr.

Months before the 1988 presidential campaign made Willie Horton a household name, California Governor George Deukmejian was asked to restate his position on supervising convicted criminals in the community instead of behind bars. The governor responded that he would embrace alternatives to incarceration when criminals embrace alternatives to crime.

That was a neat remark, especially since, as the governor spoke, California already had more than 200,000 convicted criminals on probation and more than 35,000 on parole—about three times as many offenders "doing time" on its

SOURCE: From "Punishing Smarter: Penal Reforms for the 1990s" by John J. Dilulio, Jr. in *The Brookings Review*, Summer 1989, pp. 3–12. Reprinted by permission

streets as it had locked up inside its terribly overcrowded prisons and jails.

Basic facts have a way of getting lost in discussions of correctional policy. Perhaps that is because the facts are perplexing and discouraging. I have spent much of the last decade as a researcher and consultant in the correctional trenches, and during that time things never looked quite so unmanageable as they do today.

But there are correctional strategies that, if adopted wisely and widely, will protect the public and its purse more effectively than conventional approaches. There are cost-effective ways of enhancing the life prospects of convicted criminals without betraying the legitimate desires of their victims and the general public for retribution.

A steady increase in both the number

of citizens behind bars and in the number under community-based supervision is inevitable. Yet, the 1990s can be the decade when "punishing harder" gives way to "punishing smarter." Just as the 1980s saw the emergence of an intelligent consensus on welfare reform, so may the 1990s witness the emergence of an intelligent consensus on penal reform.

For that to happen, however, the federal government must begin to treat corrections as the major national domestic public policy issue that it has become. The federal prison system may well double in size over the next 10 years, and state and local corrections systems are already desperate for help. Furthermore, unless corrections and related criminal justice issues are addressed more thoughtfully than they have been, the problems of the urban underclass can only grow worse.

SOARING CORRECTIONAL POPULATIONS

In the 1980s overcrowding behind bars has been accompanied by "overloading" on the streets. Between 1983 and 1987 the nation's probation and parole populations increased faster than its prison and jail populations. Today, about 3.5 million citizens live under some form of correctional supervision. More than 900,000 are in prison or jail, while nearly 2.6 million are on probation or parole.

Historically, minority males have been placed under correctional supervision at much higher rates than white males, while women, minority and white, have been a negligible fraction of the prison population. In the 1980s the former gap has widened while the latter gap has narrowed slightly. About 10 percent of all adult black males live under some form of correctional supervision; for adult white males, the figure is closer to 1 of every 35. In 1981 about 4.2 percent of the nation's prison population was female; by the start of 1988 that figure had

jumped to 5 percent. By the end of 1988 more than 30,000 women were imprisoned.

Like their male counterparts, women under correctional supervision have become not only more numerous but more hard core. Over 90 percent of all prisoners are violent offenders, repeat offenders (two or more felony convictions), or violent repeat offenders. But because of overcrowding and related pressures, these chronic and violent offenders—corrections workers often refer to them as "heavies"—are being released in record times and in record numbers.

A 1987 study by the U.S. Bureau of Justice Statistics showed that violent criminal (murderers, rapists, robbers, and others guilty of crimes against people) serve about half of their sentence time in the community; many classes of nonviolent offenders spend less than a third of their sentence time behind bars. In many prison and jail systems, early release programs have been institutionalized.

MORE INCARCERATION, LESS CRIME?

Has this increased reliance on community-based supervision had any effect on crime rates? In publicizing the Willie Horton incident—in which a murderer furloughed in Massachusetts sexually assaulted a Maryland woman—the 1988 presidential campaign spotlighted a general issue that corrections policymakers, administrators, and analysts have been debating for years (often with only slightly greater calm and intelligence than it was "debated" in the campaign); namely, do crime rates go down when incarceration rates go up?

Many believe that they do, and that the increased use of alternatives to incarceration, and related "liberal" penal reform measures such as prison furloughs and early release programs, are responsible for increased rates of crime, especially increased rates of violent crime.

The evidence for this view is largely anecdotal, and some of the anecdotes are more telling than others. Though the tragedy was real, the infamous Horton anecdote was hollow. Over 99.5 percent of prison furloughs result neither in a violation of the terms of the furlough nor in a new crime. In 1987, for example, some 50,000 prisoners were granted more than 200,000 furloughs, virtually all of them without incident. Most jurisdictions furlough violent offenders, including murderers. But most agencies, including the federal system, do not furlough prisoners convicted of murder in the first degree, and most grant furloughs only to inmates who are within months of their official release dates. Even though it was one of only two states that furloughed persons serving sentences of life without possibility of parole (the other was North Carolina), and even though the process by which prisoners were selected for furloughs (and monitored once beyond the walls) was arguably quite weak, statistically, the Massachusetts program that furloughed Horton was even more successful than the norm.

Before Horton, however, the anti-alternatives anecdote of choice involved a Michigan convict who committed other crimes while on parole. In 1975 Wayne Lamar Harvey wantonly killed two people in a Detroit bar. He plea-bargained the charges against him down to second-degree murder and was sentenced to 20–40 years. On his first day in prison, he received nearly 10 years of "good-time" credits. Though he committed dozens of major prison rule violations during his incarceration in a Michigan prison, his credits were never revoked. His confinement time was further reduced under the state's early release program, and he was paroled in mid-1984. Three months later he and an accomplice killed a 41–year–old East Lansing police officer, the father of six.

He then went to a nearby home and killed a 33–year–old woman as she opened her front door.

While Horton was atypical of prisoners on furlough, Harvey was typical of prisoners on early release—like most offenders who serve only a fraction of their sentences behind bars, he did not "go straight" upon release. (Harvey, in fact, spent more time in prison than most murderers—eight and a half years compared with the national median of about six.)

While furlough programs are successful, the rate at which paroled prisoners are convicted of a new crime is discouraging. Echoing the results of most previous studies of recidivism, a 1987 study by the U.S. Bureau of Justice Statistics reported that almost 70 percent of young adults who had been paroled from prisons in 22 states were rearrested for serious crimes once or more within six years, 53 percent of all parolees were convicted of a serious new offense, and 49 percent were sent back to prison. Perhaps most disheartening of all, the study found that parolees initially imprisoned for a property crime were as likely as those incarcerated for a violent crime to be rearrested for a violent crime.

Many conservatives leap from such evidence to the general conclusion that more incarceration is the key to less crime, while less incarceration is the cause of more crime. For example, writing in a recent issue of *Policy Review*, Assistant Attorney General Richard B. Abell drew a simple, seductive graph to show that in 1960, when crime rates were low, a typical offender had a 6.2 percent chance of going to prison; by 1983, when crime rates had more than tripled, the chance of going to prison was only 3.5 percent. When the probabilities of imprisonment were lowest, crime rates were highest.

There is some good to be said for juxtaposing trends in this provocative way. But the more sophisticated the statistical analysis—the more it systematically relates a host of relevant variables to each other—the weaker and more ambiguous the incarceration-crime nexus becomes.

The difficulty of determining the actual relationship between crime rates and incarceration rates has long been recognized both by analysts, like myself, who have absolutely no qualms about locking up dangerous and chronic offenders and by leading researchers and criminology institutes whom most corrections cognoscenti would label "liberal" or "pro-alternatives." For example, a 1988 report by the National Council on Crime and Delinquency ranked the 50 states and the District of Columbia according to several measures of "punitiveness"— imprisonment rates, incarceration rates (prisons plus jails), and "total control" rates (prisons, jails, juvenile facilities, probation, and parole) per 100,000 residential population. The report found such crazy-quilt variations both among and within jurisdictions that it concluded, as have many other studies, that the relationship between incarceration and crime is neither uniform nor simple.

That the incarceration-crime nexus is hard to demonstrate statistically does not rebut the commonsense view that it exists. Neither, for that matter, does it answer the moral argument (which, like most of the public, I support) that citizens who assault, rape, rob, kidnap, burglarize, deal deadly drugs, and murder ought to be punished swiftly, certainly, and proportionately: those who abuse liberty ought to be deprived of it.

IS INCARCERATION A STEAL?

Recently, the historic debate over whether it is socially desirable to widen the "net of social control" has been waged indirectly by analysts of the monetary costs of corrections. Estimating those costs is difficult, but most analysts put the national bill for corrections in 1988 somewhere in the neighborhood of $25 billion. That is a very expensive

neighborhood, especially when a decade or so ago, only $2.5 billion was spent on all correctional operations, construction, and services.

Virtually all of the money is appropriated at the state and local levels. According to the National Conference of State Legislatures, corrections spending nationwide in 1987 increased by 10 percent over the previous year, surpassing the rate of increase in spending for education for the second consecutive year. Half the states increased corrections spending by more than 10 percent; only 3 states cut it. Corrections spending grew faster than general fund spending in 36 states.

On average, it costs about $20,000 a year to keep somebody behind bars; most of that goes to pay the officers, administrators, and other personnel needed to run a prison or jail. This figure makes even grizzled analysts like me wince. No sane taxpaying person can rejoice at the fact that so much money is spent keeping people in the custody of barbed wire bureaucracies, money that could be better spent on educating children in public schools, moving riders on public transit, and doing other things we value. Nevertheless, once the costs of incarceration are weighed carefully against its benefits, it is much harder to argue that money spent on incarceration is somehow money "wasted."

In a 1987 study published by the National Institute of Justice, economist Edwin Zedlewski estimated that one year's imprisonment cost $25,000 an offender. Using various crime data, he estimated that the typical prisoner had committed 187 crimes a year and that the typical crime costs $2,300 in property losses and/or physical injuries and suffering. Multiplying these two figures, he calculated that the typical prisoner was responsible for $430,000 in total "social costs" a year. Thus, placing 1,000 typical felons behind bars costs society $25 million a year; but not placing them behind bars costs society about $430 million a year (187,000 felonies times $2,300 per felony)!

Zedlewski's finding is rather incredible; I know of no other government activity that would yield such a high benefit-cost ratio. Some of the studies on which Zedlewski based his estimates were rather dated, and his computations used averages when other measures would have yielded a lower ratio.

In a 1988 article published in the journal *Crime and Delinquency*, Franklin E. Zimring and Gordon Hawkins charged that Zedlewski's methodology inflated his findings. They cited, for example, several studies suggesting that the typical offender commits fewer than 20, not 187, crimes a year. They did not, however, recalculate the incarceration benefit-cost ratio. In fact, though, if one were to recalculate, using the most reasonable low estimates of crimes per offender and costs per crime and the most reasonable high estimates of incarceration costs, one might still get a benefit-cost ratio above one.

MORE OVERCROWDING, MORE VIOLENCE?

Whatever the monetary benefit, the sheer human toll of incarceration cannot be denied and should never be forgotten. I have been through scores of prisons and jails, federal, state, and local. Even under the best of conditions, prisons and jails are not pleasant. They are lousy places to work, terrible places to live, (and, need I add, less comfortable as research sites than most university libraries). And overcrowded prisons and jails are downright miserable places.

But is it true that overcrowding is associated with an increase in institutional violence, a disruption in work and educational programs, and other problems?

Common sense suggests that the answer to this question must be yes. Yet every meaningful study either has answered it in the negative or concluded that the impact of overcrowding on the quality of institutional life is ambiguous. For example, in my book *Governing Prisons*, I reported the results of a highly exploratory analysis of the state prison systems in Texas, Michigan, and California. This study indicated that overcrowding varied inversely with prison violence. Prisons and prison systems were most violent when they were *least* overcrowded.

Statistician Christopher A. Innes came to similar conclusions in a report for the U. S. Bureau of Justice Statistics. Analyzing the effects of overcrowding on more than 180,000 housing units at 694 state prisons, he found that the most overcrowded maximum-security prisons had a *lower* homicide rate than moderately crowded ones, and about the same rate as prisons that were *not* overcrowded. He concluded that there was little evidence that crowding levels were directly related to increased homicide rates, assault rates, or the incidence of major disorder, findings that have been echoed in half-a-dozen subsequent studies.

Unquestionably, however, overcrowding makes life harder for those who live and work in prisons and jails, just as the rise in community-based populations overtaxes probation and parole agents and hamstrings meaningful efforts to supervise offenders and to assist them in finding jobs, counseling, and other things vital to a successful return to the community. An important question, therefore, concerns the duration of the problem. Will the increase in correctional populations continue, and, if so, for how long?

The answer, I fear, is that it will continue to the end of the century, and possibly longer. Two main factors have fueled the increase, and neither will abate anytime soon.

Sentencing trends are the first factor. Widespread outrage at "revolving door" practices that free convicted criminals before they have served their entire sentences has led to mandatory sentencing and related changes in penal codes.

Many of these laws contain a strong presumption in favor of incarceration for even first-time and "petty" offenders. The result—and we are only now beginning to see the full effects—has been soaring numbers of people under correctional supervision for longer periods of time, both behind bars and in the community.

It is estimated, for example, that in conjunction with recent changes in federal sentencing guidelines, the sweeping "lock 'em up" provisions of the Anti-Drug Abuse Act of 1986 will double the federal prison population from its current level of about 50,000 inmates by the year 2000. In response, the federal Bureau of Prisons has already begun a dramatic prison construction program that, by the turn of the century, will double the number of federal facilities and cost billions of dollars. New facilities are coming on line pretty much on schedule every few months. Even so, the system's prisons remain overcrowded.

The second factor has to do with demography. Criminologists have long known that males between the ages of 15 and 35 commit most crimes. As the baby boomers began to drift out of their most crime-prone years in the early 1980s, criminologists expected to see crime rates fall. The rate of decrease, however, has not been as great as anticipated. In addition, two countervailing demographic trends are likely to contribute to increases in the crime rate. One is the "echo boom"—the sons of baby boomers who have their crime "wonder years" ahead of them. The other is the fact that the baby boom never ended among citizens living in the most economically distressed big-city ghettos.

VICTIMS AND VICTIMIZERS

In his influential book *The Truly Disadvantaged*, William Julius Wilson sought to explain the sad lot of the residents of these "underclass" neighborhoods. He focused mainly on deindustrialization

and related socioeconomic trends. It has become increasingly clear, however, that the plight of "the truly disadvantaged" is fostered and perpetuated by the behavior of "the truly deviant"—by the incredible concentrations of career predatory street criminals who live in the midst of and prey upon these overwhelmingly law-abiding, aspiring, and poverty-stricken ghetto dwellers. It is these citizens who are most directly affected by the bulge in correctional populations, and by how that bulge is being managed.

My Princeton colleague Mark Alan Hughes and I have recently completed research that supports what most corrections analysts and officials have long suspected; namely, that the ghetto neighborhoods, of the 1980s have extreme concentrations of crime and extreme concentrations of persons under correctional supervision.

Using census tract data, Hughes, a leading geographer and urban affairs expert, defined "impacted ghettos" as those neighborhoods with levels of deprivation (rates of male unemployment, welfare dependency, female-headed households, and school dropouts) that are twice the average of neighborhoods throughout the surrounding metropolitan areas. In *Poverty in Cities*, a widely circulated 1989 report of the National League of Cities, Hughes showed that between 1970 and 1980, the number of impacted ghettos in Philadelphia, Chicago, Baltimore, and other large metropolitan areas increased by 100 percent or more. As the ghettos became more concentrated geographically, the centers of economic opportunity moved farther away. Eventually, these impacted ghettos evolved into isolated, crime-torn chains of impoverished neighborhoods in which most crime was black-on-black and neighbor-on-neighbor.

• • •

The same basic picture holds for the impacted ghettos of other major cities.

For example, in more than half of Chicago's impacted ghettos, 1 of every 200 residents was behind bars in 1980; in several of them, more than 1 of every 100 residents was imprisoned; and an estimated 6 percent of the residents of Chicago's impacted ghettos were under some form of correctional supervision.

This simple geography of urban crime and correction helps to explain why blacks are victimized by crime at much higher rates than whites, and why criminals and their victims are usually the same race. Most violent crimes against blacks are committed by blacks; most crimes against whites are committed by whites. In 1986, for instance, 83.5 percent of one-offender violent crimes against blacks were black-on-black, while 80.3 percent against whites were white-on-white. For multiple-offender (gang or "wolf-pack") crimes of violence, 79.6 percent were black-on-black, and 59.6 percent were white-on-white.

Similarly, in 1988, Washington, D.C., had 372 murders, 82 percent of them committed on the streets by black males against other black males in the city's impacted ghettos. While reliable data on victim-offender relationships is hard to come by (I am working with the D.C. police to enhance their routine store of such data), my guess is that the impacted ghettos of other major cities are also home to such unprecedented and extreme concentrations of crime, criminals, and correctional supervisees.

Big-city police departments have been doing their best to help bring peace and order to these impacted ghetto communities. So far, however, their best has not been nearly good enough.

If corrections systems compound the failure of the police by doing little or nothing to direct their supervisees into noncriminal pursuits; if prisons and jails are places where the only education young criminals receive is from each other, aggressive and antisocial behavior is the norm, and brazen drug dealers and violent punks are the only available role

models; if street toughs likely to commit new crimes are released prematurely; if probation and parole agents provide virtually nothing in the way of meaningful supervision of these offenders once they are returned to their old neighborhoods; if community-based corrections programs involve no real and sustained effort to enhance the basic life skills and job prospects of those whom it would correct; then all of us must suffer, but citizens trapped in the nation's impacted ghettos must suffer most. For it is they who are most likely to be criminally victimized, or revictimized, by these convicted criminals; and it is they who must languish in poverty and joblessness in part because local commerce is stalled, stunted, or stopped by the real and perceived costs of doing business in the midst of urban crime.

GUARANTEED FAILURE...

Unfortunately, current correctional policies and practices are a recipe for failure.

The quality of life inside prisons, jails, and juvenile "lock-ups" can be defined along at least three dimensions: order, measured by rates of institutional violence such as assault and rape; amenity, measured by the incidence of good food, clean cells, recreational equipment, and other things that minimize the pains of incarceration; and service, measured by the availability of remedial reading, vocational trainings, and other programs intended to enhance the inmates' life prospects after release. On all three dimensions, the quality of life inside most of America's correctional facilities remains poor to wretched.

It has been said before, but is bears repeating: most prisons and jails are run in ways almost calculated to produce low levels of order, amenity, and service, and to reinforce inmates' uncivil, criminalistic behavior. For the most part, the nation's adult and juvenile inmates spend their days in idleness punctuated by meals, violence, and weightlifting.

Meaningful education, vocational, and counseling programs are rare. Strong inmates are permitted to pressure weaker prisoners for sex, drugs, and money. Gangs organized along racial and ethnic lines are often the real "sovereigns of the cellblocks."

Even in many maximum-security institutions, inmates are free to behave behind bars pretty much as they behaved on the streets. Aggressive horseplay is more common than serious study; opportunities for malicious mischief are easier to find than opportunities for productive work; and contraband, including drugs, is pervasive.

Meanwhile, probation and parole agents in many jurisdictions manage 200 to 300 cases apiece. "Community-based supervision" often amounts to a phone call once a month, and sometimes not even that much. With such heavy caseloads, even the most dedicated probation or parole agent cannot keep supervisees on a short leash, or assist them to find work and gain access to drug counseling and other things that may help them stay out of trouble and lead a good life.

Given that most of America's 3.5 million convicted criminals are ill-managed, undermanaged, or not managed at all—it is not surprising that so many correctional institutions are violent and recidivism rates run so high. Indeed, I am amazed that things are not worse both behind bars and on the streets.

...OR PROMISING ALTERNATIVES

This unsettling state of affairs is neither necessary nor inevitable. My own research and that of others show that different correctional policies and practices produce different outcomes. Though they are now the exceptions, three alternative approaches to both institutional and community-based corrections have succeeded for less money than we are now spending to fail. There is no insur-mountable reason why these approaches cannot be employed more widely.

HOUSE ARREST PLUS

There are many different types of house arrest programs. What I call "house arrest plus" refers to community-based programs where the typical supervisee does not have several prior felony convictions; where he is required to stay in or around his home for all but court-approved activities, such as work; where he must meet curfews and other restrictions; where he is subject to electronic surveillance as well as regular face-to-face or telephone contact with supervisors; and where he is incarcerated swiftly and certainly for any violations.

House arrest programs of this type are no picnic for the offender, which may be good, and involve more investment up front than less well-structured programs, which is bad. Especially costly are the electronic monitoring devices themselves—ankle bracelets and other computerized "prison jewelry." New Mexico, for instance, spent nearly $100,000 for its first two dozen bracelets. Moreover, the electronic systems have proven far from bug-proof. In several jurisdictions, officials have gone crazy responding to false alarms; in others, offenders have been found "out of bounds" though they were shown as being at home.

Largely, because of the hefty costs and the technical problems, only about 10 percent of the 10,000 or so offenders under house arrest in 1988 were in these highly structured supervision programs. In early 1989, however, New York City and several other jurisdictions decided to join the 20 states where house arrest has been tried, and most of them seemed to be opting for house arrest plus.

They are wise to do so. Less restrictive house arrest programs simply do not work. Offenders ignore the terms of their release. They miss court appearances. They find it easy to return to their criminal lifestyles and associates, prey upon their old neighbors, and avoid contact with their supervisors, who may have no idea of their true whereabouts. Most judges are rightly wary of placing even"lightweight" offenders in loosely structured house arrest programs.

Thus far, the most extensive experiment with house arrest plus has been made in Florida. Between 1983, when it was started, and 1988 the Community Control program had 5,000 offenders, most of them petty criminals and misdemeanants, but many of them felons. Offenders wear shockproof, tamper-resistant electronic bracelets and pay a monthly fee to defray the costs of the supervision. The program keeps track of offenders through random, computer-generated phone calls as well as through face-to-face contacts with the offender and his relatives, friends, employers, neighbors, and social workers.

Florida officials estimate that 6 or 7 of every 10 house arrestees would have been sent to prison if the program did not exist. On average, it costs nearly $30 a day to keep somebody locked up in Florida's overcrowded prisons. It costs less than $5 a day to keep somebody in its house arrest program. More than 80 percent of the offenders in the program have completed the program without incident.

COMMUNITY SERVICE SENTENCES

Another promising alternative to incarceration places offenders in the community under close supervision and requires them to perform a variety of socially useful tasks, to pay restitution to their victims, and to defray the costs of their supervision. A few dozen jurisdictions have tried various types of community service sentences. But the most extensive, and the only well-studied, community service program was administered by the nonprofit Vera Institute of

Justice in New York City. Douglas C. McDonald, formerly with the institute and now a member of Abt Associates, described and evaluated this program in his superb book, *Punishment Without Walls*.

The program began in 1979. By the end of 1983, some 2,400 offenders, convicted mainly of nonviolent property crimes, were in the program. Most of these offenders would have been sentenced to jail if the program had not existed. Each offender performed at least 70 hours of community service—cleaning nursing homes, painting buildings, cleaning vacant lots, and the like. The offenders worked in small groups supervised directly by a Vera Institutes staff member. Staff members also assisted offenders with housing, transportation, day care, and other needs.

The results of the program were mixed. For example, of 494 program participants tracked for six months after sentencing, 212 of them were rearrested 310 times. McDonald estimated that a third of these rearrests were for crimes committed when, had the program not existed, the offender would have been in jail. He found no meaningful difference in the recidivism rates of program participants and comparable offenders who had been incarcerated. And, he found that most participants declined to describe the program as a punishment; indeed, they felt that it was much less punitive and far more desirable than either jail or conventional probation.

On the bright side, however, the cost of administering the program was $920 per year per offender, a far cry from the $40,000 a year it costs to jail someone on Rikers Island. McDonald estimated that the project saved nearly 260 jail-years overall. Moreover, while he did not make explicit comparisons to conventional probation programs, few observers would doubt that the community service sentences were a better bargain for the city, and more of a boon to public protection, than the unsupervised, unstructured, and socially unproductive alternatives.

INTENSIVE SUPERVISION PROGRAMS

Probably the single most promising alternatives to incarceration are intensive supervision probation and parole programs (ISPs). Unlike conventional programs, which are largely unstructured, ISPs coordinate the offender's every move to see that he is behaving in accordance with the terms of his community-based status.

ISPs subject offenders to mandatory work, community service, and educational activities as well as to random drug and alcohol tests. Participants live in program centers that have no guns or iron bars but that do have strict rules governing chores, curfews, and interactions with other offenders and program staff (or, where there is no center, regular face-to-face contacts with program officers). Their arrest records are checked weekly. They must make payments to victims and payments to offset the costs of supervision. Any violation results in immediate incarceration.

Despite the success of these highly structured programs, the number of offenders in them remains very small indeed; only half a percent of New Jersey's corrections population participated in the intensive supervision program in 1988. Moreover, none of these programs has yet been studied in the most scientific fashion possible (i.e., using random assignment and concomitant controls).

Nevertheless, political enthusiasm has started to build around these "no-nonsense" alternatives. In particular, ISPs are perceived as a viable "intermediate sanction" that satisfies the practical and moral demands of both liberals and conservatives. Conservatives tend to like the programs because they save money and give criminals more than a mere slap on the wrist; liberals tend to like them because they represent a viable alternative to incarceration that protects the community better than conventional approaches.

While I would do nothing to scotch this budding enthusiasm, I would caution that these highly structured alternative programs probably cannot be expanded rapidly without undermining their effectiveness. For one thing they are not easy to staff and administer. For another, they could easily become less careful about keeping "heavies" behind bars and were to use the programs as a "not-too-risky" short-term way to free up beds, reduce institutional overcrowding, and trim costs.

Above all, it should be understood that any political consensus surrounding these programs will remain fragile. A similar consensus on state work-based welfare reform measures that emerged in the 1980s might or might not be weakened by the fact that these programs are performing less well than was anticipated. Politically, however, a program that fails to get x percent of poor citizens off the welfare rolls by a given time is one thing, and a program that fails to keep even one convicted criminal under correctional supervision from harming even one innocent citizen is quite another. The most well-administered ISPs will have their Hortons and their Harveys. That these programs may be more successful overall than incarceration will rarely be enough to buoy them in the wake of the resulting negative publicity, public outrage, and political pressures.

For these and related reasons, including the hard fact that many offenders are dangerous and simply cannot be trusted on the streets, we must make increased use of such promising alternative measures and a wider and saner use of incarceration.

IMPROVING PRISON ADMINISTRATION

Just as there are better ways to handle convicted criminals on the streets, so there are better ways to handle them behind bars. The quality of institutional life is mainly a function of the quality of institutional policies and practices. Let me cite three examples of good institutional management.

Example One. The California Men's Colony (CMC) is a maximum-security prison in San Luis Obispo. When I first visited the prison in the mid-1980s, it was overcrowded, operating at 120 percent of its rated capacity. More than 80 percent of its 2,000 inmates were violent offenders, and virtually all of them were repeat offenders. About 25 percent were incorrigible felons who, according to their official security classification, should have been housed in San Quentin or Folsom, the state's two highest-security prisons, but these facilities were overflowing too.

During a follow-up investigation on CMC in early 1989, I discovered that its population had increased dramatically. Indeed, for the last several years CMC has held over 6,500 prisoners, making it one of the most heavily populated, and overcrowded, prisons in the free world. And its share of hard-core and hard-to-handle offenders had increased as well.

Despite the acute overcrowding, however, CMC remained what it had been for years: the safest, cleanest, most program-oriented, and most cost-effective maximum-security prison in California, and one of the best prisons in the nation. Rates of inmate-on-inmate assaults remained low, as did rates of inmate assaults on staff. Rates of violence actually decreased as the prison became more crowded. Meanwhile, the cellblocks continued to sparkle and the prison industry programs continued to hum. Inmate participation in all sorts of educational and vocational programs grew, recreational facilities were expanded and improved, and the already far above-average institutional meals were diversified and enriched.

All of that was achieved while CMC had the highest inmate-to-staff ratio and the lowest annual expenditures per inmate of any maximum-security prison in California. Levels of order, amenity, and service at CMC were higher than at better staffed and less crowded California Prisons like Soledad where more money per prisoner was spent.

Example Two. In 1974 New York City closed the Manhattan Tombs jail, a filthy, riot-torn, dilapidated facility. Conditions in the Tombs would have made life in a medieval dungeon look good. Under federal court orders, the city built a new Tombs jail in Manhattan. Over the last five years, rates of disorder at the new Tombs have been extremely low; months have passed without a serious assault. Good remedial reading and other programs are offered, and basic amenities have been in ample supply.

It is not merely the new jail architecture that accounts for these improvements. The new Tombs features "unit management," an approach to correctional administration in which uniformed security staff and counselors work as a team in a given cellblock or wing of the jail. Under the direction of a unit manager, a sort of "mini-warden," the team is responsible for managing everything from counting, locking, frisking, and cell-searching, to monitoring inmates' disciplinary records, keeping track of program activities and release dates, and maintaining sanitation.

Despite the success of unit management at the Tombs, most observers doubted that it could be made to work at the city's jails on Rikers Island. But after lots of debate within the department, and lots of political wrangling outside of it, unit management was tried there on a limited basis. Even I was surprised by the results: a 28 percent decline in the rate of violent infractions over an eight-month period compared with the same period the previous year; even greater reductions in the rates of assault and stabbings; better inmate-staff relations, reflected in a nearly 50 percent reduction in the use of force; and a marked improvement in officer morale, reflected in a reduction in absence rates and transfer requests.

Example Three. The federal Bureau of Prisons established unit management in most of its facilities in the early 1970s. In conjunction with a book I am completing on the agency's political and administrative history from 1930 to 1988, I have visited bureau facilities around the country. Though by no means perfect, the bureau's reputation as one of the best correctional systems in the country, and the world, is well-deserved. Overall, levels of order, amenity, and service in its prisons are higher than in any other major prison system in America.

There are two popular explanations for the agency's success relative to most state and local systems, neither of them supported by the facts. One is the "Club Fed" explanation. The federal prison system, it is said, simply gets "a better class of criminals." Historically, however, the agency has never handled only white-collar offenders; in mid-1988, for example, 46 percent of its 50,000 prisoners had a history of violence; and each year the states transfer many of their "too-hard-to-handle" cases to the federal system.

The second explanation is that the federal system outspends most state and local systems. In truth, the Bureau of Prisons spends almost exactly the same as the national median spent per prisoner per year and has, so far as raw statistics permit one to tell, for most of the last 50 years. Moreover, the agency has higher inmate-to-staff ratios than any major prison system in the country.

In each of these examples, and in the dozen or so others that I could add to them, the keys to safe, civilized, cost-effective institutions are enlightened management policies and practices. The CMC, the new Tombs, and the Bureau of Prisons all use some form of unit management. But the administrative similarities among these and other successful institutions go much deeper. In essence, successful institutions are marked by five basic organizational characteristics: stable, hands-on leadership in headquarters and "in-the-field"; a strong organizational culture, high morale, and sense of mission developed around a custodial or security-risk ethic that places a premium on enforcement of the rules governing inmate behavior but that is not inimical to inmate counseling and related activities; excellent line staff training, labor-management relations, and inmate-staff communications; a results-oriented approach that brooks no excuses about security breakdowns, poor sanitation, and other performance problems; and an openness to outsiders—journalists, legislators, judges, extra departmental researchers—with the capacity to influence the institution's fiscal health, operating procedures, and public image.

To be sure, behind most institutional success stories is at least one superb administrator. CMC's Warden Wayne Estelle is a lifelong "prisons man," descended from the first warden of San Quentin and known to may of his peers as "the best warden west of the Rockies." For nearly three decades, the Bureau of Prisons was led by James V. Bennett (1937–64), an extremely intelligent and politically savvy penal reformer who dedicated his life to making the system safe and humane. Bennett's longest-reigning successor, "Big" Norm Carlson (1970–87), was in his own way even more politically savvy and administratively talented than Bennett.

Yet there is every reason to suppose that unit management and related administrative approaches can work well even where they are not put in place or sustained by managers with unique talents and extraordinary gifts. Indeed, in many jurisdictions, including New York City, that has been the case. Fortunately, the possibility of good institutional management, and improved prisons and jails, is not contingent upon "great men."

CORRECTIONS: A NATIONAL PROBLEM

Historically, correctional policies and practices have reflected the virtues and vices of federalism American-style. Those policies and practices have been nothing if not diverse. Over time, however, regional variations in Americans' views of what constitutes just punishment have become less pronounced, conversing around Judeo-Christian ideas of "revenge tempered by forgiveness." Progress in the care and custody of convicted criminals has occurred, albeit very slowly, as knowledge of "what works" has spread unevenly from jurisdiction to jurisdiction. With varying degrees of success, national organizations like the American Corrections Association have attempted to codify, deepen, and disseminate that knowledge through institutional accreditation standards and in other ways.

In recent years, the National Governors Association has been paying more and more attention to corrections; so have conferences of mayors. But the involvement of national policymakers has remained shallow. Corrections now accounts for a larger share of many state budgets than public assistance. Yet welfare reform is treated as a major national domestic public policy issue while penal reform is not. "Domestic defense" (federal law enforcement plus corrections) still accounts for a negligible fraction of the national budget.

While the Department of Justice has been receptive to weakly reasoned ideas about "privatizing" the nation's prisons and jails, no serious attention has been paid to the more pragmatic possibility by which the nation's correctional policies are made and implemented. I believe that it is time to step up the federal role. In my judgment, two unpleasant facts justify increased federal involvement.

First, like it or not, over the next 10 to 15 years, hundreds of new prisons and jails will need to be built, staffed, administered, and financed. Tens of thousands more convicted criminals will have to be supervised in the community. Second, if they are to have any real hope of succeeding, our responses to the problems of underclass neighborhoods, drug abuse, and drug-related violence cannot be police responses made almost entirely at the state and local levels. At a minimum, the government must develop nationally coordinated, intergovernmental responses that integrate courts, cops, and corrections.

As a small first step in that direction, I recommend a major federal commitment to, and a broadened mandate for, the National Academy of Corrections. The academy is a creature of the National Institute of Corrections, itself a research arm of the Bureau of Prisons with a tiny budget. The academy should be expanded to serve as a national anchor of corrections research and training that regularly brings together federal, state, and local policymakers and practitioners to share information, promote promising strategies, and educate the wider public.

This proposal is not terribly sexy or immediately far-reaching. But it is a valuable incremental move that can be made well within the budgetary and political constraints of current national policymaking. In politics and policymaking, symbols matter. If nothing else, the proposed academy would symbolize the nation's long overdue recognition of corrections as a vital area of public concern and give those who work in this most demanding and thankless area of public services a greater sense of public support.

About 10 years ago, when I began my work in the field, an old Massachusetts corrections officer, months from retirement, gave me some depressing advice. "I don't care what research gets done, or what judges or politicians or activists say, or who else is going to get involved," he warned. "Corrections will always be sensationalized, politicized, emotionalized, but most of all forgotten except when riots occur. . . . Don't waste your time on this business." I retain a faint hope that the 1990s may prove my old corrections officer friend wrong.

CHAPTER 7

City Politics

Local governments in the United States come with an almost bewildering assortment of names: county governments; municipal governments, including cities, towns, and villages; township governments; special district governments; and school district governments. A city is a special kind of municipality that is usually distinguished from towns and villages because of its larger population. Almost all cities with a large population face a myriad of problems—increasing crime rates, fewer job opportunities, and struggling school systems, to name just a few. On the other hand, many people, including those who live in the suburbs, see cities as places for leisure activities that include going to museums, theaters, and professional sports events; as locations for the headquarters of financial institutions and other major businesses; and as centers for specialized medical care. On balance, though, today's city governments have a difficult time maintaining the quality of life for people living within their political boundaries.

Of the many problems confronting cities in recent years, one of the most important has been that of economic development. A sound economic base creates jobs for city residents and generates tax revenues that enable a city to provide needed services. The pressure to maintain a viable economic base has led to extensive competition among local government officials trying to convince businesses to locate in their cities. Officials in this contest are able to offer a number of incentives to business leaders; two examples are tax abatements and debt financing. Tax abatements allow a city's elected officials to forgive a business's local financing for a number of years, and debt financing refers to low-interest loans arranged by a city.

The competitive economic environment that cities operate in is illustrated in Reading 17 by political scientist Arthur Johnson, who examines the relationship between minor-league baseball teams and local governments. City officials see the location of a professional sports team in their cities as beneficial to the local economy and to the quality of life enjoyed by the cities' residents. A limited number of sports franchises and a rather high demand for them have created a situation whereby team owners can make their own demands—frequently for new stadiums—on government officials. If these demands are met, the team will stay or move in; if not, the team's owner will probably have little difficulty finding a city that will meet the demands. This is analogous to most economic-development issues facing city officials: What kind of incentives do we have to offer to attract a new business, or retain a business that is thinking of moving? And when does the cost of these incentives exceed the probable benefits?

Johnson discovers that, in the area of minor-league baseball, cities do have quite an investment of their own funds in the construction, renovation, and operation of stadiums, even though the vast majority of teams are privately owned. Nevertheless, city officials reported that minor-league teams were important to the community and they wanted to continue to be a host community. Johnson concludes that the benefits of having a sports team need to be better documented because it could be argued that the money spent in subsidizing sports should be spent on fundamental problems such as education and the homeless.

Reading 18, by political scientists Lawrence Herson and John Bolland, provides an overview of alternative policies to assist cities. In addition, the authors make the important point that not all analysts of today's cities and their problems agree that major efforts, especially federal initiatives, should be undertaken. A number of policies are described—private sector initiatives, urban homesteading, and enterprise zones—but all have had only limited success in battling urban decay. The core problem in large cities is that of urban poverty. Herson and Bolland see no easy solution here, and argue that government-subsidized jobs and other programs will be needed to help the "deserving poor." The proposal for a comprehensive national urban policy that would control business investment and location decisions in a beneficial way for cities might be advocated by some, but it runs counter to our basic belief in a market economy, and consequently is unlikely to be adopted.

QUESTIONS FOR DISCUSSION

1. From a financial perspective, who do you think benefits more from the presence of a minor league baseball team in a community: the team's owners or the local government of the host community?

2. Should money spent by city officials to support or attract a professional sports team be allocated on other things such as education or crime prevention?

3. How do you view large cities? Are they primarily places of "disheartening poverty, crime, drugs, and physical decay"? Or are they "centers of culture and creativity"?

4. What do you think would be the best way for the federal government to help cities? Should they be helped?

17.   Professional Baseball at the Minor League Level: Considerations for Cities Large and Small

Arthur T. Johnson

Fifty American and seven Canadian cities host National Football League, National Hockey League, National Basketball Association, and Major League Baseball teams. The subsidies and the investments in sports facilities for these teams which these cities make are most often justified in terms of the benefits to the local economy which professional sports produce. Cities without major league teams frantically pursue them to create an image as a major league city and to gain intangible contributions to the local quality of life as well as any direct economic benefits that such teams produce.

Thus, local governments, often with the assistance of state governments, as a matter of public policy seek to join "big league cities" either by obtaining an expansion franchise in a particular sport or by luring a team away from its current host community. The scarcity of franchises in a particular sport relative to the demand for franchises is perpetuated by the team owners' refusal to expand the leagues.[1] Reluctance to expand has created a highly volatile market wherein the owner of a franchise can make unlimited demands on a host community and, at the same time, on any number of suitor cities, playing one off against the other. This situation has received attention from the media (more in cities which have lost teams), Congress, and scholars in public policy and law (Fulton 1988, 34–40; Berry and Wong 1986; Johnson and Frey 1985; Johnson 1983, 519–28; Noll 1974).

However, the number of communities with a major league franchise in at least one of the four principal sports is relatively small compared with the number of cities that host other professional sports teams. There are minor leagues in baseball, hockey, and basketball, as well as sports leagues claiming to be major in soccer and lacrosse. Plans have been announced to launch one or more spring football leagues by 1991. Although local government support permits many of these sports operations to be viable, virtually no scholarly attention has been given to these professional sports activities within the context of local government policy and administration.

This article brings attention to the fact that public policy decisions regarding professional sports are not exclusive to a relatively few large cities with major league sports teams. The municipal dimension of public sports policy is revealed be examining whether the relationships between minor league baseball franchises and their local governments are subject to the same political and economic dynamics affecting big league teams and their host communities.

SOURCE: From "Professional Baseball at the Minor League Level: Considerations for Cities Large and Small" by Arthur T. Johnson in *State and Local Government Review*, Spring 1990, Vol. 22, No. 2, pp. 90–96. Reprinted by permission of the author and the Carl Vinson Institute of Government, The University of Georgia.

METHODOLOGY

Data for this article were collected in a mail survey of 148 cities that hosted minor league baseball teams in 1988. The survey was conducted for the International City Management Association

(ICMA) Sports Consortium during December 1988 and January 1989. Cities with teams in AAA, AA, A, and two Rookie leagues—the Appalachian and the Pioneer leagues—were included in the sample. Telephone calls were made to each city to determine who should receive the survey. Respondents included city managers, directors of parks and recreation departments or their equivalent, and facility managers.

An overall response rate of 59.5 percent *(n=88)* was achieved. More than one-half of the cities at each league level, with the exception of AA leagues, responded. Just less than half of the cities with AA teams responded.

BACKGROUND

Historically, minor league baseball teams were owned and operated by major league parent clubs. Within these organizations, minor league operations rarely received priority from a business perspective and were harmed by the advent in the 1950s of telecasts of major league games into their home territories. Between 1949 and 1952, attendance at minor league baseball games declined from nearly 42 million fans to approximately 15.5 million (Horowitz 1974). Slowly, the major league organizations divested themselves of their minor league teams so that today fewer than a dozen teams are owned and operated by major league clubs. The majority of minor league teams are privately owned. A small number are owned and operated by local government or nonprofit organizations organized by local government (e.g., Elizabethton, West Virginia, and Ohio's Lucas and Franklin counties).

The National Association of Professional Baseball Leagues is the governing organization for the minor leagues. The association is composed of a hierarchy of leagues arranged according to the level of competition leading to the major leagues. These leagues are designated AAA, AA, A, and Rookie. The AAA and AA levels

have three leagues each. The seven A leagues are made up of five regular season A leagues, which schedule about 144 games per team, and two short season A leagues, which schedule approximately 70 games per team. Five Rookie leagues of varying degrees of stability—four in the United States and one in the Dominican Republic—also play a schedule of approximately 70 games per team. The Mexican League, not included in the survey, has an AAA designation.

Each major league team has affiliations with at least one AAA team, one AA team, and two regular season A teams. A team can affiliate with as many A and Rookie league teams as it wants or it can decide not to affiliate with any Rookie league team. Some teams at the A and Rookie league levels have no major league working agreement, but operate on a "cooperative" basis in which two or more major league teams contribute players to the minor league team.

These affiliations are negotiated and governed by a formal contract and can change from year to year, depending upon the contractual arrangement. For example, in 1987, 11 of 141 (7.8 percent) teams changed their parent club affiliation; in 1988, 21 of 144 teams (14.6 percent) did so; and in 1989, 9 of 148 teams (6 percent) changed affiliations.

The Player Development Contract between Major League Baseball and the National Association of Professional Baseball Leagues provides the umbrella agreement under which the teams operate. The Player Development Contract is fixed for each league level and cannot be renegotiated by individual teams. It requires the major league team to pay the salaries of a certain number of players on each minor league team, to cover a percentage of the traveling expenses of the minor league team, and to supply equipment within certain limits. Whatever profit the minor league team makes remains with its owners.

More than 17 million fans attended minor league baseball games in 1987 in the 15 leagues which were surveyed and more than 18 million attended games in 1988 (Baseball America 1988, 1989). Attendance at minor league baseball games in 1989 exceeded 23 million. Minor league franchises have sold recently for as much as $5 million. Franchise sales have been brisk, especially those of A league teams which have sold for as much as $3.8 million.

HOST COMMUNITIES

In 1988, more than 150 American and Canadian communities in 37 states and 3 provinces hosted minor league franchises at the AAA, AA, A, and Rookie league levels. Although there is a positive correlation between a city's size and the level at which its team plays, the size of cities which host minor league teams varies widely at each league level.

This variation has implications for league stability. Larger cities have aspirations to join the major leagues or otherwise move up in league level. Thus, AAA cities such as Buffalo, Phoenix, Denver, Indianapolis, and Columbus (Ohio) have made known their desire to obtain a major league expansion franchise.

Other large cities with teams below the AAA level also are pursuing major league franchises. For example, St. Petersburg has an A-level team, but has built a stadium in the hopes of luring an existing team from its present site. In 1988, the city nearly won the Chicago White Sox. Only a last-minute agreement within the Illinois legislature to fund the construction of a new Chicago stadium for the team kept the White Sox from relocating. San Jose, which also hosts an A-level team, had been suggested as a potential site for a future stadium housing the San Francisco Giants.

At the other end of the spectrum is franchise instability. Relatively small communities find it difficult to retain franchises. Within three of the five league levels, the smallest cities lost

their franchises for the 1989 season. In the 10 formal franchise relocations for the 1989 season, Fresno and Tampa were the only cities with a population of more than 40,000 to lose their teams.

In the smallest community at the A league level—Port St. Lucie of the Florida State League—as with many of the Florida communities, the attraction of professional baseball is not minor league baseball but rather spring training, which has become an industry with a significant economic impact. Port St. Lucie recently built a modern sports complex and is now the spring training site of the New York Mets. The Mets own and operate the St. Lucie Mets, making it improbable the team will relocate.

THE STADIUMS

Ownership and Operation

Nearly all of the stadiums where minor league baseball is played are publicly owned. A smaller number, but still the vast majority, also are publicly operated. Stadiums in 94.3 percent of the 88 ICMA survey sample communities are owned by the local government, a parks and recreation district, a public authority, or a school district. Only three of the local governments reported that their stadiums are owned by their teams. However, 23 percent of the communities reported that their teams are responsible for the operation of the stadiums, and an additional 6.9 percent of the communities reported that the local government and the team share operational responsibilities, at least during baseball season.

Age

The stadiums in which minor league professional baseball is played tend to be relatively old, but an increasing number of these are being renovated or replaced. More stadiums (12) were built in the reporting communities between 1983 and 1988 than in any recent similar period although 16 stadiums were constructed in the postwar interval between 1946 and 1951, and 13 were built in the 1935–1940 time span. It is noteworthy that the current stadium construction boom will continue into the 1990s as new stadiums are planned for construction in several cities including El Paso and Durham.

Cost/Financing of Construction/Renovation

The most striking, but the least surprising, difference between the new and old stadiums in the survey is the original construction cost. In communities reporting original cost data, no stadium built before 1960 and only 36.4 percent of those built during the 1960s and 1970s exceeded $1 million in original construction costs, but the cost of 92.3 percent of the stadiums built in the 1980s did so. Indeed, half of the stadiums in the sample which were constructed in the 1980s cost more than $4 million.

Stadiums built in the 1980s have been financed in varied ways including bonds, room (tourist) tax proceeds, and operating revenues. Community Development Block Grant funds were used for one stadium, the only reported instance of federal monies having been used to construct modern ball parks. However, in the sample of those reporting financial information, 45 percent of the 20 stadiums built before 1940 were built at least in part with federal dollars—especially WPA (Works Progress Administration) money.

As with any real estate deal, creative financing may be used to achieve a new stadium. Buffalo, for example, combined a $22 million state loan, $4.25 million in revenue bonds, and $7.7 million in city funds with more than $8 million from 12 other sources to complete its stadium in 1988. On a smaller scale, other communities building stadiums in the 1980s have tapped cable franchise fees and

exploited sale-leaseback arrangements in addition to the financing methods described above.

The stadiums built in the 1980s appear to have been built for teams which were newly arrived in a community. Nearly two-thirds (60 percent) of the stadiums built between 1980 and 1984 house teams which located in their host communities during that time period. Similarly, 77.8 percent of the stadiums constructed since 1984 house teams which located in their communities during that time span. This is further evidence that franchise instability exists in the minor leagues and that there will be increasing pressure upon communities to construct new stadiums in order to fend off the advances of other cities in search of a team.

Not only is there a boom in new stadiums, most (64.8 percent) of the reporting communities recently have been engaged in renovation of their stadiums. All but one of the 57 communities which reported completing at least one renovation project did so in the 1980s. Of the 57 renovation projects, 70.2 percent were begun in 1985 or later.

Renovation projects are most often financed by drawing upon a community's general fund; 43.4 percent of the renovations reported were paid for in this way. Bonds were used in 15.1 percent of the cases and hotel/motel (or tourism) taxes were used in 9.4 percent of the projects (mostly in Florida). Communities used a wide array of other sources to finance their renovation projects, including federal revenue-sharing funds, capital improvement funds, private foundations, state bonds, the major league affiliate of the minor league team, and the stadium's concessionaire.

THE STADIUM LEASE

Leases between cities and their teams range in duration from one month to 30 years. Cities in the sample which host

AAA and AA teams have negotiated longer leases with their teams than have cities with teams at the A and Rookie levels. Whereas nearly two-thirds (60.3 percent) of the A and Rookie league leases are for three years or less, fewer than one-third (30.4 percent) of AAA and AA leases are of such short duration. Leases of more than five years are more common at the AAA and AA levels. Nearly one-half (47.8 percent) of the cities hosting AAA and AA teams enjoy long-term leases, compared with 15.5 percent of the cities hosting lower-level teams. Overall, 75 percent of the cities which reported lease data have leases of five years or less. Leases will be renegotiated in 74.1 percent of the responding cities before the end of 1992.

The Player Development Contract between the National Association of Professional Baseball Leagues and Major League Baseball expires at the end of 1990. When renegotiating the Player Development Contract, the major league teams may demand part of the minor league teams' profits or, more likely, reduce the subsidy given to minor league team owners. This presumably would result in the latter asking host communities to lower rent and other costs tied to the stadium lease.

Beyond stadium rental fees, local governments tend not to share directly in the revenues produced by the teams. Fewer than half (47.1 percent) of the 34 communities whose teams generate parking revenue share in the parking receipts and only 4 of these local governments retain all of them. With only two exceptions, all the sample communities which disclosed financial data reported that their teams generate revenue from advertising within the ball park. However, only 19.5 percent of these communities share in stadium advertising receipts. Finally, 65.5 percent of the teams generate radio/television revenue, but only four of the reporting communities share in this revenue.

Responsibility for costs of stadium maintenance and operation during the baseball season varies a great deal. Local governments tend to assume all (52.4 percent) or a part (19.1 percent) of stadium and field maintenance costs, all (41.7 percent) or a portion (15.5 percent) of the stadium's gas and electric costs, and all (58.3 percent) or a part (4.8 percent) of the stadium's water costs. The teams tend to assume responsibility for all other game-related costs, such as security within (86.9 percent) and around (70.2 percent) the stadium, salaries of ushers (95.2 percent) and ticket takers (97.6 percent), and janitorial services (58.5 percent).

As a result, the majority of those communities which revealed operating costs in support of and revenues derived from minor league baseball for the years 1986, 1987, and 1988 reported expenditures in excess of revenues each year. In 1986, 75.4 percent of the reporting communities experienced a shortfall, as did 73.8 percent of the communities in 1987 and 75 percent in 1988. Whereas nearly all of the communities which reported excess revenues from stadium operations enjoyed surpluses of under $50,000 (85.7 percent in 1986; 75 percent in 1987; 81.3 percent in 1988), fewer were able to keep their stadium operating losses under $50,000 (58.1 percent in 1986; 53.3 percent in 1987; 52.1 percent in 1988).

Local governments, therefore, are not likely to realize an operating surplus from their minor league teams. If they do generate an operating surplus, it will probably be modest compared to the deficits incurred by many of their counterparts.

THREAT OF FRANCHISE RELOCATION

Lease negotiations offer the opportune time for a team to make demands upon its host community. Given the short-term leases which most cities employ, it is not surprising that 66 (76.7 percent) of the responding communities reported that their teams had made demands upon them within the past three years. Nor is it surprising that the most frequent demands centered around improved lease terms (32) and stadium improvement and/or expansion (56). In the responding cities, increased parking was demanded by 11 teams, and a new sta-dium was requested by 9 teams. Operating subsidies were sought by 5 teams.

Team demands for stadium improvements seem to be both justified and effective. Communities which reported renovating their stadiums most frequently cited facility deterioration (42) and team demands (41) as the reasons for undertaking renovations. Seven cities made renovations in an attempt to lure a team at a higher league level.

Of the 20 cities which reported expanding their stadiums, team demands (13) and increased attendance (10) were the most frequently cited reasons for expansion. Six communities enlarged their ball parks as part of their pursuit of a team at a higher league level.

The threat to relocate a sports franchise is often used by major league team owners to obtain compliance with their demands. Although team demands are not always accompanied by a threat to relocate, 24 of 66 communities that reported team demands described being threatened with relocation. Ten of these communities indicated that the threat of relocation actually developed into an issue.

In fact, franchise relocation is not uncommon in the minor leagues. Five franchises relocated in 1987—1 at the AA level and the remainder in A leagues. Seven franchises relocated in 1988—1 at the AAA level and the remainder at the A level. In 1989, 10 franchises relocated—1 at the AAA level, 4 at the AA level (all in one league), and the remainder at the A level.

This count understates the number of relocations because these figures only represent franchises which abandoned their home territory. Other teams moved from one jurisdiction to another, but did not leave their home territory. For example, in 1988, the Birmingham franchise relocated to Hoover, a suburb of Birmingham. Also, in 1989, the Charlotte franchise played its ball games outside the North Carolina border in Fort Mill, South Carolina.

Not every community which loses one franchise is without a team the next season. For example, Watertown, New York, was able to replace its franchise (which relocated to Welland, Ontario) for the 1989 season with an expansion franchise after much debate within the National Association. Also in 1989, Hagerstown's A franchise moved to nearby Frederick, but the city obtained an AA franchise, previously located in Williamsport, which, in turn, obtained Pittsfield's franchise.

It is often argued that a professional sports franchise seeks to relocate due to financial hardship caused by local conditions (i.e., lack of fan support, outdated stadium). The data raise questions about this and other explanations of why teams relocate. Although a slightly higher proportion (33.3 percent) of unprofitable teams than apparently profitable teams (27 percent) threatened to relocate, two-thirds of the former have not made such threats. A similar relationship holds for teams about which respondents expressed concern that financial instability/insolvency was a negative factor for the community. Therefore, it does not appear that financial hardship is a necessary cause of relocation threats in the sample communities.

In order to decrease the likelihood of franchise relocation, many major league communities seek local ownership of their teams. Local ownership is present in 52.3 percent of the reporting minor league communities. However, there is little difference between those communities with and without local ownership in terms of relocation threats from team owners. A slightly higher percentage (34.2 percent) of communities without local ownership than with local ownership (22.7 percent) has been threatened with relocation. However, nearly two-thirds of those communities with nonlocal ownership of their teams report no relocation threats. Thus, local ownership is neither a guarantee nor a necessary condition of franchise stability.

ROLE OF MINOR LEAGUE TEAMS IN THE COMMUNITY

In spite of the financial costs of hosting a minor league team and team demands for additional public expenditures, the responding communities overwhelmingly asserted that maintaining professional baseball is a priority (85.1 percent) and reported general agreement among local government officials that minor league baseball in their communities is important (84.9 percent). However, several communities which host major league spring training camps volunteered that their minor league team's importance was secondary to that of spring training activities.

Spring training has become an industry in itself with a significant economic impact. In 1987, a study commissioned by the state of Florida found that spring training had an economic impact of $295 million. The study found that 150,000 fans accounted for a 1987 attendance level of 1.1 million for 241 games played by the 18 teams which conduct spring training in Florida (*Orlando Sentinel*, September 30, 1987). Arizona claims an economic impact of $144.8 million exclusive of team spending for the seven teams which conduct spring training in that state. The California Angels, which play their spring training games in Palm Springs, California, have an estimated economic impact in that city of $15.5 million. Attendance at Cactus League (as

spring training in Arizona is called) games totaled 597,406 in 1988 (Governor's Special Task Force on Cactus League Baseball 1988, 7–8).

A majority (60.2 percent) of the reporting communities are without other significant sports activities (i.e, no major league sports, no other minor league sports, no training facilities for major league teams, and no college or university sports). More than a third (34.1 percent) of the communities are without a community theater, a symphony orchestra, and/or a zoo. Altogether, 23.9 percent of the reporting communities lack professional or collegiate sports alternatives and these cultural options. Of these communities, 63.2 percent have a population of less than 50,000. Minor league baseball, therefore, offers many communities, especially smaller ones, a significant entertainment opportunity. Asked to name benefits which their communities derive from professional baseball, respondents cited entertainment for their residents (98.9 percent), economic benefits (84.1 percent), regional prestige (83 percent), community identity (83 percent), civic pride (78.4 percent), and the attraction of nonresidents to their communities (72.7 percent).

Respondents infrequently cited negative aspects of hosting professional baseball. Those cited most often were economic in nature. For example, 34.1 percent mentioned disputes over stadium conditions, 30.7 percent identified large public subsidies to keep the team in the city, and 21.6 percent expressed concern over team solvency, a factor often exploited by a team's management for more demands in lease negotiations. Friction with team management (15.9 percent) and neighborhood disruption (17 percent) were less frequently cited as negative aspects.

It appears that communities have decided that the intangible benefits derived from the team's presence and the perceived economic benefits which are received indirectly outweigh the costs of hosting a minor league team. Very few local governments, however, have attempted to document the economic impact of minor league baseball on their communities. Only 11.4 percent of the communities in the sample have done so, and nearly half (40 percent) of these studies were done by the teams.

If professional baseball is important to a community and it is perceived to have an economic impact, it would appear to have potential for economic or community development purposes. Nearly a third (30.2 percent) of the responding communities reported that the presence of minor league baseball is a component of an explicit economic or community development strategy. Asked to describe that strategy, however, few could cite more than their belief that minor league baseball somehow aids the economy ("the multiplier effect"), helps promote the city's image ("referenced in all journals and promos," "media exposure for city"); and adds to the local "quality of life."

CONCLUSION

Minor league professional baseball is important to the communities which host these franchises. These communities perceive professional baseball as making positive contributions to the local quality of life and to the local economy.

These perceptions of local officials, however, do not appear to be based on any objective study of the impact of their teams. More systematic and rigorous research is needed on the impact of professional sports franchises. Research done thus far has been conducted by self-interested parties, such as the teams, their paid consultants, and booster groups. Without impartial analysis, those who advocate using public funds to retain or to obtain a professional sports team will be vulnerable to the crit-

icism of those who question value systems that give priority to the demands of sports entrepreneurs over more fundamental service problems (e.g., assistance for the homeless, educational deficiencies, health care problems).

Local governments, as a matter of public policy, have entered into a relationship with baseball team owners which commonly results in a publicly owned facility which a team leases so that it may produce its product—between 40 and 75 baseball games—for local residents and visitors. A variety of financial arrangements govern this relationship, but as a general rule, an operating surplus is rarely achieved by local government. Local officials, however, can expect a series of demands from team owners related to stadium and playing field maintenance and lease arrangements.

The survey data suggest that the same political and economic dynamics which characterize the relationship between major league teams and their host cities exist between minor league baseball teams and their host communities. It is important, therefore, that local officials, especially in smaller communities:

- negotiate lease arrangements which make franchise relocation more difficult;
- find other partners, especially local business interests, neighboring communities and, possibly, state government to help meet the team's escalating demands; and
- integrate the team into the community's economic and community development plans.

To accomplish these tasks, local officials must understand that professional baseball at the minor league level is no longer just "sport," but that it is made possible by their public policy decisions. Public funds are being invested in support of a generally profitable private business.[2] Regardless of their size, communities which understand this are more willing to respond to team demands with demands and expectations of their own and will be more likely to realize a greater return on their investment. From such negotiations, reciprocal partnerships may emerge.

NOTES

The author acknowledges the support for this project provided by the International City Management Association.

1. The National Basketball Association added Miami and Charlotte as expansion franchises in 1988–89 and Minneapolis and Orlando in 1989–90. The last expansion by the National Football League was in 1976, by Major League Baseball in 1977, and by the National Hockey League in 1974. [Editors' note: Denver and Miami obtained major league baseball teams that began play in 1993.]
2. Seventy-six percent of the survey respondents indicated that they believed the local team produced a profit for its owner. One recent estimate suggested that 75 percent of all minor league teams are profitable (*Time*, August 1, 1988, 38–39).

REFERENCES

BASEBALL AMERICA. 1988. *Baseball America's 1988 directory*. Durham, N.C.: American Sports Publishing, Inc.

———. 1989. *Baseball America's 1989 directory*. Durham, N.C.: American Sports Publishing, Inc.

BERRY, ROBERT, and GLENN WONG. 1986. *Law and business of the sports industries*. Dover, Mass.: Auburn House Publishing Co.

FULTON, WILLIAM. 1988. Desperately seeking sports teams. *Governing* 1 (March): 34–40.

Governor's Special Task Force on Cactus League Baseball. 1988. *Interim report*, 7–8.

HOROWITZ, IRA. 1974. Sports broadcasting. In *Government and the sports business*. Roger Noll, ed. Washington, D.C.: The Brookings Institution, 275–323.

JOHNSON, ARTHUR. 1983. Municipal administration and the sports franchise relocation issues. *Public Administration Review* 43 (November/December): 519–28.

JOHNSON, ARTHUR, and JAMES FREY. 1985. *Government and sport: The public policy issues*. Totowa, N.J.: Rowman and Allanheld.

NOLL, ROGER, ed. 1974. *Government and the sports business*. Washington, D.C.: The Brookings Institution.

18. The Future of Central Cities: Ideologies and Interpretations

Lawrence J. R. Herson and John M. Bolland

Most everyone agrees that the problems of many central cities are massive. Even to present them in barebones outline is

SOURCE: From "The Future of Central Cities: Ideologies and Interpretations" from *The Urban Web* by Lawrence J. R. Herson and John M. Bolland, Nelson Hall, 1990, pp. 447–457. Reprinted by permission.

to yield to the temptation of being discouraged about the future: homeless people living and sleeping on the streets; high rates of unemployment; housing segregation and housing decay; white flight; juvenile street gangs; drug dealing and drug wars; school dropouts; the obsolescence and breakdown of the city's physical plant (water pipes, bridges, sewage systems, and the like), which has been in place often for over a century in the older cities of the Northeast; and for many central cities a declining tax base, which limits the ability of central cities to adequately address this long list of problems.

"WHO SHALL DECIDE WHEN DOCTORS DISAGREE?"

Given the enormity of the problems confronting many central cities—especially the older, industrial cities—it should not be surprising to discover wide and deep disagreement over what, if anything, *should* be done; and there is equally wide and deep disagreement over what, if anything, *can* be done. In general, these disagreements are organized around the fault lines of ideology and the perceptions of reality framed by those fault lines.

Economic conservatives generally take the view that central-city problems are closely linked to the evolution of market societies. Capital flows to places of greatest profitability (they argue), and while dislocations (such as joblessness, housing decay, and technological unemployment) are among the social costs of a market economy, the long-term benefits to the entire society are great. It is an historic truth, they say, that market societies are the freest and most prosperous of all societies. As needed, government ought to assist those individual persons who suffer the consequences of economic dislocations, but it should not engage in massive programs to save the cities.[1]

In a related vein, Banfield (1970, 1974) argues that conditions in central cities have more to do with perception than reality:

For something like two-thirds of all city dwellers, the urban problems that touch them directly have to do with comfort, convenience, amenity, and

business advantage . . . these are "important" problems, but not "serious ones.". . . [Thus,] although things have been getting better absolutely, they have been getting worse relative to what we think they should be. (Banfield 1970, 6, 19)

Liberals, in contrast, advocate federal intervention not only to assist the cities, but also to assist those who live there. It is time, they say, for a return to the compassion that lay behind the Great Society programs; equally, it is time to try again for extensive national programs designed to solve central-city problems. And if massive national programs are not to be invoked, they conclude, then let federal government embark on a series of city-assisting, small-scale interventions.

Framing both sets of arguments is another observation that deals both with changing economic conditions and with perceptions of reality—in this case, the collective perception of the entire society. Cities, writes George Sternlieb (1971), no longer perform their historic function. Formerly, with their deep pools of immigrant labor, they provided the work force that ran the American industrial system. But now, the need for strong backs and the fifteen-hour day

has been reduced to almost nothing by the transportation revolution, which has the effect of homogenizing time and distance. Much of our labor-intensive work is now imported from abroad. Welfare legislation, minimum wages, maximum working hours, and the like have minimized the economic functions of the conglomerations of poor-but-willing people in our cities.

The city, says Sternlieb, has become a *sandbox*, a place where our society has parked those who are no longer productive, so that the rest of society "can get on with the serious things of life" (p. 17).

If our cities have indeed become sandboxes, then perhaps nothing can be done for the cities—except to make the unproductive poor who live there as comfortable as our resources and generosity will permit. And even more important, if society perceives the city as sandbox, then perhaps nothing *will* be done— except again to make the city's unproductive poor as comfortable as our resources and generosity will permit. Is this a realistic perception? Or a counsel of despair? Both perhaps, or neither? It is not so much that only time will tell, but that the idea of the city as sandbox—as a self-fulfilling perception—may get in the way of present and future plans to help the cities.

PRIVATE INITIATIVES WITH AND WITHOUT PUBLIC ASSISTANCE

Gentrification is the word commonly used to describe the process whereby single householders and small-business firms buy up and transform an entire city area. German Village and Victorian Village in Columbus, Ohio, the Lincoln Park area of Chicago, Queens Village in Philadelphia, Capitol Hill and Adams Morgan in Washington, D.C., are all examples of gentrification (Gale 1984, McGrath 1982). As the term itself suggests, gentrification not only restores to former glory the physical character of a residential neighborhood, it also brings to the area a gentry (i.e., middle) class. And perhaps more important, success in restoring one part of the city tends to encourage comparable restorations in other parts of the city.

Most gentrification projects have won the praise of city officials and civic leaders. Some are hailed as the best and surest road to city revival. But hard facts and spillover consequences also travel that same road. The pull of suburban life remains strong among the American middle class, and relatively few in that class give evidence of a desire to return

to the central city. More important and more sobering is the fact that gentrification increases property values and sends rents soaring. As a result, gentrification displaces the poor who once lived in the area, forcing them back into what is likely to be an already overcrowded market for low-rent housing.

Urban restoration is the commercial counterpart of gentrification, in which old business buildings are bought and restored through private enterprise. All forms of urban revitalization receive some form of government assistance (at the very least, an income-tax benefit for interest paid on borrowed money). But urban restoration projects also receive additional forms of government assistance. For example, in 1966 Congress enacted a law establishing the National Register of Historic Buildings. Buildings designated for inclusion in the register are protected from the wrecker's ball; more important, those who restore them are eligible to receive a restoration grant. In this way (and often with further assistance from local and state government), several cities now proudly display restored areas of Victorian and Romanesque architecture: Pioneer Square in Seattle; the former Tivoli Brewery (a Hollywood-Bavarian fantasy of shops, offices, restaurants, and cinemas) in Denver; the Old Post Office building (a multi-storied atrium, banked by restaurants and boutiques) in Washington, D.C.; the Lit Brothers Department Store Block in Philadelphia; the Ohio Theatre (a 1920s Moorish fantasy) in Columbus; and an area of small art-deco hotels in the south Miami Beach area (to name only a few such restorations).

Urban restoration projects do much to bring a sense of life and vitality back to central cities. They bring shoppers and strollers to the central business district, add jobs to the work force, and enhance the city's tax base. Perhaps most important of all, they give visual and sensual pleasure to those who appreciate the bustle of urban life and its kaleidoscopic variety. But there is also criticism of these urban restoration projects which bears an old and familiar ring. They divert money to the benefit of the privileged classes that might be better spent on overcoming the problems of the urban underclass.

URBAN HOMESTEADING

Successful public policies remain locked in memory long after they cease to be. During the Civil War, in an attempt to open the West for settlement, Congress passed the Rural Homestead Act of 1862. Under the act, settlers could stake out 160 acres of homestead. If a settler family built a house on those acres, lived there, and cultivated the land for at least five years, then on payment of a modest fee the land would belong to the family. ("A five year bet with Uncle Sam" was the refrain of a song of that time.)

Rural homesteading was a considerable success, and many Plains states families today trace their farmstead back to the Homestead Act. Recalling that success, policymakers in the 1970s, as they confronted the problem of urban decay, transferred the idea of homesteading to the central city. Baltimore and Philadelphia were among the first to try the idea of urban homesteading, and as the idea gathered wider support, Congress in 1974 authorized a national homesteading program. Under the terms of the Housing and Community Development Act, cities were invited to "designate a target neighborhood that was not severely blighted, but which contained HUD-owned one-to-four family properties" (Marshall 1985, 6).

Each city would receive from HUD money sufficient to buy a number of these properties (each valued at less than $15,000), which the city, in turn, would hand over to urban homesteaders. Homesteaders were required to live in these homes for at least three years, repair and restore them (usually with the assistance of low-interest federal loans), and at the completion of restoration and occupancy, would come into ownership of their refurbished property.

Overall, and nationwide, only a few thousand houses have been homesteaded. Some critics explain this meager success by arguing that the homesteading experience was a nightmare of government rules, regulations, and red tape. Others argue that home ownership is essentially a middle-class attribute, and those who have this attribute do not want to live in areas targeted for homesteading, while those who live (and are willing to live) in those areas are usually lacking in middle-class attributes.[2]

ENTERPRISE ZONES

Following Ronald Reagan's election to the presidency in 1980, many conservative policy planners began advocating enterprise zones (i.e., designated inner-city areas in which private enterprise would be given tax benefits and other forms of government assistance). The idea was to attract business enterprises to those areas, thus providing jobs for those who lived there. The idea behind enterprise zones is straightforward. No matter what other measures may be tried (say enterprise-zone advocates), in the end the quality of urban life will rise or fall in accordance with the success or failure of private enterprise; for it is business enterprise, not government, that provides the surest, most efficient instrument for lifting the poor out of poverty.[3]

About twenty states have enacted enterprise-zone legislation; and while many in those states have claimed success for their enterprise zones, their overall impact on the economy of inner cities has thus far been minuscule.

BUSINESS FIRMS IN THE INNER CITY

But with or without enterprise zones, several large corporations have established a presence in the inner city. Their purpose is essentially philanthropic and civic-minded (though they do benefit from federal tax programs that offer tax benefits to businesses hiring new entrants into the job market and the hard-core unemployed). In most cases, "urban-blight enterprises" are moved forward by the same rationale as the urban-enterprise zones: Business, not government, is to be the effective lever of urban transformation. For example, Control Data Corporation has built factories and hired inner-city workers in a number of cities: Minneapolis, St. Paul, San Antonio, Toledo, Baltimore, and Washington, D.C. (*Ebony*, June 1982).

As is the case with urban restoration, enterprise zones, and other private initiatives, the "corporation in the ghetto" has had many individual successes, but no overall success. Perhaps those who expect massive changes in the inner cities expect too much. Or perhaps the problems of setting up a manufacturing plant in an inner city are so great that big companies become intimidated and are too easily discouraged.

LOOKING TO THE FUTURE: URBAN ECONOMIC TRENDS

Those who scan the economic skies looking for a revival of heavy industry in America must surely be doomed to disappointment. Steelmaking, automobile making, and most of their related industries have fled to the havens of cheaper labor abroad. And textiles, electronics, and a host of other industries that once made American production a source of domestic pride and foreign envy have also gone abroad (Bluestone and Harrison 1982, Reich 1983). In cities of the Midwest, Northeast, and along the Atlantic coast, those were the industries that were major employers for skilled and semi-skilled workers. And those, too, were the industries that had once

been magnets for city-bound immigrants from rural America and from abroad.

Now those industries are mostly shut down, their jobs gone and not likely ever to return. And the once thriving textile, steelmaking, and automobile cities are riddled with unemployment and tagged with the title "rustbelt" cities. What, then, is going to take the place of employment in textiles and heavy industry? Service jobs, say most economic forecasters. To bear this out, 80 percent of the jobs created since 1980 have been in the service sector—and more than half paid less than $7,000 a year (Report, University of Michigan Business School, cited by Tom Hundley in the *Chicago Tribune*, June 20, 1988). Along the same lines, Peter Drucker (a noted writer on economic trends) predicts that, by the year 2000, the number of people holding jobs in manufacturing will have dropped from 20 percent to 10 percent of the national work force (Lockwood and Leinberger 1988).

But service jobs pay far less than manufacturing jobs, and the transition to a service economy is especially disruptive for those moving from skilled industrial jobs into the service sector. To make matters worse—at least for rustbelt cities—a significant portion of the manufacturing jobs that will be available in the year 2000 are forecasted to be in the sunbelt.

What, then, of future service jobs for most central-city workers? Who will provide them? And what will they be like? Perhaps part of an answer is to be found in a recent report on Cleveland, Ohio:

In a blue-collar neighborhood where there once were small factories and tool shops, a giant, pink granite pyramid rises above the cold smokestacks and wood frame houses. . . . This is the Cleveland Clinic, a medical complex that has gained international fame . . . and now stands as a graphic symbol of the city's transition from a manufacturing to a service economy. With 9,134 employees, the clinic is the city's largest private employer, a plateau it achieved when it passed LTV Steel, the nation's No. 2 steelmaker, which is mired in bankruptcy proceedings. . . . "It's not a healthy sign for a hospital to be the No. 1 employer in a city as big as Cleveland," said . . . the clinic's chief executive. (Hundely, in the *Chicago Tribune*, June 20, 1988).

THE URBAN POOR

Sooner or later, most attempts at improving, revitalizing, or saving our central cities lead us back to considering the urban poor. A great number of the problems considered to be big-city problems are bound up with the presence there of millions mired in poverty. During the 1980s, much thought but little policy action was given to the plight of the urban poor. There are numerous explanations for this inaction. One is an emotional weariness that followed the great expenditure of civic and policy energies on Great Society programs, along with disappointment over the perceived failures of those programs. A second is a national swing to the conservative right, as signalled by Ronald Reagan's election. A third explanation centers around a spiraling national deficit that crowds out new domestic policy initiatives. And, most telling of all, inaction can be explained by a widespread sense (and a fear) that, as far as poverty is concerned, nothing really works.

As the 1990s begin, the public temperament may be changing. Concern for the poor, both rural and urban, seems to be climbing back onto the national policy agenda. Journals of intellectual opinion pull our memories back to the riots of the 1960s and remind us of what can befall a society in which the Kerner Commission's "two nations" stand separated and intact. Many such journals have begun to make an inventory of "poverty programs that work." Many of these are

of the small-scale variety, relying on local rather than federal initiatives: for example, a Chicago bank that makes mortgage loans to inner-city borrowers; an Allegheny County program that created a community college offering job training to former steel workers; the promise of a privately funded, college education to inner-city youth who finish high school. The purpose of such inventories is not only to provide a pool of future policy alternatives, it is also to keep alive a public view that poverty programs can be made to work (e.g., *Washington Monthly*, June 1988).

In framing future poverty programs, policymakers are likely to invoke two long-standing ideas, one liberal, the other conservative.[4] The liberal idea involves an investment in *human capital*, resting on the belief that public money spent on job training and education is the surest, best way to ensure national prosperity and a rising standard of living (e.g., Reich 1983, Thurow 1980). The conservative idea establishes a distinction between the deserving poor (those who want to work and are able to work) and the undeserving poor (those who are able to work but have little wish to do so). This distinction accords with what many perceive to be traditional American values (a work ethic, a success ethic); and it also accords with a widely held belief that no one has an inherent right to an income—that "workfare" (i.e., government-subsidized employment) is preferable to welfare.

Thus, future poverty programs are likely to be grounded on the idea of an investment in human capital: job training, education to overcome illiteracy, and workshop experience that instills habits of work-force discipline. (To the extent that present policy is forerunner of future policy, we should note that Congress' welfare reform legislation of 1988—the Family Security Act—embodies these same principles.)

Time was, not long ago, that any distinction between the deserving and the undeserving poor would have given rise to fierce ideological debate. For conservatives, all who received public money were to be regarded as recipients of charity, and charity was a gift to be reserved for the deserving. For liberals, a commitment to equality of outcomes was sufficient to make the idea of charity demeaning to the human spirit and an affront to the idea of income as a social right. For them, there could be no easily established distinction between the deserving and the undeserving poor.

Complicating matters have been accusations of racism and elitism. Is a distinction between the deserving and the undeserving poor only a disguised racism, a way of doing nothing to assist poor Hispanics and blacks? Is it a way of blaming the slums on those who live there—in short, a way of blaming the victim?

However, a national belief may now be emerging that this distinction does have validity, and that the deserving poor ought to be saved from what a journal of liberal opinion has recently called a "destructive ghetto culture" (*New Republic*, June 13, 1988). It is a culture, says Christopher Jencks, of "sane, healthy adults who refuse to follow norms of behavior that most of society endorses," a culture that "approves (or at least fails to disapprove) of idleness, single parenthood, theft, and violence" (*New Republic*, June 13, 1988).

However, to identify and thus characterize a destructive ghetto culture is not to be unmindful of its many causes and sources (e.g., Wilson 1987, Auletta 1982), not least of which may be a social and economic system that has driven jobs and good housing out of urban centers; the manifold inheritances of what the Kerner Commission called white racism; and the propensity of contemporary America to see the inner city as a sandbox. But even when these things are said, it is a destructive ghetto culture that

gives greatest worry to those concerned about the future of American cities (liberals and conservatives alike), for it is a culture that stubbornly resists attempts to change it.

This growing national consensus is likely to target future poverty programs toward the deserving poor. But with this in mind, we should reexamine the statistics on poverty, which tell the story of an underclass that is, for the most part, deserving. Consider the following statistics:

- Over 50 percent of the families living in poverty have one or more members in the work force, most of whom work at least part time on a continuing basis.
- Children under seventeen account for approximately 42 percent of the people living in poverty, with the elderly accounting for another 13 percent.
- Nearly one-quarter of those heads of households who do not work are ill or disabled, with another 40 percent caring for children and/or keeping house.

Providing these deserving poor with the opportunity to escape the pathology of the ghetto represents an ideal that both liberals and conservatives applaud. Given society's commitment to a market economy, this opportunity will most likely come in the private sector, in the form of government-subsidized jobs and training programs. But it will also be costly. For example, job opportunities for mothers with small children make little sense in the absence of day-care programs. And even more critical, few families can survive on the $7,000 annual salary that many new service jobs are paying; therefore, workfare may need to be supplemented with other forms of income. But whatever its form, a rethinking of the assumptions (both liberal and conservative) about poverty may be necessary if the poverty of the cities is to be overcome. Success will require not only patience and policy inventiveness, but also a public willingness to account even small successes as major accomplishments.

A NATIONAL URBAN POLICY?

In the years to come, Congress will no doubt enact many programs designed to assist American cities. And many policy entrepreneurs are likely to suggest that the United States follow Europe's lead in establishing government programs that work at revitalizing entire regions, not single cities. (Examples include Germany's assistance to the heavy industries of the Ruhr valley and Britain's system of incentives to persuade business firms to move northward, away from the overcrowded "home counties.") Others are likely to suggest that the national government create something on the order of an Urban Development Bank, making long-term, low-cost loans to business firms willing to build (or stay) in central cities.

Still others may push for a grant-in-aid program to the states—framed with Europe's experiences in mind—to encourage the states to enact statewide controls over land development and land use, and perhaps even create a special government authority over each of the state's metropolitan areas. (Sweden, for example, has given the city of Stockholm the authority to buy up extensive tracts of land all around the city, and the city has developed a ring of satellite suburbs which are famous for their orderly planning and high quality of urban amenities; see Heidenheimer et al. 1975.)

Perhaps most visionary of all will be those who push for a comprehensive national urban policy. That policy, if it is to be truly national and truly comprehensive, would most likely authorize some form of national control over the locational and investment decisions of private business, controlling where they are to be located and the purposes for which they are to be permitted to invest

their capital (e.g., Smith 1979, Kantor 1988, Moynihan 1969b).

Of all these possible policies, only some form of an Urban Reconstruction Bank seems even remotely likely. Although economic Conservatives are likely to oppose it, an Urban Reconstruction Bank does have historic precedent (the Reconstruction Finance Corporation of the Great Depression), and it is in some degree ideologically compatible with our society's attachment to a market economy (see, for example, the writings of investment banker Felix Rohatyn 1981). In contrast, a regional development plan would run counter to the highly developed sense of localism that lies at the heart of our system of congressional government. Thus Congress is likely to be wary of any proposal to assist one region of the country at the expense (or so it will be presumed) of other parts of the nation.

Statewide controls over land use and metropolitan development run counter to our tradition of local governments as republics in miniature—not to mention our long history of land development as opportunity for the business entrepreneur and the strength of our belief that land and buildings are commodities to be bought and sold for profit.

As to the idea of a comprehensive national urban policy, its realization seems remotest of all. It, after all, strikes at almost everything held sacred by protectors of a market economy: the rights of a business to locate where it wishes and to decide how and for what purposes it is to invest its capital. And perhaps even more important as an impediment to the development of a national urban policy is the fact that as a society we have no consistent vision of what it is that we wish our cities to be, nor have we arrived at a consensus concerning the role that cities are to play in our national life. Our vision of cities is clouded by an ambivalent regard: We see them as symbols of accomplishment and as creators of culture and wealth, but we also see them as places of violence and evil that are merely to be endured. Side by side, both visions work to constrain our policy options. What, then, lies in store for our cities?

THE FUTURE OF AMERICAN CITIES

As those who read science and social fiction well know, cities have traditionally played a central role in futurist writings. From Plato onward to the early twentieth century, what was imagined as a utopian future was usually set in the city, for the city was characteristically seen as the instrument of human progress. Then, in our own century, futurist writing became darker and more pessimistic. The city remained as the place where the future was imagined; but now mankind's fate was seen to be painful and problematic. And the city was not utopia, but *dystopia*—the symbol and instrument of human suffering and political repressions.[5]

If present trends continue—barring war or a wrenching economic depression—what the future holds for many American central cities is probably something between the antipodes of utopia and dystopia. They will remain places of disheartening poverty, crime, drugs, and physical decay, but also places that will continue to fulfill many of our dreams of the good urban life: places of visual and architectural variety; places of economic opportunity and productivity; places for the stroller's enjoyment, with thronging sidewalks and (it is to be hoped) safe passage; and above all, centers of culture and creativity.

NOTES

1. See, for example, Friedman and Friedman (1981) and Wanniski (1978). For the argument that government's role is to assist the private entrepreneur, see Gilder (1981). And for extension of the proposition that democratic societies historically have evolved inside market societies, see Lindblom (1977) and Friedman and Friedman (1981).

2. Few ideas invoke more argument than defining the psychological attributes and personality structure of the middle class. Karl Marx spoke of the outlook of the bourgeois class, and to be one of its members still carries a derisive overtone. Even so, there is a good deal of agreement that to be middle class in America (whatever one's income) is to have a sense of thrift, a self-discipline that puts the future ahead of the present (and its demands for immediate gratification), and an ability to plan for that future. More than one hundred fifty years ago, Tocqueville (1945) saw these attributes as the essence of the American character, and it worries many contemporary scholars—as well as ideologists—that these attributes may be disappearing from American life. (See, for example, Riesman 1950; Gilder 1981; and for a recent inquiry into the conflict between private desires and the public good, see Bellah, et al. 1985). Even so, a fierce intellectual debate followed Banfield's (1970) assertion that the urban poor differed from the rest of American society precisely on grounds that they were outside the middle-class value structure.

3. Critics of these programs argue that economic opportunities for the underclass may be largely meaningless without social opportunities provided by improved health care, housing, and education. While these improvements may be obtained through economic opportunities, they come slowly if the poor must rely solely on their earnings; and in the meantime, substandard health or housing may threaten

continuing employment. Finally (argue the critics), without job skills, the urban poor are likely to receive only minimum wage, which may be insufficient to pull them from the cycle of poverty.

4. This, again, reaffirms a long-standing political tradition: In difficult decisions, no side is likely to leave empty-handed.

5. This pessimistic view not only pervades twentieth century fiction, but also art and films. See, for example, George Grosz's painting *Metropolis* (1917) and films such as Fritz Lang's *Metropolis* (1926) and Martin Scorsese's *Taxi Driver* (1976).

REFERENCES

AULETTA, KEN. *The Underclass*. New York: Random House, 1982.

BANFIELD, EDWARD C. *The Unheavenly City*. Boston: Little Brown, 1970.

BANFIELD, EDWARD C. *The Unheavenly City Revisited*. Boston: Little Brown, 1974.

BELLAH, ROBERT N.; MADSEN, RICHARD; SULLIVAN, WILLIAM M.; SWIDLER, ANN; and TIPTON, STEVEN M. *Habits of the Heart: Individualism and Commitment in American Life*. New York: Harper and Row, 1985.

BLUESTONE, BARRY and HARRISON, BENNET. *The Deindustrialization of America: Plant Closings, Community Abandonment, and the Dismantling of Basic Industry*. New York: Basic, 1982.

FRIEDMAN, MILTON and FRIEDMAN, ROSE. *Freedom to Choose*. New York: Avon, 1981.

GALE, DENNIS E. *Neighborhood Revitalization and the Post-industrial City: A Multinational Perspective*. Lexington, MA: Lexington, 1984.

GILDER, GEORGE. *Wealth and Poverty*. New York: Basic, 1981.

GRATZ, ROBERTA B. *The Living City:*
Thinking Big in a Small Way. New York: Simon and Schuster, 1989.

HEIDENHEIMER, ARNOLD J.; HECLO, HUGH; and ADAMS, CAROLYN T. *Comparative Public Policy: The Politics of Social Choice in Europe and America*. New York: St. Martin's, 1975.

KANTOR, PAUL. *The Dependent City: The Changing Political Economy of American Urban Politics Since 1789*. New York: Scott Foresman, 1988.

LINDBLOM, CHARLES E. *Politics and Markets: The World's Political Economic Systems*. New York: Basic, 1977.

LOCKWOOD, CHARLES and LEINBERGER, CHRISTOPHER B. "Los Angeles Comes of Age." *The Atlantic*, 1988, 261 (1), 31–56.

MCGRATH, DENNIS. "Who Must Leave? Alternative Images of Urban Revitalization." *Journal of the American Planning Association*, 1982, 48, 196–203.

MARSHALL, FOSTER, JR. "Urban Homesteading in Columbus: Success in the Politics of Perception." Unpublished Honors Thesis, The Ohio State University, 1985.

MOYNIHAN, DANIEL PATRICK. "Toward a National Urban Policy." *The Public Interest*, 1969, 17, 3–20.

REICH, ROBERT B. *The Next American Frontier*. New York: New York Times, 1983.

RIESMAN, DAVID. *The Lonely Crowd: A Study of the Changing American Character*. New Haven: Yale University Press, 1950.

ROHATYN, FELIX. "Reconstruction of America." *New York Review of Books*, March 5, 1981.

SMITH, MICHAEL P. *The City and Social Theory*. New York: St. Martin's, 1979.

STERNLIEB, GEORGE. "The City as Sandbox." *The Public Interest*, 1971, 25, 14–21.

THUROW, LESTER. *The Zero Sum Society: Distribution and the Possibilities for Economic Change*. New York: Basic, 1980.

TOCQUEVILLE, ALEXIS DE. *Democracy in America.* Henry Reeve text, edited by Phillips Bradley. New York: Knopf, 1945.

WANNISKI, JUDE. *The Way the World Works: How Economics Fail and Succeed.* New York: Simon and Schuster, 1978.

WILSON, WILLIAM J. *The Truly Disadvantaged: The Inner City, the Underclass, and Public Policy.* Chicago: University of Chicago Press, 1987.

CHAPTER 8

Politics in Metropolitan Areas

As everyone knows, the United States has become a predominantly metropolitan nation since World War II. After the 1990 census there were 284 metropolitan statistical areas—defined as urban cores of at least 50,000 people, including immediate suburbs and adjacent communities that have a high degree of economic and social interaction with the core city. The percentage of Americans living in metropolitan areas increased from 56.1 in 1950 to 77.5 in 1990. For the first time a majority of Americans (50.2 percent) live in areas of 1 million or more people.

Since 1970, a majority of those living in metropolitan areas have been located in suburbs. In the 1980s the pattern across the country was that metropolitan areas grew fastest on their fringes. Even in the Sun Belt, in places such as Phoenix and Houston, most of the population growth was suburban. As in the 1970s, the rate of growth of the Sun Belt states in the 1980s was about four times that of the rest of the country. Much of that growth was in mid-sized (100,000 to 400,000) suburbs located on interstates, some distance from central cities. For example, Mesa, Arizona, and Rancho Cucamonga, California, both grew over 83 percent in the 1980s. This pattern has created numerous satellite cities with their own business districts and industry that are largely independent of old, central cities. This can be seen in the north as well as in Sun Belt states. For example, in metropolitan Detroit, the Pistons play basketball in Auburn Hills, forty miles from downtown, and the Lions play football in Pontiac, thirty miles from downtown. Suburbanites can shop in dozens of malls while downtown Detroit doesn't have a single department store.

In the 1950s suburbs seemed to be a homogeneous group of white, upper-class, bedroom communities. Increasingly, suburbs have become more diverse: populations have aged, minorities have moved in, service jobs have been created, and as we have noted, new types of satellite cities have developed. At the same time many of the problems of big cities—crime, pollution, traffic congestion—are now problems for suburbs.

In Reading 19, political scientist Gary A. Tobin presents an overview of housing segregation in the 1980s. The articles referred to by Tobin are from a publication he edited titled *Divided Neighborhoods: Changing Patterns of*

Racial Segregation. While there are more blacks living in suburbs than in 1970s, Tobin points out that most blacks who live in suburbs live in predominantly black neighborhoods. Discrimination has been more subtle, but the effect is to maintain segregated neighborhoods and keep many suburbs overwhelmingly white. Tobin feels that we need positive government action, including investigative actions and increased development funds for integrated neighborhoods, if we are to achieve a change in the racial living patterns of America's cities and suburbs.

While there has been substantial social, cultural, and economic change in many suburbs, the basic political problem of metropolitan areas—fragmentation—remains. As data from the 1990 census make clear, the number of overlapping governmental units in metropolitan areas is at an all-time high. This means that public services in each metropolitan area are provided by an array of governments and there is little coordination of their activities. The results, as pointed out in all textbooks, are confusion, duplication of services, a lack of political responsibility, and the inability to deal effectively with many policy matters.

Most political scientists recommend greater political consolidation among cities, counties, and special district governments in metropolitan areas. In Reading 20, political scientist David B. Walker discusses seventeen distinct types of metropolitan cooperation, ranging from those that are relatively easy to accomplish to those that are very difficult. Walker believes the federal government has been hostile toward taking a role in metropolitan governance, and thus these areas must try to establish types of interlocal cooperation on their own initiative.

Consolidation efforts have met with only minimal success because there is political opposition from suburbs *and* central cities. Suburban residents and business owners fear their taxes will be raised to pay for services to poorer residents in central cities. Suburban homeowners also are concerned about losing control over the use of land and about population density if zoning changes allow a greater mix of dwellings. At the same time residents of central cities (often a black majority) are concerned that they will lose their political clout if they are submerged in a large metropolitan area where a majority of the total population is white and suburban.

Finally, some argue that fragmentation is good because it provides easier access to government officials, people feel a greater sense of personal effectiveness, and they can identify themselves better as part of a small community. It is contended that the economies of scale are overrated and that more often large government leads to greater bureaucratization and inefficiency. Services may become impersonal in big governmental units, and they become less innovative when not in competition with other localities in their metropolitan area.

The search for the ideal size of community and mix of services will continue to be a lively topic for academics. Others are content with more limited goals: better schools, lower taxes, workable recycling.

QUESTIONS FOR DISCUSSION

1. Discuss the two myths about housing segregation that Tobin debunks.

2. In what ways can we blame government for continuing racial segregation in housing? What are the prospects for change in the 1990s?

3. Which of Walker's seventeen approaches to regional service delivery have been tried in your area? How successful have they been?

4. Seek out information on Metro Toronto and compare regional government there to regionalism in the United States.

19. Housing Segregation in the 1980s

Gary A. Tobin

Patterns of housing segregation in the 1980s differ from those of the 1950s or the 1940s, but they are no less real. More than twenty years have passed since the landmark open housing legislation of the 1960s. Yet the vast majority of the nation's minorities, particularly blacks, remain locked in segregated neighborhoods throughout the United States. Segregation remains, largely as a function of continued discrimination, albeit usually more subtle than the discrimination of the past. Persistent patterns of racial segregation are also the legacy of the actions in both the public and private sectors. Discrimination was institutionalized into housing markets throughout most of this century. Although some discriminatory practices have been largely abandoned, or greatly reduced, others have become integral components of neighborhood selection, sales, and financing. The past restrains the present, but segregative actions also continue unabated.

It would be simplistic, however, to

SOURCE: From "Divided Neighborhoods: Changing Patterns of Racial Segregation" by Gary A. Tobin, pp. 8–14, Sage Publications, *Urban Affairs Annual Reviews*, Vol. 32, 1987. Reprinted by permission of Sage Publications, Inc. Copyright© 1987 by Sage Publications, Inc.

argue that nothing has changed in the past forty years. Racially restrictive covenants are no longer enforced in the courts; Realtors rarely openly refuse to show blacks houses in certain neighborhoods; and federally subsidized housing in no longer sanctioned to be racially segregated. At least on paper, through legislative and some judicial and executive actions, housing discrimination, and the subsequent segregation of neighborhoods, constitutes a violation of civil rights in the 1980s.

But two myths about the nature of housing segregation continue today. Both of them should be finally put to rest. The first myth holds that great strides have been made every decade in reducing the overall segregation of minorities. Especially in the post-1960s era, it is believed that everybody could live where they choose, and therefore "past" problems have been resolved. The second myth holds that where housing segregation has not disappeared, it is a function of two factors. The first is that minorities are poor, and housing markets segmented by income, find racial segregation as an artifact. Second, minorities cluster together because they are showing a revealed preference for living among people of their own kind.

Overwhelming evidence has always

refuted these arguments. Poor whites are no more likely to live with poor blacks than upper middle-income blacks are to live with upper middle-income whites. If class or income were really influential in patterns of racial segregation, then the levels of racial isolation should have been reduced a great deal some time ago. Of course, where the income argument fails, the revealed preference argument is introduced. Whites prefer not to live with blacks, even though blacks may prefer to live with some whites, and therefore dislocation in the market is always present. In short, whites simply do not want to live with blacks in great enough proportions to support integrated neighborhoods.

Most whites do indeed avoid black neighbors. But these preference arguments have always failed to take into account the role that institutions played in molding racial attitudes. The history of both governmental and private sector actions, a partnership of discriminatory practice throughout most of the twentieth century, set standards in which individuals made their housing choices. Racially restrictive covenants were enforced by the state, utilized by FHA as a means for evaluating neighborhood stability, and utilized by bankers, insurers, and realtors in everyday housing market operations. Federally subsidized housing was segregated by race. In many states, public schools were legally segregated, reinforcing existing housing patterns and vice versa. Blacks and other minorities were openly and blatantly refused housing in white areas.

By the 1950s, the patterns of racial segregation had been institutionalized to the point that the entry of a black into a white neighborhood signaled a rapid transition that often resulted in panic. By helping to construct a totally segregated housing system, governments at all levels and often housing market actors such as realtors, insurers, and bankers, helped mold straightforward and rigid guide-

lines for the housing consumer. The system was simply understood: If blacks or other minorities entered a neighborhood, they must be either driven out, which was often the case, or white residents should begin looking for housing elsewhere. Both of these practices continue today. In this system, individual choice becomes a nonsensical notion. Segregation could give way only to resegregation, from white to black. The sooner the white residents left a transitional neighborhood, the less risk they incurred in terms of property values declining, increased crime, and deterioration of the public schools. Purchasing a home in a transitional area also constituted a big risk. For blacks, a great "neighborhood chase" was perpetually under way, looking for stable neighborhoods that were by their very nature destabilized the moment they entered them. The legacy of these practices continues to frame housing market systems in the 1980s.

In his article entitled "Choosing Neighbors and Neighborhoods: The Role of Race in Housing Preference," Joe Darden effectively dismisses the preference for one's own kind argument. He traces the literature, and reveals the flaws in these arguments. In "Housing Market Discrimination and Black Suburbanization in the 1980s," John Kain shows that income is a very poor explanation for patterns of racial segregation. John Yinger ties these two pieces together in "The Racial Dimension of Urban Housing Markets in the 1980s." Together, the three authors definitively demonstrate that discrimination and the legacy of discrimination, not preference or income, continues to be the leading cause of segregated housing markets in the 1980s.

The legacy of the past, particularly the actions of local governments, is described by Yale Rabin in "The Roots of Segregation in the Eighties: The Role of Local Government Actions." Urban renewal projects, the location of highways, clearance of black neighborhoods, and other actions all had the effect of reinforcing segregated housing patterns. Failure to take any actions on the part of these same governments in the 1970s and 1980s to reverse the patterns that they helped create in earlier years is a major contributor to the continuation of segregated housing today. This theme is further expanded by Goering and Lief in "The Implementation of the Federal Mandate for Fair Housing." The federal government, particularly through FHA and HUD, had a long history of discriminatory housing practices. Even more damaging, the failure to take affirmative action in the 1970s and 1980s to implement the legislation and the regulations that they are mandated to enforce, helps perpetuate systematized patterns of segregation that are found in the 1980s. More than any other factor, Goering and Lief show that the failure to act on the part of the federal government remains the key and most damaging aspect of continued segregation in this decade.

How segregated are America's cities in the 1980s? John Farley found, in his analysis of the 1980 census, that blacks were only slightly less segregated in 1980 than they were in 1970. These patterns are likely repeated in the six years since the census was taken. Even the modest improvement may be an illusion. The census data show that blacks are much more likely to be found in the suburbs than a decade ago. Furthermore, it appears that some modest integration has occurred in the suburbs. On closer examination, the data reveal that most blacks who live in the suburbs live in predominantly black neighborhoods, or in neighborhoods that changed rapidly from 1970 to 1980. There is no evidence that a significant number of neighborhoods are truly integrated, and not merely showing a racial mix in a transition period from white to black. Thomas Clark has shown that black suburbanization usually repeats patterns of resegregation in lower-density areas. In most cases, however, black enclaves have merely extended beyond their central cities to include inner-ring suburbs as well.

Woolbright and Hartmann, in their article "The New Segregation: Asians and Hispanics," found most Asian and Hispanic groups highly segregated as well. Some of this segregation can be attributed to the new arrival status of many of these groups. But Puerto Ricans, for example, have been in the continental United States for a number of decades. While some Asians of high-income status can be found in relative deconcentration in the suburbs, most Asians remain highly segregated in inner-city or suburban ghettos. But neither group seems to face the magnitude of both covert and overt barriers that blacks still encounter in metropolitan America.

While the legacy of the past continues to constrain minorities within segregated housing, a number of the authors in this volume demonstrate that continued discrimination plays an important role as well. Orfield and Fossett found systematic patterns of housing discrimination in Chicago, while Hansen and James found the same in small cities in Colorado.

Discrimination in the 1980s is certainly more subtle. But coupled with the severe constraints of the past, and the ways that separate neighborhoods have been institutionalized into the housing market, any continued discrimination has extreme effects. Realtors continue to steer their clients into certain areas, and landlords refuse to rent on the basis of race. Lenders do not make critical loans in areas that are no longer officially redlined, but nevertheless loans are not made in certain areas. The combined effect of these actions is to reinforce both old patterns of housing choice, and perceptions of the inevitability of segregated neighborhoods.

The data in this volume present an irrefutable picture. First, and foremost, segregated housing patterns still persist.

They have not much changed in terms of character, and there is little evidence of their gradual disappearance. Enough blacks and other minortities have reached middle-class and upper middle-class status to achieve a modicum of integration over the past two decades. Instead, the patterns of resegregaton continue, racial transition being the norm. The economic progress of a significant proportion of the minority populations over the past few decades has not brought with it the commensurate changes in housing patterns that one would have expected.

Decades ago, apologists for a segregated housing system argued that better economic time for minorities would bring, as a natural consequence, racial integration. But the powerful combination of past discriminatory actions, and continued discrimination today, prevents what ought to be a "natural" outcome. Perhaps most importantly, the failure to take affirmative actions in the 1970s and 1980s to dismantle the segregated housing market is the most obvious problem of all. Patterns that have been institutionalized over many decades are not going to disappear on their own. Unless specific actions are taken by governments at all levels to dismantle the existing segregated housing system, there is little hope for change in the near future. The private market in housing has not existed for at least half a century. It is a highly regulated and subsidized industry. Private market forces are merely a reflection of what the government has done in the past, or what it fails to do in the present.

What governments are doing currently tends to be counterproductive. Most subsidized housing programs have been slowly but effectively phased out over the past six years. Those that do remain make no attempt in any meaningful way to integrate existing units. At the same time, the slow but steady processes of inner-city decay, and now inner-suburb decay, continue unabated. These declin-ing and deteriorating bases of black and other minority population continue to destabilize housing markets throughout the United States. As has been the case for decades, blacks and other minorities continue to seek housing in new environments, only to find transition and ultimately neighborhood decay at the other end of a series of what seem to be perpetual moves.

The pathology of transition continues to erode, and often to devastate neighborhoods. The subsidies to high-income housing through the income tax structure, and subsidies to outer suburbs' physical infrastructures continue. The federal government has never wavered from its program of high-income and high middle-income household subsidies. With it, of course, they have subsidized the transition process. Unfortunately, as has been shown throughout the literature, what "filters" down is not only housing but entire neighborhood packages as well. Schools, streets, and other urban services decline in quality or perceived quality as the transition process accelerates. As this phenomenon continues to affect inner cities and inner suburbs, the impetus for white flight from particular neighborhoods and white avoidance of those neighborhoods continues as well. These processes, of course, are themselves abetted by the failure of realtors to show whites housing in an integrated neighborhood, and the failure of lenders to act quickly and fully on loan applications in these areas.

At the same time, subsidies to selected gentrifying neighborhoods have accompanied the general decay in other parts of the cities throughout the 1970s and 1980s. But, as has been shown in the literature, gentrification affects a very small proportion of neighborhoods. Even where some modest integration is achieved in redevelopment areas, the consequences often include displaced low-income minority populations again seeking alternate housing in transition areas. It is a very old pattern that has taken new forms in the 1970s and 1980s, but with the same results. The middle class and upper-middle class continued to be subsidized in the housing market, creating dislocation and transition in other neighborhoods. The net result, of course, is continued segregation and resegregation throughout metropolitan areas.

Positive government action has been rare, even when the national will has been turned to civil rights issues. But in the 1980s, the national attention has been concentrated on many issues. War has been declared on organized crime, on pornography, and against drug use. Abortion continues to be a hotly contested issue, as it was during the 1970s. Prayer in public schools has absorbed much public attention. Tax reform has been a key focus in the 1980s, along with a stronger national defense. All of these make up a social and political agenda that rarely, if ever, includes civil rights as a component.

Indeed, concern with civil rights issues has all but vanished from public debate. The current "crisis" agenda has been determined by the social and political, and often the religious right. Affirmative action, in any form, is not only neglected but is looked upon in the current social context with scorn.

The persistence of housing segregation in the 1980s, and the persistent forms of discrimination that are demonstrated in this volume, require affirmative action. But the prospects are quite dim. Housing audits, investigative actions initiated by the federal government, increased efforts to desegregate subsidized housing, increased development funds for integrated neighborhoods, and a variety of other actions are needed to enforce existing legislation and regulations, and at the same time effectively dismantle a well-established system. It is clear that such actions are not going to take place in the current political climate.

It is useless to argue whether or not housing is slightly less segregated in the 1980s than it was two decades ago. Significant progress has not been made. The vast majority of white Americans, the vast majority of black Americans, and other minorities all still live apart from one another. It has been demonstrated over and over again that the social and economic costs, to say nothing of the moral costs, of a segregated society are extraordinarily high. It is clear from the vantage point of the mid-1980s that it is a cost that American society will continue to bear for a long time to come.

20.   Snow White and the 17 Dwarfs: From Metro Cooperation to Governance

David B. Walker

Snow White nearly lost her heart. But she overcame the hostility of her stepmother and was kept alive in the forest by a family of dwarfs.

SOURCE: From "Snow White and the 17 Dwarfs: From Metro Cooperation to Governance" by David B. Walker in *National Civic Review*, Vol. 76, No. 1, January/February 1987, pp. 14–27. Reprinted by permission.

Metro America is Snow White. Migration to suburban areas nearly took the heart out of her. Federal hostility toward taking a role in metro governance has driven metro America into a temporary disappearance from public view. The good news is that she is being kept alive by 17 distinct types of interlocal approaches, on a spectrum from intergovernmental cooperation to full regional governance.

Some view this spectrum as a path out of a dark forest of problems, toward a regional Camelot.

INCREASING NEED FOR METRO APPROACHES

The nation's metro areas are growing, and their problems along with them. Substate regionalism seeks to address problems that spill over the artificial boundaries of central city limits. As metro America expands, the substate regional drama is being played out in more arenas. Note these seven current trends:

1. More metro areas. More metro areas exist today than ever before, with a more than two-thirds increase since 1962.

2. More people in metro areas. Three-quarters of our total population is located there, compared to 63% in 1962. More people also live in suburban jurisdictions than previously—some 45% of total population compared to 30% two decades earlier.

3. Continued metro government fragmentation. Growth in metro areas hasn't meant consolidation. More of the nation's local governments are located in metro areas now: over 36% of the 82,000 total as against 27% in 1972. The average metro area still encompasses about 100 governmental units, despite the slight increase in the percentage (48% of the total) of single county and presumably jurisdictionally simpler metro areas.

4. Increased metro diversity. Compared to their situation in the 1960s, metro areas are now more diverse in (a) population and territorial size, (b) the mix of private economic functions and the range of public services offered, (c) the respective position of central cities vis-a-vis outside central city jurisdictions, and (d) the kinds of jurisdictional complexity.

5. Advisory disharmony. For officials seeking guidance from governmental gurus, theoretical harmony is more elusive than ever. More theories are in vogue as to how metro areas should be run. No wonder actual practice is more eclectic than ever before.

6. Reduced federal aid. Direct Federal aid to localities, from day care funds to revenue sharing, has been cut back year by year without a concomitant reduction in Federal regulations.

7. Reduced state aid. Because non-educational state aid has been reduced without changes in state mandates and conditions, metro (and, though not the focus of this article, rural) communities' budgets have suffered a double whammy.

These metro area trends point to regionalism as a solution because it can (a) handle certain functions (usually of a capital-intensive or regulatory nature) on a multi-jurisdictional basis, (b) achieve economies of scale in providing various services by broadening the basis of fiscal support and the demand for certain services, (c) handle "spillover" servicing problems caused by rapid urban population growth and sometimes decline, and (d) confront the necessity for retrenchment by seeking more effective ways of rendering public services.

THE 17 APPROACHES TO REGIONALISM

Regionalism is a gold mine for officials seeking to solve local problems, and 17 different miners may be put to work to extract the gold. These 17 approaches to regional service problems can be arrayed on a spectrum from the easiest to the hardest—from the most politically feasible, least controversial, and sometimes least effective to the politically least feasible, most threatening to local officials, and sometimes most effective, at least in the opinion of many in jurisdictions that

REGIONAL APPROACHES TO SERVICE DELIVERY

Easiest

1. Informal Cooperation

2. Interlocal Service Contracts

3. Joint Powers Agreements

4. Extraterritorial Powers

5. Regional Councils/Councils of Governments

6. Federally Encouraged Single-Purpose Regional Bodies

7. State Planning and Development Districts

8. Contracting (Private)

Middling

9. Local Special Districts

10. Transfer of Functions

11. Annexation

12. Regional Special Districts and Authorities

13. Metro Multipurpose District

14. Reformed Urban County

Hardest

15. One-Tier Consolidations

16 Two-Tier Restructuring

17. Three-Tier Reforms.

have made these fairly radical reforms (see box).

EASIEST EIGHT

The first eight approaches are the easiest:

1. ***Informal Cooperation***. For many up against the wall, this is the easiest of them all. This approach is clearly the least formal, and the most pragmatic of the 17. It generally involves collaborative and reciprocal actions between two local jurisdictions, does not usually require fiscal actions, and only rarely involves matters of regional or even subregional significance. Although reliable information on the extent of its use is generally absent, anecdotal evidence suggests that informal cooperation is the most widely practiced approach to regionalism.

2. ***Interlocal Service Contracts***. Voluntary but formal agreements between two or more local governments are widely used. Some 45 states now sanction them broadly. Survey data suggest a slight decline (4%) between 1972 and 1983 in their use, but well over half the cities and counties polled in 1983 had used such contracts to handle at least one of their servicing responsibilities. Metro central cities, suburbs, and counties generally rely on them to a greater extent than non-metro municipal and county jurisdictions.

3. ***Joint Powers Agreements***. These agreements between two or more local governments provide for the joint planning, financing, and delivery of a service for the citizens of all the jurisdictions involved. All states authorize joint service agreements, but 20 still require that

each participating unit be empowered to provide the service in question. Surveys indicate that the number of cities and counties relying on joint services agreements for at least one service rose from 33% in 1972 to 55% in 1983, making them slightly more popular than interlocal contracting, although usage closely parallels interlocal servicing contracts.

4. ***Extraterritorial Powers***. Sanctioned in 35 states, extraterritorial powers permit all or at least some, cities to exercise some of their regulatory authority outside their boundaries in rapidly developing unincorporated areas. Less than half the authorizing states permit extraterritorial planning, zoning, and subdivision regulation, however, which makes effective control of fringe growth difficult. Because a number of states do not authorize extraterritorial powers, and because this approach does not apply to cities surrounded by other incorporated jurisdictions, this approach is less used than other techniques.

5. ***Regional Councils/Councils of Governments***. In the 1960s, no more than 20 or 25 jurisdictions had created wholly voluntaristic regional councils. That figure had soared to over 660 by 1980, thanks largely to Federal aid and especially to Federal requirements (notably Section 204 of the Model Cities legislation) that required a regional review and comment process in all metro areas for certain local grant applications. Title IV of the Intergovernmental Cooperation Act of 1968 built on the Section 204 base to create a "clearinghouse" structure at the rural and urban regional as well as state levels. Local participation in regional councils still remained primarily voluntary, however, with jurisdictions resisting any efforts at coercion.

Regional councils, also known as Councils of Government (COGs) which

rely so heavily on interlocal cooperation, assumed far more than a clearinghouse role in the late 1960s and 1970s. Thirty-nine federal grants programs with a regional thrust sometimes utilized COGs for their own integral parts of a strong state-established substate districting system, as well. Rural COGs tended to take on certain direct assistance and servicing roles for their constituents, while the more heavily urban ones usually served a role as regional agenda-definer and conflict-resolver.

With the advent of Reagan federalism a reduction in the Federal role in substate regionalism occurred. Reagan's Executive Order 12372 put the prime responsibility for the A-95 clearinghouse role with the states, while providing a backup Federal role (48 states picked up the challenge). Twelve of the 39 Federal regional programs were scrapped, eleven were cut heavily, nine lost their regional component, and six were revised substantially; only one was left fully intact.

To survive, COGs had to adapt and the overwhelming majority did so; less than one-fifth (125) of the 660 regional councils shut their doors. Some got greater state support both in funding and in power. Many others sought more local fiscal contributions and became a regional servicing agency for constituent local units. A majority of regional councils now serve as a chief source of technical services and provide certain direct services under contract to their localities. Some state functions have been transferred to regional council and many serve as field administrator of certain state-planned and fund services. All still perform some type of clearinghouse function and some assume specialized regional planning and other related functions under at least 11 Federal single-purpose grants and loan programs as of FY 1983.

Most COGs, then, reflect a greater "nativism," "pragmatism," and service activism than their predecessors of a decade ago.

6. **Federally Encouraged Single-Purpose Regional Bodies**. Single-purpose regional bodies came into being when institutional strings were attached to some 20 Federal aid programs (as of 1980). According to the 1977 Census of Local Governments, these federally encouraged special-purpose regional units numbered between 1,400 and 1,700 depending on definitions and classifications. A less rigorous, private, and meagerly funded survey identified more than 990 such bodies in 1983. Although the actual number as of 1983 was probably higher, by 1986 the total was probably a lot less, given the number of regional program revisions, budget cuts, and eliminations during the 1983–86 period. Single-purpose regional bodies now exist only in a few Federal aid programs (notably economic development, Appalachia, Area Agencies on Aging, Job Training, and metro transportation). Continued Federal fundings make them easy to establish and they play a helpful, non-threatening planning role.

7. **State Planning and Development Districts (SPDDs)**. These districts were established by the states during the late 1960s and early 1970s to bring order to the chaotic proliferation of Federal special purpose regional programs. A state's own substate regional goals were a prominent part of the authorizing legislation (19 states) or gubernatorial executive orders (24 states) that established SPDDs. By 1979 18 states had conferred a "review and comment" role on their SPDDs for certain non-federally aided local and state projects. Sixteen conferred such authority for special district projects and 11 authorized SPDDs to assume a direct servicing role, if it was sanctioned by member governments or the regional electorate.

As a matter of practice, practically all SPDDs adhere to the confederate style of regional councils/COGs. Many regional councils have been folded into the SPDD system, although boundaries have sometimes changed. Approximately the same number of SPDD systems (43) exist today as in the late 1970s, although in the hard-pressed midwest funding problems have rendered some moribund. All of these states took on the devolved responsibilities under Reagan's Executive Order 12372 for the "clearinghouse function," as did five others. Over half fund their SPDDs but only five in a respectable fashion.

Although feasible, SPDDs are somewhat difficult because special authorizing legislation is required, state purposes and goals are involved, and the establishment of a new statewide districting system can at least initially appear threatening, especially to counties.

8. **Contracting (Private)**. Contracting with the private sector is the only form of public-private collaboration analyzed here and is the most popular of all such forms. Service contracts with private providers are now authorized in 26 states—far fewer than their intergovernmental counterparts and usually with far more detailed procedural requirements. Their use has clearly increased from the early 1970s to the present with scores of different local services sometimes provided under contracts with various private sector providers. Joint powers agreements and inter-local service agreements, however, are both more popular than contracting with private firms.

This approach rounds out the cluster of interlocal approaches that we term easiest. Contracting with private organizations has been placed last because authorizing legislation, especially non-restrictive statutes, may be difficult to obtain. Moreover, the fears of public sector unions as well as certain public employees are aroused when local officials seek to contract services privately.

MIDDLING SIX

The middle cluster in the spectrum includes four institutional and two tough procedural approaches for new and usually broader territorial service delivery systems. These approaches present somewhat greater hurdles than those in the prior group but each is a more stable way to effectively align governmental and service delivery boundaries.

9. ***Local Special Districts***. These districts are a very popular way to provide a single service or multiple related services on a multi-jurisdictional basis. Three-quarters of all local special districts serve areas where boundaries are not coterminous with those of a city or country, a situation that has prevailed for at least two decades. Forty-one percent of all special districts were found within metro areas, making special districts the most numerous of the five basic categories of local government in metro America.

10. ***Transfer of Functions***. This procedural way to change permanently the provider of a specific service jumped by 40% in a decade, according to a 1983 survey of counties and cities. The larger urban jurisdictions were much more likely to transfer functions than the smaller ones. Over three-fifths of the central cities reported such transfers compared to 37% of the suburban cities and 35% of the non-metro municipalities. Among counties, 47% of the metro-type counties transferred functions compared to only 29% in the non-metro group. Cities were likely to shift services, first to counties, then to COGs and special districts.

Despite its increased popularity, the difficulties involved in transfer of functions should not be overlooked. Only 18 states authorize such shifts (eight more than in 1974) and in half these cases voter approval is mandated. In addition,

the language of some of the authorizing statutes does not always clearly distinguish between a transfer and an interlocal servicing contract.

11. ***Annexation***. The dominant 19th century device for bringing local jurisdictional servicing boundaries and expanding settlement patterns into proper alignment remains popular. The 61,356 annexations in the 1970s involved 9,000 square miles and 3 million people. The 23,828 annexations in the first half of the 1980s affected one million citizens and 3 million square miles. Although the vast majority of these annexations involved very few square miles, they are an incremental solution to closing the gap between governmental servicing boundaries and the boundaries of the center city.

A look at the larger-scale annexations of the past four decades highlights a dozen municipalities that serve almost as de facto regional governments: Phoenix, Houston, Dallas, San Antonio, Memphis, San Jose, El Paso, Huntsville, Concord (Cal.), Ft. Worth, Omaha, and Shreveport. Most large-scale annexations have occurred in the southwest and west, thanks to the large amounts of unincorporated land on municipal peripheries and to pro-city annexation statutes. Students of public finance point out that central cities that were able to annex substantial land are usually in good fiscal shape since they have escaped the "hole in the doughnut" problems of central cities in the older metro areas of the east and midwest.

Annexation is limited by the nature of state authorizing laws (most do not favor the annexing locality); its irrelevance in most northeastern states, given the absence of unincorporated turf in their urban areas; and a reluctance to use the process as a long-range solution to eliminating local jurisdictional, fiscal, and servicing fragmentation. Annexation, then, has limited geographic application and is usually used incrementally but when it is assigned a key role in a city's development, it can transform a municipality from a local to a regional institution.

12. **Regional Special Districts and Authorities**. These big area-wide institutions comprise the greatest number of regional governments in our 304 metro areas. Unlike their local urban counterparts, these Olympian organizations are established to cope on a fully areawide basis with a major urban surviving challenge such as mass transit, sewage disposal, water supply, hospitals, airports, and pollution control. Census data show there were approximately 132 regional and 983 major subregional special districts and authorities in 304 metro areas in 1982, compared to 230 and 2,232, respectively, in non-metro areas.

Relatively few large, regional units have been established because they (a) require specific state enactment and may involve functional transfers from local units; (b) are independent, expensive, professional, and fully governmental; and (c) are frequently as accountable to bond buyers as to the localities and the citizen consumers.

13. **Metro Multipurpose Districts**. These districts differ from the other regional model in that they involve establishing a regional authority to perform diverse, not just related regional, functions. At least four states have enacted legislation authorizing such districts, but they permit a comparatively narrow range of functions.

This option clearly ranks among the most difficult to implement, with metro Seattle the only basic case study. While multipurpose districts have a number of theoretical advantages (greater popular control, better planning and coordination of a limited number of areawide functions, and a more accountable

regional government), political and statutory difficulties have barred their widespread use.

14. **The Reformed Urban County**. Because it transforms a unit of local government, a move frequently opposed by the elected officials of the jurisdiction in question, new urban counties are difficult to form. As a result, though 29 states have enacted permissive county home rule statutes, only 76 charter counties (generally urban) have been created.

In metro areas, however, three-quarters of the 683 metro counties have either an elected chief executive or an appointed chief administrative officer. The servicing role of these jurisdictions has expanded rapidly over the past ten decades or so. Since 1967, outlays for what used to be traditional county functions (corrections, welfare, roads, and health and hospitals) have declined, while expenditures for various municipal-type, regional and new federally encouraged services have risen commensurately. Overall, the range of state-mandated and county-initiated services has risen rapidly in metro counties, during the past two decades, which has necessitated a better approach to fiscal and program management.

In the 146 single-county metro areas this reform county option is excellent. However, since county mergers and modification of county boundaries are almost impossible, in the 159 multicounty metro areas the option is less valuable. It can only provide a subregional solution to certain service delivery problems, not a fully regional approach.

THE TOUGH TRIO

The hardest approaches to metro regionalism are the three general governmental options: one-tier or unitary, two-tier or federative, and three-tier or superfederative.

All three involve the creation of a new areawide level of government, a reallocation of local government powers and functions, and, as a result, a disruption of the political and institutional status quo. All three options involve very rare and remarkable forms of interlocal cooperation.

15. *One-tier consolidations*. This method of expanding municipal boundaries has had a lean, but long history. From 1804 to 1907, four city-county mergers occurred, all by state mandate. Then municipalities proliferated but city-county mergers virtually stopped for 40 years. From Baton Rouge's partial merger in 1947 to the present there have been some 17 city-county consolidations, most endorsed by popular referendum. Among the hurdles to surmount in achieving such reorganizations are state authorization, the frequent opposition of local elected officials, racial anxieties (where large minorities exist), an equitable representational system, concerns about the size of government, and technical issues relating to such matters as debt assumption. Only one out of every five consolidation efforts has succeeded in the past 25 years.

Most consolidations have been partial, not total, with small suburban municipalities, school districts and special districts sometimes left out but the new county government generally exercises some authority over their activities. In addition, the metro settlement pattern in some cases has long since exceeded the county limits, so that the reorganized government may be the prime service provider and key player, but not the only one. This, of course, is another result of rigid county boundaries.

To sum up, one-tier consolidations have generally been most suitable in smaller non-metro urban areas and in smaller and medium (ideally uni-county) metro areas.

16. *Two-Tier Restructurings*. These seek a division between local and regional functions with two levels of government to render such services. These and other features, notably a reorganized county government, are spelled out in a new county charter that is adopted in a county wide referendum. The Committee for Economic Development advanced one of the most persuasive arguments for this approach in the 1970s. Metro Toronto, which created a strongly empowered regional federative government to handle areawide functions and ultimately led to some local reorganization by the merger of some municipalities, is a model for this approach.

The prime American example of this federative approach is Metro Dade County (Miami-Dade). Unlike the incremental reform approach of the modernized or urban county, a drastically redesigned county structure and role emerged from a head-on confrontation over the restructuring issue. Narrowly approved in a countywide referendum in 1957, the new Metro government's cluster of strong charter powers and its authority to perform a range of areawide functions were steadily opposed until the mid-1960s. Since then, its powers have grown and it is widely considered a success. Witness the extraordinary responsibilities Metro Dade assumed during the various waves of immigration since the early 1960s. The level of metro-municipal collaboration is better now than it was a generation ago, but tensions and confrontations are still part of the relationship—as they are in most federative systems. In my opinion, however, its survival is assured.

17. *The Three-Tier Reforms*. This is a rarely used approach, with just two U.S. examples. However, it deals with the special problems of multi-county metro areas.

The first example is the Twin Cities (Minneapolis-St. Paul) Metropolitan

Council. Launched as a metro initiative and enacted by the state legislature in 1967, the Council is the authoritative regional coordinator, planner, and controller of large-scale development for its region which includes seven counties and a dozen localities.

It is empowered by the state to review, approve, or suspend projects and plans of the area's various multi-jurisdictional special districts and authorities; it is the regional designee under all federally sponsored substate regional programs for which the area is eligible, and has the right to review and delay projects having an adverse areawide impact. Direct operational responsibilities do not fall within its purview but it directly molds the region's future development. Like any body that possesses significant power over other public agencies and indirectly over private regional actors, the Council has become somewhat politicized in recent years but its rightful place in the governance of the Twin Cities is not questioned.

The other three-tier experiment is the Greater Portland (Oregon) Metropolitan Service District (MSD), a regional planning and coordinating agency that serves the urbanized portion of three counties. Approved by popular referendum in 1978, the MSD supplanted the previous COG, and assumed the waste disposal and Portland Zoo responsibilities of the previous regional authority. The enabling legislation also authorized the MSD to run the regional transportation agency and to assume responsibility for a range of the functions, subject to voter approval, but these options have not been utilized. A 1986 referendum on a new convention center did pass and this task was assigned to the MSD. Unlike the Twin Cities' Council, the MSD has an elected mayor, an appointed manager, and an elected council of 12 commissioners, which provides a popular accountability that the Met Council has yet to achieve.

Both three-tier examples suggest how other multi-county metro areas might approach areawide service delivery and other metro challenges but they are arduous to achieve and not easy to sustain.

SUMMARY ANALYSIS

This probe of metro Snow White's current status suggests that she is alive and well, and is being looked after by her 17 regionable dwarfs:

1. Overall growth in regionalism. Virtually all of the various approaches have been on the increase. Since the early 1970s, the use of the eight easiest approaches has seen a net increase despite a reduction in the number of regional councils and federally supported substate districts. Meanwhile five of the six middling approaches grew markedly (the exception was the metro multi-purpose authority). Even the three hardest approaches have grown in use.

2. Multiple approach use. Very few metro areas rely on only one or two forms of substate regionalism.

3. The easier procedural and unifunctional institutional types of service shifts tend to be found more in larger metro areas while the harder restructurings usually take place successfully within the medium-sized and especially the small metro areas.

4. The expanded use of at least ten of the 14 easiest and middling approaches is largely a product of local needs and initiatives, as well as of a growing awareness of their increasingly interdependent condition.

5. Jurisdictional fragmentation has not been reduced as a result of restructuring successes, but even incomplete forms of cooperation are useful. Such approaches are used extensively; in a majority of metro areas they are the only feasible forms of regional and subregional collaboration.

6. Like much else in the American system of metro governance, the overwhelming majority of interlocal and regional actions taken to resolve servicing and other problems reflect an ad hoc, generally issue-by-issue, incremental pattern of evolution. However, most of the major reorganizations were triggered, at least in part, by a visible crisis of some sort.

7. The intergovernmental bases of substate regional activities remain as significant as ever. The states, which always have played a significant part in the evolution of their metro areas, must move into a new primary role if the federal role in this arena continues to erode.

Our Snow White would be ever so happy if her Prince Charming would gallop up soon, wake her from the slumber induced by her stepmother, take her out of the forest and—please—make room in the palace for 17 hard-working dwarfs!

CHAPTER 9

Taxes and Spending

Most states and cities entered the 1990s in serious financial trouble. During the 1991–92 fiscal year a majority of states raised $10 billion in new taxes and about thirty states cut spending, laid off workers, or put a freeze on new hiring. Only months after a campaign in which he said a state income tax would be like pouring gas on the "flames of recession," the newly elected independent governor of Connecticut called on his state to establish a new personal income tax. At the same time, Connecticut's largest city, Bridgeport, became the first major U.S. city to seek relief under the federal bankruptcy code. And Connecticut has the country's highest per capita income.

After increasing state expenditures an average of 8 percent each year since Governor Mario Cuomo was elected in 1983, New York faced a $6 billion deficit in 1991. California's deficit soared above $14 billion in 1991 and it remained nearly that high in 1992 and 1993. California voters in 1992 defeated two initiatives that were aimed at improving the state's financial position. Proposition 167 would have increased the taxes of top wage earners by about 50 percent. Proposition 165, supported by Governor Pete Wilson, would have reduced welfare spending and given the governor more authority to cut state spending.

How did resurgence in the 1980s turn to distress in the early 1990s? As noted in Chapter 2, part of the problem can be traced to the New Federalism of the 1980s that gave states more responsibility for many social services, especially for health care, but cut federal financial assistance. Federal revenue sharing to states and localities was eliminated by the mid-1980s, and the recession of the early 1990s cut deeply into state revenues. The so-called tax revolt, which began with California's Proposition 13 in 1978, led about twenty states to exact limits on taxing and spending. The movement to cut taxes was strongly supported by President Reagan and by George Bush's 1988 pledge of "no new taxes." Thus states faced the recession without budget surpluses, with less money, and with tax systems that required voter approval of any new revenue measures.

Yet the pressure to spend was increased in the 1980s by federal programs that mandated action by states and cities, especially in the areas of health and welfare. Cities were doubly affected. They lost federal aid for critical programs such as low-income housing and they had to cope with mandates from Congress and their state legislatures. Moreover, there has been mounting pressure for cities to spend money in response to growing social problems such as AIDS, homelessness, and drug-related crime. In Bridgeport, Connecticut, the major causes of its financial crisis in 1991 were heavy reliance on property taxes, binding arbitration that produced expensive labor contracts, state-mandated services, and the refusal of suburbs to help pay for social services.

Reading 21 examines the impact of Reagan administration programs on U.S. cities. The authors surveyed all cities over 50,000 population to see how the New Federalism affected sources of municipal income, the delivery of public services, and the relationship between states and cities. They found that cities turned to local sources of revenue to compensate for the loss of federal funds, and thus they became considerably less dependent on aid from Washington. The price paid for this independence, however, included reduced services and greater reliance on more regressive local taxes.

Given the severe financial squeeze and the political fear of raising taxes, there is a natural tendency for states to look for quick fixes. Public employees may be laid off, college tuition increased, new lotteries proposed, and even riverboat gambling instituted as an attractive way for some states to raise money. State political commentator Neal R. Peirce suggests that the budget crisis may be a good opportunity for states to improve their long-range positions by cutting unnecessary bureaucrats (for example, in state education offices), dropping meddlesome mandates, and rethinking programs such as mandatory sentencing that have added greatly to the cost of prisons. While several states have developed innovative plans to reduce rapidly rising health care expenses, the Clinton administration is seeking a national solution to the problem.

A major part of Reagan administration proposals to deal with urban problems was support of enterprise zones. As first developed by Sir Geoffrey Howe and enacted by the British Parliament in 1980, enterprise zones were supposed to encourage economic development in the most depressed areas of British cities by removing as much government regulation as possible. In Britain they were located in abandoned areas almost devoid of population. Under the Reagan plan enterprise zones were designed to encourage small business through tax incentives and a minimum of government regulation. Unlike the British plan, U.S. enterprise zones would have encouraged neighborhood organizations to create food coops and day-care centers to improve the overall life of the community. In addition to federal actions, state and local governments would have to agree to reduce taxes and regulations.

Enterprise zones were not approved by Congress while Reagan was president. In an ironic twist, President Bush in 1992 vetoed legislation that would have created urban and rural enterprise zones. Although he supported the concept and was under strong pressure to help cities in the aftermath of the Los Angeles riots, Bush vetoed the bill because it would have increased some taxes. When making his major economic address in early 1993, President Clinton stated, "With a new network of community development banks, and one billion dollars to make enterprise zones real, we begin to bring new hope and new jobs to storefronts and factories from South Boston to South Texas, to South-Central Los Angeles."

States in the 1980s expected a federal enterprise zone program that never materialized. While awaiting action from Congress, nearly forty states have created over 2,200 enterprise zones in cities and rural areas. Although early programs had only modest tax and regulatory advantages, newer plans have done more to encourage local government planning for economic development.

In Reading 22, Stuart M. Butler of the Heritage Foundation distinguishes enterprise zones in the United States from those in Britain, and he traces their evolution as adopted by the United States. Butler notes that enterprise zones in the states have been seen as a way to revitalize poor neighborhoods through improved commercial structures as well as improved housing. The study of enterprise zones illustrates the intracacies of our federal system, with shared federal-state responsibility for taxes and the ability of the states to adopt programs to respond to local conditions.

QUESTIONS FOR DISCUSSION

1. How have cities compensated for the loss of federal aid since the early 1980s? What groups have been disadvantaged by these changes?

2. Discuss the Reagan legacy to cities in the 1990s. Will it, as Cole, Taebel, and Hissong suggest, persist at least until 1995? What hope does the Clinton economic program offer cities?

3. Explain why enterprise zones appeal both to liberals and conservatives. Why has the concept been opposed? Is a federal enterprise zone plan likely to be approved by the mid-1990s?

4. Discuss how enterprise zones are related to American federalism and what they say about the role of states as laboratories for government experiments. Has your state enacted enterprise zones? If so, where do they exist and how successful have they been?

21.   America's Cities and the 1980s: The Legacy of the Reagan Years

Richard L. Cole, Delbert A. Taebel, and Rodney V. Hissong

In a speech delivered to the National Association of State Legislators at the beginning of his presidency, Ronald Reagan predicted a "federalist revolution" resulting from the domestic policy initiatives which were soon to be introduced in his administration.[1] Later, scholars would generally agree that—if no "revolution" actually occurred—the Reagan legacy indeed is one of significant and perhaps lasting change in American intergovernmental relations. As George Peterson put it, "Ronald Reagan [was] the first president since Franklin Roosevelt to challenge not just the workings of the intergovernmental system but the prevailing federalist ideology of his time."[2] Reagan's policies, says Timothy Conlan, "permanently restructured the federal government's domestic agenda."[3]

Calling his approach the "New Federalism," Reagan proposed a plan which if fully adopted would have turned back to state and local governments exclusive responsibility for the Aid to Families with Dependent Children Program and would have assumed at the national level full responsibility for the Medicaid and Food Stamp programs (often called the "swap and turnback" features of his proposals), would have eliminated many categorical grant programs and folded a number of others into a few block (or broad purpose) grants, and would have significantly reduced feder-

SOURCE: From "America's Cities and the 1980s: The Legacy of the Reagan Years" by Richard L. Cole, Delbert A. Taebel, and Rodney V. Hissong, Institute of Urban Studies, The University of Texas at Arlington, March 1990. Reprinted by permission.

al outlays for grants-in-aid to state and local governments. All these policy objectives were in marked contrast to what Conlan calls the "normal pattern of incremental growth"—both in numbers of grants-in-aid and in federal dollars allocated through the grant programs—which state and local governments had come to expect in the pre-Reagan era.[4]

While President Reagan did not succeed in having the "swap and turnback" aspects of his proposal adopted, he was remarkably successful—especially in the early years of his administration—in accomplishing his other goals. The growth rate in grant-in-aid spending did slow dramatically in the Reagan years. Such spending actually *declined* in 1982 and 1987. The Omnibus Budget Reconciliation Act of 1981 resulted in the consolidation of seventy-seven categorical grants into nine block grants—more than doubling the previously existing number of block grant programs. The new block grants accounted for about 10% of federal aid to state and local governments. Most significant, the Reagan-supported block grants reassigned program funding and control exclusively to the *states* (in contrast to previously existing block grants—such as CETA and CDBG— whose funds mainly went directly to local governments). From 1981 to 1987 the number of categorical grants declined from 534 to 422[5] and in 1986, the General Revenue Sharing program was terminated. Over the full period of the Reagan presidency federal spending on grants to state and local governments declined by over 10 percent.[6]

Reflecting at the end of his presidency on his domestic accomplishments, Reagan concluded that he had succeeded in breaking "the federal government of its compulsion to control every breath the states take. [Power] that once was in the hands of federal agencies [was returned] to the hands of governors and state legislators." Further, the president stated that he hoped that "history will record that [he] not only talked about the need to get the federal government off the backs of the states but that [he] did, in fact, fight the use of federal grant-in-aid dollars . . . and sought to return power and responsibility to the states, where they belong."[7]

IMPLICATIONS FOR AMERICA'S CITIES

Reagan's "revolution" resulted in "a transformation in the system of intergovernmental relations in the United States,"[8] and nowhere is the effect of this transformation more directly felt than in the management and administration of local government. Under the new block grants, states have been given new and expanded administrative responsibilities, responsibilities which have reshaped state and local relationships. Local governments have had to reestablish (and, in some instances, establish for the first time) working relationships with state officials and state agencies.[9] States and state agencies have been provided considerably more influence in setting funding priorities for activities included in the block grant programs and in targeting the distribution of funds within their states. This has resulted, some have argued, in less attention to the concerns of the poor and needy[10] and in the distribution of projects and spending among larger numbers of local governments (rather than focused on the special needs of the few big cities).[11]

But, the most obvious and most important result of the New Federalism, from the perspective of the day-to-day administration and management of local government, has been the loss of federal rev-

enues which cities have experienced and the strategies which cities have had to adopt to deal with that revenue loss. Grants-in-aid represented more than 15% of total federal outlays in 1980. By the end of the decade that percentage had declined to just about 10 percent.[12] Federal outlays expended on grants to state and local governments declined by 33 percent between the years 1980 and 1987, with the largest reduction occurring in general-purpose assistance, economic development, employment and training, and social services.[13] In 1980 cities received about 16% of their total general revenue in direct federal aid. By the end of the decade federal aid amounted to less than 10% of total local general revenues.[14]

Few cities were untouched by the new financial realities, and most major cities found they were receiving considerably less direct federal aid after the Reagan initiatives than before. Los Angeles, as an example, received $269 million in direct federal aid in 1981, but only $182 million in 1986 (the latest year for which city government finances are available). Baltimore in 1981 received $220 million in direct federal aid, compared with $124 million in 1986. Dallas which received $54 million in 1981 received only $30 million of federal aid in 1986.[15] Local governments have had to make up their federal aid "losses" by generating larger proportions of revenue from other sources, by reducing services, by eliminating personnel, or by some combination of these and other "cutback" strategies.

In spite of the importance of the New Federalism programs for America's cities, little is known—beyond evidence of a speculative and anecdotal nature—about the *actual* implications of the "Reagan revolution" for local government. Just what strategies have cities pursued to compensate for lost federal revenues, and what have been the programmatic and service consequences of these strategies for local governance? Some attempts to answer these questions, of course, exist.[16] However, much of the existing literature was prepared in the early years of the Reagan presidency, prior to the time in which the full effects of Reagan's programs would be felt at the local level. Further, much of the available research utilizes a case-study approach so that generalizations beyond the experiences of any particular locale or situation are difficult. Commenting on the state of existing literature, one team of scholars recently noted, "It is safe to say that little has been settled by [currently available research]" and that "our sense of the depth of the Reagan federal revolution remains [uncertain]."[17] And another team of observers states, "In spite of the fact that the Reagan cuts have been in place for some time, speculation about the fiscal impacts of New Federalism still abounds. . . . Have [local governments] had to raise taxes, reduce or eliminate services, or have the cuts been small enough so that they have had little or no impact? [And,] have New Federalism cuts had uneven impacts on different types of cities or on cities in different regions?"[18] At this point, answers to all these questions are incomplete.

This research attempts to fill this gap by examining the full effects of the Reagan years on the budgetary and programmatic decisions of America's cities.

METHODOLOGY

In order to assess these issues, we mailed in the summer of 1989 a survey to the chief finance officer of every American city over 50,000 (exclusive of townships and villages). Dealing with issues of fiscal impact is always difficult, but we believed finance officers would be the most appropriate representative in each city to provide the sort of historical and current budgetary information called for in the survey. Also, we believed finance officers typically would be in the best

position to offer informed judgements about the relative impact of changing budgetary, taxing, and economic conditions. Following two mailings, we received usable returns from 136 respondents, for a return rate of just over 31 percent. . . .

The survey dealt with a number of issues related to the implications of Reagan's New Federalism for America's cities. Among those pursued in this paper are: (1) the impact of the New Federalism initiatives on the changing sources of municipal general revenue; (2) the programmatic and service delivery consequences of these changes; and, (3) the effect of New Federalism policies on the changing relationships between cities and states. We examine all of these issues "controlling for" region and city size, and we attempt also to account for the independent effect of local economic conditions. There are a number of ways to measure the underlying economic vitality of an urban area.[19] As our measure, we simply asked our respondents— as local experts—to assess the recent economic vitality of their city's private sector. Using these evaluations, we rank our responding cities into three groups: those with "growing," those with "declining," and those with "stable" economies. The remainder of this paper presents our findings in the areas identified above.

CHANGING REVENUE SOURCES

Probably the most well-documented consequence of Reagan's New Federalism policies, as noted above, is the declining proportion of federal aid available for America's cities. Census records show that all cities received 8.0% of their total general revenue from direct federal aid in 1986 (the latest year for which data are available), compared with 13.6% in 1980.[20] It comes as no surprise, then, to find that most respondents to our survey also report receiving less federal aid today than in 1980 (or even than in 1985). About 86% of respondents report receiving less federal aid today than in 1980, and about 80% report receiving less than in 1985.

But, the issue which concerns us most is the effect of declining federal revenues on other sources of local funds. How have local governments made up the difference in lost federal funds? We look at the total picture of revenue generation for local governments in 1980, prior to the Reagan years, compared with 1989. . . .

All cities, regardless of region, size, or condition of economic health, are receiving significantly smaller proportions of direct federal aid today than in 1980. Most cities also report smaller proportions of "passed through" federal aid or of direct state aid. Large cities in particular (those in excess of 500,000) report smaller proportions of aid passed through the states. This point confirms earlier predictions of some observers, such as George Peterson, who believed big cities would be "one of the clearest losers of federal funds under [state administered] block grants."[21]

Our data show that in compensating for these losses cities have relied more on all other forms of revenue generation, but most extensively on local revenue sources. The effect on the local tax package has been twofold. First, local sources now contribute a greater percentage of the total tax package. All categories of cities report larger proportions of their budgets to be comprised of property taxes, sales taxes, and user fees. Second, the composition—or mix—of taxes in the local tax package has been altered. The absolute increases of proportions have not produced equal relative increases. This, in turn, has resulted in significant shifts in shares of local tax revenue. . . .

Cities with populations of less than 250,000, growing economies, and which are located outside of the northeast have significantly increased in their taxing

package the proportion of sales taxes. Proportional increases from user fees have occurred in all regionals with the exception of the west. Cities with populations less than 250,000 have relied more extensively on user fees, as have cities with declining or growing economies. The proportion of property taxes has increased predominantly in small western cities with growing economies. Losses in federal aid, then, have been partially compensated by proportionate increases in all other categories of revenue source, especially in sales taxes, property taxes, and user fees.

The reduction of intergovernmental aid has also changed the *relative shares* of taxes and fees within the local tax package. Property taxes remain the major source of local tax revenue, but its share has diminished relative to sales taxes and user fees. In 1980, 78 cents of every revenue dollar was derived from six local sources. Property taxes contributed 35.50% of this, unclassified "other" sources contributed 24.13%, and user fees contributed 16.95%. In 1980, sales taxes, licenses fees, and income taxes contributed 13.74%, 5.39%, and 4.75% respectively. In 1989, 87 cents of every revenue dollar comes from local sources, and the composition is significantly different. Now, the local tax package is comprised of 33.37% property taxes, 23.21% "other" sources, 18.48% user fees, 15.13% sales taxes, 5.08% licenses fees, and 4.73% income taxes.

Economic theory suggests, with respect to annual income, that the property tax is a proportional tax for low and middle income groups and a progressive tax for upper income groups, while sales taxes and user fees are regressive.[22] The data presented here reveal that the adjustments made by local governments to compensate for the loss of intergovernmental aid have produced a significantly more regressive tax package.

In all regions with the exception of the west, the proportion of regressive local

revenue sources has increased significantly. The northeast relies most heavily
on user fees where the average share over
the decade increased 2.00 percentage
points. North central and southern cities
increased their share of sales taxes by
1.12 and 3.13 percentage points respectively. . . .

Losses in federal aid, then, have been
made up by increases in all other categories of revenue sources and the picture
portrayed is one of significant shifts
toward more regressive forms of revenue
generation. The data reported here show
that middle and low income residents of
relatively moderate to small non-western
cities which have stable or weak
economies have born a disproportionate
share of the fiscal burden of New Federalism.

But cities also may respond to revenue
loss by utilizing a variety of other management strategies, such as service
reduction, staff cutbacks, project post-
ponements, and so forth. The following
section examines these other programmatic consequences of the Reagan years.

PROGRAMMATIC RESPONSES TO
NEW FEDERALISM

Other researchers have noted that, in
responding to budget cutbacks, jurisdictions may initiate a number of "nonfiscal
cutback management" actions.[23] In order
to assess other consequences of the New
Federalism years, we asked officials if
their cities in recent years have had to
eliminate or cutback any city services,
layoff some city employees, defer
employee salary increases, or postpone
capital improvement projects. We also
asked officials to estimate whether their
actions in any of these areas were due
exclusively or primarily to cutbacks in
federal aid, local economic conditions,
or some combination of both factors. . . .

Roughly a third of all respondents
indicated that their cities have recently
had to eliminate some city service

(38.3%), layoff city employees (32.3%),
or defer employee salary increases
(34.6%). Larger proportions report having to cutback some city services
(59.7%), and to postpone capital
improvement projects (78.9%). Cities in
the north central region generally were
more likely to adopt all these strategies,
as also were larger cities and those
whose economies were defined as
"declining."

Respondents whose cities had engaged
in any cutback activities were asked to
indicate if these actions were due to
reductions in federal aid, a decline in
economic conditions, or a combination
of both factors.

About a third of respondents, report
that their actions were due "primarily"
or "exclusively" to cutbacks in federal
aid, about a third said they were due to
declining economic conditions, and the
remainder said these actions were due to
a combination of both factors. In general,
respondents from smaller cities (those
under 250,000), those in the northeast,
and those with growing economies were
more likely to attribute these actions to
federal aid cutbacks.

Our findings in this regard both conform to and also deviate from some of the
earlier studies of New Federalism's
anticipated impact on America's cities.
Bingham and James in their study of the
1981–1982 years concluded that "the
loss of federal aid is a much more critical
problem for officials [in the midwest]
than it is for officials in cities elsewhere."[24] Officials elsewhere, they
found in 1981 and 1982, were concerned
more about adverse economic conditions
(unemployment and inflation) than
about declining federal assistance. By
1989 our data show that only in the west
did officials continue to attribute any
necessary cutback management actions
mainly to adverse economic conditions.
In all other areas, loss of federal aid was
seen as at least equally important to
declining economies.

Cutbacks in federal aid, then, not only have resulted in significant shifts in revenue sources for many American cities, but they also have had important programmatic and service consequences as well. Even when considering economic conditions, respondents from many cities report declining federal assistance to be directly responsible for these actions.

New Federalism actions also have altered relationships between cities and the individual states. States and state agencies, as noted above, have been given much greater responsibility and discretion in setting spending priorities under the new block grants. We explore in the following section of this paper experiences of local officials under the new arrangements.

ATTITUDES OF LOCAL OFFICIALS TO STATE ADMINISTRATION OF THE BLOCK GRANTS

President Reagan and officials in his administration frequently argued that the reduction in federal funds which were to occur in the shift to block grant funding would be offset by significant reductions in federally-set rules, mandates, and regulations—there would be, in a word, less "red tape." David Stockman, at the time Director of Office of Management and Budget, declared in 1981 that although New Federalism would mean an aggressive reduction in funds for local areas, "services delivered need not be diminished because massive reductions in Federal administrative requirements also are being made."[25] And, in President Reagan's own words, "We are not cutting the budget simply for the sake of sounder financial management. This is only the first step toward returning power to states and communities, only a first step toward reordering the relationship between citizens and government."[26]

In attempting to assess the experience of local officials with the actual administration and implementation of the New Federalism block grants, we asked respondents to indicate whether they have experienced less federally-imposed red tape as a result of the Reagan programs, and to compare this with any increases in rules and regulations which may have been imposed by the states in their administration of the new programs. . . .

The proportion of officials reporting *state* imposed red tape to be less than that experienced when the programs were administered by the federal government is about the same as the proportion saying such red tape now is *more* extensive (9.2 percent compared with 11.0 percent). Generally, officials from the larger cities (those over 500,000) were considerably more likely to find state imposed red tape to be more extensive.

Finally, we asked officials to rate on a scale of from "poor" to "excellent" their state's administration of each of the block grant programs.[27]

Considerable variance exists in local official evaluations of state administration of the block grants. Only about 15 percent rate state administration of the Low-Income Home Energy Assistance program as "excellent" or "good," but over 38 percent give positive ratings to state administration of the Elementary and Secondary Education program. In general, the programs which consolidated the largest number of categorical grants received the highest evaluations. The Elementary and Secondary Education program, for example, resulted from the consolidation of 37 categorical grants. The Alcohol, Drug Abuse, and Mental Health program—which received high evaluations from over 29% of respondents—consolidated 10 categorical grants. The Preventive Health program—which also received fairly high evaluations—consolidated 9 categorical grants. On the other hand, the Low-income Home Energy Assistance program previously consisted of only one categorical grant, and the Social Service block grant which was a consolidation of only 2 grant programs received low evaluations.

Many factors, undoubtedly, are related to local official evaluations of state administration of the new block grants, but one factor suggested by this study is the number of categorical grants previously consolidated. Local officials seem more satisfied with state administration of those block grants which represent consolidation of a large number of categorical grants; they are considerably less pleased when the previously federally-administered program was represented by one or just a few grants. For local officials, then, the important issues may not be so much the level of government (state or federal) which administers the program as it is the nature of the grant program itself. Local officials indicate a preference for a single grant in a particular area; in this case, at least, the issue of level of administration appears secondary.

The breakdowns by region, size, and economic health reveal few deviations from these points. While some exceptions are evident, officials from smaller cities, those in the south and west, and those with growing economies generally are more pleased with state administration of the new block grant programs than are officials from cities in other categories.

SUMMARY AND CONCLUSIONS

The Reagan years have left their mark on urban America, and on intergovernmental relations in general. Although, as noted above, President Reagan was not able to achieve his full federal agenda, he was more successful than most early analysts predicted in cutting back federal grants to cities and states, in consolidating numerous categorical grants into a few block grants, and in delegating

authority to states for the management and administration of programs previously run from Washington. Conlan puts it best when he says that, "Federal spending priorities, popular expectations, and the federal policymaking environment have all been substantially altered during the Reagan presidency."[28] Further, it seems a safe bet that the changes brought about by the Reagan agenda probably will persist throughout at least the first half of the coming decade.[29]

Our study confirms what others previously have noted: cities indeed are receiving considerably less federal aid today (both direct and "passed through") than before the Reagan era began. This is true of all categories of cities, regardless of size, region, or conditions of economic health.

Some see considerable *optimism* in the current state of affairs, describing the present era as a sort of "renaissance" of federalism in America. From this perspective, New Federalism has meant a return to vigorous, active, non-federally dependent state and local governments accompanied by a return to healthy, productive relationships between state agencies and their local governments. John Herber, for example, is cheerful in his assessment of the current state of federalism and concludes that this "new sense of independence from the federal government . . . promises to be both more profound and more permanent than most people have recognized."[30]

Indeed, some elements of this optimistic assessment are evident in our study. In general, we find that the new relationships between state and local governments resulting from state administration of programs previously administered at the national level to be satisfactory, at least from the perspective of local officials. A fair proportion of local officials report greater spending flexibility than before, and relatively few report state imposed rules and regulations to be more burdensome than those previously imposed at the national level. A fairly sizeable proportion rate as "excellent" or "good" state administration of all the new block grant programs.

This generally optimistic view of the current and evolving state of federalism, however, must be tempered by other facts revealed in this study. In responding to budget cuts, cities have adopted regressive revenue policies, policies which have placed much of the revenue generation burden from New Federalism on middle and low income households. We also find that large proportions of cities in all size and regional categories have had to significantly trim service deliveries. Others previously have noted that in reducing or eliminating services, communities have targeted disproportionately programs benefiting poor and minorities.[31] Thus, whether considering new revenue generating measures adopted by cities in response to lost federal funds or service cuts made by those same cities, the evidence indicates that the burdens of new federalism have been felt most by those in the lower and moderate income groups.

Most observers, we believe, would agree that the lessening of dependence of America's cities on the federal government and the renewed vitality of relationships between cities and states probably are healthy developments in the American federal system. At least, they represent a reversal of much of the direction of intergovernmental relations of the past fifty years. But, a high price has been paid for this new "independence": reductions in urban service deliveries, and significantly expanded regressive taxing policies. The only reasonable antidote is a return to increased levels of federal involvement in and funding of urban problems. With the current talk of major cuts in military spending resulting from developments in Europe and elsewhere, many are hopeful of renewed federal funding of domestic and urban pro-

grams. Whether cities and states would be able, in the face of renewed federal domestic activism, to maintain their "independence"—a positive feature, we believe, of the New Federalism era—remains one of the most significant dilemmas in contemporary American federalism.

NOTES

1. Remarks at the Annual Convention of the National Conference of State Legislatures, July 30, 1981. *Weekly Compilation of Presidential Documents*, August 3, 1981, 834.
2. George Peterson, "Federalism and the States," in John L. Palmer and Isabel V. Sawhill, *The Reagan Record* (Cambridge, Mass.: Ballinger Publishing Co., 1984), 222.
3. Timothy Conlan, *New Federalism: Intergovernmental Reform from Nixon to Reagan* (Washington, D.C.: The Brookings Institutions, 1988), 127.
4. Ibid., 125.
5. *A Catalog of Federal Grant-In-Aid Programs to State and Local Governments* (Washington, D.C.: Advisory Commission on Intergovernmental Relations, August, 1987), 3.
6. Conlan, *New Federalism*, 127.
7. Ronald Reagan, "Flattening Hierarchies in the American Federal System," *Intergovernmental Perspective*, Vol. 14 (Fall, 1988), 5–6.
8. Peter K. Eisinger and William Gormley, eds., *The Midwest Response to the New Federalism* (Madison, Wisconsin: The University of Wisconsin Press, 1988), 3.
9. For examples see: George E. Peterson, et al, *The Reagan Block Grants: What Have We Learned?* (Washington, D.C.: The Urban Institute Press, 1986).
10. Sarah F. Liebschuts and Alan J. Taddiken, "The Effects of Reagan Administration Budget Cuts on

Human Services in Rochester, New York," in George E. Peterson and Carol W. Lewis, eds., *Reagan and the Cities* (Washington, D.C.: The Urban Institute Press, 1986), 131–154.

11. Peterson, *The Reagan Block Grants*, 21.

12. *Significant Features of Fiscal Federalism, 1988 Edition* (Washington, D.C.: Advisory Commission on Intergovernmental Relations, December, 1987), 15.

13. Conlan, *New Federalism*, 154–155.

14. *Statistical Abstract of the United States, 1989* (Washington, D.C.: U.S. Government Printing Office, 1989), 286.

15. Data taken from *Statistical Abstract of the United States* for years 1984 and 1989.

16. For examples see: Richard Nathan, Fred Doolittle, and Associates, *The Consequences of Cuts* (Princeton: Princeton University Press, 1983); "Assessing the New Federalism," entire issue of *Publius: The Journal of Federalism*, Vol. 16 (Winter, 1986); Richard L. Cole and Delbert A. Taebel, "Initial Attitudes of Local Officials to President Reagan's New Federalism," *Journal of Urban Affairs* (Winter, 1983), 57–69; Peterson and Lewis, *Reagan and the Cities.*

17. Eisinger and Gormley, *The Midwest Response to the New Federalism*, 7 & 15.

18. Richard D. Bingham and Peggy Ann James, "Local Fiscal Adaptations to the New Federalism: The Lake Michigan States and the Rest of the Nation," in Eisinger and Gormley, *The Midwest Response to the New Federalism*, 147.

19. See: Terry N. Clark and Lorna C. Ferguson, *City Money: Political Processes, Fiscal Strain and Retrenchment*, (New York: Columbia University Press, 1983).

20. *Statistical Abstract of the United States, 1989*, 290.

21. Peterson, *The Reagan Block Grants*, 21.

22. Peter Mieszkowski and George R. Zodrow, "Taxation and the Tiebout Model: The Differential Effects of Head Taxes, Taxes on Land Rents, and Property Taxes," *Journal of Economic Literature*, 27 (September,1989), 1048–1146.

23. David A. Caputo, "The New Federalism: Actual and Anticipated Impact in Midwestern Cities," and Bingham and James, "Local Fiscal Adaptations to the New Federalism," both in Eisinger and Gormley, *The Midwest Response to the New Federalism*, 121–141 and 142–162.

24. Bingham and James, "Local Fiscal Adaptations to the New Federalism," 151.

25. David Stockman, Testimony before U.S. Congress, House, Subcommittee on Manpower and Housing, 97th Cong., 1st sess., April 28, 1981.

26. Ronald Reagan, Speech before the Conservative Political Action Committee Conference, March 20, 1981.

27. Asked only of respondents whose cities received funds in each block grant category.

28. Conlan, *New Federalism*, 277.

29. A point also made by: John Kincaid, "Current of Change in the Federal System," *Intergovernmental Perspective*, 15 (Fall, 1989), 19–23.

30. John Herbers, "The New Federalism: Unplanned Innovative and Here to Stay," *Governing* 1 (October, 1987), 28.

31. As an example, see: Sanford F. Schram, "The New Federalism and Social Welfare: AFDC in the Midwest," in Eisinger and Gormley, eds. *The Midwest Response to the New Federalism*, 264–294.

22.   Enterprise Zones in America

Stuart M. Butler

When the enterprise zone concept was first unveiled in the United States, in 1979, it was hardly surprising that the radical free market development strategy should appeal to conservatives like Jack Kemp and Ronald Reagan. To both these politicians, the proposal was, in effect, a supply-side program to save the inner cities: It was the urban complement to the general conservative strategy of cutting taxes and regulation to stimulate economic growth. Kemp eagerly adopted the proposal and introduced an enterprise zone bill in May 1980, and Ronald Reagan adopted enterprise zones as the centerpiece of his urban proposals during the 1980 election. Enterprise zones became official Reagan Administration policy in 1981.

More surprising was the liberal reaction. Within one month of Kemp introducing his bill in Congress, he had persuaded South Bronx liberal Democrat Robert Garcia to join with him on a slightly modified bill. By 1981 a remarkable bipartisan coalition had assembled to support the enterprise strategy, including leading congressional Republicans and Democrats, the Reagan Administration, the congressional Black Caucus, the National Urban League, the NAACP, and the National League of Cities.

To be sure, some of the liberal support after the 1980 election was triggered by the feeling that an enterprise zone program was the only approach likely to be

SOURCE: From "The Conceptual Evolution of Enterprise Zones" by Stuart M. Butler in *Enterprise Zones: New Directions in Economic Development*, edited by Roy E. Green, Sage Publications, 1991, pp. 30–39. Reprinted by permission of Sage Publications, Inc. Copyright© 1991 by Sage Publications, Inc.

acceptable to the tax and budget cutting Reagan Administration and the Reagan-dominated Congress, but there were deeper reasons for the remarkable coalition. For one thing, urban Democrats like Garcia had seen one expensive government program after another introduced into their districts, including Model Cities, urban renewal, and urban development action grants. Some had a marginal impact, but others, such as urban renewal, literally had destroyed neighborhoods and left wastelands. Despite the plethora of federal programs, places like the South Bronx continued to deteriorate. By 1980 there was a greater willingness among liberals to try a bold change in direction, at least in a few experimental areas.

The other reason a bipartisan coalition was possible was that the original British proposal was substantially modified in its American reincarnation. While the basic idea of cutting taxes and regulations to boost inner-city redevelopment in a small number of selected areas remained the core of the enterprise zone concept, the aims and legislative ingredients in the early U.S. proposals were shaped by a significantly different view of urban development from that held by Sir Geoffrey Howe. This distinctly American view of the purposes of an enterprise zone program sat better with most liberals that did the industrial park theme in the British zone program. Admittedly, not all American supporters of enterprise zones have shared exactly the same vision—indeed there has always been a fierce internal debate within the enterprise zone coalition—but it is fair to say that the development of the concept in the United States has been   strongly   influenced   by   the approaches to economic development discussed below.

THE PRIMARY AIM OF ENTERPRISE ZONES SHOULD BE THE ECONOMIC IMPROVEMENT OF POOR NEIGHBORHOODS

The British program is based on the notion that vacant sites make the best enterprise zones, with the zones acting as a focal point for the economic improvement of a wide area. Although job opportunities for poor families close to an enterprise zone are seen as an important consequence of the zone program, they are not the primary objective. In the United States, by contrast, most supporters of the enterprise zone idea have seen it as a tool to resuscitate specific poor neighborhoods, creating jobs primarily for local people. Thus the quintessential enterprise zone has been assumed in America to comprise a distinct neighborhood, not an entire city nor a vacant area.

There has been less argument, however, regarding the idea of restricting enterprise zones to urban settings. Certainly the original British proposal was aimed at reviving cities (even though some of the British sites are in open areas on the edge of cities), and leading American supporters of the idea, such as Jack Kemp, always imagined heavily blighted, crime-ridden inner-city neighborhoods as the principal target for enterprise zones. Similarly, most of the scholarly work contributing to the proposal assumed the purpose was to resuscitate urban areas. Nevertheless, there have always been certain proponents of enterprise zones in the United States who envisioned the concept also of applying to small rural towns with chronic economic problems. Although the majority of enterprise zone proponents may be skeptical of the applicability of zones to rural areas, politics has

decided otherwise. To secure political support at both the state and federal level, enterprise zone advocates generally have accepted the principle of reserving a certain proportion of zone designations for rural locations.

Underpinning the choice of objective is a basically optimistic impression of poor neighborhoods and poor people; one that is shared by conservative as well as liberal backers of enterprise zones. For politicians and scholars at both ends of the spectrum, the assumption is that there is enormous latent potential within even the most blighted neighborhoods. Currently, that potential is smothered in red tape, excessive taxation, and a culture of welfare dependency. But with the right incentives, the argument goes, the dormant human and capital resources of a South Bronx can be brought to life. Liberals, more than conservatives, tend to feel that other ingredients than incentives are necessary to trigger growth, but both agree that enterprise zones should be a tool to revive a neighborhood, not one to destroy it in order to start again.

Furthermore, basing growth on existing but unused or underused resources means that the enterprise zone proposal in the United States has been seen as a device to improve a neighborhood without having to divert people and economic activity from elsewhere. It is not, as Jack Kemp puts it, an exercise in "zero sum economics" but an attempt to create genuinely new economic activity. For this reason, Kemp and other conservative proponents maintain, the tax reductions in an enterprise zone should not be viewed as leading to a reduction in net government revenues. If cutting tax rates triggers indigenous activity in a depressed neighborhood where virtually no taxes were being paid, then the government would receive a fraction of something rather than all of nothing.

This notion that an enterprise zone program would be a catalyst for indigenous economic activity also suggested to most of its proponents that enterprise zone designation would be temporary for a neighborhood. The special tax and regulatory status would be like an economic "jump start" for an area, to ignite local resources and overcome obstacles arising from years of blight and crime. Economic growth itself, however, would gradually eliminate the obstacles and lead to self-sustained improvement. At that point, according to proponents, the area could safely be taken off the "endangered list" and returned to the regime of taxes (and possibly regulations) prevailing in adjacent non-zone areas.

Moreover, while supply-siders in the Reagan Administration in general opposed the idea of legislation committing the government to raise tax rates in the future, there was a widespread countervailing principle held by many Reaganite Treasury officials that the federal tax system should be neutral and not fine-tuned to benefit particular areas of the country. Thus the idea of ending tax breaks in enterprise zones was not opposed by the same officials who could be counted on to attack any move to raise general tax rates. Indeed, most supply-side economists at the Reagan Treasury were either lukewarm or hostile to the enterprise zone proposal, believing it to be a distortion of basic conservative tax principles.

No real consensus has emerged on what would constitute an ideal time limit. The benchmark for the British zones, contained in the 1980 legislation, was 10 years, although the precise period was left open to agreement between the national government and the local jurisdiction. Federal legislative proposals in the United States have also included similar time limits.

The emphasis on existing neighborhoods and the local population can be seen in the design of enterprise zone legislation, particularly at the federal level.

Absent, for instance, are the deep tax incentives of the British program intended to spur major physical development. Instead, the federal bills and most state measures have contained a variety of provisions aimed at fostering modest improvement of existing commercial structures. Unlike the British program, U.S. proposals also have included incentives to rehabilitate existing housing. And perhaps most important of all, the federal bills have all included deep tax incentives to encourage businesses to recruit labor, particularly low-skilled or disadvantaged workers. The British program contains no such incentives— British enterprise zone firms, in fact, are given every incentive to employ machines rather than people.

COMMUNITY INSTITUTIONS ARE CRUCIAL TO ECONOMIC DEVELOPMENT

American proponents of enterprise zones also have been strongly influenced by the argument that urban economic development initiatives for poor people can only succeed if their designers recognize and build upon the institutions that exist within a community. This view of urban development is in stark contrast to much of the thinking in the 1950s and 1960s, when the prevailing view was more that carefully planned physical redevelopment is the key to urban revival and that people could and should be moved around to fit within newly built neighborhoods. On the contrary, countered such urban writers as Jane Jacobs, in her books *The Death and Life of Great American Cities* and *The Economy of Cities*, successful urban development depends on complex social relationships within a community.[1] Ignore these relationships, and treat residents simply as individuals who happen to live in a certain geographic area—worse still, physically disrupt a neighborhood and its institutions—and development initiatives are virtually guaranteed to fail.

The principal theme of Jane Jacob's work is that diversity is needed for an inner-city neighborhood to be economically and socially vibrant. This means the mixed use of buildings, leading to a variety of economic activity, making the area better able to adapt to changing economic conditions, and to a flourishing street life throughout the day, reducing the incidence of crime. It also means recognizing that neighborhood organizations are crucial to the development process, mobilizing local people to tackle crime and other social problems that discourage enterprise.

This emphasis on preserving and strengthening community institutions has been a strong theme in enterprise zone proposals in the United States, although it was completely ignored in the design of the British zones. In the zone selection criteria contained in the Reagan Administration proposals, for instance, the Administration stressed that it would look more favorably on applications from cities that demonstrated they were taking steps to include neighborhood-based organizations in the development process.

The argument that strengthening community institutions is essential to economic development in poor communities also is an answer to the perennial question asked of antipoverty programs: Should the emphasis be on people or places? The answer implied in the enterprise zone strategy is that in a very meaningful sense people cannot be separated from place, and that an antipoverty strategy needs to treat individuals in the context of their community. Thus, in order to improve the condition of the poor, the enterprise zone strategy assumes that the focus must be on poor communities.

SMALL BUSINESSES SHOULD BE FAVORED OVER LARGE ONES

The third influence on the evolution of the American version of enterprise zones has been the thesis that small enterprises are the key to economic growth, particularly in depressed urban neighborhoods. Proponents of enterprise zones argue that there are several reasons why a program should be geared to small firms.

The first is that a solid body of evidence points to the conclusion that small firms are overwhelmingly the most important generators of new jobs. In extensive surveys covering 80% of U.S. firms, for instance, David Birch of the Massachusetts Institute of Technology has found that about two thirds of all net new jobs are created by firms with less than 20 employees. In poor urban neighborhoods, small firms turn out to be the only net producers of jobs. The best job generators of all tend to be young small firms. By contrast, Birch points out, very large firms tend to be net destroyers of jobs.[2]

Birch also found that in comparing job losses throughout the nation, the curious fact that the rate of job terminations tends to be remarkably similar—about 8% each year—in growing and declining areas. The crucial difference explaining growth and decline is the rate of formation of new firms. This implies that the primary objective of government development officials would be to institute policies that are likely to increase the start up rate of new firms, rather than measures designed mainly to retain existing employers in an effort to save jobs. This conclusion, of course, runs against the thinking of many officials. Development strategies aimed at reducing the loss rate of jobs, declares Birch, are "as futile as telling the tide not to go out."[3]

The second reason for targeting small firms in an enterprise zone strategy is that small enterprises fit better within an approach based largely on stimulating local activity within existing buildings. Small entrepreneurs in poor neighborhoods establish small firms, not *Fortune 500* corporations. Small firms also tend to fit more easily into existing structures; large firms tend to need new facilities. Small entrepreneurs are also more inclined to recruit local, unskilled labor and take the risk of operating in a marginal neighborhood. Executives from large corporations are disinclined to do so.

Enterprise zone proposals at the federal level have stressed incentives that are more likely to appeal to smaller firms, although there continues to be a vigorous debate about how small firms can, in fact, be induced by tax incentives to open their doors. It is pointed out by small-business people themselves that reductions in corporate income tax rates are not a major factor in their decisions to start a firm or to expand, because most make so little net profit in their early years that income tax rates are irrelevant. On the other hand, these entrepreneurs point out that two of the most important determinants of their success or failure are everyday operating expenses, including the cost of labor, and their ability to obtain capital for the start-up phase and for later expansion.

The architects of enterprise zone proposals have sought to fashion tax incentives that might address these needs of smaller firms. Thus the earliest version of federal legislation, introduced by Kemp and Garcia, included employment tax credits not only to induce firms to hire local labor, but also to reduce the largest operating cost of most small firms. Later federal versions have continued such credits for the same reasons. Similarly, the most important federal bills have all included tax incentives to encourage investors to risk modest amounts of money in small enterprise zone firms. Among these have been incentives to purchase stock in such firms, and the rapid depreciation for tax purposes of limited amounts of machinery placed in enterprise zone firms. The plan advanced by the Bush Administration, and designed by Housing and Urban Development (HUD) Secretary Jack Kemp, also eliminated capital gains for certain investments in an enterprise zone.

State enterprise zone programs have focused in varying degrees on stimulating the growth of small business. Typical incentives include partial relief from property taxes and inventory taxes, as well as steps to speed up and simplify the process needed to acquire a permit to open a business. In addition, the federal proposals have sought to induce states to include such actions by noting in the designation language that applications with measures to help small business would receive more favorable treatment.

ENTERPRISE ZONES AND THE POLITICS OF FEDERALISM

The evolution of the enterprise zone idea in the United States has not been shaped only by American views of the nature and objectives of urban development. It has also been influenced by the peculiar politics and institutional arrangements of the American system of federalism.

When the enterprise zone concept was first introduced in the United States, it aroused interest almost exclusively at the federal level. With the exception of a narrowly defeated attempt at legislation in Illinois, it was legislative proposals at the federal level that constituted the template both for the debate over enterprise zones and for the design of legislation at the state level.

State legislation, however, was viewed as an essential complement to a federally designed program. There were two principal reasons for this. The first was that given the shared responsibilities for taxation and regulation, it would require state as well as federal legislation to bring about the reductions in tax and regulatory barriers envisioned in the proposal. The second reason was that the enterprise zone approach, from its very inception in Britain, was to be experimental in nature. The idea was to trigger slightly different approaches in different places, adapted to local conditions and drawing on local creativity. This required innovative state and local initiatives blended with a national framework of incentives established at the federal level.

Inducing states to cooperate by cutting their own taxes and regulations was not a simple task, however. State politicians and development officials had become accustomed in the 1960s and 1970s to a particular form of federal-state development program: In return for a certain set of actions by a state or city, federal cash would flow—but the enterprise zone proposal involved no cash. The federal government simply would reduce its tax rates on certain depressed areas if the state, and perhaps the local government, would do likewise. It was not at all clear to some development officials schooled in the more traditional what they had to gain from such a novel arrangement.

Nevertheless, there was sufficient interest in the enterprise zone concept among state and local politicians, as well as organizations with an interest in urban affairs, for there to be strong pressure for federal enterprise zone designations and the tax incentives that would accompany the zones. But perhaps not surprisingly, state and local officials were far more interested in federal tax cuts in their cities than in reducing their own taxes or assembling a package of possible expensive initiatives.

The relatively strong demand for a federal designation permitted congressional and administration architects of legislation to use a limit on the number of federal zones to force complementary state action. Thus federal legislative proposals

have all included some limit on the number and size of possible designations, and guidance on actions at the state and local level that would improve the chances of selection by federal authorities.

Reagan-supported legislation introduced during the first term of the administration, for instance, required states to submit a proposed *Course of Action* with their application for a federal designation. If the application were accepted in the competitive process, the Course of Action then in effect would constitute an agreement by the state to undertake the actions. Although the legislation did not specify precisely what should be in such a state commitment, it noted that the plan might include such items as reductions in taxes and regulation, proposals to privatize municipal services in the zone, and steps to include community organizations in the development process.

In the first two years of the Reagan Administration, several states, including Connecticut, reasoned that the best way to increase the chances of selection for the federal program—passage of which was widely assumed to be a foregone conclusion—would be to enact a state program in tune with the basic elements of Reagan-supported congressional legislation. Thus the eligibility criteria of most state measures mirrored those in the federal legislation (based on UDAG criteria), and the tax, regulatory and other measures included in legislation and programs at the state level, broadly conformed to most people's best guess of a package likely to win applause from federal officials administering an enterprise zone program.

Enterprise zone legislation, however, never did pass Congress during the Reagan Administration, other than a token and toothless measure, devoid of any tax incentives, signed into law in 1988. At the time of writing, with the Bush Administration well into its second year, enterprise zone legislation has yet to pass Congress (although the prospects for passage seem better than at any time since the early Reagan years).

The precise reasons why legislation with such wide bipartisan support became stalled in Congress are complex and still disputed. But with the chances of a federal program becoming bleaker during the Reagan Administration, the enterprise zone concept slowly and almost imperceptibly underwent another stage in its evolution. It has changed from a federally inspired concept, in which state and local governments were to play very much a supporting role, into what is today a series of state programs in search of supporting federal tax incentive.

This change in the federal-state relationship regarding enterprise zones, with the states in the vanguard, has had a profound effect on the structure of state zones. There is now a remarkable variety of state enterprise zones. Some may be considered enterprise zones in name only, because they include major government spending programs and development planning that are the antithesis of the whole concept. But others are relatively bold experiments in using tax and regulatory incentives to create an environment conducive to enterprise development in depressed areas. In this sense one of Sir Geoffrey Howe's original purposes for enterprise zones is being fulfilled: Enterprise zones at the state level are indeed a set of laboratories in which a wide variety of economic development strategies are being tested, and where successes and failures will serve as a guide to better policies in the future.

NOTES

1. Jacobs, J. (1961). *The death and life of great American cities*. New York: Random House; Jacobs, J. (1969). *The economy of cities*. New York: Random House.
2. Birch, D. (1979). *The job generation process*. Cambridge: Program on Neighborhood and Regional Change.
3. Birch, D. (1980). *Job creation in cities*. Unpublished manuscript, MIT, Program on Neighborhood and Regional Change, Cambridge, MA, p. 11.

CHAPTER 10
Community Development

Although many American cities were "planned" in the sense of the original layout of streets and parks, their great growth near the end of the nineteenth century was largely unmanaged. By 1900 most large cities were crowded and unsanitary, and land use was uncontrolled. Political reformers who introduced city managers and civil service systems early in this century also reinstituted planning as a way to beautify cities. Early planners often were engineers who focused their attention on land use. They introduced zoning and developed master plans for city growth. After World War II, planners began to take a much more comprehensive look at all aspects of city life: housing, transportation, health care, economic development, recreation, environmental control, and culture. As noted in Chapter 8, efforts to provide regional or metropolitan-wide planning have met with limited success. This chapter focuses on land use, housing, and transportation, which are core concerns of all planning commissions.

Zoning began in the 1920s as a means of protecting neighborhoods from the intrusion of business and industry. Typically, communities were divided into zones and each was restricted to a specific use. Because zoning laws impact directly on the nature of communities—determining which economic activities and which types of housing will be permitted—strong political battles often surround the creation of zoning codes and later the approval of variances from normal policy.

Perhaps most controversial has been *exclusionary zoning* that restricts the entry of certain types of people into communities. This usually occurs in suburbs where zoning and building codes may require houses to have large lots and where low-rent apartment buildings are prohibited. As noted in Chapter 8, one effect is to perpetuate racial segregation in suburbs. The most extreme form of exclusion is limited-growth or no-growth zoning laws that restrict the number of new housing units in a community. Such laws have been enacted in suburban, high-growth areas in California and Florida where often there are genuine environmental concerns. Although advocacy groups for the poor have argued that exclusionary zoning is discriminatory, the U.S. Supreme Court has not prohibited it because discrimination based on income has not been deemed unconstitutional. Some state supreme courts (notably New Jersey) have called for *inclusionary zoning*, which requires builders to provide a portion of new housing for moderate- and low-income families.

Suburbs that restrict growth drive development to the outer fringes of metropolitan areas, increasing sprawl, destroying green areas, and making people more dependent on automobiles. In addition, the rising price of suburban housing has caused some young professionals to buy housing units in the central city that might otherwise be occupied by lower-middle-class people. Other urban residents may be displaced by the restoration of run-down neighborhoods that become attractive investments for singles and young-marrieds. This process of gentrification or urban regeneration has worsened the problem of homelessness in central cities. Of course, other low-income housing has been torn down to make way for commercial development.

Financing housing for the poor has been largely the responsibility of the federal government's Department of Housing and Urban Affairs. However, in seeking federal grants, cities must show that they have established comprehensive plans for redevelopment, including the relocation of persons displaced by renewal projects.

In Reading 23, political scientist Todd Swanstrom discusses homelessness as an economic problem caused, in large part, by government policy that has not produced a sufficient supply of low-income housing. Swanstrom explains how gentrification and zoning have worsened the homelessness problem, and he is especially critical of the exclusionary zoning practices of suburban communities. Given the complex economic and political nature of the problem, Swanstrom suggests that the shelter system for the homeless is a temporary approach that is shortsighted and expensive. His solution to the problem calls on government to dismantle many existing policies and to increase affordable housing in metropolitan areas.

Transportation always has been the major factor influencing economic development. Decisions to build canals and railroads in the nineteenth century had profound economic and social effects in the United States, and current public decisions regarding the location of highways directly influence where people live, where they work, and where they shop. We have noted that metropolitan areas long have been characterized by "pave and sprawl." This has encouraged even greater use of the automobile while urban planners have been calling for expanded public transportation.

Since the mid-1950s, the construction and location of interstate highways have had profound effects on American life. Increased mobility and easier access *to* cities have had numerous unintended consequences. Highway systems have led to the abandonment of many old downtowns and the development of suburban malls; they have split up neighborhoods and displaced people from their homes; they have caused air pollution to increase; and they have permitted people to live farther from cities and still have many of the benefits of metropolitan life.

Federal spending for mass transit (rapid rail and subway systems) did not begin until 1961. Little change occurred until the 1970s, when direct federal aid increased and states were allowed to use some of their interstate highway money for urban transit systems. By that time there was the growing realization that building more freeways was not helping transportation problems. In the 1970s and 1980s, new mass transit systems were opened in Miami, San Francisco, Washington, Atlanta, Baltimore, and Pittsburgh. Both the Reagan and the Bush administrations cut funds for mass transit, arguing that it should be a local responsibility—that is, taxpayers in North Dakota should not be required to help finance a rail system in Miami. However, the 1991 Transportation Bill significantly increased federal aid to mass transit and gave state and local governments more flexibility to shift highway funds to mass transit.

In Reading 24, Peter Gordon and Harry Richardson argue against creating new mass transit systems in vast metropolitan areas such as Los Angeles. Instead, they believe that metropolitan transportation needs would be better served by well-managed automobile transport, good bus systems, and transit schemes such as "dial-a-ride" services. Much of what they say goes against the conventional wisdom of how transit problems developed (e.g., in Los Angeles) and how they should be solved. They contend that suburbanization is a fact of life, and that mass transit systems should not be built on the hope of revitalizing a downtown that may no longer exist. Despite this argument, work is underway to develop a subway line and commuter rail system in Los Angeles. After years of delay, Los Angeles opened a 4.4-mile section of its subway in early 1993. The city's policy is not to build any more freeways in the next thirty years. As discussed in Reading 24, critics argue it is a huge waste of money (projected costs over thirty years are $78 billion), contending that buses and vans could offer cheaper and more flexible transportation in the vast Los Angeles metropolitan area.

QUESTIONS FOR DISCUSSION

1. Explore the problem of homelessness in your area. Why do your local government officials believe it exists? Pick a large city in your state and examine the effects there of gentrification (begin by defining the term).

2. Do you buy Swanstrom's argument that government policies are the primary cause of homelessness? Why? What about his view of shelters?

3. Discuss and define the standard monocentric model of urban economics as it applies to large cities near you.

4. Examine the subway or rapid rail system of any city except New York and see what its problems are. Do the Gordon and Richardson proposals make good sense? If so, what is likely to happen with the Los Angeles subway system?

23.   No Room at the Inn: Housing Policy and the Homeless

Todd Swanstrom

Gradually, it is becoming clear that the problem of the "new homeless" is not primarily caused by personal pathologies such as mental illness or alcoholism. Homelessness is primarily an economic problem: in large metropolitan areas, many households simply cannot find affordable housing at the bottom of the rental market. As a result, they are forced onto the streets. In the face of cutbacks in social programs by the Reagan Administration, concerned citizens are calling on governments, at all levels, to do more to help the homeless.

While I share some of the reasoning of this emerging consensus about the issue of homelessness, I also part company with it at key points. My thesis is that homelessness is primarily caused not by personal pathologies, but by housing market pathologies. The problem in housing markets is primarily one of *supply*, not *demand*. The cause of the recent wave of homelessness is not inadequate economic demand, or poverty, but inadequate supply of housing for the low income segment of the market. Government policy, far from being part of the solution, has been a primary cause of homelessness, especially in recent years. Therefore, we do not simply need more money for homeless housing policy; we need to radically reform our housing policies across the board.

My argument can be advanced through a syllogism that I hope to prove in succeeding sections:

SOURCE: From "No Room at the Inn: Housing Policy and the Homeless" by Todd Swanstrom in *The Journal of Urban and Contemporary Law*, Vol. 35:81, 1989, pp. 81–88, 98–105. Reprinted by permission.

1. Homelessness is primarily caused not by personal deficiencies, but by structural problems in metropolitan housing markets.
2. As a housing market problem, it is primarily a matter of inadequate supply, not inadequate economic demand.
3. A major cause of the inadequate supply of low income rental housing in large metropolitan areas with expanding service economies is the unintended effects of government policies.
4. Q.E.D.: to solve the problem of homelessness, it is not enough simply to spend more money on shelters; instead, housing policies, at all levels of government, must be redirected.

HOMELESSNESS: FROM PERSONAL PATHOLOGY TO STRUCTURAL PROBLEM

Beginning about 1980, homeless people became more visible on the streets of urban America. While estimates of the number of homeless persons vary, there is little doubt that homelessness increased significantly beginning in the late 1970s and that this trend has continued in the 1980s. The evidence shows that the "new homeless" differ in important ways from the previous residents of skid row. Previously, the homeless were primarily older white males who frequently suffered from alcoholism.[1] In contrast, many of the new homeless are children or females. They are the working poor or the recently unemployed, and a higher percentage are from racial minority groups. The new homeless have a surprisingly high level of education, and many come from middle-class backgrounds. While some are chroni-

cally homeless, many have been homeless for only a short time.[2]

Survey evidence shows that the vast
majority of the new homeless do not
have any especially debilitating condition. This evidence contradicts explanations that rely on personal characteristics
of the homeless population. Explanations based on personal pathology also
suffer from an inability to explain historical change. It does not make sense to
attribute the recent rise in homelessness
to a sudden upsurge in the number of
people who are unable to cope with life
for personal reasons.

One way to salvage the personal
pathology explanation is to argue that
the number of individuals with personal
pathologies did not suddenly increase,
but the number of them on the streets
did. In other words, the deinstitutionalization of mental patients caused homelessness. Surveys of the homeless have
found, however, that only a minority has
ever been in psychiatric hospitals.[3]
Moreover, most deinstitutionalization
occurred in the late 1960s, well before
the rise of the new homeless.[4] Finally,
studies have shown that in earlier years
ex-mental patients found housing, however inadequate; only in recent years
have they been forced out onto the
streets in greater numbers.[5]

Clearly, it is necessary to focus on the
structures that individuals find themselves in, not on the individuals themselves, if we are to adequately explain
the recent rise in homelessness. Perhaps
the major structural explanation of
homelessness focuses on inadequate
income, or poverty, due to the changing
job structure in cities. The transformation of urban economies from industrial
to service functions, the argument goes,
is creating a "missing middle" in the
income distribution, with jobs falling in
either the high or the low ranges.[6] Analyses of homelessness frequently focus on
poverty as a precipitating factor.[7] Indeed,

there is a great deal of circumstantial evidence linking rising poverty to homelessness: income polarization in service
economies, increased female-headed
households, high unemployment in
cities and among the minority population, and increased levels of poverty in
general.

In addition, many examinations of
homelessness emphasize the effect of
cuts in government benefits for the poor,
such as the falling real value of AFDC
benefits and the termination of disability
benefits.[8] Overall, the problem seems to
be that many households simply lack
sufficient income to afford decent housing. Statistics show that many households, especially lower income rental
households, are paying an increasing
percentage of their income on housing.[9]
Others cannot afford any housing. In
short, the problem seems to be inadequate income.

The weakness of structural explanations of homelessness that focus on inadequate demand, or income, is that they
cannot explain the timing or the geographical distribution of the new homeless. The poverty rate was higher in previous periods, such as the 1950s, yet
homelessness was never the acute problem then that it is today. Unemployment
peaked in 1982 and has since declined,
yet homelessness increased rapidly during this period. Clearly, some states,
such as Mississippi, have higher poverty
rates and unemployment, yet they do not
have especially severe homeless problems. Homelessness is concentrated in
large metropolitan areas with dynamic
and growing white collar economies.

The poverty explanation is too simple.
To say that poverty is the cause of homelessness is almost a tautology: the homeless could be defined as those who lack
sufficient resources to purchase housing
on the private market. To argue that
poverty is the cause of homelessness is
like arguing that water in the lungs is the

cause of drowning. Of course water is the cause of drowning; the problem is how did the water overwhelm that particular individual at that particular time.

The problem today is not to explain why people are poor but to explain "why their poverty takes the distinctive form of having no place to live."[10] I will argue here that it is not poverty, or inadequate demand, that is the proximate cause of homelessness, but inadequate *supply* of housing. The problem lies not in the general class structure of capitalist society but in the pathologies of metropolitan housing markets, caused to a great extent by government policies. Putting this another way, if tomorrow the poor were suddenly given a significant increase in their incomes, the problem of homelessness would not go away. While market theory assumes that supply automatically meets demand, this is not true in metropolitan housing markets today.

The proximate cause of homelessness is not poverty-induced, inadequate demand, but inadequate supply of low income housing. Evidence for the shortage of low income housing abounds. Vacancy rates in New York, San Francisco, and Boston in recent years have averaged one percent to two percent (five percent is considered normal); increasingly, families are forced to "double up" to find housing.[11] At a time when an increasing number are seeking low cost housing, the supply of low-rent housing is shrinking. Nationwide, from 1974 to 1983, the supply of low-rent housing units fell eight percent and it is projected to decline another twenty-seven percent by the year 2003.[12] The gap between supply and demand is especially severe in large metropolitan housing markets. A study of twelve cities from the late 1970s to the late 1980s found that while the number of poor people increased thirty-six percent, the number of rental units they could afford decreased thirty percent.[13] Contrary to market theory, at the

same time that rents have been going up, the supply of rental units has been going down. In New York City for example, between 1982 and 1985, a period of rapidly inflating rents, the number of rental units actually declined 36,000.[14]

The causes of the shortage of low income rental housing are numerous. Part of the problem is the abandonment and eventual demolition of low income housing in central cities. Contagious abandonment in deteriorating neighborhoods, whether due to landlord neglect, fires, or other causes, is a major problem. In the nation as a whole, however, in recent years the rate of abandonment has fallen an estimated fifty percent from the rate in the 1950s and 1960s.[15] In New York City, the number of units lost to abandonment declined from approximately 31,000 units per year from 1970 through 1981 to approximately 23,000 units in 1985.[16] At the same time that abandonment was declining, however, the number of homeless was swiftly increasing.

While abandonment is part of the problem, more pertinent to the rise of the new homeless in recent years is the increased competition for inner-city housing.[17] This, in turn, is related to the transformation of cities from centers of industry to centers of high level white collar employment. The shortage of low income housing is intimately related to the economic restructuring of American cities.[18] In many cases, housing in central cities has been torn down to make way for office and commercial functions. One author estimated that "almost half of the nation's post-1950 gain in office employment and construction was captured by the downtowns of our large cities."[19] It is well documented that the urban renewal programs of the 1950s and 1960s tore down more housing than they replaced.[20]

More important than changing land uses is the gentrification of inner-city housing markets near concentrations of high level service sector employment in central business districts. A 1981 study estimated that every year 2,500,000 persons are involuntarily displaced from their homes. "Rent increases are the single largest cause of displacement."[21] Displacement is greatest in inner-city neighborhoods with attractive historic brickframe housing stock close to jobs in the central business district. The movement of high income professionals into such neighborhoods is call gentrification. Gentrification has today replaced urban renewal as the main cause of displacement. Under gentrification, affordable rental housing is pulled off the market by rent increases and by conversion of rental units to condominiums. Peter Marcuse estimates that 25,000 to 100,000 persons in New York City are displaced each year, directly or indirectly, by gentrification.[22]

The conversion of single room occupancy (SRO) hotels to luxury housing for the urban gentry is a documented cause of homelessness. In New York City between 1970 and 1983, the number of SRO units dropped eighty-nine percent, from 127,000 to 14,000.[23] The City of Chicago estimated that 18,000 SRO units were converted, abandoned, or destroyed between 1973 and 1984.[24] The pattern is the same across the country: the supply of low rent housing in central cities is dwindling as units are converted to luxury housing for the new urban professionals.

In short, the proximate cause of the new homelessness of the 1980s is an acute shortage of low income rental housing related to the restructuring of American cities into centers of high-level service-sector employment. The demand for housing has shifted as households have become smaller and the job structures of central cities have changed. Traditionally, the supply of housing is thought to respond slowly to changes in

demand because housing is such a "lumpy" and expensive good. In the best of circumstances, metropolitan housing markets will have trouble adapting to rapidly changing demand.

Beyond this criticism of inflexible supply, however, left-wing critics charge that private housing markets simply will not serve one segment of demand at all: the poor. As one critic asked rhetorically: "Does not the private market in fact cause much of the recent growth of homelessness through skyrocketing rents, gentrification and the conversion to other use of marginal buildings?"[25] The problem with this attack on the free market, however, is that the free market is a myth. The government is everywhere involved in housing. But contrary to the conservative view that government interventions have overwhelmingly helped the poor, overall, government policy, however well-intended, has primarily benefited the well-to-do and exacerbated the problem of homelessness.

• • •

LOCAL GOVERNMENT POLICY: THE BANEFUL EFFECTS OF REGULATION

Historically, state governments have played a minor role in housing. In recent years, however, in response to the vacuum created by the withdrawal of the federal government, they have begun to take the initiative.[26] Indirectly, however, states have always played an important role in housing through the powers they have given to local governments. The police power of the local state, and the power this implies over land use, has been used powerfully to shape regional housing markets. While the original intentions may have been progressive, the final effects were regressive. Specifically, local building regulations, housing codes, and zoning laws have worsened the homelessness problem.

Building and housing codes were first enacted during the progressive period around the turn of the century. Designed to upgrade housing to higher standards, these regulatory efforts were prompted by the concern of middle class reformers about the deplorable conditions of urban slums portrayed by muckrakers such as Jacob Riis. Building codes established minimum standards for new construction, and housing codes mandated that existing housing be brought up to minimum standards.

Basic standards to control the social costs of substandard housing and protect people's health and safety made sense. Often, however, these codes went beyond basic standards to legislate middle class norms of living for the poor. Before the progressive period, entrepreneurs supplied housing for the very poor in the form of flop houses and cage hotels (similar to SROs). While these accommodations may have been offensive by middle class standards, they were nevertheless better than living on the streets. Beginning in the 1920s, however, entrepreneurs began to withdraw from providing housing for the very poor unless government subsidies were provided. "Thus, housing reform had two contradictory effects, that of improving the quality of housing for the poor, while reducing its availability."[27] Building codes increased the cost of new construction, often beyond what was necessary for health and safety, thus helping to move the bottom of the rental market out of the reach of the very poor.[28] Recent research indicates that strict enforcement of housing codes can lead to displacement of the poor, who cannot afford the increased rents necessary to cover the repairs, thus reducing the supply of low income housing.[29]

A more important cause of the imbalance between supply and demand in large metropolitan housing markets is the exclusionary practices of suburban governments. The rationale behind zoning is to prevent incompatible uses from damaging each other. Zoning controls limit the damage resulting from market failures, specifically, the effect of negative externalities in urban real estate development, such as the noise or traffic congestion caused by a factory. While zoning controls have often been used for such valid purposes as preventing the construction of a fat-rendering plant adjacent to homes, zoning controls also have been used to limit the mobility of people, not the use of land. The most relevant zoning regulations for our purposes are those that create zones which limit residential development, prohibit multifamily construction, or require minimum lot and house sizes.[30]

• • •

Suburban municipalities are driven to exclude on the grounds that admitting low income families will swell service demands, especially for education, without providing commensurate increases in the tax base. Moreover, if cities can restrict new construction, or limit it to only the most expensive single-family homes on large lots, then existing owners, whether of homes or rental units, will see property values rise: if supply is prevented from keeping pace with demand, prices will increase.

While the effect of suburban exclusionary controls is indirect, in the long run it is significant. If cities prohibit multifamily construction and limit single-family construction to the luxury end, the filtering chain is lengthened to the point where it is doubtful that the benefits of suburban construction ever trickle down to the inner-city poor. In addition, exclusionary controls exaggerate urban sprawl, thus increasing commuting times and encouraging some members of the professional middle class to abandon the suburbs and compete with the poor for scarce inner-city housing.

The driving logic behind the deleterious actions of local governments is the desire to enhance the local tax base, relative to service demands, in competition with neighboring governments. The idea is to attract the rich and repel the poor. Under the so-called NIMBY syndrome ("not in my backyard"), all local governments oppose low income housing, especially subsidized housing. Central cities are no exception, with neighborhoods loudly protesting public housing or shelters for the homeless.

On the other hand, many central city governments have aggressively promoted the gentrification process. The result has been to promote displacement of the poor and reduce the supply of low income rental units. . . . Perhaps the most famous, or infamous, example is the 70 million dollar abatement received by Donald Trump for his Trump Tower on Madison Avenue. One bedroom units in the Trump Tower start at 4,000 dollars, and three bedroom units start at 15,000 dollars—a month![31] Both of New York's residential tax abatement programs fueled the destruction of SRO hotels, discussed earlier as a prime cause of homelessness. In addition, local governments have used their control over federal grant programs, such as CDBG and UDAG, to promote the conversion of scarce low income housing to luxury condominiums and rental apartments.

In conclusion, some city governments address the causes of the homeless problem by aiding in the construction of low income housing, usually with federal grants. On balance, however, the actions of local governments have made the homelessness problem worse. Homeless people have become urban pariahs, shunned by governments less concerned with helping the disadvantaged and more concerned with protecting exclusive residential enclaves or developing the city as a playground for the corporate service sector.

CONCLUSION: WHITHER PUBLIC POLICY?

The foregoing analysis, by placing the main blame for homelessness on government policies, not on the limits of the private market, may suggest neoconservative policy implications. Nothing could be further from the truth. The interests entrenched in contemporary housing policy are for the most part conservative. Many who praise the virtues of the free market on the job go home to white upper-class suburbs and vote for exclusionary controls over the market. The so-called free market approach of the Reagan Administration (housing vouchers), because it does not recognize the ways that the supply of housing no longer responds to increases in demand, does not address the roots of the housing problem and may even exacerbate it. Most importantly, unlike neoconservatives, I believe it is neither possible nor desirable to go back to a mythical free market. The United States needs to reform its housing policies, not abandon them.

The tragic visibility of the homeless captured the attention of policy elites. Unfortunately, policy attention has been focused on the most visible expression of the housing problem, not its underlying causes. The recent change in rhetoric from "bums," "derelicts," and "winos" to the "homeless" has recast the issue in moral terms. While bums have only themselves to blame, the homeless are victims—the deserving poor. Homelessness defines the problem in a welfare context, not in the context of basic social and economic policy. To place highest priority on sheltering the homeless is to treat the problem after it has already occurred, to put in place a social safety net that can catch people after they have fallen between the cracks. The shelter system being created for the homeless, however, is like putting pots and pans around a living room to catch the dripping water without trying to plug the leaks in the roof.

Shelterization is a shortsighted and expensive policy response. New York State and New York City have led the way in funding shelters for the homeless. New York City officials estimate that the city will spend 543 million dollars in city, state, and federal funds for its shelter system in 1987. In 1986, the system sheltered more than 50,000 people at one time or another—more than the population of Santa Fe, New Mexico.[32] Without addressing the underlying causes of homelessness, the shelter system may only become an endless sump for government revenues.

While motivated by a commendable sense of compassion, at best the shelter system provides temporary relief; at worst it perpetuates dependency and resignation among the homeless. The main problem with the shelter system is that it primarily addresses the physical needs of the homeless, not their social needs. Homelessness is more than the lack of physical shelter; it is detachment from society, detachment from the web of human relationships that integrate a person into the economy and society.[33] Without these ties, we are not fully human. From this viewpoint, a person can be homeless even if he or she has adequate shelter. The shelter system segregates the homeless as fundamentally different from the rest of us, cutting them off from society. Following the NIMBY syndrome, neighborhoods object to having shelters placed in their midst. Even if shelters provide expensive social services, they promote dependency by placing the homeless in a vulnerable situation where their needs are met by professional caretakers, not by their own actions. Ironically, while governments are funding vast shelter systems, their own policies subsidize the destruction of SROs and other low income housing alternatives where many of those presently occupying shelters were able to satisfy their physical and social needs by their own actions.[34]

The politics of compassion has succeeded in passing unprecedented government funding for the homeless. This shelter system is essentially charity, which I do not oppose. Even if housing policy were reformed tomorrow, it would take years for the supply of affordable housing to meet demand. In the meantime, shelters would be needed. And, of course, there is a small percentage of the homeless who will never be able to care for themselves. Shelterization, however, cannot take the place of a serious attack on the causes of the problem. Social welfare professionals are being set up to become fall guys for what is essentially a housing problem. If the causes of the problem are not treated, the shelter system will become more and more expensive until it will become politically impossible to meet even the bare physical needs of the homeless. At that point, there will be, indeed, "no room at the inn."

If this analysis is correct, the general direction housing policy must take is clear. The homeless problem is caused primarily by inadequate supply, not inadequate demand (or simple poverty). The supply problem is rooted in the transformation of cities from centers of industry to centers of high-level service employment. Subsidizing demand, in the form of housing vouchers, does not address the underlying shortage of low-rent housing. Federal spending programs for the poor must be targeted on increasing affordable rental housing, especially in tight metropolitan housing markets. In addition to shifting from a demand to a supply approach, housing policies should be targeted to places, not to people. Each year, in large cities with growing homeless populations, hundreds of thousands of potentially sound housing units are destroyed due to contagious abandonment. Programs should be targeted to save our existing housing resources. To accomplish this goal, comprehensive programs are needed that go beyond the physical aspects of housing to address the quality of life in the neighborhoods, including such social problems as drugs, crime, and, above all, unemployment. All this will require more intervention in markets, not less.

On the other hand, because many government policies help cause the problem, not cure it, part of the solution lies in withdrawing the government from market intervention and its broad array of misguided policies. Instead of helping those who need it the most, many policies protect the privileged position of entrenched housing interests, thereby hindering the ability of regional housing markets to adapt to changing needs—especially the needs of low income renters. Progress on the homeless problem, then, requires that we dismantle those policies that have helped cause the problem: tax incentives targeted to the wealthy homeowners, suburban zoning regulations designed to keep out low income rental housing, central city economic development policies that boost gentrification without regard to displacement—to name only a few.

The primary obstacles to solving the homeless problem are rooted in politics, however, not policy analysis. The regressive nature of United States housing policy has more to do with the power of interest groups than with the machinations of a ruling class. Our political system has been described as "broker state," or a system of interest group liberalism.[35] The fragmented nature of the state allows easy access by interest groups that cap-

ture portions of state power for their own advantage. United States housing policy has developed willy-nilly as various interests (homeowners, suburbanites, urban gentry) have entrenched themselves in different policy arenas. The result is a rigidified housing system that is incapable of meeting the needs of the politically powerless. We know what needs to be done; what is lacking is the political will to do it.

NOTES

1. Research on the earlier denizens of skid row contradicts the popular image of them as hopeless alcoholics. While alcoholics represented a larger percentage of the population of skid row than in the rest of the city, they still were only a small minority of the homeless population. *See generally* C. HOCH & R. SLAYTON, THE NEW HOMELESS AND THE OLD (forthcoming).

2. For a summary of the survey research on the demographics of the new homeless, see Ropers, *The Rise of the New Urban Homeless*, 26 PUB. AFF. REP. 1 (Oct.-Dec. 1985).

3. NEW YORK STATE OFFICE OF MENTAL HEALTH, WHO ARE THE HOMELESS? 38 (1982) [hereinafter WHO ARE HOMELESS?]; *see also* Ropers, *supra* note 3, at 3; Hopper & Hamberg, *The Making of America's Homeless: From Skid Row to New Poor*, in CRITICAL PERSPECTIVES ON HOUSING 31, (1986); COALITION FOR THE HOMELESS, STEMMING THE TIDE OF DISPLACEMENT: HOUSING POLICIES FOR PREVENTING HOMELESSNESS 26 (1986).

4. COALITION FOR THE HOMELESS, *supra* note 3, at 29.

5. Ropers, *supra* note 2, at 10–11; *see also* COALITION FOR THE HOMELESS, *supra* note 3, at 30–31.

6. *See generally* B. BLUESTONE & B. HARRISON, THE GREAT AMERICAN JOB MACHINE (1986).

7. Hopper & Hamberg, *supra* note 3, at 17–20.

8. *Id.* at 27; *see generally* M. CUOMO, 1933–1983 - NEVER AGAIN: A REPORT TO THE NATIONAL GOVERNORS' ASSOCIATION 47–50 (July 1983); Ropers, *supra* note 2, at 24.

9. Hopper & Hamberg, *supra* note 3, at 21.

10. *Id.* at 13.

11. *Id.* at 29.

12. *See generally* P. CLAY, AT RISK OF LOSS: THE ENDANGERED FUTURE OF LOW INCOME RENTAL HOUSING RESOURCES 24 (1987).

13. Wright & Lam, *Homelessness and the Low Income Housing Supply*, 17 SOC. POL'Y. 48, 51 (1987); *see also* COALITION FOR THE HOMELESS, *supra* note 3, at 9.

14. Sternlieh & Hughes, *Demographics and Housing in America*, 41 POP. BULL. 1, 31 (Jan. 1986).

15. *Id.* at 31.

16. COALITION FOR THE HOMELESS, *supra* note 3, at 6.

17. Abandonment and gentrification are not mutually exclusive processes; in fact, they reinforce one another. Gentrification, for example, siphons off people and investment from other neighborhoods and helps precipitate the process of contagious abandonment. *See generally* Marcuse, *Abandonment, Gentrification and Displacement: The Linkages in New York City*, in GENTRIFICATION OF THE CITY 153 (1986).

18. *See generally* Adams, *Homelessness in the Industrial City*, 21 URB. AFF. Q. 527 (1986).

19. Ganz, *Where has the Urban Crisis Gone?*, 20 URB. AFF. Q. 456 (1985).

20. SEN. COMM. ON BANKING, SUBCOMM. ON HOUSING AND URB. AFF., REPORT ON THE CENTRAL CITY PROBLEM AND URBAN RENEWAL POLICY 56 (1973).

21. LeGates & Hartman, *Displacement*, 15 CLEARINGHOUSE REV. 230, 236 (1982).

22. Marcuse, *supra* note 17, at 172.

23. COALITION FOR THE HOMELESS AND SRO TENANTS RIGHTS COALITION, SINGLE ROOM OCCUPANCY HOTELS: STANDING IN THE WAY OF THE GENTRY 5 (1985).

24. C. HOCH & R. SLAYTON, *supra* note 1, at 245.

25. Marcuse, *A Shame of the Cities— Why are they Homeless?*, 244 NATION 426, 428 (1987).

26. Herbers, *Economic Competition is Shifting Government Role in Low-Cost Housing*, N.Y. Times, May 20, 1987, at A18, col. 1.

27. C. HOCH & R. SLAYTON, *supra* note 1, at 106.

28. E. BANFIELD & M. GRODZINS, GOVERNMENT AND HOUSING IN METROPOLITAN AREAS 93–98 (1958); S. SEIDEL, HOUSING COSTS AND GOVERNMENT REGULATIONS: CONFRONTING THE REGULATION MAZE ch. 5 (1978); Coldwell & Kau, *The Economics of Building Codes and Standards*, in RESOLVING THE HOUSING CRISIS 57 (M.B. Johnson ed. 1982).

29. Local government regulation raises the question of the effect of rent control on homelessness. Conservatives argue that rent control dissuades entrepreneurs from investing in housing and promotes abandonment of marginal housing. C. HARTMAN, *supra* note 45, at 563–64; P. SALINS, THE ECOLOGY OF HOUSING DESTRUCTION: ECONOMIC EFFECTS OF PUBLIC INTERVENTION IN THE HOUSING MARKEt 64 (1980). Based on regression analysis, one study even concluded that rent control is "the single most important factor for predicting homelessness." Tucker, *Where Do the Homeless Come From?*, 22 N.Y. PERSP. 2 (1987). Defenders argue that rent control simply limits windfall profits by landlords and does not suppress new construction or contribute to abandonment. *See generally* Achtenberg, *The Social Utility of Rent Control*, in HOUSING URBAN

AMERICA 459; Bartelt & Lawson, *Rent Control and Abatement in N.Y. City: A Look at the Evidence*, in CRITICAL PERSPECTIVES ON HOUSING 180 (1986). This is not the place to sort out the complex issues in the rent control debate. Suffice it to say, however, that rent control basically views the housing problem as rooted in the fact that tenants are paying too much for housing. If the view here is correct, that homelessness is primarily caused by an inadequate *supply* of low income housing, then, at best, rent control does not address the homeless problem. At worst, if conservatives are correct that rent control suppresses investment in housing, it may even contribute to homelessness.

30. M. DANIELSON, THE POLITICS OF EXCLUSION chs. 3–4 (1976).; K. JACKSON, *supra* note 27, at 241–43; S. SIEDEL, *supra* note 28, at ch. 8.

31. Domurad, *It's 1985: Do You Know Where Your Tax Dollars Are?* CITY LIMITS, Aug.-Sept. 1985, at 27.

32. Barbanel, *New York Shifts Debate on Homeless Problem*, N.Y. Times, Nov. 11, 1987, § 2, at 1, col. 1.

33. Ropers, *supra* note 2, at 2.

34. *See generally* C. HOCH & R. SLAYTON, *supra* note 1.

35. G. ALPEROWITZ & J. FAUX, REBUILDING AMERICA: A BLUEPRINT FOR THE NEW ECONOMY ch. 2 (1984) T. LOWI, THE END OF LIBERALISM (1979).

24.   Notes from Underground: The Failure of Urban Mass Transit

Peter Gordon and Harry Richardson

Doomsday forecasts of crippling traffic jams now dominate discussions of urban development and form the basis of some very expensive transportation proposals. The Southern California Association of Governments, for instance, recently forecast that by the year 2000 the average rush-hour freeway speed for the Los Angeles area will fall from 35 mph to 17 mph. Under the banner "$42 Billion Needed to Avoid Future Gridlock, Report Says," the *Los Angeles Times* recently wrote that

even with severe restrictions on future driving, it will take massive spending

SOURCE: From: "Notes from underground: the failure of urban mass transit" by Peter Gordon and Harry Richardson. Reprinted with permission from: *The Public Interest*, No. 94 (Winter 1989), pp. 77–86. ©1989 by National Affairs, Inc.

on new freeways and transit to prevent the daily traffic catastrophe that many fear will define life in metropolitan Southern California by 2010, a new report . . . says. . . . More than $42 billion in construction is needed just to keep the freeways running close to today's average speeds, *already among the worst in the nation* [italics added].[1] If planners cannot alter where population growth and new jobs occur, and if drivers are not forced to change their habits, the cost could soar over $110 billion, the report says.

Studies such as these have been widely reported in the local media, and their forecasts are generally accepted. Recently these forecasts have been used to support a massive expansion of the public transit system for the Los Angeles area. The capital costs of all transit plans between 1992 and 2010 amount to $43.7 billion. A new subway is now under construction, and plans for more rail transit are being discussed. Before billions of dollars are spent in order to avert a traffic catastrophe, two questions ought to be answered. First, are the predictions accurate? And second, is a subway the solution?

Many of those who fearfully await the arrival of "gridlock" blame suburbanization, long the dominant spatial trend in U.S. cities. This trend reflects how most Americans choose to live, and it has been made possible, in great part, by the range and mobility that cars and highways afford. What the gridlock theorists ignore, however, is that industries are relocating to the suburbs in order to be close to workers' homes. Firms have learned that shorter work trips are a lure, helping them to recruit and retain employees. In addition, managers recognize productivity gains associated with shorter commutes. Today most job growth and even most jobs are suburban. Lower taxes and the greater availability of land in the suburbs have also helped to lure business away from the city. Most commuting today is suburb-to-suburb: in our twenty-five largest urban areas, only 8.4 percent of all jobs are in the central business district (CBD), and fewer than half those jobs are held by suburban residents.

Planners once believed that inefficient cross-hauling would accompany "sprawl," but it is now apparent that suburb-to-suburb trips are likely to be shorter and quicker than those to and from downtown, and that intersuburban routes can relieve some of the pressure on downtown routes. People who live and work in the suburbs—now 45 percent of the total work force—on average face a mercifully short commute of only twenty minutes. Indeed, while suburban labor may be the pull when businesses choose sites, downtown congestion is

often the push. Together, the push and the pull have left only 3 percent of the Los Angeles area's jobs in the CBD; San Francisco's CBD accounts for 11 percent of the area's jobs, and the other major urban areas fall within this range.

Even if we consider subcenters of job concentration, we find most jobs widely scattered. We have tried to identify all the subcenters in greater Los Angeles and have found nineteen major foci, using a broader definition of the downtown than the Census Bureau. Yet together these nodes account for only 17.5 percent of the area's jobs. The other 82.5 percent are so thinly spread that it is hard to identify clusters that resemble traditional "centers." Los Angeles is far from unusual in this respect; many other cities are developing similarly, because this pattern saves commuters time. Suburbanization is part of the traffic solution, not part of the problem. It is not leading to a doomsday gridlock.

Much of this essay deals with Los Angeles, but it is important to recognize that Los Angeles is more representative than exceptional. It is an extreme case only in the wild inappropriateness and the exorbitant expense of its rail-transit plans. But the same trends, such as the fading role of the central business district and the increasing dominance of suburb-to-suburb work trips, exist in all the major metropolitan areas. Although different strategies and investments may be needed in different cities, new construction of suburban-to-downtown mass transit is not justified anywhere.

USING THE WRONG MODEL

We believe that the premises, the reasoning, and the rhetoric that generate and accompany the dismal traffic forecasts are wrong. The costs of the error, judging by the *Los Angeles Times* account, approach the hundred-billion-dollar range for just one metropolis. But many other cities have incurred huge costs because their new subways have failed to attract enough riders to relieve congestion and to avoid massive subsidies. Such mistakes result from overattention to central-city traffic, which, in turn, rests on a misunderstanding of modern urban-development trends.

Conventional urban economics has misled policymakers by encouraging the rhetoric of "gridlock." The standard monocentric model of contemporary urban economics assumes that most jobs are located in the city center. Economists employ this supposition for analytical convenience and rarely subject it to study; they assume that such job concentration offers significant net benefits. The city center, in this model, is surrounded by a suburban ring of housing and roads. The model predicts that the residential ring expands outward as the city grows; average work trips must become longer because the model does not allow for any significant suburbanization of jobs. Moreover, unless the radial transport network can be expanded without limit, additional commuting to the city center will result in more congestion and slower trips.

But much of this is implausible. As we have already pointed out, the monocentric model does not square with reality; it flies in the face of evidence suggesting that employers orient themselves to workers' settlement choices rather than vice versa. We have found no empirical association, furthermore, between city size and traffic congestion. The largest cities do not have the worst traffic—precisely because they have rearranged themselves spatially to alleviate congestion. While the pace of suburban development has sometimes been so rapid that road building and other essential infrastructure investments have lagged behind, time solves many of the resulting traffic problems.

In addition, the conventional analysis overemphasizes the work trip, which is a small and shrinking share of all trips. Much congestion could be relieved simply by rationing "less essential" trips to off-peak hours—perhaps by a system of time-specific tolls, totally neglected by planners.

Why, then, does a faulty model survive? While economists use it for analytical convenience, the model appeals to policymakers because it encourages their tendency to brood over the downtown's demise and to plan big outlays to revive it. Downtown- and transit-boosters have chosen to depend upon this general model of urban economic analysis rather than to refer to the policy recommendations of urban planners such as John Kain, John Meyer, Martin Wohl, Martin Wachs, and José Antonio Gomez-Ibanez, who have overwhelmingly and repeatedly argued that fixed-rail systems cannot compete with efficiently priced and well-managed automobile transport, sound bus systems, and supplementary transit schemes like "dial-a-ride" services, jitneys, and van pools.

We have spent $45 billion in federal aid since the inception of the Urban Mass Transit Administration (UMTA) in 1964, and an almost equal amount in state and local subsidies, but the long-term decline in transit ridership persists. The funds have kept a number of inefficient bus operations in existence and have paid the bill for several low-impact rail projects.

New plans for rail systems surface intermittently in spite of the fact that the more one knows about rail transit in America, the worse it looks. There are no major subway markets outside Manhattan. San Francisco's BART (Bay Area Rapid Transit) merits a chapter in Professor Peter Hall's *Great Planning Disasters*. BART ridership now is less than 80 percent of that forecast for 1975; fares cover only about half of BART's operating costs. The costs per passenger trip remain higher than those for taking the bus or driving. Some years ago Melvin Webber predicted that BART might "become the first of a series of multibillion-dollar mistakes scattered from one end of the continent to the other."

Similarly, a one-way ride on Washington's Metro costs, in capital and operating expenses, more than $8 per passenger;[2] although the cost is comparable to that of automobile commuting, taking the subway increases travel time for all but the fortunate few who live and work near subway stations. Clearly, if commuters were expected to pay the full cost of their subway trips, the trains would soon be empty. The relatively poor subsidize the relatively well-off riders, since the subway is financed by sales taxes, which are regressive; in addition, the expected traffic, air-quality, and land-development benefits have proven to be almost non-existent. Baltimore and Atlanta have new subways that are grossly underused and whose most significant impact has been on the finances of local governments.

WHAT TO EXPECT IN LOS ANGELES

Los Angeles is unlikely to be any different. City folklore has it that a cabal between big auto and big oil interests eliminated Los Angeles's "Big Red Car" system in order to sell cars and gas. This story was recently repeated on CBS-TV's "60 Minutes"; more appropriately, it also figured in the plot of the cartoon movie "Who Framed Roger Rabbit?" But does anyone believe that most Los Angelenos are auto drivers because a conspiracy took the transit option away? Los Angeles's original rail system simply shared the fate of the American transit industry as a whole, losing in head-to-head competition with the automobile.

Transit-planning decisions continue to be made on the basis of pleasant fictions.

Opportunistic consultants grind out wholly implausible scenarios and forecasts that are almost always swallowed whole by downtown boosters and the cheerleading media. The consultants responsible for the failed Miami subway (202,000 daily riders were expected, but only about 30,000 use it) had little trouble obtaining lucrative contracts in Los Angeles, for which they made predictions that are no more believable. The developers of Los Angeles's Metrorail predict more riders per mile than any U.S. subway, *including* New York's. The L.A. forecasts look no more realistic when presented on a per-station basis; according to Martin Wohl, if the consultants' numbers are to be believed L.A.'s Metrorail can expect far greater usage per station than Toronto or Montreal. One of the authors (Peter Gordon) has developed a model that predicts ridership on the basis of system and city characteristics, including station spacing, auto-ownership rates, and population density. The model predicts less than one-third of the officially expected ridership.

Neither the transport planners nor the newspapers in Los Angeles have expressed any doubts about the consultant's model. Accordingly, construction is now under way at a cost of at least $250 million per mile (according to consultants' estimates) on the first 4.4-mile "minimum-operable" segment of an 18.6-mile "starter line." This line is intended to be part of a hybrid 155-mile system, most of which will be "light rail"—essentially streetcars. The mix reflects widespread recognition of the intolerably high construction costs of "heavy rail"; even so, a trolley can do nothing that an express bus cannot do better, and for less money.

The 22-mile Los Angeles-Long Beach light-rail line, now under construction, will cost between $600 million and $1 billion. Planners project 54,700 daily riders, yet the *faster* express bus following a parallel route on the Long Beach freeway currently carries fewer than a thousand passengers per day. The express bus will undoubtedly be cancelled when the trolley begins to run, transferring its modest number of passengers to a much costlier and slower system.

As if the consultants' mistakes were not enough, the subway component of the Los Angeles plan is being built by the Southern California Rapid Transit District (RTD), an agency that has a record of gross managerial incompetence. Recent disclosures have focused on employee drug abuse and absenteeism, a rash of bus accidents, insurance fraud, parts theft, and other abuses. According to the *Los Angeles Times*,

> Record-keeping at the RTD is so flawed that an internal investigation into whether bus parts were stolen had to be dropped because officials can neither produce the parts nor show conclusively that they are missing. . . . The new audit suggests that allegations of theft by employees may never be resolved. . . . Although RTD computers said the parts were stored in a nonexistent warehouse, more than $1.2 million in parts were actually missing or stolen.

In the hands of this agency, the new rail project will probably cost more than the estimated $250 million per mile.

But the headaches will be even bigger when operations begin. With the deficits generated by running a 155-mile rail system, bus services will suffer and fares will rise. The RTD currently operates an all-bus system, which costs about $500 million a year and serves about 1.3 million riders per day. Only about 40 percent of operations are covered by revenues. Current subsidies stand at almost $300 million. Service has been cut back, and fares have recently been increased. The system can only be further damaged

by the costs of a rail system. In fact, Los Angeles may be spending huge sums on a project that will actually reduce total transit use. (However, the recent Southern California Association of Governments' *Regional Mobility Plan* [1988] aims for a 19 percent transit share of total trips, almost four times greater than the current share of less than 5 percent.) The people deprived of bus service by the rail project—who, incidentally, will be among the poorest riders—could outnumber the rail system's patrons.

The Los Angeles story is only one of many. Urban rail transit is an 1890s idea, not suited to societies with income levels high enough to sustain widespread auto ownership. Nevertheless, there are currently more than sixty applications before the UMTA for funds to build rail.

TRANSIT MANAGEMENT AND SUBURBANIZATION

Costly rail-transit proposals draw on popular frustrations with big-city traffic congestion and rest on the assumption that new transit systems will solve the problem. U.S. politicians and planners love to take "study tours" to Tokyo and the European capitals to study their transit "successes." But the Los Angeles metropolitan area has about half Tokyo's population in twice the area; Tokyo's widespread transit use is based on very high population densities. In addition, average Tokyo commuting times exceed one hour and living spaces are minuscule by American standards. Do our planners expect or wish to promote this urban pattern for the United States?

If not, what is the rationale for the argument that transit investments will eventually justify themselves by promoting high-density developments near stations? This argument is beguiling to transit planners because it lets them point to an additional revenue source to help finance subway plans. While the principle is reasonable, planners exaggerate the magnitude of the expected rises in property values by depending on overoptimistic ridership forecasts. For Los Angeles's 4.4-mile project, consultants have become highly creative in inflating the numbers. In an attempt to show a $1.5-billion increase in property values, the consultants double- and even triple-counted: projected land-value increments were added to expected rental increases, these were added to revenue benefits, and so on.

But in any event, none of the postwar subways seems to have significantly changed local development patterns. Whenever a rail system is suggested, transit advocates and their consultants claim that tremendous corridor development will follow. But if transit systems do not generate heavy traffic, development surrounding the stations will be disappointing.

The first of the postwar rail systems, San Francisco's BART, has had twenty years and several gas crises to make an impact. Its environment could be expected to favor rail: San Francisco's population distribution is primarily coastal and linear, water barriers restrict travel routes, and economic activity is relatively centralized. At the time of BART's construction, one-third of the region's jobs were in San Francisco itself; that proportion has since declined to one-fifth and is expected to fall further. In the other subway cities the experience is the same. Development today is predominantly suburban and often far from the rail system's routes.

Apparently recognizing that the customary predictions about development rarely come true, some planners suggest that mass-transit projects be combined with suburban land-use controls to force concentrations of population and employment that would make mass-transit service "efficient." But what type of development pattern do we seek? The widespread and spontaneous trend toward suburbanization suggests that workers and their employers do not wish to live and work in densely populated areas. Mass transit exists for no other reason than to serve the local citizenry; and yet urban planners seem to want to foist undesired living patterns on the population so as to make their transit systems more efficient.

There is no single solution to traffic congestion, and the search for one has exacted high costs. Big-city life has its drawbacks, among them queuing and traffic. The issue is how to balance the social costs of traffic congestion with the costs of doing something about it. Dreams that others—such as the federal government or imaginary converts to public transit—will bail us out have no place in the discussion.

Nineteenth-century transit schemes are increasingly irrelevant in the dispersed and decentralized modern American city, which is why, time and again, new urban rail systems have failed so spectacularly. But this view is too unpopular to receive a fair hearing in an atmosphere charged with boosterism. Transit proposals are associated with the drive to put an empty convention center into every major American downtown and to overinvest in downtown renewal. With rare exceptions, these anachronisms have been expensive and wasteful. The support they garner is based on a misunderstanding of American cities. The downtowns of the 1890s cannot be re-created. Collectively, most Americans have chosen to live and work anywhere but downtown.

Is there then no relief from traffic congestion? There is no simple answer, but some trends and some policies can help us. Since, in the end, suburbanization and decentralization are potent traffic decongestants, planners and politicians should facilitate these spontaneous processes. There are suburban congestion spots, but they reflect the overallocation of metropolitan transportation investments to central core areas instead of suburban locations. Problems arise when restrictive zoning measures prevent industrial deconcentration or when "slow-growth" or "growth-control" policies limit it. Most growth controls tend to counter the natural tendency for businesses and residences to be located together in newly settled areas; to the extent that they do so, the result is longer trips and deteriorating traffic conditions.

Metropolitan transportation planners should begin by improving the management of transport facilities already in place. "Transport system management" has had some successes, as in the effort to reduce congestion during the 1984 Los Angeles Summer Olympic Games.[3] Sound management would make the best possible use of existing facilities, *before* deciding what to build next. Techniques might include peak-load pricing on freeways (or at least extending Los Angeles's ramp metering to other cities), reducing cycle time on traffic signals, and fining truckers—who account for almost one-half of Los Angeles's freeway congestion—a cash sum equivalent to the time-delay costs of any accidents or hold-ups for which they are found liable. Traffic management also means ending the folly of subsidized parking and making more serious efforts to tow away parked cars illegally obstructing traffic during peak hours. (To its credit, the City of Los Angeles already tows three thousand cars daily during the afternoon peak, and illegal parkers during peak hours are said to have an 85 percent chance of being ticketed or towed.)

There are many more common-sense measures appropriate for a variety of urban settings. These receive too little attention because planners and politicians seem to prefer big-expenditure (but low-benefit) projects, the grand designs

rather than the modest steps. Urban-transportation proposals cannot be effective so long as they fail to recognize the established growth patterns of contemporary American cities. People have voted with their feet in favor of suburbanization; it is folly to devote vast stores of public funds to a transit system built around a "downtown" that may no longer exist.

NOTES

1. While speeds may have slowed since 1980, Los Angeles seems to compare very favorably with other large cities. Los Angeles's median commuting time in 1980 was 23.4 minutes; New York's was 30 minutes. Of the top ten metropolitan areas, Los Angeles ranked ahead of all but two according to this measure. It benefits from the dispersion of its population.

2. This estimate is based on 1981 data; annual capital costs of $483 million and operating costs of $94.2 million are distributed over 290,000 weekday trips.

3. Transport system management (TSM) improves the effectiveness of an existing system by using strategies that are not capital intensive to increase system capacity and by influencing travel demand to reduce peak-period vehicle trips. During the Olympics TSM strategies included scheduling events for off-peak hours, encouraging spectators to use public transit, promoting fewer nonwork trips, rearranging work schedules, rescheduling truck traffic, creating one-way streets, and closing freeway ramps. As a result of these strategies, traffic conditions during the Olympics were better than usual; the specter of a "Black Monday" never materialized.

CHAPTER 11
Social Issues

Historically, two policies that have been within the purview of state and local governments are those of welfare and education. The federal government plays a more important role in these policies today than it has in the past, but it would be a mistake to think that the federal government has eclipsed the states and localities. In this chapter we look first at welfare policy where the federal government and the states play almost equal roles, and then at educational policy where local governments are particularly important in deciding policies and delivering services.

The federal role in welfare policy started during the Great Depression, when state and local governmental programs could not cope with large numbers of unemployed people (25 percent of the population) and a collapsed national economy[1]. Under the leadership of President Franklin D. Roosevelt, the Social Security Act of 1935 became law. This act, and amendments added over the years, forms the basis of welfare policy in the United States. In 1989, well over one-half of the $115 billion spent on major social welfare programs (Aid to Families with Dependent Children, Supplemental Security Income, general assistance, food stamps, and Medicaid) came from the federal government.

Welfare reform is discussed continually in the United States. In 1988, Congress passed, and President Reagan signed into law, the Family Support Act. The goal of this law, and the Job Opportunities and Basic Skills (JOBS) Training Program it created, is to help people on welfare obtain jobs so they can support themselves and their families. In other words, welfare recipients will move from depending on government to depending on themselves. They will become economically self-sufficient. To a considerable extent, it is state and local welfare agencies that are responsible for achieving this goal. They are changing from simply providing case assistance to providing an array of services, including education and training, that will bring those on welfare into the labor force.

It may appear that since the federal government has adopted a new approach to welfare, state and local agencies have only to follow federal guidelines. But nothing could be further from the truth. Reading 25, by Susan Blank of the Foundation for Child Development in New York City, argues that JOBS could serve as a basis for states to develop a two-generation

---

[1] Ann O'M. Bowman and Richard C. Kearney, *State and Local Government* (Boston: Houghton Mifflin, 1990), p. 63.

approach for families receiving AFDC. This approach would combine adult employment and training services with support for the children, especially child care and health services. Blank also identifies various ways welfare agencies have started to implement JOBS, demonstrating the accuracy of Justice Louis Brandeis's statement in 1932 that states are the "laboratories of democracy." Minnesota is screening the health needs of children of JOBS participants, and San Diego, California, has a program that helps parents become more supportive of their children in school.

It is no secret that American public schools, especially those in our large cities, are not doing a satisfactory job in educating many of their students, Almost all of the evidence is disheartening: high school dropouts, adult illiteracy, declining SAT scores, and below-average performance on international math and science tests. In Reading 26, Paul Hill, a researcher at the Rand Corporation in Washington, D.C., notes that urban schools need more revenues, but he does not think lack of money is the most important factor contributing to the failure of public schools. He argues that school systems are highly regulated. Teachers and principals must comply with rules from local school boards, legislatures and educational agencies at the state level, Congress and Department of Education at the federal level, and state and federal courts. Rather than take responsibility for students' learning, teachers and principals work in an environment that forces them to make sure they follow rules and regulations. Unfortunately, a teacher's saying, "I get paid whether you learn this or not" too often becomes the norm.

Hill believes the problems of today's schools can be solved only by fundamental change that creates an alternative public school system. This alternative system would take school boards and superintendents out of the day-to-day operations of schools and give them the role of setting basic goals and hiring contractors to operate individual schools. Contractors, operating under an agreement with the school board that specifies performance, cost, and duration of contract, might be a local child-development organization, a university's school of education, or a teacher's union.

The hope is that this system would require school boards to focus on what students need to learn and the hiring of contractors that are effective in educating students to the level required by the board. Teachers and principals (employed by the contractor) would focus on providing students with a quality education or they would lose their contract.

QUESTIONS FOR DISCUSSION

1. Do you think the two-generation approach to helping families on welfare is a better idea than concentrating on developing the educational and job skills of adults so they can enter the labor force?

2. Based on your experience, how would you rate the performance of elementary and secondary schools you attended? If changes are needed, what kind would you recommend? Is an alternative school system needed to bring about the kind of changes you want?

25.   JOBS as a Two-Generation Intervention

Susan Blank

The JOBS Program, the welfare-to-work program created under the Family Support Act of 1988, is most often discussed in terms of its implications for adult welfare recipients. However, JOBS also offers an opportunity to target assistance to some of the most vulnerable children in our society—children in families receiving Aid to Families with Dependent Children (AFDC).

The historian of 2030 will only be able to study whether or not the Family Support Act and its JOBS programs improved welfare policy in the 1990s; we, however, have the opportunity to become actively engaged in ensuring that the Family Support Act's full potential for reform is realized. Clearly, that means paying attention to the law and the adequacy of its funding. It also means careful policy analysis to determine how the Family Support Act and JOBS can be used most effectively.

In this article, I describe early implementation experiences in JOBS programs as a basis for understanding more about the Family Support Act's potential for addressing the needs of the whole family. JOBS, according to the Foundation for Child Development, can stimulate the development of two-generation interventions that combine adult employment and training services with supports to help children grow up healthy and ready to learn. These dual-focus interventions are a potentially powerful new approach to fostering genuine family self-sufficiency.

One shortcoming of many past efforts to improve the lives of at-risk families is

SOURCE: From "JOBS as a Two-Generation Intervention" by Susan Blank from *Public Welfare*, Summer 1992, Vol. 50, No. 3, pp. 46–51. Copyright © 1992 Foundation for Child Development. Reprinted by permission.

that they often have proceeded down only one of two tracks. Welfare-to-work programs serve adults but typically have not attended to children's needs. Meanwhile, child- and family-oriented programs, even quality early childhood interventions, usually have given little priority to efforts to help parents become more employable. In contrast, a two-generation intervention could ensure that both sets of needs are addressed simultaneously. It would reduce short-term risk factors in children's lives through services such as preventive health care and quality child care; at the same time it would target poverty, a serious long-term risk factor, by helping parents achieve long-term economic independence.

Ideally, a two-generation intervention consists of six elements:[1]

- assessment of child and family needs,
- quality child care and early childhood education,
- services that strengthen parenting,
- preventive health services for children and parents,
- self-sufficiency services leading to employment and a living wage, and
- case management that supports the dual goals of economic self-sufficiency and healthy child development.

For two reasons, JOBS programs seem to be promising catalysts for the creation of these two-generation interventions. First, through JOBS, the Family Support Act provides new funding for several services that are essential to a two-generation intervention: education, skills training, and job readiness activities; child care; transitional Medicaid; assessment; and case management. Second, JOBS can be linked to other important family service programs, such as preventive health care programs, family literacy programs, and Head Start, bringing both the program's own resources and those of the other interventions to bear on the needs of one family.[2]

Despite these advantages, objections could be raised to casting JOBS in the role of catalyst for two-generation interventions on the grounds that, in an era of fiscal constraints, delivering services to adult welfare recipients is difficult enough. Designing welfare-to-work programs with little or no regard for family needs, however, presents a greater ultimate risk than integrating family supports with employment and training services because, for many families, employment and training services alone are not enough to end the cycle of intergenerational poverty.[3]

Convinced that the two-generation approach is feasible even at a time of great stress for the welfare system and for JOBS, the Foundation for Child Development decided to find out what that approach looks like in practice. Extensive telephone interviews, consultations with experts, and selected site visits did not uncover any examples of interventions that fully fit the ideal two-generation model—in other words, interventions that contain a perfect or near-perfect mix of the model's six elements. The investigations did reveal, however, a variety of innovative JOBS policies and practices around the country that are moving the welfare-to-work system toward two-generation services. What follows is a discussion of each of the six elements, with illustrations from various sites.

ASSESSING CHILD AND FAMILY NEEDS

JOBS programs must conduct an initial assessment of participants, taking into account family circumstances as a part of the determination of employability. Programs can, if they choose, expand this assessment to identify the basic needs of the family and its children. Doing so is an important first step toward transforming JOBS into a two-generation intervention. Both the Hawaii and Denver JOBS programs conduct far-reaching family assessments, designed to help the family identify its strengths and to bring to light health, developmental, and family problems that could make the family more vulnerable to long-term dependency.[4]

Three general guidelines are relevant to the initial assessment:[5]

- Assessment information is best used to maximize available supports for families. Ideally, quality services to address identified needs will be available; and the JOBS Program can play an important role in making these accessible to families. When serious service gaps exist, however, a full assessment of basic child and family needs still may have great value, since documenting unmet needs is critical to program development that will ultimately benefit families.

- Assessment of basic family and child needs should be conducted for all JOBS participants. Children of parents who are judged to be "job ready" may have needs that are as urgent as the needs of children whose parents are assigned to education and job training activities.

- Information from a single source should not be used to exclude a child or other family member from services. In most cases, needs are best understood through multiple sources, including parental reports, observations by professionals, and formal assessments.

Many children in families receiving welfare are not screened for health and developmental problems until they reach school age, thus precluding earlier and frequently less expensive and more effective treatments. JOBS, however, is in contact with many families when their children are younger and thus can facilitate timely identification of problems, both through its own assessments and by encouraging participating parents to take advantage of other screenings. An excellent program for identifying children's health needs is the Early and Periodic Screening, Diagnosis, and Treatment (EPSDT) program, which operates under Medicaid and is available automatically to children in families receiving welfare. EPSDT has been underused, despite evidence that it successfully identifies treatable conditions and can save money by promoting early intervention. Recognizing the value of EPSDT services, some states are conducting EPSDT outreach in JOBS programs. The state plan for Minnesota's JOBS Program mandates outreach to enroll children of JOBS participants in EPSDT.

CHILD CARE AND EARLY EDUCATION

Stable child care that meets the developmental and educational needs of children can positively influence not only parents' ability to participate in JOBS but also children's well-being and development. Welfare-to-work programs, however, often have treated child care as ancillary, analogous to transportation subsidies whose sole purpose is to enable parents to work or take part in training. That approach gives programs little encouragement for seeking out the highest-quality care available for the child. But the level of vulnerability among AFDC children indicates that placing them in excellent developmental child care should be a priority concern. Children of JOBS participants often are the very same children targeted for Head Start and other enriched early childhood interventions. Thus, it is shortsighted to treat the decision about what kind of child care they need as less important just because they come to our attention

through the JOBS Program rather than through another route, such as a Head Start referral.

Ensuring that children of JOBS participants receive quality care is a two-step process. First, parents must be offered information and counseling about how to identify quality care. Second, families' access to good care must be improved by means of adequate reimbursement rates, efforts to improve the supply of quality care, and arrangements that foster JOBS families' participation in Head Start and other exemplary early childhood programs.

When the Maryland JOBS Program, Project Independence, began operations in Baltimore, Department of Social Services staff were overwhelmed by the search for child care for JOBS participants. To help negotiate the complex task of finding child care arrangements that would meet each participant's needs, Project Independence turned to LOCATE: Child Care, a child care resource and referral agency. Before serving the JOBS Program, LOCATE held contracts with a number of corporations; however, LOCATE is now offering low-income parents the same quality of care as the program gives its corporate clients. In the first year of working with Project Independence, LOCATE found child care for 70 percent of children in JOBS families who used the service.

A different kind of child care effort is under way in Illinois through the Child Care and Development (CCD) section of the state Department of Public Aid. While other subsidized child care, including the new federal Child Care Block Grant, is handled through the Illinois Department of Children and Family Services, CCD oversees child care for the state's AFDC recipients exclusively. The focus in this program is on active state-level problem solving. CCD has used a variety of mechanisms, including client surveys, informational campaigns, and training, to provide better child care options for JOBS families.

One particularly promising strategy for improving child care under JOBS is to promote children's enrollment in Head Start so that families can take advantage of its comprehensive child and family services. Across the country, JOBS and Head Start programs are beginning to intersect. In Philadelphia, for example, most of the more than 3,500 children enrolled in the city's seven Head Start agencies are from families eligible for AFDC and at risk of long-term welfare dependency. Because of the considerable overlap in the population served by Head Start and the families targeted by JOBS, administrators of these two programs had a number of shared concerns and goals that led to an interest in collaboration. In an evolving relationship between the Philadelphia JOBS and Head Start systems, two local Head Start directors have signed a formal agreement with the city's JOBS Program, New Directions, to facilitate joint enrollments. The Head Start programs also will try to extend their hours to accommodate the needs of parents participating in JOBS and whose children are enrolled in Head Start.

SERVICES THAT STRENGTHEN PARENTING

When a parent on welfare takes steps to become economically self-sufficient, the process has implications not just for that adult, but also for the entire family. The experience can affect the parent-child relationship in both positive and negative ways. For example, a parent involved in education or training may have a more hopeful outlook on the future, but she may also face new stress as demands on her time increase. Two-generation programs can help parents cope with problems that adversely affect parenting. At the same time, they can affirm parents' interest and investment in their children's futures—and this affirmation, in turn, can be a powerful motivator for parents to succeed in their own efforts to become economically self-sufficient.

JOBS programs can provide parenting activities directly. For example, many parents need help in learning how to support their children in school. San Diego's JOBS Program—Greater Avenues for Independence (GAIN)—has developed a workshop on parent involvement in schools that is offered to participants engaged in job search or education activities. The workshop covers home teaching, strategies for helping children succeed in school, effective parent-teacher conferences, and similar topics.[6]

Another way JOBS can assist participants with parenting issues is to establish connections with other programs that support families. In several Kentucky counties, for example, special efforts are made to coenroll JOBS parents in Parent and Child Education (PACE), the state's highly regarded family literacy program. In Lexington, Kentucky, and Denver, some JOBS participants are enrolled in sites of the federal Comprehensive Child Development Program (CCDP), which provides exceptionally comprehensive, sustained intervention to low-income families with young children. And Portland, Oregon's, Teen Parent Program, which serves teenage JOBS participants in school, includes a site of the federal New Chance demonstration program, which offers unusually intensive services to teens and their children.

One reservation that could be advanced about linking JOBS to other family initiatives is that programs like PACE, CCDP, and New Chance are by definition enriched interventions and by no means typical of services available to most welfare families. Nevertheless, many communities are home to at least one of these programs; and where they exist, they are an important resource upon which JOBS programs can draw. JOBS officials routinely should survey their states and communities for the presence of these programs and then consider whether joining forces with them would be useful. Furthermore, especially with recent increases in federal funding, Head Start programs could be widely available as partners in joint initiatives with JOBS.

PREVENTIVE HEALTH SERVICES

Preventive health care for both children and parents is critical to achieving family self-sufficiency. Yet the prevalence of health problems among AFDC children is well documented, and growing evidence shows that the health of mothers on welfare is similarly deficient.[7] In the face of these problems, JOBS programs offer a natural opportunity to encourage families to use preventive health services. A regular part of JOBS orientations in some Tampa programs are preventive health workshops operated by the district Medicaid office. The workshops stress EPSDT, family planning, and other aspects of good preventive health care. The supervisor of the district Medicaid office is pleased that JOBS orientations allow her staff to target a key audience with information about health care. The sessions encourage parents to take an active role in securing good health care for their families. Before states adopt policies to make the level of a welfare benefit contingent upon whether or not a mother secures health care for her child, they may want to consider this simpler and more direct way of using JOBS programs as an opportunity for outreach and education on preventive health care.

TOWARD EMPLOYMENT AND A LIVING WAGE

Even when their parents are employed, low-income children are at high risk of poor social adjustment and school failure—predictions of poverty in adulthood. This pattern suggests that simply moving parents into the ranks of the working poor is often not enough to fortify children against negative outcomes.

Family supports like those mentioned here—quality child care and early childhood education, parenting education, and preventive health care—provide additional protection; but over the long term, a two-generation intervention should help the family escape poverty.

Many questions remain unanswered about the intensity, structure, and content of welfare-to-work services most likely to further this goal. Moreover, it has been widely argued that, regardless of how well welfare-to-work services are designed and delivered, they must be reinforced with additional assistance, such as improved provision of child support, family allowances, and tax credits, if the family is to have adequate financial support. But, despite the many open questions about welfare-to-work services, some research indicates that the Family Support Act is on the right track in placing new emphasis on education and training as opposed to shorter-term interventions such as job search that prevailed in many initiatives of the 1980s. The Kentucky, Hawaii, and Denver JOBS programs, all of which define themselves as family interventions, enroll significant numbers of participants in education and training designed to help them leave welfare permanently and earn decent wages.

It is also important to provide ongoing practical support and encouragement to help parents successfully participate in education and training and make the transition to work. Project Match, a Chicago welfare-to-work program, is unusual in giving recognition to the small, first steps a client may take toward self-sufficiency—such as volunteering in a Head Start program or keeping appointments—and provides encouragement and assistance to parents even after they find jobs. Similar recognition of the importance of making a long-term commitment to participants has led Portland's Teen Parent Program, which serves many JOBS teens, to hire transition coordinators to monitor the progress of participants after they graduate from high school and leave the core teen parent program.

CASE MANAGEMENT

A genuine two-generation approach to JOBS rests on consistent oversight by case managers of the entire effort to attain long-term self-sufficiency. Several of the programs discussed in this article have managed to maintain relatively low caseloads for JOBS case managers, thus facilitating the provision of careful guidance and support to families. For example, case managers in the Hawaii program typically carry caseloads of 70 participants and are expected to be in contact with their clients weekly.

As with parenting education, a second strategy that JOBS can use to strengthen case management is to establish links with other programs. JOBS participants coenrolled in the Denver and Kentucky federal CCDP programs and in the New Chance teen demonstration sites in Portland and Kentucky are assigned to case managers who get to know them very well because of the intensive nature of family services provided. In the Denver CCDP program, a combination of two funding streams enables JOBS case managers to be outstationed to the CCDP site. Elsewhere, case management responsibilities are shared between JOBS and the family program. When two programs do assume joint responsibility for case management, they formally should establish mutual goals and concrete methods for reinforcing these goals in working with families.

The Foundation for Child Development's investigations have led it to conclude that a new approach to welfare reform is possible. While certainly not the dominant theme in JOBS nationwide, the two-generation strategy nevertheless persists, often in the face of severe fiscal constraints. In a 1991 report that dis-

cusses the feasibility of using the welfare system to meet the needs of children and that examines programs implemented before the Family Support Act was enacted, Olivia Golden—then a scholar at Harvard University's John F. Kennedy School of Government—concluded that addressing child and family needs through the welfare system is difficult but by no means impossible.[8] The foundation's examination of programs in the early stages of JOBS implementation confirms that conclusion.

JOBS officials who wish to give their programs a two-generation focus should first take stock of how well their programs are meeting families' needs currently. Five major indicators can be used to assess the extent to which a JOBS program, in conjunction with other institutions and programs, is supporting children's health, development, and prospects for school success and future self-sufficiency:[9]

1. Is the JOBS Program guided by explicit policy objectives that include the goal of actively supporting children's healthy development?
2. Do training activities provide clear guidance to frontline workers about how JOBS and related services can address child and family needs?
3. Does the JOBS employability assessment seek to identify basic needs of children and family circumstances that affect children's well-being?
4. Is the JOBS Program coordinated with other essential child and family services so that JOBS participants and their children have access to needed supports? Does this coordination create a network of JOBS and JOBS–related services that includes the six elements of a two-generation intervention?
5. Are key program administrators, representing a range of child, family, and adult self-sufficiency services, organized to work together on improve-

ments in the JOBS Program that lead to stronger support for both family self-sufficiency and children's healthy development?

We still have much to learn about the kinds of services that will be most helpful to families with different characteristics and needs. Nevertheless, a two-generation model of intervention reflects our current knowledge of conditions that are likely to help parents move from welfare to work and to support the well-being of children and their social and academic development. This knowledge has informed many of the new two-generation Head Start and family literacy program models and is beginning to influence the implementation of JOBS. Taken together, our improved understanding of how to help families out of poverty, and the emergence of new program models and funding streams, create the best opportunity in decades to transform assistance to welfare-dependent families in ways that benefit children.

NOTES

1. Sheila Smith, Susan Blank, and Ray Collins, *Pathways to Self-Sufficiency for Two Generations: Designing Welfare-to-Work Programs that Strengthen Families and Benefit Children* (New York: Foundation for Child Development, 1992).
2. Ibid., 6–7.
3. Sheila Smith, "Two Generation Models: A New Intervention Strategy," *Social Policy Report* (Spring 1991):8.
4. *Pathways*, 36, 43–44.
5. Ibid., 15.
6. Telephone interviews with Vonnie Ellis and Marilyn Stewart, San Diego GAIN program.
7. Nicholas Zill et al., *The Life Circumstances and Development of Children in Welfare Families* (Washington, D.C.: Child Trends, Inc., 1991).
8. Olivia Golden, *Poor Children and Welfare Reform: Executive Summary of the Final Report* (New York: Foundation for Child Development, 1991).
9. *Pathways*, 90–91.

26. Urban Education

Paul T. Hill

HOW THE SYSTEM IS STACKED AGAINST BETTER PUBLIC SCHOOLS

Why did we get schools that are different from what everyone wants? The answer is complex and, because it lacks a single villain, unsatisfying. We, the adult Americans who vote, pay taxes, and badger or praise elected officials, made them

SOURCE: From "Urban Education" by Paul T. Hill in *Urban America; Policy Choices for Los Angeles and the Nation*, edited by James B. Steinberg, David W. Lyon, and Mary E. Vaiana, The Rand Corporation, 1992. Reprinted by permission.

that way. We made them through the gradual accretion of small decisions, not by design. Since the mid-1960s, when schools first became the focus of social policy, they have been subject to layer after layer of rules, regulations, court orders, teacher contract provisions, and other formal rules that bind and delimit what teachers and principals can do. Do schools have too few or too many minority students or does a desegregated school have too many segregated classes? The answer is a rule or court order. Are handicapped children neglected in some schools? The answer is a new legal principle and access to the courts for aggrieved parents. Do some students need extra help in school? The answer is a series of federal and state categorical programs, each with its own set of controls designed to ensure that the services bought with federal and state monies go to the intended beneficiaries and no one else.

Taken one by one, most of these policies and programs seem reasonable. So do the literally hundreds of other rules made by local school boards, state legislatures and state education agencies, Congress, the U.S. Department of Education, and federal and state courts. So do the many rules governing when schools open and close, how many minutes teachers may teach, and how a principal may supervise and evaluate a teacher, all agreed to one by one by school boards who chose to make work rule concessions rather than meet teachers' union salary demands. [1] In the aggregate, however, the accretion of rules has created schools that no one would have consciously designed and that do not work.

A highly regulated school system does not work because no one is personally responsible for whether children learn. The people inside the system, teachers, principals, and administrators, are responsible for performing tasks specified by regulations and contracts and for respecting the turf of others. Most teachers and their supervisors care about children, and many complain that their schools are hurt by a few "time servers" who do not work hard and will not cooperate with efforts to upgrade instruction. Poor performers are safe if they can demonstrate compliance and rectitude. Parents and community members who complain about poor results are often told that nothing can be done as long as no rules have been violated. School boards, caught in the web of their own rules, can do little about failing schools. Los Angeles and every other big city has dozens of schools that have abjectly failed students for years, producing sev-

eral times more dropouts, truants, and semiliterate graduates than the local average. The board or superintendent may take marginal actions (e.g., replacing a principal or adding a new program to supplement the school's inadequate core program). A school is seldom changed fundamentally as long as it complies with all applicable regulations.

Public schools that focus on education and offer their students a specific approach to learning are rare because our system of public control naturally produces a different kind of school. On important matters where school boards are divided, policies are very carefully drawn to satisfy as many people as possible and to compensate pressure groups that lose on one issue with a win on another. The natural result is a system of schools in which all are constrained by the same thicket of requirements.

The foregoing is enough to explain much of the critique of public schools. It certainly accounts for the fact that public schools try to be all things to all people and are unable to develop coherent philosophies of education. Something else is needed, however, to explain why schools in poor areas are usually worse than schools in wealthy ones. District revenues are, of course, part of the picture. Differences in local property tax valuation and the general economic plight of big cities limit the funding available for city schools.

But some of the most striking differences in school quality are evident *within* city school districts. Even with their limited revenue bases, cities like Chicago and New York are able to create some of the best schools in the country that coexist in the same system with some of the worst. There are two keys to this striking inequality within cities. The first is politics: to hold on to middle class students and demonstrate their commitment to quality, city school systems often create "flagship schools." These schools may or may not get more public funds than others, but the staff members are free to develop instructional themes and adapt curriculum to students' needs. Many of these flagship schools also get support from national foundations and reform networks, which further enhance their independence and flexibility.

The second key to inequality within cities is teacher allocation. Teachers' union contracts with big city public school districts all give senior teachers first choice about jobs and school placements. Not surprisingly, senior teachers tend to congregate in schools located in safe and attractive neighborhoods with supportive parents and responsive students. Schools in less attractive neighborhoods have trouble attracting and keeping senior teachers. They have to accept newer, less-experienced teachers and, in many cases, teachers who lack complete training or who scored poorly on state teachers' exams.

The teacher allocation process leads to staff instability in low-income area schools. Many teachers with good qualifications leave such schools as soon as they have the seniority to do so. It also leads to lower *de facto* funding for poverty area schools. Schools are billed for teacher salaries as if all teachers cost the same amount. But senior teachers cost two and one-half times as much as beginning teachers in most cities. Since over 70 percent of all school costs go for teachers' salaries, schools with all senior teachers can cost nearly twice as much as schools with all junior teachers. The recent settlement of a lawsuit, *Rodriguez v. Los Angeles Unified School District*, may lead to the elimination of some of these funding inequities.

Job protections for senior teachers pose another problem for cities with rapidly changing populations like Los Angeles. . . . As a recent study of immigrant education showed, many schools serving immigrant populations are dominated by teachers who are left over from earlier times when all students were native born. [1] During times of budget crisis, school systems can neither create vacancies to hire new teachers with the appropriate language skills nor change school staffs rapidly as student needs change.

Not all inner-city schools are defeated by these factors. A few schools in every city attract and keep dedicated staff members and work aggressively to meet students' needs. But these schools work despite the system, not because of it. Like all systems, the public schools operate pretty much as they were designed most of the time. The result is that most inner-city public schools are bureaucratic, weak, unlikely to change on their own, and resistant to change from the outside.

In the past few years, superintendents and civic leaders in a number of cities have recognized that their schools were not working and have tried to create an instantaneous reform. They have declared "site-based management" an opportunity for principals and teachers in existing schools to use their own judgment in changing school programs to meet the needs of children. Site-based management plans in places like Miami, Chicago, Los Angeles, and New York gave teachers and parents greater influence over school-level decision making. But, as a recent . . . report shows, the roles of the superintendent, school board, and central office bureaucracy did not change. [2] School communities, though urged to change themselves, are still tied up by the same inequitable school budgets, limitations on the use of funds, teacher contract provisions, and central office regulations. Some parent councils in Chicago exercised their authority to fire their principals; others elsewhere found new ways to use the few thousand dollars of flexible equipment and supplies money available to each school. But very few were able to focus on a basic review of the school's performance and devise significant improvements. The existing system had kept its strings on them.

The big city system of governance and finance that produces weak public schools is robust and persistent. Though many teachers and administrators criticize the system, most find their individual jobs safe and tolerable. Civil service protections and union contracts ensure that schools deal fairly and consistently with adults, even if they do not work well for children. The system also deals very efficiently with challenges. Outstanding principals and community leaders can flout convention, but they are isolated and few; when they leave or retire, their schools usually regress toward the systemwide mean. Schools that receive special attention from outside funding sources and reform leaders are also allowed to distinguish themselves. But they too often become Potemkin villages, protecting the system from criticism by focusing attention on its few excellent schools.

Can a city like Los Angeles create a public school system that is less bound by its rules and adult protections and more able to promote school quality and adaptiveness? The final section in this [reading] argues that the answer is yes.

AN ALTERNATIVE PUBLIC SCHOOL SYSTEM

A solution to the problems of today's schools must overcome tendencies that are inherent in the structure of large urban public school systems. An alternative school system must free the schools from micromanagement by the school board and other political bodies; it must remedy the inequities of funding and teacher allocation that exist within most urban districts; it must allow development of schools with specific approaches to education so that staff members can feel responsible for what they produce and parents can hold them accountable; it must force school boards and superintendents to act when they discover that a school is consistently failing its students.

A radical solution preferred by some is school choice based on consumer initiative. [3] The plan would give every child in a locality a voucher worth the current per pupil cost of public schooling. Parents could use the voucher to pay for tuition at any school, public or private. Parents would, presumably, seek out the better schools and avoid the weaker ones. Drawn by the possibility of lucrative tuition payments, entrepreneurs would offer alternatives to unpopular schools. In the long run, weak schools would be eliminated, strong ones would take their place, and all schools would feel the pressure of competition to maintain quality.

A choice plan including private schools raises the spectre of public funds being used to support Catholic and other sectarian schools. Some choice advocates have therefore proposed an all-public choice scheme, in which parents could choose any public school.[1]

The advantages of school choice are evident in light of the foregoing discussion of public school problems. School boards would not have to agree on what is the one best model of schooling for all students. Diverse tastes and demands could be satisfied by diverse schools. Schools would compete on quality, but like other sellers of complex services, they would also have to differentiate their product to appeal to purchasers' tastes and loyalty. Parents and students would therefore know what to expect from a school. Though schools could not discriminate in admissions, they could impose requirements related to student attendance and effort. As the research on magnet schools makes clear, students who choose a particular school knowing what it requires (even if they only consider it their least-bad alternative) have a greater incentive to meet its requirements than students who have no choice about where they will go. [4,5]

Schools would be forced to attract students and would therefore pay close attention to student needs and parent preferences. Funding would be explicitly based on attendance, not driven by the locational preferences of senior teachers or political negotiations. Schools would live and die on their reputations; teachers and principals would therefore have a strong incentive to collaborate, to press one another for good performance, to weed out weak staff members, and to work as hard as necessary to build their school's clientele. Like private schools, these schools would have to be concerned about their graduates, whether they could succeed in jobs and higher education and cope with adult life.

But choice plans, whether all-public or public-private, have a glaring problem. Vouchers may increase parents' capacity to demand better schools, but it is not clear where alternatives to the existing bad schools are to come from. Even in New York City, where Catholic schools educate over 100,000 students and constitute the twelfth largest school system in the country, there is no room for the 1,000,000 public school students. If choice is to provide new opportunities for all students, a much larger supply of good schools must be created.

For choice to have any appreciable effect on the quality of schooling in Los Angeles, a massive effort to create new schools or redevelop existing ones would be necessary. That is unlikely to happen purely through private investment. Some investors and community service organizations might venture to start one or two schools each, but only a few are likely to consider troubled central city areas the best place to start. The demand for better schools is high in inner suburbs and in minority working class areas, but prudent entrepreneurs will start in less challenging environments.

For the foreseeable future, a reform built solely on consumer choice will leave central cities with the problem they started with (i.e., how to create a large enough supply of good schools to

serve all students). Choice does not eliminate the need for a strategy to improve public schools.

There are promising approaches to the supply problem. Several national organizations are creating new designs for schools and are building the capacity to help public school systems form new schools (or redevelop existing ones) around these designs. These design organizations are sponsored by foundations such as RJR Nabisco, Macy, and Exxon, and many work out of major universities. Professor Henry Levin runs such an organization at Stanford, and others exist at Harvard, Yale, and Brown. Other design organizations (e.g., Christopher Whittle's Edison Project) are privately sponsored and hope either to work under contract to local school districts or to run private schools with money from education vouchers.

These design organizations could provide the supply side of the market envisioned by choice advocates. They could develop school concepts, test and demonstrate their feasibility and appeal, and then offer them to parents in one or many localities. Like Montessori and the Catholic religious orders, they could ensure that the staff of a school were properly trained to run it and that a competent parent organization was available to monitor quality and help solve problems.

A national effort to create such design organizations is sponsored by the New American Schools Development Corporation (NASDC), a coalition of business leaders. Among the projects sponsored by NASDC is a Los Angeles-based effort to design an inner-city school that will use older students as tutors for younger ones and focus the efforts of all neighborhood adults on education. Other designs sponsored by NASDC include a school based on old-fashioned character building and study of the classics; schools in which students learn basic skills in the course of research projects; and schools using computers in all phases of instruction. Within three years, NASDC's design teams will be available to help communities all around the country use its designs to build new schools or redevelop existing ones.

Some public agencies are creating their own design and assistance organizations. The school systems of Philadelphia and New York City are both creating new "theme" schools that take over the buildings of failed neighborhood schools and offer students choices among simple, focused, goal-oriented schools. State governments in Ohio, Oregon, and Wyoming are also developing capacities to help school systems identify and redevelop their weakest schools.

All these organizations are creating alternatives to existing public schools. None seek to become the universal model for all the schools in a locality. They are creating a menu of alternative approaches that school systems can use as they try to improve or redevelop their worst schools. The designers sponsored by NASDC, in particular, intend within five years to offer their services to any school system that wants to adopt one or more of the new designs.

However, with the exception of the efforts sponsored by the New York and Philadelphia schools, new designs for individual schools do not change the ways that public school systems do business. One or two well-designed new schools in inner-city Los Angeles (or several hundred schools nationwide) do not amount to a solution to the problems of urban education. Today's urban public school systems are built to manage large numbers of schools via regulation and compliance enforcement. They are not built to create and nurture a variety of schools or to invest in the redevelopment of schools that have gone bad. Unless we find a new way to govern whole systems of urban schools, the new designs can only slightly increase the number of exemplary-but-not-imitated public schools.

Can we find a way to govern public schools that permits and encourages variety and that moves quickly to supply better schools in place of ones that have failed their students or that nobody wants? Can we build a public school system that nurtures the development of clear, coherent educational approaches in individual schools so that parents have real choices?

A rough blueprint for a public school system that offers the benefits of choice is suggested in David Osborne and Ted Gaebler's new book, *Reinventing Government*. [6] They argue that the key to improving schools and other public institutions is to separate governance from the delivery of services. Governance bodies like school boards naturally tend to create uniformity. Because they have formal authority over schools, they find it difficult to resist constituent pressure to settle every problem or complaint with a rule that prevents the offending circumstance from arising again. The result is that a problem that arises in one school leads to rules that constrain all schools—even those in which the problem had either been handled smoothly or had not arisen at all. Because many such problems concern the treatment of employees, public bodies like school boards gradually constrain the schools—and themselves—with elaborate civil service employment rules and union contracts.

Osborne and Gaebler argue that public bodies can be saved from their own tendency to overregulate. Their strategy for separating policy-making bodies from the day-to-day management of services is to have services delivered under contract. Public decision-making bodies can set basic goals and principles of operation (e.g., nondiscrimination in student admissions and teacher hiring), but services will not be delivered by public employees. Services will, instead, be delivered by contractors, operating under limited-term and fixed-cost agreements. Public bodies could retain the right to terminate contracts for nonperformance, and contractors would have no automatic rights of renewal.

Under the contracting scheme, school boards could manage a number of different contracts—with a child development organization for some elementary schools and with a university school of education for others; with an organization like Ted Sizer's Coalition for Essential Schools for some high schools and with a college of arts and sciences or career training academy for others. Nothing would prevent a group of teachers in existing schools from organizing themselves as a contractor. Teachers' unions might offer to run a few schools in one locality; a successful local union might land contracts to provide schools in another school district or even another state.

Public school systems would still need superintendents and some form of a central office, but their roles and powers should be modest. The superintendent's job would be to advise the board on contracting—how to attract good offers; when to warn a failing contractor or reassign some or all of its schools to other contractors. The school system's central office would support the superintendent in this basic monitoring function, but it would not directly supervise principals or teachers or provide in-service training. Contractors organizations would be responsible for those functions. The school board could set general requirements for teacher qualifications and might even negotiate with contractors and the teachers' union about general wage scales. Contractors could be required to hire teachers from the existing city teaching staff, but they would be able to pick those who best fit their schools' approaches to education. The teachers' union might operate as a guild, helping teachers find placements and trying to upgrade the skills of teachers who could not readily find work.

Contracting may be the framework for the solution of many problems of urban schools. It could, if properly imple-mented, allow school boards to focus on the core issues of what children need to learn and how to save children from schools that are failing them. It could also relieve school boards of the obligation to resolve every complaint about any aspect of school operations. Contracting with statewide or national design organizations such as those discussed above would force school boards to make an explicit allocation of funds to each school, thus eliminating the current within-district inequities in school funding. Many of the teachers and administrators would come from the current teaching force, but they would work in organizations that must maintain quality and will therefore reward good teachers and retrain or replace ineffective ones.

Schools would remain public: they would be funded from tax dollars and would operate under contracts that guaranteed fair admissions, nondiscrimination, and the rights of the disadvantaged. The state could still establish requirements for teacher certification. Local school boards would be, in effect, public investment managers, deciding which contractor's approach best fits a neighborhood's need. Parental choice would force school boards and superintendents to pay special attention to their shakiest investments. Schools that had become unpopular would lose students and force a reallocation of district funds. When troubled schools became too small to run economically, contractors would be forced either to negotiate for higher per pupil payments or default on their contracts. In either case, the board and superintendent would face an action-forcing event. Even if the board shirked its duty during the life of a contract, the end of a contractor's term would force a new decision.

A board that could not get contractors to bid on a particular set of schools would know quickly that it needed to offer more money or more realistic terms. This might be a warrant for selectively allocating federal or state categorical program funds. If a school district consistently had trouble attracting contractors for its schools, the state government would have a clear signal that something must be done—a review of the district's contracting methods and specifications, special incentive funding for contractors, or reconstitution of the local school district. Failure would be evident and the remedies would be readily available. There would no longer be any justification for tolerating school failure or for leaving generations of children from inner-city neighborhoods in the same ineffective hands.

Contracting with school design organizations, such as those sponsored by the NASDC, can provide a supply of schools that make parental choice meaningful. It also provides a way out for communities like Los Angeles whose schools have collapsed under the old system. No such dramatic change can be instantaneous, but effective steps can be taken now if community leaders and the school board focus on the worst inner-city schools and commit to redeveloping them via contracts with universities and design organizations that will provide a range of focused alternatives for students.

Contracting for schools will not solve all problems. Some contractors may be inadequate and will have to be assisted by others or fired. Some parents may not exercise their rights of choice aggressively and may unwittingly help deficient schools survive. School boards will have to overcome their tendency to "solve" a problem by enacting a new policy (e.g., a new specification for contractors to meet) rather than by looking into the causes and providing needed resources. But contracting will entirely eliminate two sources of problems for today's public schools. First, it will eliminate the central office bureaucracy that is built to control and regulate schools from the outside, replacing it with a much simpler organization built to assist the board in the selection and audit of contractors. Second, it will eliminate the

need for the school board to resolve disputes by making rules that apply to all schools. Parents or interest groups with particular tastes in schooling can be encouraged to find a school that suits them rather than petitioning for general policy changes.

CONCLUSION

Many things must change before the immigrant and black students of South Central [Los Angeles] have the same life prospects as the students of Pacific Palisades and Woodland Hills. Schools cannot overcome all the problems of poverty, unemployment, crime, and community disintegration. They also need stable funding, something that only a more responsible state government can provide. But schools can do much more than they are doing.

The public school system must change fundamentally. Enabling changes in state laws and state and federal funding programs are necessary. But the greatest change must be local. School systems must allocate money to schools fairly. School boards, superintendents, and teachers' unions must all change their modes of operation to work with contractors who operate schools. School system central offices would change most dramatically, from regulators of a monopoly enterprise to evaluators and managers of a set of contracts.

None of these changes is likely to come about solely through the initiative of superintendents, school boards, or teachers' unions—the changes they face are too uncomfortable. Broader community initiative, led by the heads of neighborhood and civil rights organizations, local general purpose governments, and key businesses, is necessary. It is obvious that regulation, exhortation, and pressure on the existing school system cannot do the job. Only a concerted community effort to change the way that the community governs education can save the public schools.

NOTES

1. In any case, as Elmore has shown, parent choice of schools would require some degree of government administration. Disputes over the fairness of admissions policies and accuracy of schools' claims would inevitably lead to legal action and mandates for government oversight for publicly funded schools. [7]

REFERENCES

1. McDonnell, Lorraine M. and Anthony H. Pascal, *Teacher Unions and Educational Reform*, Santa Monica, Calif.: RAND, JRE-02, 1988.
2. Hill, Paul T., and Josephine J. Bonan, *Decentralization and Accountability in Public Education*, Santa Monica, Calif.: RAND, R-4066-MCF/IET, 1991.
3. Chubb, John E., and Terry Moe, *Politics, Markets, and America's Schools*, Washington, D.C.: The Brookings Institution, 1990.
4. Hill, Paul T., Gail E. Foster, and Tamar Gendler, *High Schools with Character*, Santa Monica, Calif.: RAND, R-3944-RC, 1990.
5. Crain, Robert, et al., *The Effectiveness of New York City's Career Magnets*, Berkeley, Calif.: The National Center for Research on Vocational Education, 1992.
6. Osborne, David, and Ted Gaebler, *Reinventing Government*, Menlo Park, Calif.: Addison-Wesley, 1992.
7. Elmore, Richard, *Choice in Public Education*, New Brunswick, N.J.: Center for Policy Research in Education, 1986.

Index